RELIGIOUS REFLECTIONS
ON THE HUMAN BODY

RELIGIOUS REFLECTIONS
ON THE HUMAN BODY

EDITED BY

JANE MARIE LAW

INDIANA UNIVERSITY PRESS

Bloomington and Indianapolis

The paper used in this publication meets the minimum requirements of
American National Standard for Information Sciences—Permanence of
Paper for Printed Library Materials, ANSI Z39.48-1984.

 ™

Manufactured in the United States of America

Library of Congress Cataloging-in-Publication Data

Religious reflections on the human body / edited by Jane Marie Law.
    p.   cm.
    Includes bibliographical references (p. xxx–xxx) and index.
    ISBN 0-253-33263-X (alk. paper). — ISBN 0-253-20902-1
(paper : alk. paper)
    1. Body, Human—Religious aspects. I. Law, Jane Marie.
BL604.B64R45   1995
291.2′2—dc20   94-4436

1 2 3 4 5   00 99 98 97 96 95

To the
gentle memory of
Ioan Petru Culianu
January 5, 1950–May 21, 1991

CONTENTS

I. Classical Views of the Body in Religious Traditions

II. The Gendered Body in Religious Discourse

PREFACE

One inescapable fact of human existence is that it is experienced in a body. How this fact determines the parameters of religious experience and discourse and, conversely, how religious thought and practice construct understandings of the human body is the subject of this volume. This collection of essays cannot claim to exhaust the scope of issues raised by a focus on the intersection of the human body and religious life. Yet the diversity of geographical foci and methodological approaches contained herein makes it possible to explore a wide range of topics and problems central to a discussion of the human body and religion.

This volume is the culmination of a two-year project which brought together fifteen scholars from ten universities in five different countries to reflect upon the central concern of the human body and how it has been constructed, deconstructed, cultivated, imagined, represented, despised, adored and adorned, transposed onto geographies, and transformed in ritual by different religious traditions. The scholars whose work appears in this volume represent the disciplines of Anthropology, Classics, Comparative Literature, History, History of Religions, Philosophy, and Sociology. We represent the subject specializations of the history of ancient and medieval Christianity, Islam in the Ottoman Empire, Indian Buddhism, Jewish studies, Japanese popular religion, Buddhist studies, Malaysian and Chinese popular religion, Buddhist philosophy, Chinese Taoism, Islamic literature, and classical Japanese theatre and literature. In April 1991, we convened at Cornell University in Ithaca, New York, to present and discuss our work and to develop the structure that has become this volume. Each of us had in common the desire to see a single collection of essays which focused on the human body as it is understood within religious traditions, a volume able to do justice to the scope of issues raised by such a focus, while at the same time respecting the cultural depth each case requires. As we are a group representing diverse methodological approaches to our subject matter, in this volume we have articulated these differences, often comparing our essays to others in the volume, at the level of both content and method.

The volume is introduced by Ioan P. Culianu's excellent discussion of constructions of the human body in Western civilization, which he presented as a keynote lecture at our April 1991 meeting. His essay in this volume is based on the unedited manuscript he presented at our conference. Since his death was a month after this meeting in Ithaca, he did not have the opportunity to revise the manuscript further. Therefore, with the exception of minor points in the citation, we have left the wording as Professor Culianu originally wrote it, including the handwritten additions he added to the manuscript itself. His lively discussion, an overview of recent studies on the body in Western civilization, is organized according to topical emphasis in various periods of history: in studies about late antiquity, the emphasis lay on the male body and male sexuality; in studies concerning the Middle Ages, the emphasis lay on women's bodies and nutrition; and in studies in the modern period, the emphasis lay again on women's bodies and a variety of topics concerning fashion and what Culianu calls the "secularization of penitential practice." The breadth of issues raised in this essay makes it a natural introduction to the volume.

In the first section, "Classical Views of the Body in Religious Traditions," each essay explores some central aspect of how a given religious tradition (or tradition of discourse) expresses a construction of the human body. Recognizing that it is not possible to talk about "the Christian view of the body" or "the Buddhist view of the body" in an artificial and monolithic fashion, we nevertheless felt that it was necessary to provide a foundation for the topics raised later in the volume. Each essay in this section reveals the centrality of an understanding of the human body to the given tradition and lays the groundwork for the more specific essays in the volume. While we have not been able to cover every religious tradition on the globe, all of the essays in this section point to issues which cannot be limited to one tradition alone. Pheme Perkins's essay on the creation of the body in gnosticism explores the gnostic origins of the dualistic evaluation of the body in Christian thought—on one hand natural and even sacred and on the other hand negative asceticism. Her discussion presents excerpts from a number of key gnostic texts which directly address the relationship between body and spirit. Michael Winter provides an overview of Islamic discourse on the body, with special attention to the Qur'anic notions of the human body. He addresses the attitudes of medieval Muslim scholars and jurists, including Abu Hamid al-Ghazzali, the Sufis, and modern Muslim fundamentalists, and makes prudent comparisons with Jewish views of the body. Sue Hamilton's essay on Theravāda Buddhism explores the view of the body in this tradition and its actual role in the soteriological process for Theravāda Buddhists. On the basis of a reading of canonical Pali literature, she argues that the seemingly negative attitude toward the body and the general world-denying position of this tradition are largely late in development, not found until later commentary material was compiled. Each of these essays presents some formulation of the body which can be considered normative within the tradition itself and hence seen as a position which exerts a strong ideological influence on subsequent developments within the tradition.

The second section, "The Gendered Body in Religious Discourse," explores the primacy of gender as an ideological construction in religious traditions. Three of the essays reveal a similar mode of constructing images of women's bodies, although they scan three different cultural settings. In these settings, the female body and feminine desire are seen as dangerous and cunning, even at times concealing putrefaction of the spirit. Fedwa Malti-Douglas presents a discussion of a punitive religious discourse in Islam by focusing on the insistence within the tradition that women's bodies, and their faces in particular, be covered and left unadorned. She contrasts these rules concerning women with visions of the male body in Islam. Her discussion includes vivid examples from both popular and classical Islamic writings. Elizabeth Wilson's essay explores how the image of a beautiful woman in post-Ashokan Indian Buddhist tales is used to reveal the impermanence and impurity of the body, with the most striking example being the image of the beautiful female form concealing a rotting corpse. Susan B. Klein discusses a similar theme in the famous Dōjōji story of Japan as presented in two versions, the late-Heian-period (794–1185) tale-literature (*setsuwa*) version and a Muromachi-period (1392–1569) Noh play using the Heian tale as its basis. In the tale, a woman's desire transforms her into a snake capable of "burning up" the object of her carnal desire, a Buddhist priest. Klein suggests that the vision of women presented in such tales comes close to becoming a justification for excluding women from the soteriological path of Buddhist enlightenment. Howard Eilberg-Schwartz discusses the meaning of passages in the Hebrew Bible which refer to the body of the divine, arguing that the hidden nature of God's body is a matter best understood within gender analysis.

The third section, "Transformations of the Body and Spirit in Ritual Practice," deals with the interesting and seemingly omnipresent problem in religious discourse of the relationship between flesh and spirit. A number of problems hinted at in earlier essays are given center focus. Three essays explore formulations of this problem in different religious traditions and geographical locations. Jean DeBernardi's treatment of the Chinese hungry ghosts festival contrasts Chinese popular religious images of control and transcendence of the material body with images of desire and attachment. Thomas P. Kasulis's discussion of Kūkai's major treatise *Sokushinjōbutsugi* (The significance of attaining Buddhahood in this very body) shows how this text of the ninth-century Japanese Buddhist master provides a fundamental paradigm for understanding the sacralization of the body in religious practice. Kasulis discusses the radical Shingon idea of the cosmos as the body of the eternal Buddha, a notion of corporeality which fuses the phenomenal and absolute worlds. Poul Andersen's essay includes a general discussion of the symbolism of the body in Taoist liturgy, discusses the Taoist idea of *bianshen* ("transforming the body" in ritual to establish a cosmic identity or personify a particular deity), and presents connections with similar ideas in Chinese popular theatre. Each of these essays points to the centrality of the body in ritual studies.

The fourth section, "Body Relics, Transpositions, and Substitutes," presents three cases in which body-related concerns are transposed onto physical entities to be explored and ritually resolved. Bernard Faure's discussion of Chan/Zen Buddhism presents examples of meditation practice which

challenge the commonly held assumption that Zen Buddhist practice can
be characterized as radically antinomian and against cultic meditations of
traditional Buddhism. Faure explores both the metaphor of "the embodiment of the dharma" as expressed in the cult of icons and the practice of
"self-mummification" by certain Buddhist practitioners. He suggests that
Chan/Zen Buddhism, far from being solely the "School of the Mind," was
obsessed with whole or fragmented bodies of its masters. Daniel Gold's
essay explores the extension and transposition of the physical body of a
guru onto the landscape of the ashram. This study, based on an actual
ashram in New York State, reveals the primacy of the body of the teacher
in organizing sacred space. Jane Marie Law's essay on ritual puppetry in
Japan explores how this tradition is directly concerned with a number of
body-dependent issues, with special focus on the problem of death and
grief and on revitalization of the contact between human and divine worlds
in a ritually prescribed setting. Her study, drawing on the field of ritual
studies, explores the interaction between myth, ritual, and performance
context to reveal how the analogical enactment of vitalization in the form
of a human body substitute—the puppet—renders a rite of revitalization
efficacious at a symbolic level.

Together the essays in this volume present an overview of the geography
of the body in religious traditions and discourse around the world. It is our
hope that scholars and students in a number of fields will find this volume
helpful in their research and reflections.

                                                        J.M.L.
                                                        Ithaca, New York
                                                        January, 1994

ACKNOWLEDGMENTS

The publisher wishes to acknowledge the permission of the following: Jiro Nakamura for permission to use his photograph of Professor Ioan Culianu; Princeton University Press for permission to reprint Bernard Faure's "Substitute Bodies in Chan/Zen Buddhism," which originally appeared in his *Rhetoric of Immediacy: A Cultural Critique of Chan/Zen Buddhism* (1993); the SYDA Foundation for permission to print the photograph of Gurumayi Chidvilasananda in Daniel Gold's essay, "Guru's Body, Guru's Abode"; the Pali Text Society for permission to print a photograph from C. A. F. Rhys Davids's *Psalms of the Brethren* (1913 edition) and Dover Publications for permission to print plate 184 from Ananda Coomaraswamy's *History of Indian and Indonesian Art,* both in Elizabeth Wilson's essay, "The Female Body as a Source of Horror and Insight in Post-Ashokan Indian Buddhism"; Fudō Bin, of Hyōgo-ken, Mihara-gun, Ichimura, Sanjo, Japan, for permission to use the photograph taken by his father, Fudō Shūichi, used in Jane Marie Law's essay, "The Puppet as Body Substitute: *Ningyō* in the Japanese *Shiki Sanbasō* Performance." All other printed art work and photographs in this volume are either in the public domain or were taken by the authors of the essays in which they appear. No photo may be reproduced without the permission of the author.

Scholars in various fields, and colleagues, students and administrators at Cornell University have contributed a great deal to the transformation of this volume from idea to reality. Funding for this project was provided by the East Asia Program of Cornell University. The Religious Studies Program at Cornell also offered generous support, as did the Faculty Fellows Program, which made it possible for the students in Religion and Asian Studies classes to work with the scholars during their visit to Ithaca in 1991. Karen Brazell, Director of the East Asia Program from 1987 to 1991, and Laurie Damiani, Assistant to the Director of the East Asia Program, were instrumental in helping to locate funding.

A most unusual group of students served as committee when scholars on this project convened in April 1991. They drove, cooked, photocopied papers, distributed flyers, and took care of endless details with remarkably good spirits, often getting up before dawn and going to bed well after midnight. My special thanks to Kathryn Allen, Charles Chen, James Henry Holland, J. Maya Iwata, Allison Lakin, Jennifer Lichtman, Jiro Nakamura, and Deborah Riley. This project could never have happened without their selfless contributions of time and endless energy.

Since 1990, the students in my seminar at Cornell entitled "Religious

Reflections on the Human Body" have taught me a great deal about this field of inquiry and the various discourses relating to the body in religious traditions, and I acknowledge their unnamed contributions.

My colleagues at Cornell have provided valuable editorial advice and support. Special thanks to Chris Minkowski from the Department of Asian Studies and Ross Brann and David Owen from Near Eastern Studies. John McRae, also of Asian Studies, deserves a separate accolade for his generous guidance as a senior faculty member. John Badgley, Curator of the South Asia Collection of Olin Library at Cornell, provided sound advice on a number of aspects of the project.

The late Joseph Kitagawa from the University of Chicago was instrumental in the formulation of the project. For this and more, I will always be immensely grateful to him.

Contributors to the volume could not have made the task of editor more painless. Each gave timely and good-spirited responses to editorial inquiries. I would especially like to mention the excellent advice offered by Pheme Perkins and Fedwa Malti-Douglas. Although it is hard to imagine two more productive and busy people, they were most generous with their time and support.

Adam Law provided help with the technical side of this manuscript (which has often meant giving up his laptop computer for days on end), and has been most supportive. I thank him for his steady patience and tenacity.

Ioan Culianu's enthusiasm for this project has been an inspiration to all of us. From our first conversations about this project in the fall of 1990, he was my most reliable sounding board and the book's staunchest supporter. When all the participants met in Ithaca, he was most generous with his time and comments. The students working on the project will never forget the spellbinding evenings spent talking with him about their work and lives. It was with great sadness that those of us working on this project heard of his murder in Chicago on May 21, 1991. He had been a central participant in the project from its inception, a respected and valued colleague, and a trusted friend to many of us. We open the volume with his essay, which he prepared and developed in this project, and dedicate this book to his memory.

RELIGIOUS REFLECTIONS
ON THE HUMAN BODY

INTRODUCTION
THE BODY REEXAMINED

Ioan P. Culianu

> The Soul . . . is full ȯf the Body.
>
> John Smith (the Cambridge
> Platonist)

If the proliferation of scholarly research about the body is a fact, and this volume part of it, it is perhaps less obvious that what we take for an exploration of history is in reality a discourse about ourselves. Most of us may still be convinced that present day insistence on the body is one part of a strategy of liberation from a millennial tradition of neglect of the body and privilege of the soul, that it represents the rightful resort to literary justice of that part of us which, through oppression and repression, has been prevented from speaking up. Much of the credit for having unseated this tenacious attitude goes to Michel Foucault, under whose long shadow all recent research on the Western history of the body abides. In the introduction to his *History of Sexuality,* Foucault has revealed the shocking truth that sexual oppression and repression do *not* explain what we take to be our recent and compensatory interest in sex, believed to have begun with Freud. On the contrary. According to Foucault, speaking of sex is part of the confessional practices of Christianity firmly installed in the thirteenth century. "We have since become a singularly confessing society," writes the French philosopher. "Western man has become a confessing animal."[1]

Similarly, talking about the past of the body actually means talking about the present of our mind. And if we believe that in speaking of the bodies of women we repair the millennial wrong done to women who could not speak for themselves, we should still bear in mind, along this research, that, where indeed women speak little with words, their bodies are the most spoken of because they have the most to tell. Again, is this language of women's bodies man-made and therefore an effect of oppression, or, on the contrary, is it woman-made and therefore an effect of manipulation of

1

men? Does the body of woman speak *about* male oppression, or *to* the manipulable male? The conclusion that it would be preposterous to deny women of the past the initiative of dialogue changed the emphasis of studies about the body from oppression by men to manipulation of man.[2]

The territory of scholarship on the Western history of the body is extremely vast and traversing it requires expert guidance. The recent survey I wrote, published in *The Journal of Modern History* (March 1991), already has to be supplemented with new material.[3] My conclusions remain useful for attempting a periodization of historical emphasis on particular aspects of the body. I deal rather thoroughly with sexuality, nutrition, cleaning and clothing, and rather marginally with birth. I deal less with health care and death, being that these themes are the object of other vast bodies of literature; and not at all with excretion, not because it is not an important topic, but because, for some reason, we still lack histories of Western excretion, and the (rather modest) literature on sewage and disposal reveals not so much a dimension of the human body as of the body of the city.

From the bulk of data and interpretations of the past few years there has emerged a rather marked periodization of the focus of scholarship on the body. Roughly speaking, the emphasis during Late Antiquity lies on the body as metonymy for sex, and sex is endowed with serious to violent negativity; during the Middle Ages the body is in first instance metonymy for nutrition, from which some particularities of medieval mysticism, especially as practiced by women, would ensue; finally, the body after the Reformation is scattered in a number of topics, with an emphasis on the sexual dangers of womanhood. Here permissiveness comes to a halt, religious symbols are secularized and reduced to accessories of fashion. The body is now complex: sex, nutrition, symbol, biology. Reading the body becomes increasingly difficult, and its ambivalences are exploited by its users. After the eighteenth century, fashion is "feminized," signals are unconsciously transmitted and deciphered. The most influential decoders are psychoanalysis and neo-Darwinian sociobiology.

1. Ancient Bodies: A Body of Metaphors

The last two volumes of Michel Foucault's unfinished *History of Sexuality*, dealing with Greek antiquity and late Hellenism, have set the tone for recent research.

Aline Rousselle's *Porneia: On Desire and the Body in Antiquity,* a wonderful book now available in English translation,[4] displays the powerful codes of sexual restraint to which both men and women were submitted in ancient Greece and Rome. Rousselle's work was published in French in 1983, one year before Foucault's book was in print. Later on, she felt that she had not been radical enough in her conclusions, and resumed her thesis in a version permeated by Foucault's teachings.[5] Contrary to common opinion, the Roman Empire was ruled by a set of rigid moral regulations. Married women would often practice sexual continence, for reasons the author calls "demecologic" (demographic and ecological), and encourage their husbands to seek pleasure elsewhere, especially with slaves (of both sexes) and concubines. Sexual behavior in general was regulated by the invisible borderline that separated "decency" from "indecency" (male passive homosexuality, for instance, if public, would fall in the latter category, being punishable by death). Despite what may seem to us an exuberant sexual life, the Roman citizen of both sexes had to stay within certain limits. Both before the law and in sexual practice, the relation of husband and wife was dissymmetrical: a woman could not bring her husband before the court for adultery, and a unilateral repudiation meant she had to part with her dowry.[6]

Between slaves and masters, a large group of professionals of both spectacle and pleasure, the *famosi* (fame and infamy together are the destiny of the historian), would seek their customers under the *fornices* (wherefrom "to fornicate")—arches of public circuses and baths—in order to submit to their most pressing needs. The picture, inevitably reminiscent of Broadway in the middle seventies, still looks very permissive if compared with the idea we have of the austere Christian Middle Ages. Yet, on the one hand, this apparent permissiveness was regulated by precise rules and, on the other, the Middle Ages were less austere than we think.

More radical than Rousselle, Michel Foucault shows that sexuality in ancient Greece was regulated by a code of fear and mistrust which closely resembles the early Christian spirit. Yet the codification of conclusions varies in the two cultures.[7] The closer we move toward the beginnings of ascetic Christianity, the closer the two cultures are:

> A mistrust of the pleasures, an emphasis on the consequences of their abuse for the body and the soul, a valorization of marriage and marital obligations, a disaffection with regard to the spiritual meanings imputed to the love of boys: a whole attitude of severity was manifested in the thinking of philosophers and physicians in the course of the first two centuries (. . .). Moreover, it is a fact that the Christian authors borrowed extensively—with and without acknowledgment—from this body of ethical thought. And most historians today recognize the existence, strength, and intensification of these themes of sexual austerity in a society known by its contemporaries, and, more often than not, reproached, for its immorality and dissolute ways.[8]

Foucault's rhetorical reference to "most historians" was certainly exaggerated. Yet, if they were not yet persuaded of the existence of sexual restraint and decorum in hellenized Roman society, they became so in the aftermath of Foucault's own work.

Most eager to follow in Foucault's footsteps was Peter Brown in his *The Body and Society*.[9] Not only would Roman legislation put restrictions on the free exercise of sexuality, but Roman sexual ethics would strongly discour-

age dissoluteness. The Roman sexual ideal was sober. If this is so, the rise
of the Christian moralizing ethics is not an isolated fact at all. According
to Brown, "Pagans and Christians alike," during the last centuries of the
Empire, "lived by codes of sexual restraint and public decorum" which, in
their denial of the Self, attempted to imitate the alleged virtues of archaic Rome.[10]

The novelty of Christianity over the old Platonic dualism of body and
soul resides in the transfiguration of the body virginal, which becomes the
miraculous body of the saints and prefigures the body of resurrection.[11]
Yet during the whole period the body is certainly to be chastised and mas-
tered, and mastership over the flesh means in the first place mastership
over one's sexuality. Augustine's doctrine of concupiscence is instrumental
in ensuring the triumph of the rigorously ascetic trend of Christian ethics.
By the end of the fifth century, bishops stop marrying, sexuality and feasts
are censored,[12] the monastic institutions grow, and Christianity begins to
assume those anti-mundane traits that have become familiar to us for having been reemphasized by the Council of Trent under Protestant pressure.
Yet between the sixth and the sixteenth centuries Christian attitudes toward
the body undergo drastic change. Only artificially would they revert to
their earlier severity.

2. The Body as Metaphor

If Peter Brown often hesitates before running counter to the generally
and tacitly admitted Nietzschean thesis that Christianity is Platonism in
disguise, Caroline Walker Bynum reads medieval women's mysticism in a
key in which body and soul are actually not opposed to each other. Around
1200 a new spirituality appears which marks "a turning point in the history
of the body in the West."[13] This contention already belongs to Rudolph
Bell's *Holy Anorexia*,[14] a work which, although written from a different
perspective, has much in common with Caroline Walker Bynum's own chal-
lenging *Holy Feast and Holy Fast*.[15] Both Bell and Bynum show that, if in
Late Antiquity the body was mainly associated with control of sexuality, in
the Late Middle Ages the emphasis shifts to control of nutrition and pain
(generally self inflicted). Bell analyzed the biographies of several women
mystics in Italy between the early thirteenth and the seventeenth centuries,
drawing a parallel between their pattern of abstention from food and the
modern syndrome known as *anorexia nervosa*, which especially affects
young women in their teens. In both cases the symptoms are lengthy and
radical abstention from any food intake, interspersed with episodes of bu-
limia or binge-eating; yet the individual is hyperactive and euphoric. Comparing the earlier with the later cases, Bell comes to the conclusion that the
Reformation radically modifies the interpretation of holy anorexia, which
becomes the sign of diabolic possession. Bell views the Reformation as an

attempt of male authorities to obtain total control over women. Because of increased male scrutiny into these women's lives, former mystics turn into witches. The phenomenon ceases thereafter to have any strong *religious* significance (although women mystics like Therese Neumann or Simone Weil would show anorexia symptoms). Bell does not interpret modern *anorexia nervosa* as mere secularization of holy anorexia; nor does he succeed in explaining the latter by the former, for the social context of *anorexia nervosa* seems to vary. Noelle Caskey[16] suggests a complex involving rejection of fat as an attribute of femininity (increase in weight at puberty precedes the first menstrual period) and rejection of the mother as representative of a feminine stereotype. A family background of emphasis on food and diet and personality disturbance in one or both parents occurs in many anorexics.[17] Bell tries to establish statistically such a pattern in medieval cases, emphasizing the spiritualized relation between daughter and father.

Bynum dismisses Bell's interpretation that the medieval mystics are early instances of anorexics who give their experience a religious dimension. She believes in a basic difference between the social sphere over which males and females exert control: men would control sexuality, women would control nutrition. Therefore, the scenarios of holiness are gender differentiated.[18]

For medieval (and not only medieval) women, being in charge of food is also a highly symbolic function, which means that they have mastery over food intake. Nothing can show this better than suppression of food intake. The mystical focus of holy anorexics is the Eucharist, in which Christ's body becomes bread. In the same way, by suppressing food, women *become food* themselves.[19] Bynum's conclusion is, therefore, that medieval asceticism is not rooted in Platonic dualism; the body has a positive function.[20]

There is another aspect to the Eucharist, emphasized by Piero Camporesi,[21] which may add a new dimension to the psycho genesis of anorexia: the radical negativity of the "pit of the stomach." "With concern and anxiety, theologians follow the descent of Christ's body into the *antrum,* the damp and smelly bowels."[22] In order to ensure the holy host a proper reception, the abominable stomach must be purified by fasting. Thus, the *theological* emphasis on Eucharist would have strong dualistic undertones (the body is a tomb) and would likewise encourage anorexia. Camporesi's position is the reverse of Bynum's.

Soul/body is not the only dissymmetrical relation established by antiquity and the Christian tradition. The gender relation is dissymmetrical as well. Its intellectual history has been reconstructed in Prudence Allen's book *The Concept of Woman.*[23] Allen traces the origins of the prevalent positions concerning gender differentiation back to an ancient medical debate about the contribution of women's seed to the generation of a new being. The Aristotelian theory of Sex Polarity would prevail, according to which woman is "a deformed male" (*de generatione animalium* 716a), for although not deprived of semen, her seed is cold, infertile and soulless. In conclusion, man and woman are to each other in the same relationship as the soul to the body: the former is active, rational, made to rule, the latter is passive, irrational, made to obey. Man is hot, fertile, perfectly formed and contributes soul to the generation of a new being, woman is cold, infertile, deformed and contributes the body. In Roman times, the Aristotelian theory of sex polarity was the most influential.

Early Christian theologians were generally not consistent with any theory. Augustine, in particular, does not mind incurring contradictions. Yet he would keep the road to women's sainthood completely open. In his *Periphyseon* (537d), John Scotus Erigena (800–875) holds the view that gender will disappear with the Resurrection. All this shows that the Aristotelian view was not adopted by Christianity before the Late Middle Ages. It would first appear in the Arabic and Jewish commentators, and would be taken over by Western scholastics like Albert the Great and Thomas Aquinas.[24]

Bell's thesis that Reformation was a totalitarian attempt of male authorities to control what was supposed to be "disorderly" womanhood finds support in the chronology of the penetration of radical Aristotelian views of sex polarity. The ultimate monument of misogyny is the German inquisitors Henry Institoris and Jacob Sprenger's 1486 *Malleus maleficarum,* whose Book one, Chapter six lists the reasons why the majority of witches are women and, using an impressive apparatus of ancient authoritative quotations, demonstrates the intrinsic inferiority of women. In summation, woman is "an imperfect animal" (Aristotle), carnal, naturally evil for lack of faith, impulsive, untrustworthy for lack of memory, emotional, destructive, naturally mendacious.[25] This attitude is very characteristic of the European pre-Reformation and Reformation, a Christian fundamentalist revival whose theology was mainly Augustinian, yet whose basic assumptions were Aristotelian as well.[26] As is usually the case, the seeds of repression hidden in the "Aristotelian Revolution" of the twelfth and thirteenth centuries coincided with the increase in permissiveness which characterized the same period and culminated in the fifteenth and first two decades of the sixteenth century. The very complexity of this historical process defies any unilateral explanation, as we will shortly see, of two institutions meant to satisfy basic needs of the human body: prostitution and public baths, both used as examples in different theories of culture.

The history of Western bordellos, both state and privately owned, starts with the Greek *dikterion* of sixth century B.C.E. Athens. In Rome, the *lupanarium* (from *lupa*, lit. "she-wolf," actually "bitch") seems already to loom behind the mythological metaphor of the founding of the city by an orphan nurtured by a *lupa.*[27] Like the Greek *dicteriadae*, the Roman *meretrices* were registered for life with the authorities. All possible categories existed, from the highly expensive courtesans to the cemetery-prostitutes called *bustuariae,* who also acted as paid mourners at funerals. Roman bordellos were equal opportunity establishments: males would also sell their charms. Public baths disguised as massage parlors were already the most common place for quick fornication.[28] Whoever believes that the institution was suppressed in the Christian Middle Ages is wrong. There was only a temporary suppression by the Germans after the fall of the Western Empire in 476. Yet among the great inventions and discoveries claimed by the sixth century, among which the most prominent are the plough and the bed, one rediscovery stands out: the brothel. Feudal bordellos would accompany moving armies in a tent and would settle in houses of business in the cities, where they would generally be tolerated. In Paris around 1230 the Quartier Latin is depicted by Jacques de Vitry as an ancient version of Rue Saint-Denis or Place Pigalle, where prostitutes would apparently drag clerics to the brothels or, if they declined the offer, would call them sodomites. Yet according to Leah L. Otis,[29] who analyzed the history of the establishment in Provence between the thirteenth and sixteenth centuries, even earlier the Church would recognize prostitution as a *malum necessarium*, condemning only procurement as sinful encouragement of debauchery. In the thirteenth century, bordellos are often expelled from the center of the cities, yet tolerated *extra muros*. In the late fourteenth and early fifteenth century prostitution is institutionalized, the women becoming literally public, for, like the establishments themselves, they were property of the municipality, and would occasionally perform their patriotic duty by enlivening parades. They greeted Frederick III in Nuremberg in 1471 and later, when the emperor Charles V came to visit the city, they appeared in front of him dressed with garlands of flowers only.

The evolution of prostitution is the object of Jacques Rossiaud's excellent book *Medieval Prostitution*.[30] Rossiaud notices that the situation of medieval prostitutes is the opposite of that of Roman prostitutes: in Rome, to be a prostitute means to be denied by the State of any rights and privileges, whereas medieval prostitutes toward the end of the fifteenth century are literally owned by the State. The reason for this change of attitude is partly the ecclesiastical rehabilitation of pleasure, and partly the felicitous integration of prostitution in the social order, where, in exchange for the acknowledgment of their social and moral role, prostitutes are held responsible for the maintenance of civil order. Interestingly enough, medieval marital relations, like those in Greece and Rome, continued to be dissymmetrical.[31]

All of a sudden, under the influence of a complex of misogynous ideas conveyed by the Protestant Reformation, bordellos are suppressed by the mid sixteenth century.[32] Pre-Reformers had already set standards in the fight against harlotry and pagan feasts.[33]

The example of Geneva is eloquent. Prostitution was a state institution, with street prostitution forbidden. The main bordello in 1428 was located near Saint Christopher gate, in a neighborhood much frequented by clerics. From 1413 the prostitutes elected a highly respected queen. Between 1481 and 1491 the attitude toward prostitution (including the queen) and mixed public baths changed dramatically. Denounced by outraged neighbors for indecency and other offenses, many establishments of both kinds would close during the first decades of the sixteenth century. Calvin suppresses them altogether in 1543.[34] Examples could be multiplied. The city of Venice, as usual, does not follow the main European pattern: major establishments are not closed until the eighteenth century (between 1747 and 1774),[35] this because the city was proud of its unequaled institution of the "cortegiane," geishas of a sort who would appear in public wearing twenty inch high platform shoes (an imitation of the Arabic *kapkap*,[36] similar to the Spanish *chapines*). A sixteenth century *cortegiana* was a highly paid professional, very educated, who could sing, dance and play musical instruments. She was a model of elegance, good manners and cleanliness for all of her contemporaries. Although the life of a *cortegiana*, who received a salary from six or seven constant lovers and was allowed to entertain foreigners at night time in her luxurious houses, was full of hazards, the profession attracted a few among the most respected women intellectuals of the Renaissance.[37]

The history of public baths closely follows the pattern of prostitution. Georges Vigarello has published a history of baths in France[38] between the thirteenth and eighteenth centuries. Vigarello ascertains that public baths close all of a sudden in all major French cities between 1510 and 1561, allegedly because they provided avenues of contamination by plague. Baths were a creation of the twelfth through thirteenth centuries, probably under the influence of the Moorish hammām;[39] in 1292 Paris had twenty-six public baths. In seventeenth century Paris no such establishment remained.[40]

Historians of Protestantism seem to agree today on the negative views of woman, sexuality and marriage held by the sixteenth century Reformers,[41] against the common misinterpretation, deriving from Karl Kautsky's *sui generis* history of communist institutions,[42] of the Reformation as a movement of liberation of women. On the contrary, recent research tends to emphasize rather sharply the *negative* character of Protestant marriage, which is not a sacrament, but an almost evil institution necessary only because of the weakness of the flesh, or, in Luther's own terms, "ein Spitall der Siechen," a "hospital for the sick."[43] Luther abolished prostitution, closed the brothels and the convents, and made marriage compulsory for every woman. According to the radical Aristotelian tradition of sex polarity in which he was raised, Luther saw in every woman an instrument of the devil whom the marital bonds were meant to chastise. This created in German history an opposition, still powerful under the Nazi regime, between married and unmarried women. The latter were the object of social contempt and faced the everyday hazards of a precarious existence.[44]

Pierre Darmon[45] would also indicate the Reformation as the principal cause of the spread of misogyny in France in the sixteenth and seventeenth centuries. The specialty of all great seventeenth century preachers consists of fulminating against the flesh and particularly against women's fashions which exposed half of the breasts. Protestants and Catholics alike began the offensive around 1550. "La bataille du sein" would continue to the end of the seventeenth century. In the 1630s several preachers advised that women, even if regrettably they cannot follow the salutary Chinese fashion of foot binding, which would naturally prevent them from leaving their homes, should nevertheless not appear in public unveiled.[46] Womanhood is especially denounced for being *concupiscent* (Augustine and Luther). Most seventeenth century religious authors would insist on women's *sexual insatiability*, on the abnormal sexual relations they engage in by reason of their unquenchable lust for sex. All of them adhere to the venerable patristic tradition which ascribes to women a larger capacity for sex than men.

As shown in a recent book by Thomas W. Laqueur,[47] another factor besides the Aristotelian theory contributed to enforce sex polarity. For a long time in medical history, the sexual organs of the woman had been interpreted as isomorphic with the male organs, more exactly as a hollow penis. This view, which present day embryologists do not find entirely incorrect, was supplanted by a new medical model, in which the woman was transformed from merely an inversion of man into a "second sex." Several events led to this episode in what Foucault defines as the eighteenth century "hysterization of women."[48] In 1492 Christopher Columbus discovered America, in 1559 Renaldus Columbus discovered a new continent of the female body: the clitoris,[49] defined for centuries to come as a miniature penis. The news must have caused a shock comparable to that of the acknowledgment of women's "solitary vice" by the mid nineteenth century, for it was actually the precondition for autoerotic practices and even, as Ambroise Paré had already remarked (16th c.), for tribadism or homoerotic gratification. Another fresh suspicion cast on women by many respectable anatomists starting with Ambroise Paré stems from the controversy around the hymen, whose very existence is doubted. This adds one more grief against women to the many accumulated previously, for if the precious membrane of chastity is an invention, then the price of virginity, for whose loss, according to Saint Jerome, not even God can make up, may after all not be so high.[50] Even if twentieth century physicians have come to the incontrovertible conclusion that the hymen does exist, the issue of the physicality of this membrane may actually be unimportant. What matters is the meaning attached to it by the human mind. The same applies to the body as a whole: it is an extension of the mind, and a play of the mind as well. The mind turns the body into a complex metaphor.

3. Body and Bodice

Why does the body have to be clothed? Two polar theories exist, one especially influential between Augustine and the end of the nineteenth century, the other one thereafter. The former is usually known as "modesty" or "lust-shame" theory: human beings are to cover their body out of

modesty and decency. Women's clothing is supposed to be both an obstacle
to the eye and a sign of male ownership. Between 1880 and 1890, anthropologists came to think that dress functions as a sexual stimulant, not as a
depressant. This led to the theory of "immodesty," according to which dress
is meant not to cover, but to *uncover*. Freud tried to combine the two by
emphasizing the gender related occurrence of scoptophilia or the "libido
for looking" and exhibitionism or "libido for being looked at." Men would
be highly scoptophilic, women highly exhibitionistic. The Freudian J. C.
Flügel, author of *The Psychology of Clothes*,[51] emphasizes two basic aspects of
clothing: its *ambivalence*, stemming from the fact that clothes cover the body
yet at the same time attract attention to it, and its being the result of
the *displacement* of one's unconscious conflict between exhibitionism and
modesty. It follows that public feelings about fashion are actually displaced
feelings about sexuality.[52] This is a way to explain the phenomenon called
"feminization" of fashion that started toward the end of the eighteenth
century, when creativity in fashion became almost exclusively reserved to
women, men's fashion being functional. Yet the preferred alternative is
still Thorstein Veblen's theory of "vicarious consumption":[53] the aristocracy
used clothing to display conspicuous consumption as a sign of wealth, and
therefore of conspicuous leisure and conspicuous waste. Religious Puri-
tanism brought into the sphere of clothing the visible sign of inner-worldly
asceticism, and for a while it was fashionable for both sexes to dress incon-
spicuously. Yet, if men's clothes stabilize and do not show major changes
after the end of the eighteenth century, women continue to display conspicuous leisure. This is the famous "vicarious consumption" theory, according to which the woman endorses vicariously the man's need for
conspicuous consumption. For men, vicarious consumption is actually a
form of conspicuous waste: in a beautiful dress the wife or mistress cannot
engage in any productive activity.[54] Apparently women's liberation from
conspicuous leisure in fashion coincides with World War I;[55] and shortly
before (ca. 1900–1905) corsets had become discrete and were worn next
to the body.[56]

If clothing is an extension of the body (J. C. Flügel) and the body signifies
an extension of the mind, then the significance of the body corseted is
difficult to read. One would be tempted to treat the corset as one of the
many symbols of captivity turned into status symbols which end up emphasizing conspicuous leisure and waste.[57] Yet this would be too simple. Let us
examine the shocking revelation that the undressed body of the mystic
Colomba da Rieti (b. 1466) presented to a bunch of rapists who assailed
her on Friday, August 22, 1488, when she was wandering far from home:

> They began to rip off her clothes, stopping only momentarily when they
> heard what they took to be the jingling of coins in her pocket, but that
> turned out to be the noise of her crucifix hitting her flagellum (. . .). Still
> they tore away her vestments, stripping Colomba down to the iron belt

three fingers wide with which she punished her naked hips and then to her
hairshirt with two studded iron chains strapped around her neck and across
her breasts.[58]

Colomba's body is no body: it is flesh recklessly chastised for the kingdom
of heaven, in memory not only of the sufferings of Christ's human body,
but also of so many lives of ancient women saints like Barbara, Catherine,
Juliana and Margaret, whose exquisite beauty aroused the lust of a powerful pagan pretender. Rejected, the man turned into a beast and committed
the innocent charms of the saint to ferocious hangmen. Her body, first
whipped in public, was atrociously mutilated: breasts and feet were cut off,
and then the head. Otherwise the saint was hung and then dismembered,
or directly cut into small pieces.[59]

The bodice functions as an ideal deterrent (especially if it is an iron cage)
and instrument of self-chastisement (as the hairshirt), yet ironically it is
also an instrument of fashion in use since the "fashion revolution of the
twelfth century" (a new trait to be added to the twelfth century Renaissance), which sees for the first time loose clothing turning into tight-fitting
and waisted clothes with lacing. In the sixteenth century all sorts of corsets
were in use. By the mid sixteenth century a cage similar to the corset is
used to support the weight of an extremely wide dress. It comes from
Spain, where it is called *verdugado* (from *verdugo*, "stick"); in English it
becomes "farthingale." Around 1855 the cage-crinoline, a new version of
the farthingale, appears in England. Ten years later it is replaced by the
bustle behind, made of horsehair and dimity and worn with *cuirasse* bodices,
poitrines adhérentes made of rubber, and other such accessories. The Pre-
Raphaelite woman gives up the corset and the conspicuous waist, to return
to the "antique waist," and the movement of "rational dress" would reduce
the tortures inflicted upon the woman's body to a rational minimum.[60]

David Kunzle, an expert on cosmetic martyrdom, wrote a history of body
sculpture in the West with particular emphasis on tight-lacing.[61] He interprets post-Reformation painful feminine body-sculpture as a *secularization*
of medieval penitential practices; accordingly, the nineteenth century
woman would keep up, to some extent, Colomba da Rieti's body chastise-
ment, endowing it with variable significance and thereby combining asceticism with sexual allurement.[62] The author perceptively notes that the corset
fashion stems from the Protestant secularization of pain. Valerie Steele
shares Kunzle's overall conclusions: the symbols of oppression worn by
Victorian women (tight-laced corset, high-heeled shoe, bustle, etc.) were
actually semantically turned into symbols of domination over males.[63] Victorian fashion was not so much opposed by feminists as by Puritans, and
it is doubtful that women's emancipation went hand in hand with the elimination of the cumbersome Victorian attire.[64]

However suggestive, the secularization theory endorsed by both Kunzle and Steele shows the same ambivalence as clothing itself: it uncovers one part of the truth, and covers the other.

4. A Body for Nobody

The category of "monster" or "mutant" may well apply to the changes operated by body sculpture on women, yet it is too vague. Some theories, often contradictory, have been devised to uncover the deep meaning of artificial yet durable corrections brought about by fashion in order to create from an existing body the shape of a non-existing, new species. We will follow this process in reference to a few body-sculpting devices such as high-heeled shoes and makeup.

The existence of platform shoes in Venice, a shocking novelty of fashion introduced by courtesans, was for the first time described in 1494 by Pietro Casola, a pilgrim to Jerusalem. Women walking on *zoccoli* looked in his bewildered eyes like giants, and could not walk unless supported by a maid-servant on each side. In Christian Spain the Chapines had made their appearance at the beginning of the fifteenth century. From Spain, the Chapines found their way into France and England, apparently with the blessing of the Church, which saw in them unexpected allies in its fight against women's dancing.[65] In Elizabethan England the Chapines (or, more frequently, Chopines) would reach the unbelievable height of twenty-four inches.[66] From around 1850 high-heeled shoes make a steady return in women's fashion, being occasionally inhibited though never completely suppressed.

What is achieved by wearing high-heeled shoes?

The Chinese custom of foot binding may shed some light on the parallel Western fashion of high heels, which is said to derive from the platform shoes of the sixteenth century. Foot binding is more ancient.[67] Into the early twentieth century, all middle and upper class Chinese girls had their feet bound, starting from the age of five.[68] The procedure, which turned the Chinese woman into a symbol of conspicuous leisure and waste, was extremely painful.[69]

The result is that *the foot is actually changed into a hoof.*[70] This must result in a radical change in bodily posture and leg musculature. Van Gulik[71] notes that no other part of the body of a Chinese woman was surrounded by such interdictions as the bound feet, not even the genitals. Sexuality seems to be displaced on this artificial creation, whose secret was jealously guarded.

Among the many theories trying to explain the significance of high heels fashion none is entirely compelling. Most of them emphasize their erotic function, which remains however vague. The phallic symbolism of high heels has been stressed by many, and the acquisition of phallic feet seems to fit into the Freudian pattern of fetishist "displacement," with the woman acquiring predatory traits.[72] Fashion historians like Steele and Kunzle would generally adhere to the more complex interpretation offered by William A. Rossi,[73] which explains the attraction of high-heeled shoes in terms of the modification of the bodily posture ("back arched, thrusting the bosom forward") and of the modification of "the apparent contour of the legs, ankles, and feet." The woman becomes a living contradiction: her long legs seem made to take off at great speed, yet she hardly can walk; she is aggressive, yet passive for being immobilized.[74] Another result is the enhancement of "hip action."[75]

Alternative explanations have been offered by sociobiology. The basis for the sociobiological interpretation of fashion has been established by the work of Desmond Morris[76] and certain European ethologists. A synthesis has been offered in a personal work by Russell Dale Guthrie, whose interpretations differ largely from Morris's.[77]

Two basic concepts are taken over by Guthrie from Desmond Morris's work. The human species is highly *neophilic* (fond of novelty), and *neotenic* (fixated on youth and youthful traits; from the Greek *neotes*, "youthful") to such a point, that we may owe our lack of furlike bodily hair to this latter characteristic.[78] Accordingly, neoteny is fundamental as both a process and a result in fashion, especially women's. The neotenic explanation has been adopted from Morris by John Liggett in his history of facial makeup.[79] Liggett notes that the female face shows the attributes of childhood. Accordingly, cosmetics are used to enhance these attributes: white makeup produces bulging cheeks, a touch of rouge is reminiscent of a healthy, sporting child, red lips, long eyelashes and artificially enlarged pupils likewise.[80] Another interpretation devised by Morris, to which Liggett adheres, concerns the sexual function of the human face.[81] Guthrie would further expand on this theory of "automimicry," which together with the concept of *neoteny* provides the conceptual structure of his book.

Among the several categories of social automimicry, the most important in its application to human fashion is sexual automimicry. Instances thereof are displayed, e.g., by the male mandrill, whose face is a duplicate of the genitals, or by the female Gelada baboon, whose chest displays a genital pattern. Desmond Morris's interpretation of female human breasts as a duplicate of the buttocks adapted to coital frontal positions has met with wide acceptance in sociobiology.[82] His interpretation of the use of lipstick as an attempt to transform the mouth (or the entire face) into a duplicate of the female genitals has been contested on the ground that red lips are a neotenic signal. According to Guthrie, many signals transmitted by women's clothing or makeup have to be interpreted in neotenic key; to those already mentioned before, we should add the miniskirt and the stocking, whose function is to suggest youthful smoothness of the skin. Blond hair is a neotenic trait selected by nature (children's hair tends to be lighter than the hair of adults), men shave their beards to appear youthful.

However, notwithstanding the human frontal coital position, humans have in common with primates the buttocks as the most erogenous zone, signaling the "hot spot" of the vulva. According to Guthrie, the signaling function extends down to the posterior part of the legs. "The lines of the buttocks, thigh, calf and ankle have a native sexual stimulation, but this can be increased with high-heeled shoes; the curves are exaggerated when the heel is lifted. These curves are particularly apparent in a ballerina's toe stance."[83] Thus, rump display would be the key to the attractiveness of high heels.

It is, however, only one key. Like bound feet, high-heeled shoes endow woman with an artificial hoof, turning her into a graceful monster, perhaps half woman and half horse, endowed with the elegance of the animal, but not with its speed.

Once we come to a conclusion acceptable to a certain extent, the most difficult part still remains to be accomplished: how are we supposed to evaluate fashion and cosmetics? Do they enslave woman, transforming her according to male fantasies, or, on the contrary, do they allow woman to express creativity within a given context which, for a long time, did not offer her many alternatives? Kunzle and Steele would emphasize women's creative, almost religious, concern with fashion. On the contrary, a recent book by Bram Dijkstra[84] sees only negativity in nineteenth century images of women, entirely determined by male fantasies of evil.

From recent research on the "flappers," single and emancipated women of the 1920s,[85] it appears indeed that fantasies associating womanhood with evil were part of our culture until recently. Yet, instead of confirming Dijkstra's conclusion, the case of the "flappers" or "superfluous women," as a certain press would label them, shows the contrary: that the signals given by women's fashion were experienced as bodily disturbing by traditional, patriarchal society. The interpretive dilemma remains. After all, the bodies and minds of men and women seem to be inextricably linked by a hermeneutical circle which, metaphorically at least, comes close to an intercourse. Any research on the body is the product of much intercourse.

NOTES

1. Michel Foucault, *The History of Sexuality: An Introduction*, vol. 1 (*La volonté de savoir*), trans. R. Hurley (New York: Vintage Books, 1990). The other two volumes of Foucault's work, *L'usage des plaisirs* and *La souci de soi*, have been published as *The Use of Pleasure* and *The Care of the Self* (Vintage Books, 1986).

2. For an analysis of the two trends in the interpretation of gender history, see Edmund Leites, *The Puritan Conscience and Modern Sexuality* (New Haven: Yale University Press, 1986), p. 17.

3. I. P. Culianu, "A Corpus for the Body: A Review Article," *Journal of Modern History* 63 (March 1991); the survey was written in reference to Michel Feher, Ramona Naddaff, and Nadia Tazi, eds., *Fragments for a History of the Human Body*, 3 vols. (New York: Zone, 1989) (hereafter cited as *Fragments*). The work contains

forty-three essays by French, Italian, and English-speaking scholars (together with a few texts commented upon by some of them), a purely iconographical section with twenty-eight plates and an extensive alphabetical bibliography by Barbara Duden.

4. Aline Rousselle, *Porneia: On Desire and the Body in Antiquity* (New York: Blackwell, 1988).

5. Aline Rousselle, "Personal Status and Sexual Practice in the Roman Empire," in *Fragments,* 3:300–33.

6. Rousselle, *Porneia,* p. 95.

7. Foucault, *The Use of Pleasure,* p. 138.

8. Foucault, *The Care of the Self,* p. 39.

9. Peter Brown, *The Body and Society: Men, Women and Sexual Renunciation in Early Christianity* (New York: Columbia University Press, 1988).

10. Ibid., p. 22.

11. Ibid., p. 444.

12. Ibid., p. 428ff.

13. Caroline Walker Bynum, "The Female Body and Religious Practice in the Later Middle Ages," in *Fragments* 1:162.

14. Rudolph M. Bell, *Holy Anorexia,* with an epilogue by William N. Davis (Chicago: The University of Chicago Press, 1985).

15. Caroline Walker Bynum, *Holy Feast and Holy Fast: The Religious Significance of Food to Medieval Women* (Berkeley: University of California Press, 1987).

16. Noelle Caskey, "Interpreting Anorexia Nervosa," in *The Female Body in Western Culture: Contemporary Perspectives,* ed. Susan Rubin Suleiman (Cambridge: Harvard University Press, 1986), pp. 175–89.

17. Ibid., p. 186.

18. Bynum, *Holy Feast,* p. 25.

19. Ibid., p. 206–7.

20. Ibid., p. 294–96.

21. Piero Camporesi, "The Consecrated Host: A Wondrous Excess," *Fragments* 1:221–37, translated from his *La casa dell'eternità* (Milan: Garzanti, 1987).

22. Ibid., p. 228.

23. Prudence Allen, R.S.M., *The Concept of Woman: The Aristotelian Revolution, 750 BC–AD 1250* (Montreal: Eden Press, 1985). See also, Giulia Sissa, "Subtle Bodies," in *Fragments* 3:133–56, esp. pp. 137–40.

24. Allen, *Concept of Woman,* p. 251.

25. On the *Malleus,* see my article in Mircea Eliade, ed., *Encyclopedia of Religion* (New York: Macmillan, 1987), s.v. "Sacrilege," by I. P. Culianu.

26. See Jean Delumeau, *La Peur en Occident, XIVe–XVIIIe siècles* (Paris: Fayard, 1978), especially 305–44; and Pierre Darmon, *Mythologie de la femme dans l'Ancienne France, XVIe–XIXe siècles* (Paris: Seuil, 1983).

27. Around the beginning of the Common Era there were 32,000 prostitutes in Rome, for a population of approximately one million.

28. See Emmett Murphy, *Great Bordellos of the World: An Illustrated History* (London: Quartet Books, 1983), pp. 32f.

29. Leah L. Otis, *Prostitution in Medieval Society: The History of an Urban Institution in Languedoc* (Chicago: University of Chicago Press, 1985).

30. J. Rossiaud, *Medieval Prostitution,* trans. Lydia Cochrane (Oxford: Blackwell, 1988).

31. Ibid., p. 75.

32. See Otis's excellent analysis, Otis, *Prostitution in Medieval Society,* pp. 42–45.

33. One of the most zealous was Johannes Geiler of Kaysersberg (1445–1510), Basel Theology Doctor (1475), hired as a preacher of the Strassburg cathedral in 1477 and later chaplain to the emperor Maximilian. Geiler, who at his death was one of the most influential and respected German humanists, had opposed, "like

a bronze wall, the stream of vices" of the city of Strassburg. In particular, he fought to suppress a number of innocuous and very ancient feasts and carnivals which took place in the Cathedral (among which the widespread rite of reversal celebrated by the choir boys on the day of the Innocents), to ban prostitution from the city, to enforce sumptuary laws, and he inveighed against indecent fashion among women. Between 1480 and 1482 the City Council yielded and some of the fierce preacher's reforms were enacted, although not the penalty of death he had proposed for blasphemy. This was only a prelude to the repressive legislation brought about by the Reformation forty years later.

34. See Henri Naef, *Les Origines de la Réforme à Genève*, vol. 1, *La cité des évêques; l'Humanisme; les signes précurseurs* (Geneva: Droz, 1968), pp. 219–30.

35. Antonio Barzaghi, *Donne o cortigiane? La prostituzione a Venezia: Document di costume dal XVI al XVIII secolo* (Verona: Bertani, 1980).

36. On the history of the Venetian *zoccoli*, see Giovanni Grevemborch, *Gli Abiti de Veneziani di quasi ogni et' con diligenza raccolti e dipinti nel secolo XVII* (Venice: Filippi, 1981), 1:136; Paul Weber, *Schuhe: Drei Jahrtausende in Bildern*, (Aarau, Stuttgart: AT Verlag, 1980), pp. 54–56. On the European and British expansion of the *chapines* fashion, see Florence E. Ledger, *Put Your Foot Down: A Treatise on the History of Shoes* (Melksham: Colin Venton, 1985), pp. 66–74.

37. Barzaghi, *Donne o cortigiane?*, pp. 155–67.

38. Georges Vigarello, *Le propre et le sale: l'Hygiène du corps depuis le Moyen Age* (Paris: Seuil, 1985); English translation, idem, *Concepts of Cleanliness: Changing Attitudes in France Since the Middle Ages*, trans. Jean Birrell (New York: Cambridge University Press, 1988).

39. About hammāms or public baths in Muslim Spain there is a rich literature. See Philip Aziz, *La civilisation hispano-mauresque* (Geneva: Famot, 1977), pp. 160–73; Rachel Arié, *España musulmana (Siglos VIII–XV)* (Barcelona: Editorial Labor, 1987), pp. 302–5. It is a fact that Christians believed the hammām to be a house of promiscuity and pleasure. In most cases this was wrong: Moorish baths were not promiscuous, and Muslim sexology discouraged intercourse in bath houses: "Nor is the bathhouse the place for coitus," says the early fifteenth century Shaykh Nafzawi, *The Glory of the Perfumed Garden: The Missing Flowers. An English Translation from the Arabic of the Second and Hitherto Unpublished Part of Shaykh Nafzawi's Perfumed Garden* (London: Neville Spearman, 1975), p. 227.

40. The only, almost clandestine, baths were functioning in private aristocratic hotels. Only a very few houses owned a bathtub. The Versailles court loved water, yet for the eye, not for the body. There would be no comeback of the bath (private) until the eighteenth century.

41. See Martin Marty, *Protestantism* (New York: Holt, Rinehart and Winston, 1972), pp. 242–50.

42. Karl Kautsky, *Communism in Central Europe in the Time of the Reformation*, trans. J. L. and E. G. Mulliken (London: Fisher Unwin, 1897; reprint, New York: Kelley, 1966).

43. See especially Dagmar Lorenz, "Vom Kloster zur Küche: Die Frau vor und nach der Reformation Dr. Martin Luthers," in *Die Frau von der Reformation zur Romantik: Die Situation der Frau vor dem Hintergrund der Literatur- und Sozialgeschichte*, ed. Barbara Becker Cantarino (Bonn: Bouvier-H. Grundmann, 1987), pp. 7–35.

44. According to Lorenz, although a Catholic, Hitler shared the values of a good German Lutheran. Ibid., pp. 29–30.

45. Darmon, *Mythologie de la femme*, pp. 33ff.

46. Ibid., pp. 44–45.

47. Thomas W. Laqueur, *Making Sex: Body and Gender from the Greeks to Freud* (Cambridge: Harvard University Press, 1990).

48. Foucault, *History of Sexuality*, vol. 1, pp. 103ff.

49. Actually, the clitoris was known in Greek and Arabic medicine (see Laqueur, pp. 108–9). Columbus *rediscovers* it.

50. Sissa, "Subtle Bodies," pp. 143–54.

51. J. C. Flügel, *The Psychology of Clothes* (London: Hogarth, 1930).

52. See Valerie Steele, *Fashion and Eroticism: Ideals of Feminine Beauty from the Victorian Era to the Jazz Age* (New York: Oxford University Press, 1985).

53. Thorstein Veblen, *Theory of the Leisure Class,* rev. ed. (New York: Random House, 1934).

54. See Quentin Bell, *On Human Finery,* 2d ed. (New York: Schoken Books, 1976), pp. 118ff.

55. Ibid.

56. See Elizabeth Ewing, *Dress and Undress: A History of Women's Underwear* (New York: Drama Book Specialists, 1978).

57. See Mary Lou Rosencranz, *Clothing Concepts: A Social-Psychological Approach* (New York, London: Macmillan Collier, 1972), 131ff. Rosencranz would treat as reversed symbols of slavery the nose rings used by Kuna and San Blas women in Panama, Arabian heavy anklets, Chinese bound feet, Western platform shoes in the sixteenth century (by 1530, not 1430, as she states on p. 133), and long fingernails in Ancient China.

58. Bell, *Holy Anorexia,* pp. 153–54.

59. See Brigitte Cazelles, *Le Corps de Sainteté, d'après Jehan Bouche d'Or, Jehan Paulus et quelques vies des XIIe et XIIIe siècles* (Geneva: Droz, 1982).

60. For the history of the corset, see Ewing, *Dress and Undress,* pp. 18ff.

61. David Kunzle, *Fashion and Fetishism: A Social History of the Corset, Tight-Lacing and Other Forms of Body-Sculpture in the West* (Totowa, N.J.: Rowman & Littlefield, 1982).

62. Ibid., pp. 11–12.

63. Steele, *Fashion and Eroticism,* p. 4.

64. Ibid.

65. Weber, *Schuhe,* p. 54.

66. Ledger, *Put Your Foot Down,* pp. 72–73.

67. See Robert van Gulik, *Sexual Life in Ancient China: A Preliminary Survey of Chinese Sex and Society from ca. 1500 B.C. till 1644 A.D.* (Leiden: Brill, 1961), chap. 12.

68. R. L. McNabb, *The Women of the Middle Kingdom* (Cincinnati, New York: Jennings Eaton, 1903), pp. 21–22. See also Rev. Justus Doolittle, *Social Life of the Chinese: With Some Account of Their Religious, Governmental, Educational and Business Customs and Opinions,* vol. 2 (New York: Harper and Bros., 1865), pp. 197ff.

69. McNabb, *Middle Kingdom,* pp. 22–23.

70. See van Gulik, *Sexual Life in Ancient China,* plate 12.

71. Ibid.

72. Kunzle, *Fashion and Fetishism,* p. 16.

73. William A. Rossi, *The Sex Life of the Foot and Shoe* (London: Routledge & Kegan Paul, 1977).

74. Kunzle, p. 18.

75. Ibid., p. 22.

76. R. Dale Guthrie, *Body Hot Spots: The Anatomy of Human Social Organs and Behavior* (New York: Van Nostrand-Reinhold, 1976).

77. Desmond Morris, *The Naked Ape,* 2d ed. (New York: Laurel, 1984).

78. Morris, *The Naked Ape,* p. 35.

79. John Liggett, *The Human Face* (New York: Stein and Day, 1974).

80. Ibid., pp. 21–25.

81. Ibid., pp. 158ff., based on Morris, p. 63.

82. Guthrie, *Hot Spots,* p. 104.

83. Ibid., p. 95.

84. Bram Dijkstra, *Idols of Perversity: Fantasies of Feminine Evil in Fin-de-Siècle Culture* (New York: Oxford University Press, 1986).

85. Editor's note: Professor Culianu added this last passage on "flappers" to his manuscript by hand. Although he indicated a note should occur here, no note was written.

I.

Classical Views of the Body in Religious Traditions

CREATION OF THE BODY IN GNOSTICISM

Pheme Perkins

The body situates human persons in the physical, social, and religious world. How it is marked, washed, anointed, and clothed, as well as its ritual postures and ascetic deprivations or indulgent feasting, serves as a reminder to the adherents of a religious tradition that they belong to a world which includes divine powers. Religious observances separate believers from outsiders, mark stages in individual progress toward religious perfection, and sometimes mark radical divisions within a religious group. Jesus' followers are distinguished from those of John the Baptist or the Pharisees by their refusal to fast (e.g., Mark 3:18–20)[1] or to observe certain customs of ritual washing before meals (Mark 7:1–8).

What began as rejection of established washings and rituals to mark the emergence of a new social group, the followers of Jesus, led to a sharp separation between body and spirit. Christians today find it difficult to understand the concern with cleanliness and bodily pollution found in other religious traditions. Michael Winter's essay in this volume provides an excellent example of cultural and religious options that Christianity came to reject. In a dramatic break with other Jewish sects, early Christians began to argue that it was not necessary to "live according to Jewish customs"[2] and, consequently, they did not require non-Jewish converts to the sect to undergo circumcision, that special mark in the male human flesh which set Jews apart from their unbelieving neighbors. Instead, the ritual immersion of converts in baptism, symbolic of participation in the death and resurrection of the sect's founder, came to designate the boundary between insider and outsider, between life and death (e.g., Rom. 6:1–4), and even between belonging to the "old humanity," in which persons are divided by race, status, and gender, and membership in a "new humanity," in which such distinctions are abolished (Gal. 3:26–28).[3]

The stories of early Christian martyrs and ascetics show a persistent concern with the body and "new life in the Spirit." Frequently, bodily limitations are transcended, so that the martyr or ascetic images for the rest of the faithful the possibility of living like the heavenly angels.[4] To nonbelievers, who lived relatively comfortably with their bodily desires and needs,[5] this early Christian preoccupation with the body must have seemed peculiar. The Jewish Essene sect known to us through the Dead Sea Scrolls had described the human being as torn by the warfare between two spirits. The spirits could be depicted as warring angels or as two spirits which God had set within the human heart (e.g., 1 QS 3,20-4,24).[6] In that example, the conflict is either externalized, the result of warring angels, or internalized, a division within the human heart. Though Christian ascetics often spoke of doing battle with demons (see Eph. 6:10–17), the body frequently becomes the source of evil influences. Christians inherited a dualism from the Pauline tradition in which "the flesh" was the source of those passions which led humanity to turn against the law of its creator (e.g., Gal. 5:16–26; Rom. 7:14–25).[7]

How did this dualistic evaluation of the body become established in Christian thought? One important line of development leads from first-century Jewish readings of Genesis into the mythological systems of second-century gnostic authors. In the second century, the most active gnostic sects were within or marginally related to the larger Christian community. Like other Christian teachers, gnostic teachers in second-century Rome and Alexandria gathered circles of disciples around them. Gnostics claimed to expound the esoteric teachings of the Savior, in contrast to the exoteric teachings found in what came to be the canonical gospels and the orthodox churches.[8] Some of the more prominent gnostic sects, such as that founded by Valentinus, appear to have developed their own system of sacraments and worship as well as speculative mythologies about the origins of the cosmos. Other gnostic writings employed the same mythological traditions as Valentinus and his disciples but were opposed to the Christianization of gnostic speculation. The mythological reading of Genesis presupposed by most second-century gnostic teachers appears to have emerged concurrently with and largely independently of the New Testament.[9]

Sethian gnostic texts[10] include extensive reworkings of the stories in Gen. 1–2.[11] The creation of Adam's body figures prominently in several of these writings. It is the work of the archons, or demonic powers which administer the material creation. Gen. 1:26 speaks of light or spirit above the waters of chaos and of the fashioning of humans in the divine image. This tradition generates some ambiguity about the status of the body. As the source of passion it is opposed to the spirit. But the body cannot be entirely derived from the darkness of chaos. Gnostic mythology holds that the reflection of a heavenly being in the waters inspired the archons to fashion Adam's body. Then the lower powers were tricked into endowing their creation with the spirit that had been lost by the divine Mother (Wisdom) in her attempt to create something without a counterpart. Consequently the body is also the vessel through which that divine light is gathered and saved.[12]

Body against the Spirit

Ascetic exhortation in gnostic writings exhibits hostility toward the body, which appears to be untouched by the ambiguity of its creation. The mythological underpinnings of this hostility are found not in Genesis but in a tale of the soul's fall from the heavenly world into the material one. An example from a gnostic tract called *Authoritative Teaching* provides a classic instance of this mytheme.

> In this very way, when the soul was cast into the body, it became a brother to lust and hatred and envy, a material soul. So therefore the body came from lust, and lust came from material substance. For this reason the soul became a brother to them.
>
> And yet they are outsiders, without power to inherit from the male, but they will inherit from their mother only. Whenever, therefore the soul wishes to inherit along with the outsiders—for the possessions of the outsiders are proud possessions, the pleasures of life, hateful envies, vainglorious things, nonsensical things . . . (23,12–33)[13]

When the soul turns away from the passions through ascetic conduct (*Authoritative Teaching* 31,24–30), she puts on heavenly bridal garments and returns the body to the evil powers who had fashioned it.

> She gave the body to those who had given it to her, and they were ashamed, while the dealers in bodies sat down and wept because they were not able to do any other business with that body. . . . They endured great labors until they had shaped the body of this soul, wishing to strike down the invisible soul. They were therefore ashamed of their work; they suffered the loss of the one for whom they had endured great labors. They did not realize that she has an invisible spiritual body, thinking, "We are her shepherd who feeds her." But they did not realize that she knows another way, which is hidden from them. This her true shepherd taught her in knowledge. (32,18–33,3)[14]

The false shepherds, in this instance, appear to be orthodox Christians. They are said to live in bestiality, not seeking God and persecuting anyone who asks about salvation (33,4–25). Unlike the pagans, who recognize a god higher than their idols, the orthodox do not hear the call to return to their heavenly dwelling (33,25–34,10).

The dualism which pits the soul and its "spiritual body" against the "material body" with its desires serves a double function. For the gnostic ascetic, the body is to be overcome and handed back to the powers who made it. At the same time, the body hides the gnostic's true identity from the world. Images of food and drink as imprisoning the soul which appear in *Authoritative Teaching* suggest that fasting played a major role in conquering the

passions associated with the body. Though the heavenly garment is described as "placed upon her in beauty of mind, not in pride of flesh,"
(32,6–7), analogies with the practices of other ascetic groups suggest that
a ritual clothing of the candidates may have symbolized entry into the
ascetic life. However, the addressees are also said to be "hidden" from their
persecutors. Apparently the gnostics still participate in rites for which the
false shepherds provide the food.[15] Thus the gnostics did not publicly make
their bodily appearance different from that of orthodox Christians.

Both Jewish and Christian readers found warrant for a distinction between body and soul in Genesis. God first creates Adam "in our image"
(1:26). Later, God fashions a being of the dust of the earth into which he
breathes life (2:7). The first-century Jewish philosopher Philo of Alexandria
distinguishes the heavenly image of God from the earthly Adam formed
of mind and body. The earthlike mind was rescued from the corruptibility
of matter when God breathed the power of life into it. Thus ensouled
humans are capable of conceiving of God and practicing virtue (see Philo,
Allegorical Interpretation i 29–40). The "image of God" referred to in Gen.
1:26 does not designate human beings as they exist in bodies, subject to
mortality and separated by gender. It refers to the archetype of humanity,
"a certain form or type or seal, grasped by thought, immaterial, neither
male nor female, incorruptible by nature" (Philo, *On the Creation of the
World* 134).[16]

Though Philo avoids vilifying the body by insisting that it was made of
the best matter and shaped more beautifully than the rest of material creation, the body has no place in the divine world.[17] Some gnostic writers
asked the obvious question: if the body has not been formed as an image
of the divine Word, whose image is it? Surprisingly, some gnostic exegetes
concluded that the bodily form of humanity was partly derived from a
heavenly image and partly from the demonic rulers of the lower world.
Because of its heavenly form, the body provides evidence that humanity is
superior to the god who claims to be creator and lord, the god of Genesis.

Creation of Adam in Sethian Gnosticism

Gnostic exegesis inverts the ordinary values attached to the actors in
Genesis. Jewish and Christian interpreters commonly assumed that the
male Adam reflected the image of God while the female Eve represented
the inferior world of sense perception, which required the ruling activity
of the rational male.[18] In a treatise called *Nature of the Archons*, this assumption is overthrown.[19] The female is associated with the heavens and the
male with the demonic. The heavenly image which inspires the archons to
shape Adam's body is feminine.[20] The maleness of the demonic archons is
emphasized in the narrative by their repeated attempts to rape and defile
the female bearers of the Spirit, Eve, and later Seth's sister, Norea.

The rulers see the image of the female savior, Imperishability, or divine Wisdom (Sophia), above the waters of chaos. Their lust for the spiritual image leads them to create man out of the earth (87,12–33). They combine the spiritual image with that of their own body, which is like an androgynous abortion with the head of a beast (87,29). This myth picks up the major points of the Genesis account: creation according to a divine image (Gen. 1:26f; 87,31–33); out of the dust of the ground (Gen. 2:7; 87,24–30), breathing in Spirit (Gen. 2:7; 88,3–5), Adam became a living soul (88,15).

The powers apparently thought that the maleness of their Adam would attract the heavenly form. They would be able to overpower the spiritual image when it came to Adam (87,34–88,1). In this version of the myth, masculinity is not "divine" but a projection of the lust of the archons.[21] The powers attempt to ensoul their creation by breathing in its face but fail despite the storm winds that they generated (88,4–10). Adam only becomes a "living soul" when the Spirit comes to him from above (88,15).

The creation of Eve follows the lead of Genesis in depicting the spiritual Eve as the true "mother of the living." The powers thought that by opening Adam's side like a woman's birth canal they could trap Adam in ignorance and extract the spiritual power Adam's soul had received (89,4–17). When they see the spiritual Eve talking with Adam, the powers seek to rape her. Eve leaves a fleshly image in her place which they pollute with their seed (89,17–30). The fleshly Eve has been defiled. She reflects humanity's involvement with base passions. Cain is the offspring of Eve and the archons, Abel of the fleshly Eve and Adam. But Seth and his sister, Norea, are offspring of the spiritual Eve.[22]

When the powers attempt to rape Norea, she rejects their claim that she should submit because her mother had done so (92,18–21). She asks the revealing angel who came to her rescue whether she belongs to the "matter" of the archons. The reader learns that the gnostic elect have a different origin.

> You and your offspring are from the primal father; from above. Their souls come out of the imperishable light. Thus the authorities cannot approach them because of the spirit of truth within them; and all who have come to know this way exist deathless in the midst of mortal humanity. (96,19–28)[23]

The knowledge which the gnostics possess is not completely contained in *Nature of the Archons*. The gnostic race is to appear "after three generations" when the Immortal Man will anoint them with eternal life (the Spirit) and teach them about the heavenly world (97,1–4).[24] Two lower stages of knowledge are represented in the text. The tale of Adam and the spiritual Eve focused on the difference between spiritual reality and imitations created by the powers. The story of Norea's rescue focused on the nature of the powers. They have no power over those who belong to the spiritual world. However, the powers are not destroyed until the Immortal Man comes.

As the text proceeds, the significance of Adam's bodily creation fades. Initially, lust for the fleshly Eve appeared to be manipulated by the spiritual Eve to deprive the archons of the light contained in their seed. This interpretation of the mytheme is developed in another gnostic treatise, *Origin of the World* (117,15–28).[25] But the Norea story and the concluding reference to the gnostic race suggest an even more radical separation between the spiritual and bodily realm than the one suggested by the use of a material image of Eve to dupe the powers. When all of the elect have been freed from ignorance and returned to the heavenly world, the archons are stripped of their power and the lower world collapses. Material creation dissolves along with its rulers.

The female saviors in *Nature of the Archons* demonstrate the tension between sexuality and the Spirit. The demonic powers attempt to use sexual passion to defile and imprison the Spirit. Humanity will be divided between the elect, children of the spiritual Eve, and those descended from the fleshly Eve. Conversion of the soul appears as turning away from the rule of the god of Genesis toward the Spirit depicted as "mother of the Living." This persistent use of female imagery for the spiritual world does not imply harmony between the spiritual and material aspects of human beings. But it may suggest an unusual asceticism which developed the image of God's feminine Wisdom as the appropriate spiritual counterpart for the soul. With an irony that is typical of gnostic reading, Adam abandons the powers who are his material "father and mother" in order to take his true wife, not the fleshly but the spiritual Eve.

Nature of the Archons is unusual in its persistent use of female images for the true spiritual power. *Origin of the World* expands on a number of the mythemes found in *Nature of the Archons* in a way which shifts the emphasis toward the more common male redeemer figures. *Nature of the Archons* suggests that the archons defiled the fleshly Eve simply because they lusted after the beauty of Adam's spiritual counterpart. *Origin of the World* provides a more extended explanation. The powers recognize that Eve is an image of the original vision they had seen. They wish to pollute her with their seed so that she will be unable to return to the heavenly world from this one (116,13–19).[26]

The shift toward a masculine redeemer figure is evident in the treatment of the creation of Adam. Unlike the figure in *Nature of the Archons*, the image which appears in the heavens is not feminine but that of the heavenly Adam, "the Adam of light." The author interprets this name to mean "luminous man of blood." A wisdom figure, now fallen into the lower world and identified as Pronoia (forethought) seeks to embrace him but is unable to, since she is mixed with darkness. Instead, she spills her light (blood) upon the earth (108,4–109,1). This passion is the origin of Eros. Creation of Paradise follows before the Light Adam withdraws from the lower world. These events are linked to the first three days of an eight-day creation cycle in which the presence of the Light Adam shaped the heavens and organized the lower world. The author has incorporated day four of Gen. 1:14–16 into the second day of this new creation myth.[27]

The powers decide to create a human being out of earth according to their image and that of the Light Adam in order to keep the Light Adam from destroying their work. The reader is told, however, that this plan will fail because the "molded form" they create is to become a container for light. It will lead to the destruction of the powers (113,5–10). The feminine side of this Adam stems from a counterplot by Sophia, who initiated the process by casting a drop of light into the waters, which became androgynous, first a female, then in the likeness of the mother (the heavenly Man). This androgynous Eve/Adam is the "mother of the living." She embodies the souls of those who are to appear on earth (113,21–114,17). The twelve months of her creation (113,29) link the soul to the signs of the zodiac which had been set up in the lower heavens.

In the initial cosmogony, the chief archon had six sons. The second, Sabaoth, rebelled against his father upon seeing a vision of the heavenly Wisdom. He was subsequently installed in a heaven above the seven planetary realms, along with Sophia's daughter Sophia-Life (103,31–106,18). His place as ruler of the sixth heaven is taken by Death, who engenders forty-nine androgynous demons representing all the negative passions and suffering of human life (106,19–107,1). Sophia-Life responds by creating seven good androgynous forces who generate other good spirits (107,2–18). The "souls" are presented to Sabaoth and commanded to "multiply and improve. Rule over all the creatures" (114,16–20; cf. Gen. 1:28). They will be imprisoned in bodies according to their destiny, hence the association of the soul with the Eighth, the zodiac.[28] At the same time, the rulers of the zodiac are also the source of all the virtues and blessings which come to humanity. Thus the soul is naturally suited to become the vehicle of salvation.

The material body is associated with seven planetary powers and through them with death, the passions, and all the evils which beset humankind. The chief archon forms the housing for the soul, the brain and spinal cord. The serpentine shape of that creation makes it an appropriate dwelling for the "Instructor," the soul-Adam generated by Wisdom, which will become the serpent of the Genesis story.[29] Ironically, the chief archon who wishes to hold Adam/Eve captive has created the image of liberation. The resulting "soul-Adam" proves superior to his creators.

> Then each of them cast his sperm into the navel of the earth. Since that day, the seven rulers have fashioned man with his body resembling their body, but his likeness resembling that man that appeared to them. His modelling took place by parts, one at a time. And their leader fashioned the brain and the nervous system. Afterwards he appeared as prior to him. He became a soul-endowed man. And he was called Adam, that is, "father," according to the name of the one that existed before him. (114,26–115,3)[30]

Origin of the World expands the account of how the bodily Adam is en-souled. At first Adam is inanimate, like an abortion. The chief ruler aban-dons the form because he remembers a word from the heavenly wisdom figure (Pistis, "faith") that the true man would enter the form and rule over it. After forty days, Sophia-Life breathes in Adam's face, enabling the protoplast to move on the ground. This episode recalls Gen. 1:26. God creates Adam to have dominion over what creeps on the earth on the sixth day. When questioned, the spirit within Adam tells the powers that he has come to destroy their work. They acknowledge Adam's superiority and place the figure in Paradise (115,16–30; cf. Gen. 1:28–30).

The powers rest on the Sabbath. On the eighth day, Wisdom sends Life/Eve, that is, the soul-Adam she had created, to ensoul the form created by the powers, Adam, and enable him to stand. He is no longer one of the "creeping things" on the earth but a human being. Adam recognizes her as the "mother of the living" (115,30–116,8). To keep Adam from following Eve/Wisdom, the powers create the fiction that Eve has been taken from Adam's rib and is to be subservient to him. They also defile the shadow image of the spiritual Eve through both natural and perverse sexual activi-ties. They begin by defiling her mouth, hoping to eradicate the word which had announced the existence of a higher God (116,8–117,14). The Eve-image bears seven sons by each of the powers and offspring from the other angels.

At this point the author injects his own commentary on the account of the myth that he has given. This is all a divine plan to deprive the powers of their seed by enclosing it in the forms created by them. These forms will condemn the powers. A tripartite schema is used to sum up the tale of Adam's creation. On the first day, the spiritual Light Adam appeared. On the sixth, the soul-endowed Adam appeared. On the eighth, the third Adam made of earth, the man of the law, appears (117,15–36). This divi-sion does not reflect the more complex division in the creation of the soul-endowed Adam that we saw in the narrative. Some scholars argue that it represents a Valentinian gnostic editing of the older mythological ac-count.[31] The "man of the law" represents the Jews. The psychic Adam represents orthodox Christians and the spiritual Adam stands for the gnos-tics themselves.[32]

When the author turns to instruct his reader about the present state of humanity, he introduces another division. The true elect are a "kingless race," apparently the offspring of the Light-Adam or Immortal Man, sent into the "molded forms" to reveal gnosis (123,34–125,13). Unlike the other three races of humanity, they do not belong to the rulers of the eighth. The powers are unable to conquer these luminous beings by mixing their seed with them (124,21–25).[33] These avatar figures teach gnosis in different lands among the churches made up of all kinds of seed (124,25–125,1). At the end of the age, each type returns to its source. Only the race without a king attains the unbegotten God (127,8–15). This eschatology makes no use of the elaborate account of body and soul in the cosmogony. The molded forms are merely vessels for various mixes of seed. The "kingless race" (the gnostics) evade contamination by the seed of the powers altogether.

Our final example of gnostic reworking of Genesis, the *Apocryphon of John*,[34] picks up several of the mythemes employed in *Origin of the World*: the creation of Adam's body by the powers, the luminous female helper who makes Adam superior to the powers, and an eschatological division of humanity. The formation of Adam takes place in five stages. The first stage is the manifestation of the First Man, the image of the Foreknowledge, Mother-Father, in the heavens. The likeness is a "human form" (CG II 14,26–33). This stage is followed by the creation of Adam by the powers according to the "image of God" and their likeness (15,1–12), the demonic creation of the anatomical parts (15,12–18,1) and the soul substance with the passions (18,2–19,12), the raising up the prostrate Adam by breathing power from Wisdom into his face (19,13–33), and finally, the darkening of Adam's light by encasing him in a material substance, which makes him subject to ignorance and mortality (20,28–21,13).

This schema is built on a tripartite division: heavenly image, psychic bodily image, and material body. The heavenly Man is the image of the Father's image, the Mother-Father. His human "form" is the "image of God" used by the powers. Adam participates in the divine image through the psychic body, not merely through the rational soul as in Philo's account. Consequently, the psychic body is introduced as a positive element in the soteriological system of the treatise even though it has been fashioned by the powers.[35]

Later in the anthropogonic myth, a dualistic system of two spirits is introduced. The counterfeit spirit, which emerges along with the cruel bondage of fate, leads astray the souls which fail to master it. The origin of that spirit is traced to the mytheme of the demonic powers defiling the worldly Wisdom figure in order to darken the superior wisdom of Adam (26,25–28,32).

The details of Adam's creation differ somewhat in the long version of the text and the short version. In the short account, the image in the waters is simply a male form: "The holy, perfect father, the first man, appeared in the form of a man. The blessed one revealed to them his likeness" (BG 48,1–5).[36] The powers then decide to make a man after the image and likeness of God (Gen. 1:26). In the long version, the image is male-female and the resulting creation shares the likeness of both the heavenly figure and its demonic creators: "He showed himself for them, the holy Mother-Father and perfect Providence (Gk. *pronoia*), the image of the invisible one who is the father of the universe, the one through whom all things came to be, the first man, since his likeness appeared in the shape of a man" (CG II 14,18–24).[37] Since both versions go on to speak of the image used as that of the perfect man, the short version may have dropped the mythic theme of a female component in the heavenly revelation of God. We have seen that this feature plays a prominent role in other versions of the tale.

The *Apocryphon of John* departs most strikingly from the other accounts of Adam's creation by inserting a description of the "soul-body." Both versions have a basic system in which each of the seven planetary demons creates the "soul" attached to one of the major organ systems (CG II 15,14–24). Each is also correlated with a divine attribute: divinity (or "goodness") with bone, lordship with sinew, fire with flesh, providence with marrow and bodily structure, kingdom with blood, insight with skin, wisdom with hair.[38] This scheme has its origins in Greek medicine, which was then attached to astrological speculation about the cosmic harmonies between various parts of the body and the planets.[39]

Instead of planetary names, each system is correlated with a divine attribute. This correlation is evidence that the structure of the body was created according to the image of the Perfect Man, which the powers saw reflected in the water. Another version of this speculation occurs in writings of the third-century Christian theologian Origen, who rejects the possibility that the body itself could be made in the image of God. He argues that there are similar names for material parts and the true "image" to which they refer. His prime example is the well-established association of blood with the soul.[40]

The long version of the *Apocryphon of John* follows the basic schema with an extended catalogue of particular body parts and the names of their creators (CG II 15,29–17,29). Another group of seven angels rules over the psychic abilities by which humans interact with the sensible world (CG II 17,29–18,1). Four more angels are guardians of the four "humors," or elements, as they affect the body (CG II 18,2–14). The final catalogue employs a common Stoic schema, which derives the various passions from four chief sources: pain, pleasure, desire, and fear (CG II 18,14–35).[41] However, this list appears to be taken from a source which did not endorse the Stoic view that a person had to become passionless. It concludes with an observation about ". . . all those of the sort which are useful and which are evil; but their true thought (Gk. *ennoia*) is sense perception[42] which is the head of the material and the psychic" (CG II 18,32–35). The combination of Greek astrological medicine and philosophic speculation suggests that the source from which the author has taken this rather elaborate system claimed to be able to manipulate the passions according to whether a given passion is useful or evil. The accumulation of demon-names suggests that the manipulation was a matter of magical practice of some sort.

Ascetic manipulation of the body in the corresponding esoteric tradition in Origen apparently developed in a different direction. Each bodily part has an "inner name" which reflects its true reality. The ascetic can obtain the desired goal of controlling that member of the body by focusing on the ideal which corresponds to it.[43]

The soteriological sections of the *Apocryphon of John* suggest some form of ascetic practice. The Spirit of life is said to exist within the elect, so that they are purified from all wickedness and evil. They are able to live in the flesh without the passions, such as anger, envy, jealousy, desire, and greed (CG II 25,23–26,7).[44] Yet the creation of Adam's psychic body suggests that the passions are aroused by the astrological demons which control them, a view which also appears in Christian ascetic writers of the period.[45] The *Apocryphon of John* refers to two spirits, the spirit of life and an opposing spirit which Ialdabaoth creates to imprison humanity (CG II 26,25–28,32). The power of the latter is associated with the final stage of the tripartite creation of Adam, humanity's imprisonment in a body made out of the material elements (CG II 20,28–21,13).[46] Only when enclosed in the material spirit does humanity become mortal, subject to desire and ignorant of its true spiritual nature.

The gnostic author would not agree with the Stoic doctrine that the wise are superior to the fate which controls their material bodies because they can control what is "in their power," passions, evaluations, and the other mental responses to the sensible world. Both the fate and the passions themselves have been subjected to demonic powers in their creation.[47] Purification by the Spirit is required for the perfect to separate themselves from the passions. It would appear to have been associated with some form of ritual or ascetic practice, since the *Apocryphon of John* insists that the perfect who have received the Spirit have not "done these works." The Spirit has strengthened such souls and preserved them from falling into wickedness (CG II 26,7–19). Such souls will be taken up to eternal rest (26,23–31). Others will be reincarnated until they are connected with a soul that contains the Spirit of life (26,32–27,21). Only those who are apostates from gnosticism perish forever (27,22–31).

The catechesis on the fate of different souls is framed by accounts of the origin of the opposing Spirit, which exploit the ambiguous sexual history of the Genesis ancestors. The earthly Eve is seduced by Ialdabaoth, who begets children by her and implants sexual desire in human offspring. Sexual intercourse serves as the mode by which copies of the original bodies are reproduced. Prior to the descent of the holy Spirit, the bodies are animated by the opposing (or "counterfeit") Spirit (CG II 24,16–31). The second explanation ties the origin of the opposing spirit to the myth of the seduction of human women by the fallen angels (Gen. 6:4). Fate, a chain which holds the material world in bondage, is created when the powers commit adultery with Wisdom (28,5–32). The powers come as angels to the daughters of men but seduce them by appearing to be the women's husbands. This adultery fills the human women with the counterfeit spirit, which resembles the divine spirit. Humanity then begins to beget children endowed with this false spirit and remains enslaved until the coming of the gnostic revelation (29,16–30,12).

The role of sexuality in generating bodies endowed with the false spirit suggests that the primary expression of gnostic perfection was the rejection of marriage and childbearing. If all adherents were required to refrain from sexuality, then the condemned souls, those who had received the spirit of life but had turned away, may have been lapsed ascetics.[48] This sharp dualism is required by the *Apocryphon of John's* conviction that once received, the Spirit of life is stronger than the counterfeit spirit. The psychic body was a mixed creation capable of being enlightened and animated by the divine spirit, just as Adam had been enlightened by the heavenly wisdom associated with Eve. Only the second formation of Adam, his entombment in matter which operates under the influence of fate, made humanity mortal and ignorant of the divine.[49]

Though clearly dependent upon first-century Jewish interpretations of the dual creation of Adam in Gen. 1:26–27 and 2:7, the *Apocryphon of John* has not remained content with shifting Gen. 2:7 to the soul which animates the lower appetites and bodily functions as in Philo. Instead, the author adds an episode in which the material body is fashioned in order to cut off any possibility of human improvement from the spiritual awareness that Adam's soul had received. This addition serves to underscore the maliciousness of the creator god. In the end, the creator and his powers cannot prevail against the superior power of the spiritual world. Because they are blind to spiritual reality, Wisdom is able to undermine their efforts by introducing counterimages into the formation of the human soul, which can be awakened by the coming of revelation.

The gnostic exegetes represented one of a number of ascetic movements in second-century Christianity. They saw sexuality as the prime example of the body's power to reduce human beings to the level of beasts. To recover its divine image, the soul must cling to the Spirit and reject all the impulses which come from the body.[50] Instead of "explaining away" the bodily creation of Adam in God's image by referring the Genesis account to God's heavenly image, the Word, and to the psychic image, the human soul, the gnostic exegetes treated the contradictions evident in Genesis by referring to two powers active in shaping Adam, the hidden Wisdom and the lower creator and his offspring.

Nature of the Archons draws a striking portrait of the rulers of the material world as lust-driven rapists. As ascetic Christianity struggled to disengage itself from the demands of marriage and family that apparently were supported by ecclesiastical authorities (e.g., 1 Tim. 3:1–13; 5:9–16), refusal to marry was perceived as an attack upon the social and the divine orders. Attempting to ward off the suspicions of hostile outsiders, Christian bishops were not ready to encourage such behavior—especially not by marriagable women. Norea's plea to the angel must have echoed the sentiments of many young women and men attracted by the ascetic ideal but forced by their families to take on the obligations of marriage and family.

Christian ascetics had to engage in elaborate footwork to explain why Christ appears to accept the Genesis command to marry (e.g., Mark

10:5–9). The Syrian writer Tatian explained that once Adam had abandoned his true "father and mother," God and the Spirit, he was subject to death and forced to cling to woman through physical intercourse. When the soul regains its true Spirit, it is raised above mortality and must abandon marriage.[51] The gnostic exegete has a "cleaner" solution to the dilemma. The commands to marry, propagate, and obey found in the Genesis narrative all derive from the demonic powers, who know that if their hold on humanity is broken, they will cease to exist. *Nature of the Archons* reads Gen. 2:24 as a command to abandon the demon "fathers and mothers" for the spiritual Eve, who is the soul's true companion.

Both *Origin of the World* and the *Apocryphon of John* provide evidence of speculative interest in the creation of the body and soul of Adam. Astrological correlations between the body and the zodiac, the planets, and even the temporal divisions of days, weeks, and years explain the ebb and flow of passion. Origen's use of a similar tradition suggests that such speculation formed part of the arsenal of Christian ascetics. Techniques for manipulating the soul or body are necessary to overcome the dominating power of the passions.

All gnostic exegesis is marked by a spirit of revolt, a rejection of the conventional readings in the Jewish and orthodox Christian communities. The "image" of God does not apply only to Adam's soul. Those who know recognize the image of heavenly Wisdom or the Immortal Man in the physical body as well as in the psychic body. Among the ironic correlations made by gnostic authors we find the chief archon shaping the brain and spinal cord to look like the serpent, the Instructor through whom the spiritual Eve will speak to Adam. The body may be no more than the suitable container for light, which is to return to the heavenly world, but the image on the container is double-edged. For the spiritually blind, it bespeaks bondage to the powers of the material world. For the enlightened, it is the path of liberation.

NOTES

1. As transmitted in Mark, the episode has been revised to indicate that after the death and resurrection of Jesus, the Christian community returned to the practice of fasting common among pious sects of Jews. Matt. 6:16–18 creates a new way of separating the two communities: Christians reject the outward signs of a person who is fasting. See W. D. Davies and Dale C. Allison, *The Gospel according to St. Matthew, Volume I. Introduction and Commentary on Matthew I-VII* (International Critical Commentary; Edinburgh: T. & T. Clark, 1988), 617–21. Outsiders saw fasting as a practice peculiar to Judaism (618).

2. The Greek verb *ioudaizein*, which lies at the heart of Paul's dispute with those who do insist that gentile converts come under the law (Gal. 2:14), means to adopt a Jewish style of life (see Charles H. Cosgrove, *The Cross and the Spirit* [Macon: Mercer, 1988], 6).

3. See Hans D. Betz, *Galatians* (Philadelphia: Fortress, 1979), 181–201. The Pauline tradition developed from a mythological identification of the Christ with the primal, androgynous human (199). The body of the risen Christ into which the believer is incorporated by baptism came to be given cosmological significance. The risen Christ, whose body is the church, was understood to be the incarnation of God's creative Wisdom (Col. 1:15–20; Eph. 1:15–23). These developments provide a point of comparison with the assimilation of the body of the believer, the body of the Dainichi, and the cosmic Buddha body described in Thomas P. Kasulis's essay in this volume, though they lack the metaphysical grounding found in the Japanese example.

4. See Peter Brown, *The Body and Society* (New York: Columbia University Press, 1988), 83–189.

5. See P. Veyne, *A History of Private Life in Antiquity: From Pagan Rome to Byzantium* (Cambridge: Harvard University Press, 1987), 202–5, and E. R. Dodds, *Pagan and Christian in an Age of Anxiety* (Cambridge: Cambridge University Press, 1965), 29–36.

6. This text from a book of communal rules can be found in G. Vermes, *The Dead Sea Scrolls in English*, 3d ed. (Baltimore: Penguin, 1987), 84–85.

7. See P. Perkins, "Pauline Anthropology in the Light of Nag Hammadi," *Catholic Biblical Quarterly* 48 (1986), 512–22.

8. Kasulis's essay provides a different example of how an esoteric tradition reformulates the doctrine of an orthodox religious community.

9. See G. Stroumsa, *Another Seed: Studies in Gnostic Mythology* (NHS XXIV; Leiden: E. J. Brill, 1984).

10. "Sethian" refers to a collection of gnostic writings whose mythological scheme links the saving gnosis with the figure of Seth. See John D. Turner, "Sethian Gnosticism: A Literary History," in *Nag Hammadi, Gnosticism and Early Christianity* ed. C. W. Hedrick and R. Hodgson, Jr. (Peabody, Mass.: Hendrickson, 1986), 55–86.

11. See B. Pearson, "Biblical Exegesis in Gnostic Literature," *Gnosticism, Judaism and Egyptian Christianity* (Minneapolis: Fortress, 1990), 29–38.

12. See Richard Valantasis, "Adam's Body: Uncovering Esoteric Traditions in the *Apocryphon of John* and Origen's *Dialogue with Heraclides*," *Second Century* 7 (1989–90), 153.

13. The translation is taken from James M. Robinson, ed., *The Nag Hammadi Library in English*, 3d revised ed. (San Francisco: Harper & Row, 1988), 306.

14. Ibid., 309.

15. A similar dualism in which the gnostics are "hidden" among orthodox Christians is explicitly described in the *Apocalypse of Peter* (CG VII 75,26–76,4; *NHLE*: 375).

16. See Thomas Tobin, *The Creation of Man: Philo and the History of Interpretation* (CBSMS 14; Washington: Catholic Biblical Association, 1983), 102–34.

17. Ibid., 136–48.

18. This schema is assumed by Saint Paul in 1 Cor. 11:7–8; on Philo's use of Eve for sense perception, see Tobin, *Creation*, 143.

19. Robinson, *Nag Hammadi Library in English*, 162–69.

20. See the detailed study by Ingvild S. Gilhus, *The Nature of the Archons: A Study in the Soteriology of a Gnostic Treatise from Nag Hammadi (CG II,4)* (Wiesbaden: Otto Harrassowitz, 1985).

21. See Gilhus, *Nature of the Archons*, 48–51.

22. Ibid., 60–62.

23. Robinson, *Nag Hammadi Library in English*, 169.

24. Gilhus, *Nature of the Archons*, 112f.

25. Ibid., 115f.

26. Gedaliahu A. G. Stroumsa, *Another Seed: Studies in Gnostic Mythology* (NHS XXIV; Leiden: E. J. Brill, 1984), 43.

27. See Michel Tardieu, *Trois mythes gnostique: Adam, Eros et les animaux d'Egypte dans un écrit de Nag Hammadi (II,5)* (Paris: Etudes Augustiniennes, 1974), 94–98.

28. *Nat. Arch.* (95,13–96,3) contains a version of Sabaoth's rebellion, but it is not connected with the creation of Adam.

29. See Tardieu, *Trois mythes*, 124f.

30. Robinson, *Nag Hammadi Library in English*, 181.

31. For a characteristically Valentinian account of the three types of human being and their salvation, see the *Tripartite Tractate* (CG I 5, 118,14–122,12; *Nag Hammadi Library in English*, 94–96).

32. See Francis Fallon, *The Enthronement of Sabaoth: Jewish Elements in Gnostic Creation Myths* (NHS X; Leiden: E. J. Brill, 1978), 120–21.

33. Cf. the attempt of the powers to defile Norea, the ancestor of the gnostics, in *Nat. Arch.* (92,28–93,2).

34. This writing exists in several copies. A complete copy of the longer recension found in the second codex from the Nag Hammadi library (CG II) can be found translated in Robinson, *Nag Hammadi Library in English*, 105–23. The shorter recension found in the Berlin Gnostic Codex (BG) can be found in W. Foerster, *Gnosis 1: Patristic Evidence*, translation ed. R. McL. Wilson (Oxford: Oxford University Press, 1972), 105–20.

35. See Richard Valantasis, "Adam's Body: Uncovering Esoteric Traditions in the *Apocryphon of John* and Origen's *Dialogue with Heraclides*," *Second Century* 7 (1989–90), 153f.

36. Foerster, *Gnosis 1*, 113; (translation given here is that of the author).

37. Robinson, *Nag Hammadi Library in English*, 113; (translation here is that of the author).

38. See M. Tardieu, *Codex de Berlin* (Paris: Editions du Cerf, 1984), 300–304.

39. Ibid., 304–8.

40. See Valantasis, "Adam's Body," 158f.

41. See Takashi Onuki, *Gnosis und Stoa* (Göttingen: Vandenhoeck & Ruprecht, 1989), 35–48; also Tardieu, *Codex*, 313–16.

42. For this reading of the lacuna, see Onuki, *Gnosis*, 50. Many translators emend the text to "not useless" and read "necessity" in the lacuna so that the conclusion becomes an affirmation of Stoic teaching.

43. Valantasis, "Adam's Body," 161.

44. See Michael Williams, *The Immovable Race* (NHS XXIX; Leiden: E. J. Brill, 1985), 127f.

45. Ibid., 130.

46. Tardieu, *Codex*, 320f.

47. Onuki, *Gnosis und Stoa*, 51.

48. The common reading of this passage (see Tardieu, *Codex*, 338f.) treats it as an expression of a gnostic dualism of natures or demythologized eschatology.

49. An earlier form of the tradition probably had the angels create Adam's body, rather than the bodily soul; see B. Pearson, "Biblical Exegesis," 32–34, and R. van den Broek, "The Creation of Adam's Psychic Body in the Apocryphon of John," *Studies in Gnosticism and Hellenistic Religion Presented to Gilles Quispel* (EPRO 91; Leiden: E. J. Brill, 1981), 38–57.

50. See P. Brown, *Body and Society*, 83–102.

51. Ibid., 92.

ISLAMIC ATTITUDES TOWARD THE HUMAN BODY

Michael Winter

This survey of the dominant attitudes toward the human body in Islam is based on texts which are considered normative within the Islamic tradition and which to a large extent determine the believer's views and practices. These texts—the Qur'an, the holy book of Islam, and the "traditions of the Prophet" *(ḥadīth)*—are considered to be God's revelation to humankind through the prophet Muhammad. Approaching a tradition's view of the human body through its canonical texts, though undeniably correct, cannot claim to exhaust the subject, since no religion exists merely as a set of texts. Scriptures interact with the everyday lives of people in the civilizations in which a religious tradition is situated. Islam, far from being only a dogma based upon text, is a culture and civilization that is based upon the Qur'an and hadith but develops far beyond these sources. Dance, dress, amulets, painting (particularly miniatures), popular literature, and contemporary film, and medical theory and practice can tell us a great deal about the wide variety of attitudes toward the human body in Islamic cultures.[1] The methodological strategy of the present discussion, however, maintains that the textual views of the body within Islam exert a normative influence in the tradition. Thus by outlining these positions, we can clearly see one of the important and essential sources for Islamic views of the human body. Moreover, this discussion focuses on normative Islam (although a few examples from Sufism are discussed). Popular Islam reveals a rich variety of notions and customs concerning our subject which cannot be dealt with in an introductory survey such as this.[2]

In addition to the Qur'an and hadith, I will draw from the writings of great Muslim theologians such as Abu Ḥāmid al-Ghāzalī to show how laws regarding bodily behavior have been interpreted by believers. I will also bring in the Sufi case, for Sufi fundamentalism provides a rich context for studying Islamic attitudes toward the human body. I will treat issues of cleanliness, eating, male-female relationships, marriage, and sexual behavior and briefly examine the attitudes behind present-day dress codes for Muslim women.

The basic Islamic attitudes toward the human body can be summarized as follows:

1. Like Judaism and Christianity, Islam accepts the Biblical dogma that human beings are created of dust and return to dust and that the dead will be resurrected on the day of judgment. The tension between the fragility and ephemeral nature of the human body and the religious meaning of human life is superbly, if brutally, expressed in the Jewish Rabbinical literature: "Reflect on three things, and you will not come within the power of sin: Know from where you came, whither you are going, and before whom you are destined to give a future account and reckoning. From where you came—from a fetid drop; whither you are going—to a place of dust, worms and maggots; and before whom you are destined to give future account and reckoning—before the supreme King of Kings, the Holy one, blessed is He."[3]

2. Islam makes no distinction between the religious and the profane— neither in public life nor in private matters. Hence it regards the human body as it does all other things—in religious terms. Nothing is seen as secular or as religiously neutral.

3. Like Judaism but unlike Christianity, Islam emphasizes "orthopraxy," right behavior or practice, rather than orthodoxy, right belief. In other words, one participates in the meanings of being a Muslim through ritual action, not merely through a profession of faith. Adherence to the prescriptions of the *Sharīʿa* Holy Law is more important than dogma (although the latter has its place in Islamic religious life). Islamic law stipulates in detail how believers should treat their bodies. In the spirit of the Torah (especially the book of Leviticus) and the Jewish *Shulhan ʿAruch,* the manual for orthodox Jewish life, Islamic Holy Law leaves nothing to the Muslim's imagination or discretion as to how one should conduct one's life. Nothing is considered too personal or too intimate to be overlooked by the *ulama,* the religious scholars of Islam, who evolved, studied, and applied the Sharīʿa.

4. Islam is sometimes described as the most "natural" religion: it accepts in a matter-of-fact manner all natural phenomena, including the human condition. The physical imperfections and weaknesses of human beings are rarely seen as a source of embarrassment or as a problem.

5. While the duality between body and soul is not unknown in Islam, the important distinction is between this lowly world *(al-dunyā)* and the hereafter *(al-ākhira),* the latter being immeasurably more valuable. It is interesting to note that the common Arabic term for soul is *nafs,* meaning "the self," the appetitive soul, or that part of personality which harbors desires and ambitions—the crafty and naturally selfish part of human beings. The struggle against the *nafs (mujāhadat al-nafs,* sometimes referred to as the bigger *jihād,* or holy war), is incumbent upon Muslim moralists, particularly Sufis.

The most authentic expression of the spirit of Islam is found in the Qur'an, the text Muslims regard as God's direct speech to the prophet Muhammad during the period 610–632. The Qur'an, like the Bible, has much to say about the question which occupies us in this volume. According to the Qur'an, human beings are created from dust or clay, or water, as one verse has it. From there the human develops into semen or sperm, which becomes an embryo, then a shapeless lump of flesh (another verse says: a chewed-up lump). The lump of flesh becomes a child and finally an adult. The man or woman will die but will be raised from the dead on the day of resurrection.[4]

On cleanliness, a religious matter since it must precede each of the five daily prayers, the Qur'an says:

> O believers, when you stand up for the service of prayer, wash your faces and hands up to your elbows, and also wipe your heads, and wash your feet up to the ankles. If you are in a state of seminal pollution, than bathe and purify yourself well. But in case you are ill or are traveling, or you have satisfied the call of nature, or have slept with a woman, and you cannot find water, then take wholesome dust and pass it over your face and your hands, for God does not wish to impose any hardship on you. He wishes to purify you.[5]

Like the Bible, the Qur'an addresses itself to questions related to women and sexual relations. There is no doubt that Islam improved women's conditions and status in comparison with their situation in Arabia before the appearance of Muhammad. Nevertheless, the Qur'an presupposes a male-dominated society, in both legal and personal matters. It says in the Qur'an: "Men have a rank above them [women]."[6] Also: "Your women are like a field to you; so seed them as you wish."[7] The Qur'an allows a Muslim man to marry up to four wives, provided he treats them justly and equally.[8] A husband may divorce his wife, yet he must wait the legally prescribed period of three months to prevent a dissolution of the marriage while the woman is pregnant.[9] Some Qur'anic verses are devoted to menstruation, described as "a period of stress,"[10] and to breast-feeding.[11]

Both the pleasures awaiting the just in heaven and the tortures awaiting evildoers in hell are corporeal, even sensual, and are graphically described in the Qur'an. In paradise, the deserving ones will recline on couches, suffering from neither the heat of the sun nor intense cold. They will be served by boys of everlasting youth. They will enjoy rivers of pure water, rivers of milk, wine (forbidden to Muslims in this world), streams of honey, and fruit of every kind. God promised to pair the male dwellers of paradise with maidens with large black eyes (*hūr al-ʿīn*)—full bosomed young women who will preserve their virginity for them, never touched by man or jinn.[12] According to a Muslim tradition, women will meet their husbands in paradise. Those condemned to reside in hell will live forever in fire and be given boiling water to drink which will cut their intestines to shreds.[13]

God's promises and threats in this regard are unequivocally clear. The orthodox attitude was not to question but to accept the text literally, "without how" *(bilā kayfa)*. Yet, Ibn al-Nafîs, a thirteenth-century doctor and theologian, although generally adhering to orthodox positions, explains that the Prophet could not have presented the life to come as spiritual, because the intellects of most people fall short of appreciating spiritual pleasures and pains. If a common man were told that as a reward for his loyal worship and just behavior, Allah would transfer him to a world where there are no bodily pleasures and where one must continually praise and glorify God, this common man would more than likely rather miss out on that happiness. Ibn al-Nafîs concludes that the Prophet had to present future life as composed of body and soul (yet the Qur'an says nothing about the spiritual side of otherworldly bliss).[14]

After the Qur'an, the best source for Islamic attitudes is the Prophet's customs *(sunna)*, as preserved in the hadith, or traditions about Muhammad's sayings and actions. The sunna are the recorded behaviors of the Prophet, and as such the second source of the Holy Law. The Prophet's is the model way of life which every Muslim must try to emulate. Like the Qur'an, the sunna's position on the human body and the human condition is generally "natural," uncomplicated, and straightforward. The figure of Muhammad is entirely human; in the Middle Ages, Christian polemicists attacked Islam, pointing to the Prophet's humanity, even sensuality. The contrast with the figure of Jesus was striking in this respect. According to a well-known hadith, Muhammad said, "I am not an angel, but the son of a woman from [the tribe of] Quraysh who used to eat sliced, dried meat."[15]

Indeed, the sunna provide descriptions of Muhammad's outward appearance. A great deal is reported about his way of dressing, eating, and sleeping and about his sex life. Muhammad was known for his extraordinary sexual drive and virility. Various traditions give the number of his wives as between nine and fourteen. One of the best authorities on the Prophet's daily activities, preferences, and temperament was 'Ā'isha, his favorite wife. He married her when she was six years old and consummated their marriage when she was nine. Other information was transmitted from other people who had the privilege of being near the Prophet and observing his behavior. Muhammad saw it as his religious duty to guide the Muslim community, not only by God's revelation in the Qur'an but also by his own personal example, which came to be regarded as a part of the revelation and therefore legally binding. It was said of Muhammad that despite his natural shyness, he taught his followers everything, even how to relieve nature. It is inconceivable that similar information would have been attributed to the founder of any other religion. Not surprisingly, similar details were reported about the personal lives of certain renowned leaders and teachers of early Islam.

Abū Hāmid al-Ghazālī (d. 1111), one of the great exponents of Islamic civilization, was arguably the greatest Muslim theologian and one of the most profound religious thinkers of all time. In his monumental *Ihyā' ʿulūm al dīn,* the "Revivification of the religious sciences," al-Ghazālī sets up a practical and spiritual program for Islamic living. His purpose was to combine the principles of orthodoxy which he upheld with the spirituality of Sufism, thus bestowing on the religious ordinances an inner symbolic meaning beyond the outward actions prescribed by the Sharīʿa. Al-Ghazālī does not shy away from dealing extensively with the most minute physical actions incumbent upon Muslims, as can be seen, for example, in two parts of the *Ihyā'.* The first part is about bodily purity as a precondition of prayer (significantly, he calls this chapter "the mysteries of cleanliness"), while the second part is a marriage manual.

Al-Ghazālī's treatise on cleanliness states that "the Prophet said: 'Religion is founded on cleanliness. Cleanliness is the key to prayer.' God said: 'Therein there are men who love purity, and God loves the pure.' The Prophet said: 'Cleanliness is one-half of belief.'" In his didactic way, al-Ghazālī explains that "purity has four stages: (1.) The purification of the external organs from excrement and filth. (2.) The purification of the bodily organs from sins and faults. (3.) The purification of the heart from evil traits and vices. (4.) The purification of the inner self [or heart] from anything except God. This is the stage of Prophets and saints."[16] Al-Ghazālī characteristically makes a distinction between simple Muslims who cannot and must not proceed beyond the external, prescribed ordinances and the elite *(khāssa),* who alone are able to understand the religious realities.

Again, al-Ghazālī provides guidance in such things as how ablution *(wudūʾ,* performed after a "minor" pollution) and bath *(ghusl,* performed after a "major" bodily pollution) should be carried out, at what point water ceases to be pure and becomes unclean, and which substances cause uncleanliness. These are primarily religious matters, not matters of personal hygiene, although al-Ghazālī and other religious scholars were not unmindful of their hygienic aspects. Al-Ghazālī says: "A man should not shave, trim his fingernails, sharpen the blade [with which he shaves], cause blood to flow, or reveal any part of him while in a state of major ritual impurity [*janāba,* usually as a result of sexual intercourse]; for all parts of his body would be restored to him in the hereafter, and he would thus return to a state of major ritual impurity. It is said that every hair will demand an account for the infraction it committed."[17]

To make al-Ghazālī's manual more concrete, I wish to use one example— not a very nice example, but as the hadith says, "There is no shame in religion." When relieving nature it is forbidden to face the *qibla,* the direction of Mecca, since it is the direction of Muslim prayer; nor is it permissible to sit with the back toward Mecca, for obvious reasons. However, dispensation is given if one is inside a building.[18]

Al-Ghazālī's marriage manual reveals a similar attitude toward the psychological and moral aspects of married and sexual life. Here too the primary motivation is religious. Because marriage is sanctioned by the example of the Prophet, it has the advantage of preventing sinful behavior or thoughts. Like other religions, Islam disapproves of masturbation as a way to seek sexual relief. Al-Ghazālī says: "A youthful bachelor is torn among three evils: The least of these is marrying a bondmaid, which would lead to enslavement of the child; worse than that is masturbation; and the most abominable of the three is fornication."[19]

Celibacy was never encouraged in Islam. In an anti-Christian polemical strain, a certain hadith says: "There is no monasticism in Islam." Junayd, one of the great early Sufis, allegedly said: "I am as much in need of sexual intercourse as I am of food, so the wife is definitely nourishment and a means for the purification of the heart."[20]

Al-Ghazālī carefully explains how a husband ought to behave during his wife's menstruation, the limits on sexual relations during that period, and how to teach his wife or wives which prayers to perform or omit while in this condition. It should be noted that the Islamic laws regulating menstruation are more complicated and severe than the Christian parallels but less so than those in Judaism.[21] Discussing at length the etiquette of intimate relations, al-Ghazālī prescribes which verses should be said at each moment.[22]

The question of preventing pregnancy by *coitus interruptus* is also addressed. Al-Ghazālī says that "the ulama have split into four groups over whether it is permissible or reprehensible: There are those who consider it unconditionally permissible under all circumstances . . . those who forbid it in all circumstances . . . those who say it is permissible with her consent . . . [and] those who say it is permissible with a bondmaid but not with a free woman." Al-Ghazālī himself sides with those ulama who sanctioned the practice. Here we have evidence that leading authorities in medieval Islam approved of birth control, even if its purpose was, in al-Ghazālī's words, "preserving the beauty of the woman and her portliness in order to maintain enjoyment, and protect her life against the danger of childbirth or the fear of excessive hardship on account of numerous offspring, and guarding against the excessive pursuit of gain and against the need for resorting to evil means. This too is not prohibited, because encountering fewer hardships is an aid to religion."[23]

It is worth looking at Sufi attitudes concerning the human body. Sufism is an integral part of Islam, not an esoteric sect; but it is a multifaceted phenomenon, and what applies to one Sufi order or shaykh may not apply to others. For example, there are vast differences between orthodox, Sharīʿa-abiding Sufis and antinomian Sufis. Some unorthodox Sufi orders, the Rifāʿiyya, for example, were famous for their dervishes' practice of overcoming the natural bodily limits through spiritual power. The Rifāʿiyyas were able to swallow cacti, eat glass, handle venomous snakes, swallow fire, and pierce themselves with sharp spikes without wounding themselves. In a ceremony called *dawsa* (trampling), the shaykh of the Saʿdiyya order, an Egyptian offshoot of the Rifāʿiyya, reportedly rode on horseback on top of dervishes who were lying prostrate without causing them any harm.²⁴ Such practices, in which the power of the spirit proved stronger than the body, were introduced into Sufism under Indian influence and were frowned upon by orthodox ulama and orthodox Sufis alike. It is noteworthy that while some Sufis adhered to asceticism, others led (and even preached) decidedly nonascetic lifestyles. A Sufi is defined by mysticism, not by denial of bodily pleasures.

Concerning the questions of sexuality and bodily needs, Sufi attitudes tend to be more nuanced and complicated than those of other Muslims. While orthodox Sufis adhere in principle to the Prophet's sunna of marriage, some wished to remain celibate in order to seek the One unhindered by marriage and family.²⁵ ʿAbd al-Wahhāb al-Shaʿrānī (d. 1565), the most prominent Sufi writer of his time, pays much attention to the idea of waraʿ, or scrupulousness, especially with regard to food, thus expressing an original, if somewhat crude, Sufi attitude. He believes that eating morally tainted or suspicious food (harām or shubha) is harmful to both the soul and the body. The less a Sufi eats, the better. A Sufi should refrain from food not only out of fear that it may be ill-gotten, but also because one should be ashamed of the needs of the body while in the constant presence of God. Shaʿrānī is virtually obsessed with this idea. He states that unlawful food is the source of evil. He maintains that Adam's sin was not disobedience but eating unlawful food in Paradise. Adam's sin caused human bodily needs for which Paradise was not the proper place, and that was the real reason for Adam's expulsion from Paradise.²⁶

The concept of the soul-body dichotomy, which Islam received from a variety of sources—gnostic, Eastern, and others—is also represented in Sufi literature. According to the Persian mystic Farīduddīn ʿAttār, the body is the soul's cage. In the hereafter, the body will become soul, and one must prepare for it in this world. In one of the fables told by ʿAttār, the body and soul are two servants in a king's orchard, one blind and the other lame. The lame man climbs on the blind man's back and steals some figs. The king is not deceived, however, and both are punished. Likewise, God will punish both one's soul and one's body, even if both try to cast blame on the other.²⁷

The philosophers dealt extensively with the duality of body and soul, but despite their immense contribution to Islamic culture, their attitudes were not considered characteristically Islamic. Many of their conceptions of the human body (as well as other matters) were directly inspired by Greek philosophy. This applies to medical theories and the functions of the organs of the human body as parallel to functions of the different classes of society. It is interesting to see how Ibn Nafīs—an imaginative but orthodox theologian—addressed this question:

> Man is composed of body and soul; the body is this thing which can be perceived, but the soul is that to which one refers when one says "I." That

to which one refers in this case cannot be the body or its parts, because everyone knows with inevitable certainty that it remains the same from the beginning to the end of his life, whereas the body and its parts are not so, because the body of man as an infant is different from his body as an old man, and likewise the parts of the body, because both the body and its parts are continuously in dissolution and reconstruction, and unavoidably in constant change. But that to which man refers when he says "I" is not so, because it remains constantly the same.

Another argument is that man may often be unconscious of his body and its parts, such as the heart, the brain, etc., but it is impossible for him to be unconscious of his soul, which is the thing to which he refers when he says "I." Therefore the soul must be something different from the body. The body is, no doubt, material and perceptible by the senses, but not so the soul, which is pure substance because it is impossible that it should be an accident.

The soul of the man can exist only after the existence of matter mixed in a manner corresponding to [the nature of] man, and the existence of this matter is a prerequisite for the existence of the soul of man.

This matter is generated from sperm and similar things, and when the soul becomes attached to it and then begins to feed and to produce the organs, the body is generated from it. This matter is called coccyx. [This is *ʿajb al-dhanab*, "the root of the tail," meaning the extremity of the spine, an organ which is declared to be the nucleus of the creation of the human body and of its resurrection as well, and not subject to decomposition in common with the rest of the body.]

The soul with which it remains continues to be perceiving and noticing, and at that time it experiences pleasure or pain; these are the pleasures and pain in the tomb. Then when the time for resurrection [*maʿād*] comes, the soul stirs again and feeds this [nucleus of] matter by attracting other matter to it and transforming it into something similar to it; and therefrom grows a body a second time. This body is the same as the first body inasmuch as this [nucleus of] matter in it is the same, and the soul is the same. In this way the resurrection takes place.[28]

Finally, a look at Islam's present situation is in order. In recent years, with the increasing activity of fundamentalist Islamic groups and organizations, questions of sexual freedom are at the center of public debate. One of the fundamentalists' main efforts is directed at the separation of the genders. Fundamentalists insist that women should avoid men's company in public places, such as public transportation, universities, and workplaces. Women are encouraged and even pressured to wear Islamic attire, which covers all their body except the face. Some variants of dress even involve veiling the face. Fuʿād Zakariyya, an Egyptian philosopher and one of his country's most outstanding and outspoken intellectuals, has this to say about the widespread phenomenon:

> The Islamicists pay little attention to the real social and economic problems; instead they concentrate on secluding women, to whom they want to assign an inferior status. Dictators flatter their public but despise it; likewise, the

fundamentalists want to perpetuate women's subservient and marginal place in society, yet call them "well-guarded jewels." They believe that women are controlled by passion and emotion. Women should cover their bodies, since this guarantees spirituality, the Islamicists claim. They assume that a woman's body is a constant source of temptation, and it is the center of her whole identity. The religious fundamentalists would like women to combine extreme modesty in public with unbridled passionate sexuality with their husbands.[29]

Such a contrast inevitably creates complexes, Zakariyya asserts. Religion is full of prohibitions—men and women should not intermingle, a man should not shake a woman's hand, he should not look at a woman a second time—and all these restrictions cause sexual hunger and frustration among young people. Women become mere sex objects, not persons. But Zakariyya also believes that Western promiscuity creates sexual complexes.

The modern secularist may be angry at the fundamentalists, accusing them of ignoring social and economic problems and criticizing them for being preoccupied with sexual modesty. Yet it should be borne in mind that in this way, fundamentalists are continuing a long religious tradition. Al-Ghazālī too was indifferent to social and political issues not directly related to religion, and as we have seen, he devoted much attention to questions of modesty, bodily cleanliness, and purity. This is the same spirit which speaks of the salvation of the soul and the knowledge of God yet regards the human body as the tool and inevitable first stage toward achieving these lofty religious goals.

NOTES

1. See, for example, Fedwa Malti-Douglas's essay, "Faces of Sin: Corporeal Geographies in Contemporary Islamist Discourse," in this volume. Malti-Douglas has rightly pointed out that studies of Islamic attitudes toward the body are in their infancy.

2. See, for example, E. W. Lane, *The Manners and Customs of the Modern Egyptians* (in several editions).

3. *Pirke Avot,* 3:1.

4. Qur'an, 4:1; 16:4; 22:5; 23:11ff; 25:54; 32:7; 40:67.

5. Ibid., 5:6.

6. Ibid., 2:228.

7. Ibid., 2:223.

8. Ibid., 4:3.

9. Ibid., 2:228, 230.

10. Ibid., 2:222.

11. Ibid., 2:233.

12. Ibid., 2:25, 214; 5:65; 10:26; 19:60, 61; 26:85; 29:58; 44:51–57; 47:15; 52:17–27; 55:46–76; 69:21–24; 76:5–6, 12–21.

13. Ibid., 13:23; 43:70; 47:15.

14. See Max Meyerhof and Joseph Schacht, eds., *The Theologus Autodidactus of Ibn al-Nafis* (Oxford: Oxford University Press, 1968), 57.

15. Ibid., 45, n. 2, citing Ibn Saʿd, *Kitāb al-tabaqāt al-kabīr*, ed. E. Sachau et al. (Leiden, 1905), i/I.4, 11.14f.

16. Abū Hāmid al-Ghazālī, *Ihyāʾ ʿulūm al-dīn*, vol. 1 (Cairo, 1387/1967), 170.

17. Al-Ghazālī, *Ihyāʾ*, quoted in Madelain Farah, *Marriage and Sexuality in Islam: A Translation of al-Ghazālī's Book on the Etiquette of Marriage from the Ihyāʾ* (Salt Lake City, 1984), 108.

18. Al-Ghazālī, *Ihyāʾ*, 1:177. See also H. Laoust, *La profession de foi d'Ibn Batta* (Damascus, 1958), 82 of the Arabic text.

19. See Farah, *Marriage and Sexuality*, 64.

20. Ibid., 62.

21. Ibid., 102–3. See also *Encyclopedia of Islam*, 2d ed., s.v. "Hayd," by G. H. Bousquet.

22. Farah, *Marriage and Sexuality*, 106.

23. Ibid., 108–13.

24. See, for example, J. S. Trimingham, *The Sufi Orders in Islam* (Oxford, 1971), 37–40.

25. Farah, *Marriage and Sexuality*, 26–27.

26. See Michael Winter, *Society and Religion in Early Ottoman Egypt: Studies in the Writings of ʿAbd al-Wahhāb al-Shaʿrānī* (New Brunswick, N.J., 1982), 159–60.

27. See Helmut Ritter, *Das Meer der Seele: Mensch, Welt, und Gott in den Geschichten des Farīduddīn ʿAttār* (Leiden, 1955), 186, 582.

28. *Theologus Autodidactus*, 57–59.

29. Fuʾād Zakariyya, *al-Sahwa al-islāmiyya fī mīzān al-ʿaql* [The Islamic awakening in the balance of reason] (Cairo, 1989), 141–50.

FROM THE BUDDHA TO BUDDHAGHOSA
CHANGING ATTITUDES TOWARD THE HUMAN BODY IN THERAVĀDA BUDDHISM

Sue Hamilton

Buddhism, like most other major world religions, is a vast and complex religious tradition which has been, and still is, practiced in many forms. This essay is concerned with early Buddhism in two of its aspects.

On one hand, this essay makes use of a body of texts known as the Pali Canon. These are the earliest Buddhist texts we have, written in a language called Pali. They consist of some thirty or more books which comprise the canonical material of the only early Buddhist school to survive to this day, Theravāda Buddhism.[1] Others have written about the way this material was preserved and recorded,[2] and I share the view of most scholars of early Buddhism that the earliest stratum of this material contains the nearest we can get to the teachings of the Buddha himself. For this essay, I have used as my primary source of reference that part of the Pali Canon, known as the *Sutta Piṭaka,* which is concerned with the doctrinal teachings of the Buddha. And in so doing, I take the doctrines as found in the *Sutta Piṭaka* to represent what one might loosely call "the Buddha's point of view."

On the other hand, this essay is concerned with the way Theravāda Buddhism has traditionally interpreted the canonical texts. In many religious traditions, the "orthodox" view is developed over a period of time, often being given definitive form by certain important historical figures within the tradition. Theravāda Buddhism has been no exception to this process: what is now Theravāda "orthodoxy" developed considerably later than the time the canonical texts were written. It was given definitive form by a man named Buddhaghosa, a highly influential figure in mainstream Theravāda Buddhism, perhaps comparable with Augustine or Thomas Aquinas in Christianity. Buddhaghosa lived in the fifth century C.E., many hundreds of years after the time of the Buddha. Most of the commentaries on the canonical doctrinal texts were written or compiled by Buddhaghosa, and he also composed an independent work, the *Visuddhimagga*. He claimed to be merely an exegete of the canonical texts of early Buddhism, and the Theravāda tradition has accepted that claim: his views came to be regarded as representing the orthodox Theravāda position.

Perhaps because Theravāda Buddhism is the only early Buddhist school to survive to the present day, and perhaps also because its canonical texts are the earliest Buddhist texts we have, its views are frequently assumed to be representative of what is called "early Buddhism" or "Pali Buddhism," in contradistinction to any later developments in the Buddhist tradition as a whole. And perhaps because of Buddhaghosa's claim to be merely an exegete, it is frequently taken for granted that the specifically Theravāda position reflects that of the Pali canon. In this essay, my aim is to show that Theravāda Buddhism is not necessarily representative of the earliest Buddhist teachings contained in the Pali Canon, and that its position should therefore be more clearly defined than simply "early Buddhism" or "Pali Buddhism" as a whole. More specifically, my point is to show that in writing about the human body, Buddhaghosa diverges significantly from the relevant material in the Pali Canon, and that one can therefore suggest that the Theravāda tradition's attitude toward the human body represents a considerable change from that of the Buddha.

Pali Buddhism as a whole (that is, the Pali Canon, its commentaries, and other Theravāda texts, including those written by Buddhaghosa) is often considered by scholars and Buddhists alike to have a negative attitude toward the human body. Before considering what Buddhaghosa writes on this subject, I will consider whether the analysis of the human being given in the *Sutta Piṭaka* of the Pali Canon supports this view of a negative attitude toward the human body. I will also consider the reasons why such a view might have come to prevail. In the course of this, we can establish what we might call the Buddha's attitude toward the human body, which can then be compared with Buddhaghosa's attitude toward the human body.

In considering the material contained in the *Sutta Piṭaka*, we have to consider an apparent paradox.

On one hand, we find statements about the body which appear to be distinctly negative: we read, for example, that the body is a "heap of corruption" (*pūtisaṇḍa*),[3] that bodily functions are "impure" (*asuci*),[4] and that only a completely deluded (or ignorant) fool would think of the body as beautiful.[5] A passage in the *Aṅguttara Nikāya* describes the body as a boil which has nine open wounds,[6] with impure (*asuci*), bad-smelling (*duggandha*) and loathsome (*jegucchi*) discharges.[7] According to the *Sutta Piṭaka*, the human being is analyzed into five constituents, called *khandhas*. These are the body, feelings, apperception and conception, volitional activities, and awareness. I will return to these shortly. The point I want to make here is that in some contexts it would appear that it is one's body that leads one astray, at least as much as the other parts of our fivefold psychophysical makeup. We

are told, for example, that "[our] teacher, friends, is one who speaks of the
driving out of desire and passion . . . in the body, in feelings, in apperception, in mental formations, in consciousness."[8] Another passage states that
we are to "get rid of that desire and passion which are in the body, feelings,
apperception, mental formations, consciousness."[9] Such references are not
uncommon and are particularly relevant, since passion and desire are the
very source of karmic bondage in Buddhism: we are told in the second
Noble Truth that it is passions or desires which tie us to the cycle of rebirth.
Apart from canonical statements which attribute passion and desire in like
measure to all the *khandhas,* from some translations of Pali texts it seems
that it is the body alone which leads us astray. For example, in a Pali Text
Society translation of the *Sutta Piṭaka,* we read that it is from the body that
"passion and hatred have their origin," and thoughts which "toss up the
mind" arise from the body.[10] And in Müller's translation of *Dhammapada*
202 and 203 it is stated: "there is no pain like the body" and "the body is
the greatest of pains."[11] The importance of such translations should not be
underestimated, as they are widely disseminated as representing the canon
of Theravāda Buddhism and as such are source books for students and
believers alike.

On the other hand, it is cardinal to Buddhism that karmic consequences
accruing to any particular individual are entirely dependent on his or her
mental volitions. Karma is defined in the *Sutta Piṭaka* as follows: "O *bhikkhus,* I say that volition *(cetanā)* is karma. Having willed, one acts through
body, speech and mind."[12] This definition is central to the Buddha's message; indeed, it is precisely what distinguished his teaching from that of
other Indian religions of his time: in interpreting action (karma) as volition,
he uniquely ethicized the law of karma. From this standpoint, it is clear
that the Buddha qualitatively distinguished volitions from the body so far
as the function of the law of karma is concerned. This qualitative distinction
is particularly significant, because according to the Buddha's teachings all
things are equally impermanent and dependently originated (or conditioned) in their constitution.

Given the Buddha's definition of karma, it seems prima facie unlikely
that it is from the body that passion, desire, and hatred, all of which are
volitions, originate. But to understand quite specifically the status of the
body with regard to the arising of such volitions and thus to justify or
disprove such negative statements as mentioned above, we need to look
more closely at the fivefold analysis of the human being. This brings us
back to the five *khandhas,* and it is here that we will start investigating the
paradox as presented.

The Buddha taught that all things, of whatever nature, are dependently
originated, or conditioned *(saṃkhata).* This means that all things are impersonal, or selfless *(anattā).* It is ignorance of this fact that binds us to the cycle
of rebirth, *saṃsāra,* and insight into it brings liberation from the cycle—the
goal of the Buddhist path. In the light of the teaching on selflessness, the

Buddha taught that what we commonly think of as an "individual" or "being" is in fact a combination of conditioned processes which form the physical and mental continuum of an individual life. These processes are classified into five constituents, the *pañcakkhandhā*. The precise relationship between these five constituents is more complex than can be explained in an essay of this length, but each is constituted in precisely the same way metaphysically: all the different aspects of the human being are dependently originated. I will go through the five *khandhas* briefly.

One, the *rūpakkhandha,* consists of everything the human body needs to function as a living body: various organs, faculties such as breathing, temperature, and so on. The *vedanākhandha* is usually understood to be feelings, which are classified according to whether they are agreeable, disagreeable, or neutral. They are more than mere sensation, and a better translation of *vedanā* might be "experiences." The *saññākhandha* is the faculty of apperception and conception, by which one apperceives or recognizes what one experiences and by which one is able to have conceptions or ideas. The *saṃkhārakkhandha* is the faculty by which we have desires, cravings, volitions, and intentions at every conceivable level. It includes both overt greed and sensual desire and, at the other end of the spectrum, the life force, of which we are more or less unaware until we are very spiritually advanced. That all volitional activity, both good and bad, is included here means that karma comes under this *khandha.* Neither feelings nor apperceptions and conceptions are considered volitional, so they do not in themselves produce karmic consequences. Finally, the *viññāṇakkhandha* is the faculty by which we are aware of things. It is particularly important in Buddhism, because if we are to overcome the karmic link between our intentions and being reborn, then we need to be aware of them. All these *khandhas* function cooperatively in our everyday experience: the body *(rūpakkhandha)* provides our physical sense organs, for example, through which we are able to have experiences *(vedanākhandha).* These experiences are recognized, or identified, by the faculty of apperception *(saññākhandha),* and we are aware of them through the faculty of awareness *(viññāṇakkhandha).*

The very fact that the human being is analyzed into five constituents in itself suggests that each constituent is, in some way, distinct from the others, even though they are of equal status; there are distinctions both between the bodily functions and between what are usually referred to as mental functions, and also between different aspects of mental functioning. From the limited description of each of them presented above, it does not appear likely that passions and desires arise from the body. Yet it can nevertheless also be seen how closely interdependent and mutually conditioning they are: they function together as the psychophysical continuum of an "individual," and they work together in our everyday experience. In discussing whether the body could in any way be the origin of passion, hatred, and thoughts which "toss up the mind," I shall treat these two aspects—the distinctiveness and the interrelatedness of the *khandhas*—separately.

In considering first their distinctiveness, I shall draw on descriptions in the Pali Canon of the practice of *sati*, mindfulness. I refer particularly to this practice for two reasons. First, the subjects on which the mindfulness meditation is to be practiced include the body, feelings, and volitions, and each subject is distinguished from the other in the meditation exercises, emphasizing their distinctiveness. Second, according to the *Sutta Piṭaka*, mindfulness is a particularly important meditational practice: it is a key meditation exercise for a monk. For example, we read in the canon: "There is one way, O monks, for the purification of beings, for the overcoming of grief and sorrow, for the ending of suffering and misery, for the attaining of the (right) Path, for the realising of *Nirvāṇa;* this [way] is the four foundations of mindfulness."[13] In the *Suttas* on mindfulness and in related passages, we read that the four meditational objects for the mindfulness exercises are the body *(rūpa)*, feelings *(vedanā)*, states of mind or thoughts *(citta)*, and abstract mental objects *(dhammā)*. In this context, volitions are included in the general term *citta*. According to the sources which describe the practice of mindfulness in detail, all four of these meditations are to be practiced in precisely the same way. But we nevertheless read elsewhere in the canon that mindfulness concerning the body *(kāyagatā sati)* is sufficient in itself for the attaining of *Nirvāṇa*.[14] So, though the practice of all four of the exercises is advocated, liberating insight can be gained simply by meditating on the body. As an aside, it is interesting to recall that according to Buddhist tradition, it was observation of the impermanent nature of the human body—through seeing in turn an ill person, an old person, and a corpse—that prompted the Buddha to go forth from home on the journey that was to lead to his enlightenment.

The *Sutta Piṭaka* contains detailed descriptions of the method to be followed in the mindfulness exercises, and all procedures are to be followed by first using the monk's own body, feelings, states of mind, and abstract mental objects as the object of meditation, then using the body, feelings, and so on, of someone else. With regard to the body, the monk is to center his attention on the body qua body, not on the feelings or anything else he might associate with the body but which are the subject of another specific mindfulness exercise (and the techniques are essentially identical for the other three meditational objects mentioned above). Then the monk is to concentrate in turn on different aspects of the body, such as breathing, posture, bodily parts and functions, and so on. Included here are the stages of decay of the body, including a corpse in progressive states of decomposition. The monk trains himself to "experience" *(paṭisamvid)* each object of meditation very precisely, to the exclusion of everything else other than that it is a part of the body. In this way the monk establishes that while the body—or part thereof—exists, he also becomes aware of and observes its impersonal and conditioned nature: there is nothing which constitutes a "being" to be found therein. The *Satipaṭṭhāna Suttas* put it as follows: "his mindfulness is present precisely to the extent necessary for knowledge, sufficient for mindfulness, and he proceeds unattached, not grasping [i.e., identifying] anything in the world."[15] The monk's knowledge of a bodily constituent, activity, or function is simply the apperception of something of which he is aware and does not involve, or lead to, false identification with the body or any part thereof.

The *Suttas* also strongly imply in these exercises that there is nothing about any particular part, or condition, of the body that is intrinsically desirable or repugnant; be it breathing or posture, hair or pus, a young body or a rotting corpse, a monk is merely to observe it quite free from any connotation. The purpose of such mindfulness exercises is so to concentrate on each specific subject of meditation that there follows clear comprehension of its precise nature, which is that it is impersonal and conditioned. The exercise is purely analytical, and in experiencing each of the objects of meditation in this way as distinct from each other, a monk understands that there is nothing inherently disgusting, hateful, desirable, or anything else about the body; nor is there anything inherently desirable or repugnant about pleasurable or painful feelings.

Desire *(sarāga citta;* literally, "a state of mind with desire") and hatred *(dosa)*, along with other volitions, are meditated on as part of the mindfulness exercise on *citta,* the third of the four objects described in the *Satipaṭṭhāna Suttas.* In this exercise the monk observes and understands every state of mind he experiences. And he sees desire, disgust, hatred, repugnance, and so on, to be volitions, which are directed *toward* the body and *toward* feelings by the mind; and that such volitional activity is entirely due to lack of insight. Moreover, he now knows that both the body and feelings can be present without such volitional activity necessarily being present at the same time.

So from the point of view of the distinctiveness of the five *khandhas,* we can see that there is no foundation for saying that the body is the origin of passion, hatred, and thoughts which toss up the mind.

What about the attitude toward the body and the origin of passion, hatred, and thoughts which toss up the mind in the light of the interrelatedness of the *khandhas?* As already stated, it is together that the *khandhas* produce the psychophysical continuum called an "individual." Each of the *khandhas,* and part thereof, has precisely the same conditioned *(saṃkhata)* status, and as such is characterized by impermanence *(aniccatā)*, unsatisfactoriness *(dukkhatā)*, and impersonality *(anattatā)*, what the Buddha called the "three characteristics of existence."[16] They are unsatisfactory precisely because they are impermanent, or transitory, in that they have no independently existing identity. Their very lack of independently existing identity is the most fundamental aspect of their interrelatedness. This interrelatedness is emphasized by the fact that the *khandhas* are collectively defined in the *Sutta Piṭaka* as what constitutes *dukkha,* the unsatisfactoriness that characterises *saṃsāra*.[17] This definition should not surprise us. Given that it is as individual human beings, or, one might say, as individual bundles of *khandhas,* that we experience conditioned, *saṃsāric,* existence, this is essentially the meaning of the first and second Noble Truths.[18]

In the brief description of the five *khandhas* above, I stated that it is the faculty of apperception (the *saññākhandha*) which recognizes, and so identifies, that of which consciousness (the *viññāṇakkhandha*) is aware; and also that the body *(rūpakkhandha)* provides the sense organs which are a necessary part of what we feel or experience through the *vedanākhandha.* This is more precisely expressed in the *Sutta Piṭaka*'s descriptions of the arising of feeling or experience. Feeling is dependent on the simultaneous presence of several factors: awareness, at least one of the six organs of sense, contact between the organ and its corresponding external object of sense, and recognition. So, for example, a passage describing visual feeling states: "Visual awareness arises because of eye and [visible] forms; contact [occurs] when there is a combination of the three; feelings are caused by contact; that which one feels, one apperceives (or recognizes)."[19] Here we can clearly see that the organs of sense are within the *rūpakkhandha;* awareness is the function of the *viññāṇakkhandha;* apperception takes place in the *saññākhandha;* and these three *khandhas* are involved in the activating of what is experienced in a fourth, the *vedanākhandha.*

A particularly notable point which arises from this, apart from the obvious confirmation of the interrelatedness of the *khandhas,* is that for a feeling to arise there need be absolutely no involvement of the *samkhārakkhandha.* I have mentioned this in connection with the analytical meditation exercise above, but here we have an unequivocal passage in the *Sutta Piṭaka* which indicates that the presence of a feeling, be it physical or mental, agreeable or disagreeable, is not dependent on there being a concomitant volition concerning it. This point is highly relevant to what we are looking at here, and I will return to it below.

We can now clearly see that it is misleading to say that volitions such as passion, hatred, and thoughts which toss up the mind arise from the body. The body is indeed present, but it is completely "unactivated," as it were, unless the faculties of awareness, apperception, and feeling are simultaneously present. And this confirms that it is from the *samkhārakkhandha* that the volitions actually arise. Regardless of the fact that one apparently experiences such volitions within the body itself, it is clear that they do not have corporeality as their source. It is thus possible to state quite specifically that all karmic effects—which in Buddhism axiomatically arise from passions and desires—are produced by the *samkhārakkhandha* and do not originate from the body, the *rūpakkhandha.*

The Buddha's attitude toward the body is therefore not a negative one. In fact, it is neither positive nor negative. As we have seen perhaps most clearly in looking at the mindfulness exercises, one is to have a purely analytical attitude toward one's body.

Why, then, are there statements in the *Sutta Piṭaka* which appear to refer to the body negatively? Why is there the apparent paradox I mentioned earlier? Before addressing the specific quotations I have given above, I will suggest a few possible general reasons for the presence in the *Sutta Piṭaka* of what appear to be negative references toward the body.

The first and most obvious reason is the Brahmanical and *śramaṇa* milieu in which the Buddhist teachings were first promulgated. Some of these traditions taught that the body and its secretions were polluting, and many advocated physical asceticism and mortification of the body. The practice of overtly subjugating the body to physical duress, combined with the view that it is polluting, indicate that the body was considered to have a negative effect on one's chances of salvation. In the *Sutta Piṭaka* itself, apart from a very few exceptions, the Buddha taught that extreme physical asceticism and self-denial were unnecessary. Indeed, they were potentially as misleading as indulgence. The texts tell us that the Buddha himself, before he attained enlightenment, spent six years as a wandering ascetic, subjecting his body to extremes of heat, cold, hunger, thirst, and so on. It was not until he realized the futility of such behavior from the soteriological point of view and relinquished it that he was able to become enlightened.[20] If, however, the negative view was widespread, then it is likely that some of the people who were converted to the teaching of the Buddha were influenced by this earlier attitude.

Second, Buddhist teachings allow room for what one might call a healthily negative attitude toward the body. This is represented by the Buddha's reaction to his observation of the human body before he went forth from home. And its relevance is to the impersonality which lies at the heart of the Buddha's teaching. Insight into this impersonality is liberating knowledge itself, and ignorance of it is what binds us to *saṃsāric* existence, the cycle of rebirth. If one has a slightly skeptical or detached attitude toward one's body, one is less likely falsely to identify with the body.

That having been said, we do tend to identify with our bodies. And this leads us to the third possible reason for negative statements about the body in the *Sutta Piṭaka*. Faced with the Buddha's teaching that we are to realize that all things are impermanent, unsatisfactory, and impersonal, one might instinctively apply this teaching to the body rather than to mental processes, at least initially. Our experience is of a mind which is ever changing, flickering here and there constantly. But our bodies seem relatively permanent to us, and we intuitively identify to some degree with our bodies.

That we also identify other people to some degree with their bodies is clearly illustrated in a well-known story in the *Sutta Piṭaka*,[21] where we read the Ānanda, the Buddha's closest friend and disciple, remained, in spite of his advanced wisdom, so attached to the physical presence of the Buddha that he did not achieve enlightenment until after the Buddha died and Ānanda was able to eliminate this attachment once and for all. It is precisely to avoid the kind of mistake made by Ānanda that the mindfulness exercises are to be practiced both on one's own and on someone else's body.

The Buddha himself recognized the apparently greater permanence of the body. It is related in the *Sutta Piṭaka*[22] that the Buddha stated that anyone looking for something permanent and lasting would do better to try the body, which lasts up to a hundred years, than the mind, which changes every moment. For anyone struggling against false notions of permanence, what more obvious object is there on which they can concentrate their efforts and subsequently vent their frustrations than the body?

For any or all of these reasons, some monks might have been predisposed, even unconsciously, toward making negative statements about the body. In turning now to the quotations from the *Sutta Piṭaka* cited above, however, we also see that in some cases a deeper consideration of their context shows them to be less negative about the body than at first appears.

The statement that "only an ignorant fool would regard it [the body] as beautiful" can perhaps be explained as follows: anyone ignorant as to the real nature of the body, who has not cultivated the foundations of mindfulness in order to see it as it really is, has not analyzed it into its constituents. Such a person has not perceived the body merely and precisely as body but has a view of the body which is meta-physical, or what some modern writers might call holistic. In Buddhist doctrinal terms, what this means is that a person still erroneously identifies in some way with his or her body. Because there is no room for such a view in the process of cultivating the penetrating analysis of the bodily complex necessary for liberating insight and because anyone who has cultivated such insight is considered wise, anyone holding such a view might be deemed to be a fool, certainly from a relative point of view; and the more so because it is only from the holistic point of view that the body could possibly be considered beautiful: its constituent parts, activities, and functions are merely parts, activities, and functions.

In the reference to the body being a "heap of corruption," the Pali term translated here is *pūtisaṇḍa*. Other meanings of the word *pūti*, apart from corruption, include "putrid," "rotten," "decayed." While "heap of corruption, rottenness, or decay" appears prima facie to be unequivocally negative about the body, in fact what such a term is doing is serving to emphasize the body's impermanence, rather than that one should feel negative about it. This interpretation is confirmed by the fact that *pūtisaṇḍa* is found in contexts which include other terms, such as *bhindana*, which means "breaking up, brittle, falling into ruin," and *pabhaṅguna*, which means "brittle, easily destroyed, perishable."[23]

I also referred above to the presence in the *Sutta Piṭaka* of statements that the body is impure. There are many Pali words for "impure," but perhaps the one most frequently found in connection with bodily functions is *asuci*. *Asuci* is used in the passage to which I referred above, which describes the body as a boil from whose nine open wounds impurity *(asuci)*, stench, and loathsomeness ooze out.[24] To refer to purity in such a context clearly overlooks the meaning of purity in Buddhist doctrinal terms. The Buddha teaches that salvation is obtained by progressing from ignorance to insight. His prescription for how to achieve insight is given in terms of following a path which can also be described as a process of purification. The path to purity cannot, however, be understood to mean that a disciple is to overcome or avoid the body or its functions and secretions because they are impure in the way suggested in the passage quoted here. We read elsewhere that the Buddha taught that impurity, or defilement, comes from hurting others, stealing, lying, adultery, greed, anger, delusion, and so on, and has nothing to do with bodily functions (nor, incidentally, with what you eat).[25] These defilements represent karmic bondage and therefore must be eradicated. Purity, in Buddhist teaching, is freedom from such defilements, and it is in this sense that practicing Buddhist teachings means following a purificatory path. In ethicizing the law of karma, the Buddha taught that defilement was moral or psychological and only indirectly connected with the physical body insofar as one's body is a channel for one's intention, or will to act. So I suspect that "impure," when used in connection with the body and its functions, is present in the canon as a result of the Brahmanical background in which the teaching took root.

I suggest the passage quoted from the *Anguttara Nikāya* comparing the body to a boil from whose nine openings impurity, stench, and loathsomeness ooze out is also couched in such terms as a result of non-Buddhist influence.[26] If one looks carefully at the context of the passage, the body is first of all described according to a stock canonical phrase as being made up of the four elements and begotten of mother and father. The passage then goes on to state—and this is its point—that this body so made up is impermanent, subject to erosion and decay, and perishable, subject to destruction.[27] In Pali, it finishes: *Tasmā ti ha bhikkhave imasmiṃ kāye nibbindathā ti.* E. M. Hare, in his translation for the Pali Text Society, gives this sentence as "Wherefore, monks, be ye disgusted with this body."[28] It is equally correct philologically, and in my opinion far more appropriate both in this specific context and in the wider context of Buddhist teachings as a whole, to translate it as "So, monks, be indifferent toward (or disenchanted with) your body."[29] The purpose of this passage is not to encourage monks to feel disgust toward their impure bodies but to discourage them from seeking anything permanent in, or identifying with, their bodies. The terms in which the description of the body itself is couched are surely the result of non-Buddhist, and certainly nondoctrinal, influence.

I turn now to the translations I cited. In Norman's translation of *Sutta Nipāta* 271, we read that passion, hatred, and thoughts which toss up the mind arise from the body. The word *body* has been supplied by the translator; it is not present in the Pali at all, which reads:

> *Rāgo ca doso ca itonidānā,*
> *aratī ratī lomahaṃso itojā,*
> *ito samuṭṭhāya manovitakkā*
> *kumārakā dhankaṃ iv'ossajanti.*[30]

Norman translates: "From this (body) passion and hatred have their origin. From this (body) aversion and delight and excitement are born. Arising from this (body) thoughts toss up the mind, as young boys toss up a (captive) crow."[31] At the front of his translation, Norman states: "Words in round brackets are those which need to be supplied in the English translation, although not found in the original Pali." The key word in Pali, to which Norman feels it necessary to add the English *body*, is *ito*, literally "from this."

The context is that the *yakkha* Sūciloma, to test whether the Blessed One is a real ascetic or just looks like one, has asked him where passion and hatred have their origin. Immediately following on from the verse quoted above, we read: *Snehajā attasambhūtā nigrodhasseva khandhajā*. Norman's translation of this text is "(They are) born from affection, arisen from oneself, like the trunk-born (shoots) of the banyan tree."[32] In an earlier edition of his translation, Norman gives an alternative rendering at the end of the story, translating *ito* as "from within."[33] In the context of Sūciloma's question and the subsequent verse, this would seem to me to be far preferable to, and one might say more accurate than, "from this body." The commentary on this passage, which was written considerably later, glosses *ito* as *attabhāvato*. *Attabhāva* is a term used to denote the conventional individuality experienced by an unenlightened person. In later material it is sometimes used when either the body or the five *khandhas* are erroneously taken in the sense "this is my self."[34] In Buddhist Sanskrit, *ātmabhāva* is used for "body"; but this is usually in conjunction with *pratilambha*, again meaning bodily existence in its broad sense.[35] None of these points would seem to support the translation of *ito* in the earlier *Sutta Piṭaka* text as "from this body."

In Müller's translation of *Dhammapada* 202 and 203, it is stated: "there is no pain like the body" and "the body is the greatest of pains."[36] The Pali sentences from which these translations have been made are, respectively: *n'atthi khandhādisā dukkhā* and *saṃkhārā paramā dukkhā*. The first of these is clearly repeating the definition that the *khandhas* are what constitute *dukkha*. With regard to the second, as well as specifically being one of the *khandhas*, *saṃkhāra* does on occasion have the broad meaning of bodily existence in its totality, but it never means "body" in the sense of corporeality. So what this sentence is saying is that the greatest *dukkha* is *saṃsāric* existence, which is precisely the content of the first Noble Truth. The same mistake is made in the article entitled "The Body (Buddhist)" in the *Encyclopedia of Religion and Ethics*, where it states that "the body is the sphere of suffering" and "the body is the origin of suffering."[37]

The Pali word *nibbidā* is often found in contexts in the *Sutta Piṭaka* which refer to the human body. We saw it above in the passage about the impermanence of the body. The way *nibbidā* is translated frequently tends to further the view that the early Buddhist attitude toward the body was negative. *Nibbidā* can mean disgust, revulsion, indifference, or disen-

chantment. In contexts where it must mean indifference or disenchantment, translating it as "disgust" or "revulsion" is highly misleading.
A frequently occurring phrase in the *Sutta Piṭaka* is that a certain practice
leads to *nibbidāya virāgāya nirodhāya upasamāya abhiññāya sambodhāya nibbā-
nāya*.[38] One translator of this phrase renders it as "downright revulsion,
dispassion, cessation, calm, full comprehension, wisdom, *Nirvana*," "downright revulsion" being the translation of *nibbidā*.[39] Another renders *nibbidā*
in the same context as "complete disgust."[40] In my opinion it cannot in
this context mean anything other than indifference or disenchantment:
"downright revulsion" or "complete disgust," directed toward the body or
anything else, would be a karmically binding volition quite inappropriate
for a monk at this stage of the path. Even if one were to understand the
qualities referred to in this sentence, disgust or indifference, dispassion,
cessation, calm, full comprehension, wisdom, Nirvana, as being qualities
which are acquired sequentially, it seems highly improbable that disgust
would immediately precede so many other qualities which are more associated with detachment.

There are a multitude of similar examples, but these will suffice to make
my point. Scholarly works other than translations can be just as misleading
in statements about the body, possibly because they have relied on the
translations.

We can now sum up the attitude toward the human body in the *Sutta
Piṭaka* and reconcile the apparent paradox referred to above. We have seen
that the doctrinal position according to the Buddha's teaching is that the
attitude toward the body should be analytical. This correlates with his
teaching that karma is volition: it is one's state of mind, not one's body,
which is the source of desire, hatred, and other karmically binding states
which determine the nature of one's future rebirth. The presence in the
Sutta Piṭaka of statements which appear to be negative about the body is
probably the result of outside influence or doctrinal confusion which arises
because of the demands of the spiritual struggle. Many such statements
are in any case not as negative as they at first appear if read in their context
or if translated more appropriately.

But what about Buddhaghosa's attitude toward the human body? My
citations are drawn mainly from the *Visuddhimagga*, Buddhaghosa's huge
compendium concerning the path to salvation written in the fifth century
C.E., but I will also refer to the commentaries on the Pali canon which he
is believed to have compiled. Many people composed the material Buddhaghosa included in the commentaries, however, so one must acknowledge that he was not the only one to write in such a way. Nevertheless,
Buddhaghosa's *Visuddhimagga* is consistently and exaggeratedly negative
about the body. I can choose only a few examples.

First, an example of the difference between the *Sutta Piṭaka* and its commentary. Though it is relatively minor, it nevertheless clearly illustrates
the difference between simple analysis, which is found in the former, and

descriptive value, which is added to the latter. In several places in the *Sutta Pitaka* we are given a list of the constituents of the body.[41] The list is invariably given without comment as follows: "There are in this body head-hairs, body-hairs, nails, teeth, skin, flesh, sinews, bones, bone-marrow, kidneys, heart, liver, membranes, spleen, lungs, intestines, mesentery, stomach, excrement, bile, phlegm, pus, blood, sweat, fat, tears, serum, saliva, mucus, synovic fluid, urine, and brain." This list, which is used in the exercise of mindfulness on parts of the body, clearly illustrates the extent to which each and every part is to be observed in the same objective light as part of the analytical meditation exercise. This is regardless of whether it is, say, a tooth or mucus or pus.[42] In itself, each part has nothing that is to be regarded with anything other than complete neutrality. In the commentary on this list, however, qualitative words are added, so the body and its constituents are described as vile *(kucchita)*, impure *(asubha* and *asuci)*, and loathsome *(jeguccha)*.[43]

In the section of the *Visuddhimagga* which describes the practice of mindfulness on the body, not only does Buddhaghosa give a substantial description (as opposed to an analysis) of each of the parts of the body to be meditated upon, rather than merely giving a list as the *Sutta Pitaka* does, but he also introduces many negative adjectives which are not in the *Sutta Pitaka*. Thus of mere head hairs we read that they are subject to a "fivefold repulsiveness" *(pañcadhā)* as to color *(vanna)*, shape *(santhāna)*, odor *(gandha)*, habitat *(āsaya)*, and location *(okāsa)*.[44] As a specimen from a lengthy passage, I quote: "[Head hairs are] repulsive in colour as well as in shape, odour, habitat and location . . . Just as a baby's excrement, as to its colour, is the colour of turmeric and, as to its shape, is the shape of a piece of turmeric root, and just as the bloated carcase of a black dog thrown on a rubbish heap, as to its colour, is the colour of a ripe palmyra fruit and, as to its shape, is the shape of a drum left face down, and its fangs are like jasmine buds, and so even if both these are not directly repulsive in colour and shape, still their odour is directly repulsive, so too, even if head hairs are not directly repulsive in colour and shape, still their odour is directly repulsive."[45] Other similes used in this passage are village sewage, a dunghill, a charnel ground.[46]

Buddhaghosa uses the body in the chapter of the *Visuddhimagga* where the meditation subject is loathsomeness or impurity. He sums up his lengthy description of the body's nature by quoting some verses as follows:

> Fools cannot in their folly tell;
> They take the body to be fair,
> And soon get caught in Evil's snare
> Nor can escape its painful spell.
>
> But since the wise have thus laid bare
> This filthy body's nature, so,
> Be it alive or dead, they know

There is no beauty lurking there.
For this is said:

"This filthy body stinks outright
Like ordure, like a privy's site;
This body men that have insight
Condemn, is object of a fool's delight.

"A tumour where nine holes abide
Wrapped in a coat of clammy hide
And trickling filth on every side
Polluting the air with stenches far and wide.

"If it perchance should come about,
that what is inside it came out,
Surely a man would need a knout
With which to put the crows and dogs to rout."

The passage concludes: "So a capable *bhikkhu* should apprehend the sign wherever the aspect of foulness is manifest, whether in a living body or in a dead one, and he should make the meditation subject reach absorption."[47] Even allowing for poetic license, this is in striking contrast to the analysis in the *Sutta Piṭaka* by which a monk also arrives at the conclusion that there is nothing inherently desirable about the body.

Buddhaghosa is traditionally thought to have been born a Brahmin. I think this is almost certainly true, judging from the terminology he uses in describing the body. So far as I am aware, his concern is not with the origin of volitions such as passion and hatred but with the physical aspects of the body.

One further example will serve here—a section of Buddhaghosa's description of the body's nature. The description begins relatively objectively but becomes wonderfully lurid as it goes on:

[The body] is a collection of over three hundred bones, jointed by one hundred and eighty joints, bound together by nine hundred sinews, plastered over with nine hundred pieces of flesh, enveloped in the moist inner skin, enclosed in the outer cuticle, with orifices here and there, constantly dribbling and trickling like a grease pot, inhabited by a community of worms, the home of disease, the basis of painful states, perpetually oozing from the nine orifices like a chronic open carbuncle, from both of whose eyes eye-filth trickles, from whose ears ear-filth, from whose nostrils snot, from whose mouth food and bile and phlegm and blood, from whose lower outlets excrement and urine, and from whose ninety-nine thousand pores the broth of stale sweat seeps, with bluebottles and their like buzzing round it, which when untended with tooth sticks and mouth-washing and head-anointing and bathing and underclothing and dressing would, judged by the universal repulsiveness of the body, make even a king, if he wandered from village to village with his hair in its natural wild disorder, no different from a flower-scavenger or an outcaste or what you will. So there is no distinction between a king's body and an outcaste's in so far as its impure stinking nauseating repulsiveness is concerned.[48]

If this is Buddhaghosa's apology for Buddhism against the caste system of the Brahmanical religion (which is based on a complex structure of purity and pollution), in my opinion it fails dismally! What we read here is riddled with concern about the polluting effects of bodily secretions and, in my view, is nothing more than the Brahmanization of Buddhist hermeneutics.

Further on in the same passage, we read: "So men delight in women and women in men without perceiving the true nature of [the body's] characteristic foulness, masked by adventitious adornment. But in the ultimate sense there is no place here even the size of an atom fit to lust after."[49] Buddhism certainly teaches that lust, or desire in general, is misplaced. But *not* because the body is foul. It is misplaced because insight into the transient nature of all things brings the knowledge that what one is desiring is momentary, impermanent, and therefore unsatisfactory. Buddhaghosa appears to have missed this point altogether. What he is doing is Brahmanizing Buddhist teaching.[50]

I return to the point made twice above that one can be aware of one's body and sensations without having any concomitant volition. It is fundamental to a monk's progress on the path to liberating insight that he achieves indifference, or detachment. It is nonsensical in a Buddhist context to cultivate antipathy toward the body or anything else. Because of the Buddhist practice of meditation on impurity *(asubha bhāvanā)*, it is sometimes argued that revulsion can be used as a meditational tool or catalyst for a monk. But as we have seen, the term *asubha* is used in contexts where the point is to understand impermanence, not that one should be disgusted. What the monk is aiming for is indifference. Not only does this follow from the doctrinal teaching that one should aim for freedom from all volitions, but it is explicitly stated in several places in the *Sutta Piṭaka*. We read, for example, that "[a monk who] lives detached from sensual pleasures, detached from unwholesome conditions," experiences ease *(sukha*, the opposite of *dukkha)*;[51] that one should aim to "cast out both wickedness and [all the work of piling up] merit";[52] and that in a certain meditation a monk "pervades, drenches, permeates and suffuses his body with *sukha* without associating it with pleasure."[53] In a later Pali text, the *Milindapañho*, we also read that "the Enlightened have neither attraction nor antipathy."[54]

Having an attitude of disgust or revulsion toward anything would constitute a karmically unwholesome, and therefore binding, "view," just as much as would considering something to be beautiful or desirable; the monk must see through and transcend all views and attain a karmically neutral position. We have seen this point borne out in what is said in the canonical descriptions of meditation: there is nothing in them which is designed to induce any specific negative (or positive) attitude, merely a detached observation of what is.

The question of gender is relevant here. To have a positive or negative attitude toward male or female would be just as much a karmically binding view, and the point is to be neutral. So one might say that doctrinally or philosophically speaking, there is no room for sexism in early Buddhism.

Because the cultivation of indifference, or detachment, is so central to understanding Buddhist teaching, in my opinion Buddhaghosa did a grave disservice to Theravāda Buddhism in his writing about the body. He went far beyond mere exegesis of the *Sutta Piṭaka,* and his elaborate reinterpretations resulted in a teaching which bears little relation to that contained in the original material.

We have seen clearly that it is not from the body itself that the karmically binding passions and desires arise. We have seen, too, that the point of meditation exercises is to see the human being as it really is, and so to understand that there is nothing toward which any volition is justifiable. Thus one might say that there is nothing either desirable or repulsive about the body but thinking makes it so. All volition is due to ignorance concerning the fundamental impersonality of all phenomena, physical or mental. It is for this reason that the chain of dependent origination which the Buddha taught to illustrate the impermanence and impersonality of all things is described in canonical texts as beginning with ignorance.[55]

To sum up: volitions have mentality rather than corporeality as their constitutional source and ignorance as their psychological source. According to the *Sutta Piṭaka* of the Pali Canon, there is little or no room for a negative attitude toward the body, and the negative terminology used by Buddhaghosa diverges widely from the original material. The earliest Buddhist attitude toward the body is neither positive nor negative; it is analytical.

NOTES

1. Theravāda Buddhism is the predominant form of Buddhism in Sri Lanka, Burma, and Thailand.
2. For example, see E. Frauwallner, *The Earliest Vinaya and the Beginnings of Buddhist Literature* (Rome: Serie Orientale Roma VIII, 1956); E. Lamotte, *Histoire du Bouddhisme Indien* (Louvain: Publications Universitaires, 1958); L. S. Cousins, "Pali Oral Literature" in P. Denwood and A. Piatigorsky, eds., *Buddhist Studies: Ancient and Modern* (London: Curzon, 1983); E. Zürcher, *Buddhism: Its Origin and Spread in Words, Maps and Pictures* (London: Routledge & Kegan Paul, 1962).
3. *Dhammapada* 148, M. Müller, trans., *The Dhammapada,* Sacred Books of the East Series, vol. 10 (Oxford: Clarendon Press, 1881), p. 41.
4. For example, *Sutta Nipāta,* 197, 205. (I have used the Pali Text Society editions of all Pali material unless otherwise stated.)
5. *Sutta Nipāta* 199: *Subhato nam maññatī bālo avijjāya purakkhato.*
6. Cf. the *Bhagavad Gītā* V.13, where the body is described as a "nine-gated city."

7. AN.IV.386.
8. SN.III.7: *Rūpe kho āvuso chandarāgavinayakkhāyī satthā vedanayā saññāya samkh-āresu viññāne.*
9. SN.III.27: *Rūpasmim chandarāgo tam pajahatha* (and so on).
10. K. R. Norman, trans., *The Group of Discourses* (Oxford: Pali Text Society, 1992), p. 30.
11. Müller, trans., *The Dhammapada.*
12. AN.III.415: *Cetanā'ham bhikkhave kammam vadāmi. Cetayitvā kammam karoti kāyena vācā manasā.*
13. Beginning and end of the *Satipaṭṭhāna* and *Mahāsatipaṭṭhāna Suttas*—MN.I, sutta 10; DN.II, sutta 22; cf. also SN.V. 141ff, 180, 183, 294.
14. AN.I.43; cf also *Milindapañho* 248, 336.
15. MN.I.56; DN.II.290: *assa sati paccupatthitā hoti yāvad eva ñāṇamattāya patissatimattāya, anissito ca viharati na ca kiñci loke upādiyati. na ca kiñci loke upādiyati* is glossed at MN.I.250 as *lokasmim kiñci rūpam vā—pe—viññāṇam vā ayam me attā vā attanīyam vā ti na ganhāti:* "he does not grasp at [false notions] such as having a soul, or thinking 'this is my self' of anything in the world, whether it be the body or any of the other *khandhas.*"
16. AN.I.286; *Dhammapada* 5–7, 277–279. Cf. also MN.I.336; DN.II.157.
17. SN.V.421: *samkhittena pañcupādānakkhandhā dukkhā* (in short, these five aggregates are *dukkha*); SN.III.158: *Katamañ ca bhikkhave dukkham. Pañcupādānakkhandhātissa vacanīyam* (O *bhikkhus,* what is *dukkha?* It should be said that it is the five aggregates of attachment).
18. The Buddha's Four Noble Truths included (1) a diagnosis of the human condition (it is characterized by unsatisfactoriness, *dukkha*); (2) an explanation of its cause (it originated in desire or craving, *tanhā*); (3) a good prognosis (unsatisfactoriness can be overcome, *dukkhanirodha*); and (4) a prescription for how to achieve this good outcome (by following the Noble Eightfold Path, *magga*).
19. MN.I.111: *Cakkhuñ-c'āvuso paticca rūpe ca uppajjati cakkhuviññāṇam, tinnam sagati phasso, phassapaccayā vedanā, yam vedeti tam sañjānāti.*
20. MN.I.16off.
21. DN.II.142ff.
22. SN.II.94f.
23. SN.I.131: *iminā pūtikāyena bhindanena pabhaṅgunā; Dhammapada* 148: *bhijjati pūtisandeho.*
24. AN.IV.386.
25. *Sutta Nipāta* 24off. Cf. also Rahula, "The Buddha on Man, His Nature and Destiny," in *Zen and the Taming of the Bull* (London: Gordon Fraser, 1978), p. 49f.
26. The reference to nine oozing openings will be seen again when we consider what Buddhaghosa has to say.
27. AN.IV.386: *Aniccucchādana-parimaddana-bhedana-viddhamsanadhamma.*
28. E. M. Hare, trans., *The Book of the Gradual Sayings,* vol. 4 (London: Pali Text Society, 1955), p. 258.
29. The translation of *nibbidā* is discussed later in this essay.
30. *Sutta Nipāta,* 271.
31. Norman, trans., *Group of Discourses,* p. 30.
32. Ibid., p. 47.
33. K. R. Norman, trans., *The Group of Discourses* (London: Pali Text Society, 1984), p. 47.
34. This is discussed in Steven Collins, *Selfless Persons: Imagery and Thought in Theravāda Buddhism* (Cambridge: Cambridge University Press, 1982), p. 156f.
35. Cf. T. W. Rhys Davids and William Stede, eds., *Pali English Dictionary* (London: Pali Text Society, 1986), p. 22.
36. Müller, trans., *The Dhammapada,* p. 54.

37. J. H. Bateson, "The Body (Buddhist)," in J. Hastings, ed., *Encyclopedia of Religion and Ethics*, vol. 2 (London: T. & T. Clark, 1908).

38. For example, SN.V.82.

39. F. L. Woodward, trans., *Gradual Sayings*, vol. 5 (London: Pali Text Society, 1986), p. 153.

40. E. M. Hare, trans., *Gradual Sayings*, vol. 3 (London: Pali Text Society, 1988), p. 68.

41. E.g., MN.I.57; Kh.2.

42. Pus has the same status as saliva, bone, sinew, and so on. A certain quantity of it is assumed always to be present in the body, and so it does not necessarily have the negative connotation which it does in English, since we associate pus with something gone bad.

43. *Paramatthajotikā*, p. 38f.

44. *Visuddhimagga*, p. 249.

45. Ñāṇamoli, trans., *The Path of Purification*, 2d ed. (Ceylon: A. Semage, 1964), p. 269.

46. Ibid.

47. Ibid., pp. 202–3; *Visuddhimagga*, p. 196.

48. Ñāṇamoli, trans., *Path of Purification*, p. 201f.

49. Ibid., p. 202.

50. Damien Keown, in "Morality in the Visuddhimagga," *Journal of the International Association of Buddhist Studies* 6 (1983), no. 1, states that Buddhaghosa's treatment of Buddhist ethics in the *Visuddhimagga* is far more concerned with practices than with intentions. This would seem to support my point.

51. DN.II.214: *Asamsaṭṭho viharati kāmehi asamsaṭṭho akusalehi dhammehi. Tassa asamsaṭṭhassa kāmehi asamsaṭṭhasa akusalehi dhammehi uppajjati sukham.*

52. SN.I.182: *Yo 'dha puññān ca pāpañ ca bāhitvā.*

53. DN.I.75: *Evam eva kho bhikkhu imam eva kāyaṃ nippītikena sukhena abhisandeti parisandeti paripūreti parippharati.*

54. *Milindapañho* 44: *n'atthi majārāja arahato anunayo vā paṭigho vā.*

55. Cf., for example, AN.II., chap. 1.

II.

The Gendered Body in Religious Discourse

FACES OF SIN
CORPORAL GEOGRAPHIES IN
CONTEMPORARY ISLAMIST DISCOURSE

Fedwa Malti-Douglas

The face of the Muslim woman is a source of controversy.[1] It is the ground on which usually begins the contemporary textual war over women, their modesty, and their adornment. More than simply a physical entity to be covered, woman's body, led by her face, becomes the locus for a kind of punitive Islamic religious discourse.[2] It is aspects of this discourse that will occupy our attention in this essay.

The Egyptian physician and feminist Nawāl al-Saʿdāwī may certainly have had her scriptoral pen on the pulse of the controversy when she titled one of her most provocative books *al-Wajh al-ʿArī lil-Marʾa al-ʿArabiyya*, which means literally "The naked face of the Arab woman."[3] It is perhaps not a coincidence—or one devoid of irony—that the translation of this work into English as *The Hidden Face of Eve* expresses another and opposite set of obsessions.[4] To hide or not to hide: that becomes the question. A woman relates

> I became very ill after a tooth extraction from which I suffered agonizing pain, and was prevented from tasting sleep or food for an entire month, since the stabbing of the pain did not stop night or day. The inflammation increased to the point that my cheek nearly exploded and it spread to my neck and head, closing my eyelids. Physicians and surgeons were confused by my case and medicine could do nothing nor could drugs. But, behold, God's hand stretched out and erased the disease and slowly healed the wound. During the illness, a woman visited me and said: "You do not deserve this punishment. You are a believer, and a pilgrim to Mecca." But I objected saying: "Do not say that. God does not treat people unjustly in any way, but it is people themselves who do wrong. I am a sinner. I deserve this punishment—and more. This mouth which God punished [*addaba*, a word that carries also the notion of education] with pain and disease used to be painted with red. It used not to enjoin the good and forbid the evil. And this swollen face: it used to be beautified with powder. And this bedridden

body: it used to adorn itself with fashionable clothing. And this aching head, burning with the fire of the fever did not cover itself completely with the veil. I did not cover myself with the veil of modesty so God covered me with the veil of pain. I put makeup on my face, and beautified my mouth and face with it—so God slapped them with pain and shame. . . . Then I was cured and made happy with true repentance—and I abandoned all that."

This story comes from the *Zād al-Musāfirīn ilā Ghayr Bilād al-Muslimīn* (loosely translated "Guide to travel outside the lands of the Muslims"), by Rabīʿ ibn Muhammad al-Saʿūdī.[5] The proliferation of written materials surrounding the Islamic revival in the Middle East has made works such as the *Zād al-Musāfirīn* widely—and cheaply—available. The aim of the work is clear: to guide Muslims traveling to non-Muslim countries. A land of moral danger, these countries play a role familiar to readers of the Western tradition, with its image of the city as the world of cosmopolitan irreligious corruption. This, indeed, is an anti-travel guide to the new Babylon.[6]

Physical travel, in al-Saʿūdī's vision, is, however, a male activity. The case of the woman with the tooth extraction is introduced as that of someone who has "tasted the poison of infatuation with the superficial aspects of deceptive secular civilization." Her temptation need not have come to her through travel. Her depravity (through exposure to Western values) is, in fact, paradigmatically related to man's moral vulnerability in the lands of the unbelievers.

The moral aspect of this woman's dramatic story is clear. Her saga is introduced as "the experience of a Muslim sister," unnamed. It is in another contemporary tract, this one written by a woman, that the veil is lifted (if the image be excused). Niʿmat Sidqī's fifty-three-page pamphlet entitled *al-Tabarruj,* a term referring to female adornment and display, has received critical attention both in the Arab world and in the West.[7] Despite its small size (or perhaps because of it), it is an extremely popular work, frequently reprinted and one of the most visible works in bookstores and souks from Egypt to Morocco.[8] Valerie J. Hoffman-Ladd notes that it is published by al-Jamāʿa al-Islāmiyya, "a university-based group that constitutes the primary locus of the 'Islamic movement,' which is the grass-roots alternative to the government-controlled establishment Islam."[9]

Niʿmat Sidqī, in her own introduction to her pamphlet, relates, in the first person, a more protracted and embellished version of the story of the tooth extraction.[10] In her account, both the medical establishment and the female visitor play greater roles. The cure effected through divine intervention leaves the physicians surprised, and they proclaim in humility the power of the deity, who is able to revive decayed bones. The female visitor, on the other hand, responds after the cure that the behavior of the narrator is by no means unusual and that many a woman beautifies herself. This provides the victim with the opportunity to reply that God has indeed done her a favor because she has been cured. This is a deity, we learn, who tests his worshipers when He loves them and purifies them through punishment. Then when He so desires, He cures them, for which they are grateful.

Our victim expresses her thanks not only for this useful lesson but for all she has endured: the pain, the punishment, and the disease. How can she, after all, not be thankful for this care and how can she not obey Him who has protected her in this way? Though she has come out of her sickness weak of body, she is nevertheless strong of will. She has also understood how her head and her face are to be covered by the veil, "as God had shown" her, and how her mouth and tongue are to pray to Him in thanks, fear, and obedience. This woman has been transformed; she is not the person she was before the illness. And what is more, this benefit was not simply bestowed on this fortunate victim, but it also extended to those around her, saving her daughters as well as many of her acquaintances and family.[11]

What a fascinating story! From a mere tooth extraction, the reader has been transported into the realm of female modesty, female covering, and a corporal discourse that recalls that of the punishments inflicted in the Muslim Hell. The female body—in its sexual and beautified nature—is mapped out as the locus of sin. Every wrongful act is met with its concomitant punishment. The lipstick on the mouth brings about the pain and disease. The face powder engenders the swollen face. The fasionable clothing leads to the bedridden body. The incomplete veiling causes the aching head. But this is not enough. This repentant adorned woman redefines the entirety of her experience. She does not cover herself with the veil of modesty, so God covers her with the veil of pain. She places makeup on her face and mouth, so God slaps them with pain and shame.

This one-on-one relationship between the sin and the punishment is direct and mimetic—and, I might add, semiotically transparent, for the relationship between signified and signifier is obvious. More interesting is the role played by the deity. This God, though He effects a cure, is violent. And His punitive actions parallel the woman's actions, but in a stunning reversal. When she does not completely cover herself with the veil of modesty, He covers her with the veil of pain. Her act of placing the makeup on her face and mouth is paralleled by the deity's slapping these two body parts with pain and shame. He partakes at once of the physical (e.g., the slapping) and the metaphorical (e.g., the pain and shame).

Woman's body becomes a pawn between the sinful female and the punitive deity. But perhaps this woman and we should be ultimately grateful: she has, after all, been cured. The vivid portrayal of her ordeal makes it clear, however, that she came close to eternal damnation. Had not her aching head, after all, been burning with the fire of the fever? The word *nār* is suggestive, to say the least, carrying connotations of Hellfire.

Yes, a woman may be a *hājja*, a pilgrim (as was pointed out so nicely to this toothache victim), but that does not place her body in safe harbor.

Rather, the female body, we learn, is the locus of an eloquent corporal geography of sin and perdition. It is no wonder, then, that it should in its entirety partake of ʿawra, a wonderfully elusive concept that at once means the pudenda, shame, the parts of the body that must be covered, etc. The medieval Muslim legists and theologians did not, as our modern story does, shy away from elaborating this concept and delineating the limits of what is and is not shameful in woman's body. The Ahkām al-Nisā' works, tracts of legal injunctions for women, are perhaps the most visible examples of this, mapping out and delineating with great care ʿawra in all its manifestations.[12] True, man's private parts also fall within the domain of ʿawra, and therefore covering them is enjoined upon the believer.[13] Thus, if for a man it is essentially the pelvic region which is ʿawra, for a woman all of her body can be considered ʿawra, and even, as one authority puts it, her voice.[14] ʿAwra implies covering, but also speaks to modesty. Modesty and the concomitant avoidance of sexually provocative dress are the keys to the discourse of the toothache victim. It is not only to makeup which this argument objects (after all, there is also a Western feminist antimakeup discourse)[15] but also to any improper exposure, including that of the head.[16]

There is, by contrast, a geography of the male body, and a beautiful one at that, in Muslim stories of the Prophet Joseph. This paragon of beauty of Islam has an entire sūra devoted to him in the Qur'ān (Sūrat Yūsuf, XII), detailing his adventures with the Egyptian ruler's wife, in a seduction scene that has entered the Muslim unconscious and speaks as eloquently to woman's perfidy as it does to Joseph's inner strength and beauty.[17] The great historian and Qur'ānic commentator, al-Tabarī (d. 310/923), presents the interchange: The ruler's wife, in an attempt to lure the young man, says to him: "O Joseph! How beautiful is your hair," to which he replies: "It is the first thing that will fall out of my body." She then says: "O Joseph! How beautiful are your eyes," to which he replies: "It is the first thing of my body that will flow to the ground." She continues: "O Joseph! How beautiful is your face," to which he replies: "It is for the dust to eat it."[18] The eloquence of this corporal dialogue lies in its tension and movement between physical beauty and physical destruction. The woman is the uncontrollable sexual entity who tirelessly moves from one body part to the next, undaunted by the Prophet's morbid replies. The body parts she elaborates are the same ones our modern diseased female accentuated. But the two morals are drastically different. The male's beauty, admired by the female seductress, turns into a commentary on the fragility of the human body. The modern female attempting to beautify herself is punished appropriately.

Does this mean that the male body can evade punishment? Certainly not, especially if one examines the Islamic discourse on Hell. The nār, the fire, of the fever that was plaguing our tooth-extraction victim should alert us that something more is at stake in this solitary female's corporal geography of sin. The nār of the fever is but one step from Hellfire, al-Nār.

The close relationship in the Muslim imaginary between women and Hell represented by a much-discussed *ḥadīth* that the majority of the inhabitants of Hell are women is not what is at issue here. Despite its importance for the creation of a particular gender discourse, it does not really exploit a corporal language.[19]

It is on the Prophet Muhammad's miraculous journey, the Miʿrāj, that he was privy to images both of Heaven and of Hell. In one of the numerous accounts of this journey, a modern compilation gleaned from medieval sources ranging from the theological to the historical, the Prophet beseeches his guide, the Angel Gabriel, to show him Jahannam. And the images of corporal punishment the Prophet watches vie with those in Dante's *Inferno*.[20] Before his eyes, sinners of both genders are made to endure various tortures.

But whereas the physical ailments of our contemporary victim were mimetic, those in the Muslim Hell are not necessarily so. The language of the body differs from the modern, more didactic example. Let us take the two areas our contemporary narrator isolated: her face, which was soiled with makeup and not veiled sufficiently, on one hand, and her fashionable clothing, on the other. These two sins appear in the Prophet's description. When he sees women being dragged by their necks, with iron chains made of fire around their necks, he asks the Angel Gabriel who these women are. The angel replies: "Those are the ones who uncovered their faces and their heads to other than their husbands."[21] The punishment here is centered on a body part, the neck, that was nòt directly involved in the sin. Were we working within a completely mimetic system, the disfigurement would have to involve the face and head directly, as in the case of the modern nontraveler. When the Prophet sees women whose flesh is being consumed by fire that is being kindled under them, he asks the Angel about them. Gabriel answers: "Those are the ones who dressed themselves for other than their husbands."[22] Total physical destruction awaits these women. Semiotically, these punishments partake not of the mimetic relationship of the icon but of the logical one of the index. In the case of the iconic or mimetic sign, the signifier is the image or equivalent of the signified; the index posits a logical relationship between signifier and signified.

This shift from one type of sign (defined by the nature of the relationship between the signifier and the signified) to another is itself a sign, on another level of discourse, of a shift of emphasis, of focus. Sidqī's one-on-one relationship of body parts kept attention focused directly on her body (whether or not it was adorned) and by implication her treatment of her own body. The punishments in the Muslim Hell, as they depart from corporal equivalencies, shift attention away from the body to the larger problem of its implications in relationships between individuals. Chains represent servitude or connection or both. (The other punishment is so close to a generic punishment in Hellfire that it communicates little about the nature of the sin.) The transgressions of these women were not really those of adornment or uncovering but those of adornment or uncovering for other than their husbands. The sinners have evaded the bonds of matrimony. It is appropriate that bonds of fire now hold them. The shift from mimetic to logical codes echoes that from personal behavior to social relationships.

By contrast, Sidqī's sin is part of a dialogue between herself and the deity alone. In fact, rather than conforming to social injunctions, she is violating contemporary norms represented by the woman who observes that there is nothing wrong with wearing makeup. This is part of what makes Sidqī's story essentially modern despite the apparent neotraditionalism of its moral injunctions. If we were to view it in Western terms, we would say it is both more individualist and more liberated. The Miʿrāj story is the more traditional, with its attention to sanctioned forms of social control. Finally, Sidqī's story is woman-centered in a way that is not at all typical of classical Islamic discourses on women and sin.[23]

Despite the similarities in transgression represented by the lack of modesty, the women at whom the Prophet gazes on his otherworldly tour are, of course, punished after their physical demise. And this is the opposite of the victim of the tooth extraction, whose punishment is inflicted on her while she is still of this world. The loci for punishment are significant. One of the conclusions we can draw from the experience of our modern-day female narrator is that her earthly lessons will assure her that she will not taste the tortures of the hereafter. Lest we misunderstand, we have the other female character in Sidqī's narrative. She represents everywoman and, more important, everywoman in a state of potential perdition, arguing as she does for the normative behavior of physical adornment and external religiosity. Her questions and objections permit the saved heroine to defend her position.

But in fact, more is at stake here than a mere lesson on adornment. The saga of this heroine is one that involves a journey from a diseased body to a healthy spirit. As Niʿmat Sidqī herself notes in her introduction to this story, the disease in her body "brought health and vitality back to my soul and my heart."[24] In that sense, her journey is a more dramatic parallel to the spiritual saga outlined in Karīmān Hamza's *Rihlatī min al-Sufūr ilā al-Hijāb* (My journey from uncovering to the veil).[25] In that work, a spiritual transformation is echoed by a sartorial shift from exposure to veiling.[26]

Different also is the emphasis in Sidqī's pamphlet on the body, specifically the female body. Her tirades against makeup and improper clothing are particularly virulent and distinguish themselves from much other modern Islamist material on adornment.[27] The colored eyelids, be they blue or black, are compared to those of monkeys and dogs, and the arched eyebrows recall those of devils. And what about women's painted red fingernails? These are closer to the claws of a rapacious animal, dyed with the blood of its prey.[28] It is the bodies of old women and ugly women who come in, however, for the harshest treatment. The faces of the old women, eaten by time, become like "swamps." The woman who goes out with her hair clipped and fluffy is carrying a jungle on her head. The woman who uncovers herself to reveal swollen legs or even thin ones frightens people. Her legs remind one of grave dwellers and decaying bones.[29] Yet this misogynist attack on the aging body brings Sidqī's argument closer to that of the Prophet Joseph when he contrasted youth with decay. Strikingly, in their severity Sidqī's descriptions go past adornment (not to speak of improper adornment) to an attack on the beauty of the female body in its natural state. As such, they echo traditional misogynist arguments used to encourage male celibacy.[30]

This state of being near death is certainly not foreign to the subtext of Sidqī's opening moral story with the tooth extraction. The narrator had very eloquently informed us that the physicians were helpless in the face of this mysterious illness. When the deity saved the woman, they proclaimed His ability to revive "decayed bones." These rotted body parts signal a state of near death, when not of death itself. The deity is able to effect a sort of resurrection for this lucky woman. Those whose legs are like decaying bones will hopefully learn their much-needed lesson.

More than death is at stake here. The physicians work in the realm of science and the deity, in the realm of religion. A tension is created between these two systems. We learn from our modern morality tale that religion triumphs over medical science.

The importance of medicine can be seen in an eloquent image used by our tooth-extraction victim. When elaborating her body parts that have transgressed in one way or another, she mentions the head, which did not cover itself with the appropriate Islamic garb. Instead, it is now veiled with medical bandages.[31] This substitution of medical bandages for a traditional head covering has been exploited, but in a humorous bisociation, by the Syrian cartoonist and artist ʿAlī Farzāt. In a comic strip sequence in the Syrian children's magazine *Usāma,* Farzāt presented the famous medieval traveler Ibn Battūta (d. 770 or 779/1368-69 or 1377), lost in a modern city. In the final scene, he replaced the great traveler's comically oversized turban with bandages, the result of a traffic accident.[32] But where Farzāt has used the similarity to ridicule tradition, Sidqī used a similar bisociation to valorize the traditional at the expense of the medical, here associated with disease and pain. Unlike Ibn Battūta, however, our female victim is freed from the medical veil but can, with the help of divine intercession, replace it with the appropriate Islamic one.

If the face of Helen launched a thousand ships, that of the contemporary Muslim woman bears an equal burden of conflict and controversy. Sin and punishment, adornment and disfiguration, covering and uncovering, the inevitable decay of the body—all play across her features.

NOTES

1. On Western attitudes to the face, see, for example, John Liggett, *The Human Face* (New York: Stein and Day, 1974); Jean-Jacques Courtine and Claudine Haro-

che, *Histoire du visage: XVIe–début XIXe siècle* (Paris: Editions Rivages, 1988); Arline and John Liggett, *The Tyranny of Beauty* (London: Victor Gollancz, 1989), pp. 64–130.

2. Studies of Islamic attitudes to the body are in their infancy. The otherwise excellent *Zone: Fragments for a History of the Human Body*, ed. Michel Feher et al., vols. 3, 4, and 5 (1989), contains nothing on Islam or the Middle East. For an evaluation of these volumes in the context of other scholarship on the body, see Ioan P. Culianu, "A Corpus for the Body," *Journal of Modern History* 63 (1991), pp. 61–80. Leila Ahmed's "Arab Culture and Writing Women's Bodies," *Feminist Issues* (Spring 1989), pp. 41–55, seeks to understand a short story by Alīfa Rifʿat against the context of classical Arabic medical lore. My own *Woman's Body, Woman's Word: Gender and Discourse in Arabo-Islamic Writing* (Princeton: Princeton University Press, 1991) is a gender exploration of woman's body as it relates to her discourse in the rich Arabo-Islamic textual tradition.

3. Nawāl al-Saʿdāwī, *al-Wajh al-ʿArī lil-Marʾa al-ʿArabiyya* (Beirut: al-Muʾassasa al-ʿArabiyya lil-Dirāsāt wal-Nashr, 1977).

4. Nawal El Saadawi, *The Hidden Face of Eve: Women in the Arab World*, trans. Sherif Hetata (Boston: Beacon Press, 1982). I have discussed the Western bisociation of the Middle Eastern woman with the veil elsewhere. See Fedwa Malti-Douglas, "Views of Arab Women: Society, Text, and Critic," *Edebiyât* 4 (1979), pp. 256–73; Malti-Douglas, *Woman's Body, Woman's Word*, p.3.

5. Rabīʿ ibn Muhammad al-Saʿudī, *Zād al-Musāfirīn ilā Ghayr Bilād al-Muslimīn* (Riyad: Dār al-Fitya and Cairo: Dār al-Sahwa lil-Nashr, 1988), pp. 22–23.

6. See Fedwa Malti-Douglas, "An Anti-Travel Guide: Iconography in a Muslim Revivalist Tract," *Edebiyât*, vol. NS 4, 2 (1993), pp. 205–213.

7. Niʿmat Sidqī, *al-Tabarruj* (Cairo: Dār al-Iʿtisām, 1975); Valerie J. Hoffman-Ladd, "Polemics on the Modesty and Segregation of Women in Contemporary Egypt," *International Journal of Middle East Studies* 19 (1987), no. 1, pp. 29–42; Sanā al-Misrī, *Khalf al-Hijāb: Mawqif al-Jamāʿāt al-Islāmiyya min Qadiyyat al-Marʾa* (Cairo: Sīnā lil-Nashr, 1989), p. 36.

8. The introduction by Saʿd Khumayyis in Sidqī, *al-Tabarruj*, p. 3, praises the work and also notes its popularity and its numerous reprintings.

9. Hoffman-Ladd, "Polemics," p. 29.

10. Sidqī's story is summarized in Hoffman-Ladd, "Polemics," pp. 29–30.

11. Sidqī, *al-Tabarruj*, pp. 9–11.

12. See, for example, Ibn al-Jawzī, *Ahkām al-Nisāʾ* (Beirut: Dār al-Kutub al-ʿIlmiyya, 1985); Ahmad ibn Hanbal, *Ahkām al-Nisāʾ*, ed. ʿAbd al-Qādir Ahmad ʿAtā (Beirut: Dār al-Kutub al-ʿIlmiyya, 1986).

13. For a discussion of *ʿawra*, see Malti-Douglas, *Woman's Body, Woman's Word*, pp. 49, 90, 121–22, 126–27.

14. See, for example, Ibn al-Jawzī, *Ahkām al-Nisāʾ*; Ahmad ibn Hanbal, *Ahkām al-Nisāʾ*.

15. See, for example, Naomi Wolf, *The Beauty Myth: How Images of Beauty Are Used against Women* (New York: William Morrow, 1991).

16. Cf. Hoffman-Ladd, "Polemics," p. 24.

17. On this story and its significance, see, for example, Malti-Douglas, *Woman's Body, Woman's Word*, pp. 50–53, 55–59.

18. Al-Tabarī, *Taʾrīkh al-Umam wal-Mulūk*, ed. Muhammad Abū al-Fadl Ibrāhīm (Beirut: Dār Suwaydān, n.d.), vol 1, p. 337.

19. See Malti-Douglas, *Woman's Body, Woman's Word*, p. 49 and n. 96 on the same page; Jane Idleman Smith and Yvonne Yazbek Haddad, *The Islamic Understanding of Death and Resurrection* (Albany: State University of New York Press, 1981), p. 162.

20. Comparisons between the Islamic and Dantean traditions have already been made. See, for example, Miguel Asin Palacios, *Islam and the Divine Comedy*, translated

and abridged by Harold Sunderland (Lahore: Qausain, 1977). For another perspective, see I. P. Culiano, *Out of this World: Otherworldly Journeys from Gilgamesh to Albert Einstein* (Boston: Shambhala, 1991), pp. 218–31.

21. Sharīf Sayyid, *al-Isrā' wal-Miʿrāj* (Beirut: Muʾassasat Bint al-Hudā lil-Tibāʿa wal-Nashr wal-Tawzīʿ, n.d.), p. 35.

22. Sayyid, *al-Isrā'*, p. 37.

23. See Malti-Douglas, *Woman's Body, Woman's Word.*

24. Sidqī, *al-Tabarruj*, p. 9.

25. Karīmān Hamza, *Rihlatī min al-Sufūr ilā al-Hijāb* (Beirut: Dār al-Fath lil-Tibāʿa wal-Nashr, 1986). On this book, see Fedwa Malti-Douglas, "Gender and the Uses of the Ascetic in an Islamist Text," in *Asceticism,* ed. V. L. Wimbush and R. Valantasis (New York: Oxford University Press, forthcoming).

26. I am investigating this issue in a book currently in progress.

27. For a more representative work, see, for example, ʿUkāsha ʿAbd al-Mannān al-Tībī, *al-Tabarruj: Akhtar Maʿādil al-Hadm wal-Tadmīr fī al-Mujtamaʿ al-Islāmī* (Cairo: Maktabat al-Turāth al-Islāmī, 1989). See also Fedwa Malti-Douglas, "The Islamist Body Social," Schell Center Working Paper Series, Orville H. Schell Jr. Center for International Human Rights, Yale Law School, 1993.

28. Sidqī, *al-Tabarruj*, p. 24.

29. Sidqī, *al-Tabarruj*, p. 27.

30. Elizabeth Wilson develops this theme beautifully for post-Ashokan Buddhism. See her essay in this volume.

31. Sidqī, *al-Tabarruj*, p. 10.

32. ʿAlī Farzāt, "Ibn Battūta," *Usāma* 196 (1977). For a discussion of this Syrian children's comic strip, see Allen Douglas and Fedwa Malti-Douglas, *Arab Comic Strips: Politics of an Emerging Mass Culture* (Bloomington: Indiana University Press, 1994), chap. 7.

THE FEMALE BODY AS A SOURCE OF HORROR AND INSIGHT IN POST-ASHOKAN INDIAN BUDDHISM

Elizabeth Wilson

If her bowels and flesh were cut open, you would see what filth is covered by her white skin. If a fine crimson cloth covered a pile of foul dung, would anyone be foolish enough to love the dung because of it? . . . There is no plague which monks should dread more than woman: the soul's death.[1]

> But, my dear nothings, take your leave:
> No longer must you me deceive,
> Since I perceive
> All the deceit, and know
> Whence the mistake did grow.
> If I gaze now, 'tis but to see
> What manner of death's head 'twill be,
> When it is free
> From that fresh upper skin,
> The gazer's joy and sin.[2]

As objects of sexual desire, women are often seen as obstacles in the celibate path of the male renunciate, sensual stumbling blocks to be avoided at all costs. But absolute avoidance is not a practical strategy; nor is it always the most effective. To vanquish desire, the enemy must be encountered, engaged, and exposed as the cause of suffering.[3] In this pursuit, encounters with beautiful women are extremely useful to the renunciate, offering him a field in which to engage and overcome his desire. Like the young women who shared Gandhi's bed during his "experiments in *brahmacarya*," tempting female bodies may be drafted into the service of male celibacy.[4] In narratives drawn from several genres of post-Ashokan literature, the female body becomes salvific for the renunciant spectator by taking on a horrific appearance. These are shocking stories in which the erotic and the repulsive aesthetic moods are deliberately collapsed, evoking in the responsive listener or reader a transformative experience analogous to that gained through the monastic practice of contemplating dead bodies (Pali, *asubha-bhāvanā;* Sanskrit, *ashubha-bhāvanā*).[5]

This essay uses literary critical and sociohistorical methods to explore the literary and symbolic conventions that constitute the female body as a locus of horror and insight in post-Ashokan Buddhist literature.[6] Arguing that the redaction of narratives featuring horrific representations of the female body served the interests of a renunciant male counterculture intent on remaining celibate, this essay supports the work of other feminist historians who question the purported gender egalitarianism of Indian Buddhism.[7]

The biography of the Buddha provides a paradigmatic example of the liberating power of gynophobic horror. On the eve of his renunciation, a gruesome transformation takes place before Gotama's eyes in the women's apartments.[8] At the end of an evening of dancing and dalliance, divine supporters of the Buddhist teaching put the women in a state of cadaverous sleep. One woman's hair, clothing, and ornaments are disheveled "like a woman crushed by an elephant and then dropped."[9] Another has saliva dribbling out of her mouth, lying "as though sprawled in intoxication."[10] Others, sleeping in distorted positions with open, motionless eyes, "lay without any beauty as if they were dead."[11] Looking at these bodies grotesquely transfigured by sleep, Gotama concludes: "Such is the nature of women, impure *(ashuci)* and monstrous *(vikrita)* in the world of living beings; but, deceived by dress and ornaments, a man becomes infatuated by a woman's attractions."[12]

With their bodies contorted in sleep like stiffening corpses, the women of Gotama's harem no longer inspire lust. They have become "impure and monstrous in the world of the living," for they have taken on the features of death in their unconscious state. Continual decay being the natural condition of all impermanent beings, this soporific body language transmits a profound message to the renunciant prince: the bedroom is a charnel ground where pleasure is snatched from the teeth of death. In the biographies of the Buddha, the sight of these cadaverous women is the final spectacle in a series of visions (the Four Signs, beginning with the sight of a decrepit old man, seen during four excursions from the palace) that reveal the ephemeral nature of life in the world. Significantly, it is this final vision of women ravaged by death that prompts the bodhisattva to renounce the world. Where the other visions occur some days prior to his leaving home, the harem vision immediately precedes the Great Renunciation whereby Gotama flees from the palace of desire in which his father has made him a prisoner.[13] Thus in the biography of the founder, horrific figurations of the feminine play a key role in the transformation of the young prince into a world-renouncer, serving as catalysts that galvanize the bodhisattva's resolve to leave the world.

Most women, however, do not oblige the would-be renouncer by miming death. Although subject by nature to continual decay, women are said to

A Sri Lankan monk contemplating a pile of bones.
The monastic practice of *asubha bhāvanā* allows the
practitioner to choose from among ten types of
dead bodies, selecting the type that best suits his
or her disposition. By permission of the Pali Text
Society.

mask their "impure and monstrous" condition with cosmetics, jewelry,
clothing, and alluring gestures. The artificial beauty of women thus resembles the bait used by hunters to lure unsuspecting prey—a dissimulation
that entices the senses with false promises of gratification. Because their
false advertising threatens the equanimity of his monks, the Buddha of the
*Nikāya*s views women as traps laid by Māra, the Evil One.[14] Furthermore,
because women bear children, they represent to the renouncer the illusion
of reproductive immortality, the folly of continued life in an impermanent
world ravished by death.[15] As creatures whose bodies transmit promises of
pleasure and continued life, women are generally considered a dangerous
obstacle to the renunciant male. The Buddha is said to have recommended
avoiding them altogether—hardly a viable solution to the problem, since
women frequently wait on monks who beg alms at their homes.[16]

This essay examines a different strategy for dealing with women and the desires they personify, a rhetorical strategy masterfully employed in various types of post-Ashokan Buddhist literature. Attractive women whose bodies speak of the pleasures of life become palimpsests on which the marks of impermanence and pain are superimposed. In the stories to be related, some women are disfigured by bodily mutilation, some by death. In each case, the transformation yields a horrific "heroine," with the disfigured woman triumphantly presented as an edifying moral lesson on the impurity of the body and the folly of lust.[17]

Spectacular Mutilation

One of the most gruesome forms of horrific transformation found in post-Ashokan texts is the use of bodily mutilation for the edification of the spectator. The display of disfigured female forms exhibits the symbolic logic of corporal punishment Michel Foucault describes in *Discipline and Punish,* his history of European penal reform movements: the nature of the crime is iconically inscribed on the body of the criminal.[18] By amputating, piercing, or branding the offending body part, the crime is graphically displayed for all to see. In several post-Ashokan narratives, women's bodies are disfigured in symbolically significant ways. Body parts that lend themselves to ornamentation are cut off and the disfigured female body becomes an object of contemplation for the edification of certain members of the *sangha,* or monastic order. The use of earrings and nose-rings and the application of henna and cosmetic pastes to the hands, feet, and breasts were conventions used by Indian women of the period to adorn and eroticize the body. Thus amputation of the ears, nose, hands, feet, and breasts of adulterous women (as specified in Indian law books) mortifies the erotic body, punishing and displaying the nature of the crime at the same time. Such punishments operate as signifiers within a fairly systematic grammar of punitive torture by which the amputation of various offending extremities inscribes the body of the criminal with punitive marks or insignia *(cihna)* indicative of the nature of the crime.[19]

In the punitive Islamic religious discourse described by Fedwa Malti-Douglas in her contribution to this volume, there seems to be a rather similar grammar that links the lipstick-reddened lips and powdered cheeks of the adorned female body with their concomitant forms of punishment, such as the divinely inflicted toothache and swollen cheeks mentioned in the *Zād al-Musāfirīn ilā Ghayr Bilād al-Muslimīn.* There is, furthermore, a similar disparity between the topographies of male and female bodies as loci of shame and punishment in the Indic and Islamic punitive religious discourses. In Islamic discourse, the focus of male shame (and presumably punishment) is limited to the genital region, while the focus of female shame and punishment extends to the extremities of the body. There is a similar focus in Indic punitive discourse on the male genitalia as the natural site of punitive marking. Whereas the bodies of males guilty of sexual transgressions are generally punished by castration or symbolic castration (the shaving of the head, for example)[20] if touched by punitive marking at all (paying fines being a legitimate form of punishment for certain men's sexual offenses), the punishments for female sexual transgressions are less predictable.[21] The bodies of the female transgressors are punished in a variety of places. Some punishments, such as the cutting off of the nose, may be seen as symbolizing clitoridectomy, or female "castration."[22] But there is virtually no end to the number of female body parts that may, according to Indic legal discourse, legitimately be inscribed with punitive marks. Since women have no external organs of reproduction indicative of sexual arousal comparable to male genitals, it follows that virtually the entire female body is apt to be regarded erotically and subject to punitive measures in the case of sexual transgression.

But even more important than punishing the perpetrator is the salutary effect of punishment on the spectator. As Foucault has emphasized, the audience plays a crucial role in "the spectacle of the scaffold." Corporal punishment is intended to impress upon all citizens the absolute power of the king to uphold the moral order. In the Buddhist context, the spectacle of the mutilated woman serves to display the power of the Buddha, the king of the Truth (Dharma), over Māra, the lord of the Realm of Desire.[23] The Buddha reigns supreme by virtue of his superior insight into the link between desire, impermanence, and suffering. By erasing the sexual messages conveyed by the bodies of attractive women through the horrific spectacle of mutilation, the superior power of the king of Dharma is made manifest to the citizens of the realm of desire.

The story of Upagupta and Vasavadattā illustrates this punitive form of horrific transformation. The *Ashokāvadāna* presents Upagupta's encounter with Vasavadattā as a significant episode in the premonastic life of this "Buddha without the marks" who later in life would become an important leader of the sangha and adviser to king Ashoka. Vasavadattā is a celebrated courtesan in the city of Mathurā. She hears of a young perfume merchant named Upagupta and is so impressed that she sends her servant to Upagupta to arrange a tryst. When Upagupta refuses, Vasavadattā sends her servant back to make sure that Upagupta understands the situation: her services are complimentary; no money is asked in exchange. Again Upagupta refuses. One day, Vasavadattā eliminates her current lover in order to acquire a wealthier patron. Her crime is discovered and reported to the king. The king orders his men to cut off Vasavadattā's hands and feet (a punishment appropriate for a murderer) as well as her nose and ears (a punishment often meted out to adulteresses, parallel to the emasculation of an adulterer). Thus disfigured, Vasavadattā and her dismembered parts are deposited in the cremation ground. There, in the place where those engaged in ascetic practices contemplate the foulness of decaying bodies, Upagupta goes to see the woman he had not wished to visit before. Vasavadattā, still accompanied by her servant, instructs the girl to hide the amputated body parts with a cloth and then asks Upagupta: "Why have you come here to see me now that my body is unfit to be looked at, plastered with mud and blood, causing fear, having lost its wonder, joy, pleasure, and play!"[24] Upagupta replies:

> Sister, I have not come to you impelled by desire, but have come to see the intrinsic nature of desires and impurities.[25] When you were covered with clothes, ornaments, and other variegated externals conducive to passion, those who looked at you could not see you as you truly are, even when they made the effort. But now, free from outer trappings, your form may be seen in its intrinsic nature.[26]

Upagupta goes on to compare the human body to a living corpse in a continual state of putrefaction: "unlearned and wicked are those who take pleasure in this gross, living carcass."[27] The message of this punitive spectacle is certainly not lost on Upagupta, who attains the status of a nonreturner as a result of his encounter with the mutilated courtesan.[28]

A more ambiguous message is transmitted to the wayward monk Nanda.[29] The story of Nanda is a very popular, much repeated example of how the Buddha on occasion uses the power of untoward desires to lure a wayward monk back to the path.[30] Nanda, the half-brother of Gotama, does not freely choose to become a monk. On the very day of his marriage to the beautiful Janapāda-Kalyāṇī, he enters the sangha only out of deference to the Buddha. Soon Nanda begins to long for Janapāda-Kalyāṇī. To prevent the discontented monk from returning to the life of a householder, the Buddha takes him by the arm and transports him to the heaven of Indra, where five hundred celestial nymphs entertain the king of the gods with music and dance. The Buddha promises Nanda that if he will remain in the sangha, he will win for himself these five hundred celestial Apsarases.

Along the way to the heaven of Indra, however, Nanda sees a very unpleasant sight which foreshadows the subversion of desire that is the final outcome of the story. "The Blessed One pointed out to Venerable Nanda in a certain burnt field, seated on a burnt stump, a female monkey who had been seduced and whose ears and nose and tail had been cut off." Nanda does not grasp the significance of this sight immediately; when the Buddha asks Nanda whether the five hundred celestial nymphs are not more enticing than Janapāda-Kalyāṇī, Nanda confesses that Janapāda suddenly seems to him as ugly as this mutilated monkey. However, by the end of the story Nanda has become an Arhat (one who is liberated through the eradication of desire). No longer troubled by desire of any kind, he releases the Buddha from his promise. Thus the Buddha initially lures Nanda back to the path with enticing female flesh.[31] But the desire that he encourages in Nanda is ultimately subverted through the power of horror unleashed by a mutilated female form.

I know of no comparable scene in Indian Buddhist literature that pre-

An *apsaras*, or celestial nymph, with her maid. From Ananda Coomaraswamy, *History of Indian and Indonesian Art.* New York: Dover Publications, Inc., 1985 (orig. pub. 1927).

sents a mutilated male body as an edifying spectacle. While it is true that self-mutilation in the service of hungry beings plays a role in the bodhi-sattva career, the removal of portions of flesh from the bodhisattva's body is a voluntary act of sacrifice with no discernible punitive dimension. Furthermore, depictions of this heroic act do not underscore the impurity of the bodhisattva's body. To the contrary, the bodhisattva's self-mutilation serves to reveal his adamantine body, since the cutting off of his flesh is compared to the cutting of gems.[32]

Charming Cadavers

An equally horrific figuration of the feminine appears in narratives that depict monks achieving insight while scrutinizing dead bodies of women—especially beautiful women struck down suddenly in the full flower of their youth. Doctrinally speaking, there is no reason to focus on the female body as a special locus of impurity and impermanence.[33] Male bodies are, quite obviously, just as subject to old age, disease, death, and decay as female bodies.[34] But the absence of male corpses used as objects of contemplation is as conspicuous as the presence of male subjects in various post-Ashokan tales of edifying encounters in the cremation ground. Given the pan-Indian tendency to hold women responsible for the arousal of desire, this division of labor between male subject and female object serves an obvious function. The contemplation of decaying beauty provides an unparalleled opportunity for suppressing those desires that threaten the commitment of individual monks and the integrity of the sangha as a celibate community.

Where most examples of the charming cadaver theme tell the story of a particular named monk who encounters the dead body of an unnamed woman, the story of Sirimā reverses that pattern. In this narrative, which appears in the commentary to the *Dhammapada* under the title "Sirimā's Story" *(Sirimā-vatthu)*, we are told quite a bit about Sirimā but very little about the lovesick monk who encounters her dead body.[35] Sirimā's story begins with a brief description of the circumstances that prompted Sirimā to renounce her profitable career as a courtesan to become a lay follower of the Buddha.[36] But although the story begins with Sirimā as the subject, by the end of the tale Sirimā no longer occupies the subject position. Her convenient death makes her body an ideal object of meditation for a lovesick monk.

Sirimā's story is atypical in another respect. Where other narratives featuring charming cadavers describe private encounters involving a single monk or a small group of monks, Sirimā is put on public display at the request of the Buddha. The moral opportunity afforded by Sirimā's dead body is deemed so salutary to the general populace that all citizens are made to contemplate her fly-blown corpse. There is, however, one aspect of Sirimā's story that provokes no surprise. The public display of Sirimā's body is set within an already familiar frame story: the Buddha cures a monk of lust by capitalizing on the intensity of the monk's desire.

The *Dhammapada* commentary *(Dhammapadāṭṭhakathā)* explains that after her conversion, Sirimā becomes a generous patron of the sangha. Spending sixteen *kahāpaṇas* per day on food, she regularly provides lavish meals for eight monks.[37] A certain unnamed monk hears about Sirimā from a visiting monk who has just eaten at her home. As the visiting monk raves about how Sirimā's beauty is even more pleasing than the delicious foods she serves, the unnamed monk falls in love with this woman whom he has never seen. He immediately sets off and walks through the night to take alms at her home in the morning. But that very evening, as the monk sets off to see her, Sirimā falls ill. In the morning she has a high fever and is unable to wait on the monks personally. Nevertheless, Sirimā instructs her servants to carry her into the presence of the monks so that she can pay her respects. The lovelorn monk sees her, and instead of receiving the dharmic message transmitted by the diseased body of Sirimā, he decides that if she is this lovely when ill, she must be even more beautiful when well. "Then passion, accumulated during many millions of years, attacked him. He fell into a stupor and lost all interest in food."

That evening, Sirimā dies. When the teacher hears of her death, he sends the king the following message: "There's to be no cremation for Sirimā. Have her body laid in the charnel field and post a guard, so that crows and dogs will not devour it."

> The king did so. Three days passed, one after another. On the fourth day the body began to bloat, and from the nine openings of her body, which were like gaping wounds, maggots poured out.[38] Her whole body had burst open like a cracked vessel of rice. The king caused a drum to go through the city and the following proclamation to be made, "Let everyone come see Sirimā. Except for youngsters guarding houses, all who refuse to come will be fined eight *kahāpaṇas*."
>
> Now that young monk had laid for four days without touching food, hearing nothing anyone said to him. The rice in his bowl had gone putrid and moldy. Then the other monks who were his companions came and told him that the Teacher was on his way to see Sirimā. When the young monk, lying there, heard the word "Sirimā," he jumped to his feet. Someone said to him, "The Teacher is going to see Sirimā, are you coming too?" "I'm coming," he answered. And tossing the food out of his bowl, he washed it and put it in his bag and then set out with the company of monks.

The young monk rushes along with the others to the burning ground, where all the citizens have assembled, monks and the Buddha on one side of the body, nuns, laypeople, and king on the other. The Buddha establishes that this corpse is indeed the lovely Sirimā and then instructs the king "Send a drum through the city and let it be known that whoever will pay a thousand *kahāpaṇas* for Sirimā may have her." When no one expresses any interest, the king informs the teacher: "They won't have her, Blessed One." And the Buddha responds: "Well then, great king, lower the price."

By dropping the price in gradual increments, the fact that no man will have Sirimā at any price is made evident to all spectators, especially the lovelorn monk. The teacher concludes:

> "Monks, look at this available woman adored by so many people. In this very city men used to pay a thousand *kahāpaṇas* for the sake of spending one night with this woman. Now there is no one who will take her even for free. Her beauty has perished and decayed." Saying, "Monks, look at this diseased body," he spoke the following verse [*Dhammapada* 147]: "Look at this decorated image, an elevated mass of wounds. This diseased thing is highly fancied, (although) it's neither permanent nor stable."

The lovelorn monk is cured of his dangerous condition by an elaborate spectacle orchestrated by the king of Dharma. With his passion aroused by the thought of seeing Sirimā in all her glory, the hapless monk ends up instead contemplating Sirimā as a fly-blown corpse. Here, just as in the story of Nanda and the celestial nymphs, the Buddha encourages the monk's desire only to subvert it in the end.

The proximity of lust and aversion in these stories is reminiscent of a modern form of therapy which the Great Physician might have approved of—behavior modification through aversive stimulation.[39] Given that lust, in the Buddhist scheme of things, is a life-threatening condition and knowing that the Great Physician was not given to wasting time over elaborate diagnosis when an effective cure lay readily at hand, I think that the analogy of aversion therapy is not inappropriate.[40] The lust of the male spectator is engaged in a repulsive spectacle by which that lust is transformed into aversion and thus effectively subverted. The charming cadaver transmits two messages simultaneously: desirability and extreme impurity. The ironic message of the charming cadaver is fairly self-evident in any context. But in the context of Indian culture, with its concern for avoiding the impurities of death, the macabre spectacle of putrefying beauty is extremely potent. And its rhetorical effect on the responsive reader may be as powerful as the actual practice of contemplating corpses *(asubha-bhāvanā)*.[41]

In *Dhammapadāṭṭhakathā* 11.4, the Buddha orchestrates an arousing encounter in the charnel field to chasten a group of forest-dwelling monks.

> Five hundred monks, having been in the presence of the Teacher and gotten their meditation subjects, went to the forest. After great exertion and struggle, they achieved success in meditation. (Saying) "We've accomplished our duty as renouncers by avoiding the afflictions *(kilesānaṃ)*; let's notify the Teacher of the virtues we've attained by ourselves," they left the forest. At the moment they reached the gateway, the Teacher told the Elder Ānanda: "There's no reason, Ānanda, for these monks to come in and see me. Let them return to see me after they go off to a charnel ground."[42] The Elder went and told them. They didn't ask why they were to go to the charnel ground. They just assumed that the omniscient Buddha must have a good reason for doing this. Going to the charnel ground, they saw corpses that had fallen one or two days ago. They experienced aversion for those bodies, but at the same time found that they felt desire for the freshly fallen bodies *(patitesu allasarīresu)*. At that moment, they knew that afflictions existed in them.
>
> The Teacher, seated in the Perfumed Chamber, suffused them with radiance and, as if they were face to face, said: "Is it really appropriate, monks, for you to experience passionate appreciation on seeing such a collection of bones?"

The Tamil poet Cāttaṉār utilizes the rhetorical power of the charming cadaver theme in his *Maṇimēkhalai*, a sixth-century Buddhist epic about a courtesan's daughter who renounces her hereditary occupation to become a Buddhist nun. Turning classical Tamil poetic conventions on their head for Buddhist rhetorical purposes, Cāttaṉār inverts standard images of erotic love in portraying a ghoulish wedding feast in a cremation ground called the "Cosmic Place."

> A boy named Cāṅkalaṉ went inside the Cosmic Place *(cakkaravāḷa)* all alone, thinking it was a well-fortified city. Instead he met with sounds pro-

claiming to people who love the body that it is only flesh, blood, and bones: there was the ceaseless, exultant howl of a jackal clutching in his jaws a corpse's foot decorated with red cosmetic paste, a lump of wormy decaying flesh. Then he heard the drawn-out shriek of a vulture piercing and consuming a naked mound-of-venus, the unrestrained howl of an evil dog who had snatched and torn apart a severed arm, stacked with bangles, and the crunch, of the hungry kite seizing and eating beautiful, erect, young breasts adorned with sandal paste.

These sounds served as the beats of the *muḷavam* drum played on a stage created out of white ashes from once-lovely bodies. A female ghoul gleefully mounted onto that stage. She did not ask herself, "What are these, clouds or a woman's tresses? Carp or eyes? Is this a *kumiḷ* flower or a nose? Are these lips or *kavir* flowers? Teeth or pearls?" She did not show any mercy. Dancing with joy on her cloven feet, she gouged out the eyes of that head and ate them with insatiable glee.[43]

The *muḷavam* drum, used in South Indian marriage ceremonies, suggests imminent sexual consummation. But the poet has inverted the erotic mood, lingering on the dismembered parts of the female corpse as a lover fixates on certain features of the beloved's body. As the translator of this story, Paula Richman, notes, Cāttaṉār has transformed the vocabulary of erotic love "into a catalogue of cannibalism."[44] This macabre marriage ceremony contains an element of necrophagy not evident in other post-Ashokan tales of insight achieved through horror. But the necrophilia of Cāttaṉār's "wedding" feast only amplifies the necrophilia implicit in so many other instances of the charming cadaver theme.

In the *Theragāthā,* a collection of verses ascribed to elder monks of the early sangha, several monks tell of having succumbed to the necrophilic charms of relatively undecayed female corpses while practicing cremation-ground meditation. Their stories, detailed in the commentary to the *Theragāthā,* show the dangers of selecting bodies of the opposite sex as supports for *asubha bhāvanā.*[45] One man, named Rājadatta, had squandered his fortune on a courtesan living in Rājagaha.[46] Hungry and destitute, the wretched man wandered around aimlessly until one day he heard the Buddha teaching. Impressed by what he heard, Rājadatta joined the sangha and began to spend time in cremation grounds practicing *asubha bhāvanā.* The courtesan, in the meantime, committed a theft, was caught, and was put to death. Her body, left to rot in the cremation ground that Rājadatta frequented, was still relatively undecayed when Rājadatta encountered it and selected it as an object of meditation. Even though portions of it had been savaged by dogs and jackals, Rājadatta nevertheless found himself aroused by the courtesan's body. Fleeing from the scene and meditating elsewhere in order to regain his composure, the monk finally returned to the body, recommenced the meditation, and achieved Arhatship.

Whereas Rājadatta was able to overcome necrophilia and achieve insight on his own, the monk Kulla required the assistance of the Buddha.[47] A sincere monk who is plagued by lust, Kulla is given *asubha bhāvanā* as a meditation subject. The hapless Kulla continues to have lustful thoughts, even in the cremation ground. Knowing Kulla's tendencies, the Buddha accompanies the monk to the cremation ground one day and through the exercise of his psychic powers creates a magical display. The Teacher conjures up an undecayed body for Kulla to observe—the attractive body of a young woman who had died quite recently. As soon as he perceives that Kulla is aroused, the Buddha causes this body to become extremely disagreeable in smell and appearance, with maggots pouring from every opening. Thanks to this horrific transformation, Kulla achieves Arhatship.

Desire, as Peter Brown has recently shown with regard to the Desert Fathers tradition, can serve as an accurate seismograph of the soul.[48] In the case of the overconfident monks, necrophilic arousal provides a clue to the need for further effort. Yet however useful necrophilic arousal may be in helping the meditator to gauge the purity of his mind, such forms of desire can easily defeat the purpose of contemplating dead bodies. One way to overcome necrophilia is to subject the charming cadaver to further transformation through burning. Thus the dead body that should be repulsive but instead provokes desire can be made into a thing of horror by cremation. In the first book of the *Dhammapada* commentary, in a section devoted to the past and present lives of the chief disciples, there are two notable instances of insight achieved through the cremation of a female body.

The story of Yasa begins like the account of the bodhisattva's departure from the palace. Yasa is a young man from a wealthy family in Benares who flees in horror from the women's apartments in the middle of the night. Like Gotama himself, Yasa sees his bedroom turn into a cemetery; immediately after this experience, he goes to the Buddha for ordination. Once he joins the sangha, he and fifty-four of his companions come to play leading roles in the community. The commentary ascribes the present-life achievements of Yasa and his friends to insights the fifty-five men gained in a previous life through the cremation of a pregnant female corpse (*Dhammapada* 1.8). Long before the time of the present Buddha, these men had banded together to perform good deeds. Mainly they devoted themselves to cremating abandoned corpses. One day, they saw the dead body of a pregnant woman. Yasa and four of his companions took the body to the burning ground while the rest went back to the village.

> The young Yasa achieved awareness of impurity while burning that body, piercing it with stakes and turning it over and over. To the other four men he said: "Brothers, look at this impure, foul smelling, disagreeable body. Here and there the skin has broken open, resembling (that of) a mottled cow." They also attained awareness of the impurity right there. These five people then went to the village and told the rest of their friends. And young Yasa went home and told his mother, father, and wife. They all meditated on impurity too.

> Because of this work of merit, awareness of the cremation ground arose
> within Yasa's mind in the women's quarters.

This encounter with a horrifically transformed female body led not only
to Yasa's edification but also to that of many others. As a result of one
cremated cadaver, fifty-eight people came to know the impurity of the body.

In another narrative from the *Dhammapadāṭṭhakathā*, an ascetic older
monk named Mahākāla (the older Kāla) watches as the flames transform a
still-alluring female corpse into a charmless—and harmless—tangle of
limbs.[49] It is one of several past life stories about the Kāla brothers, and
the point of the story is to contrast the spiritual success of the older brother
with the failure of the younger. The younger brother requests ordination
only to be with his older brother, Mahākāla, whom he hopes to lure back
to the householder's life. By the end of the story, the younger monk is
literally defrocked by his spurned wives, who taunt him for failing to con-
sult them about his decision to leave the world and then tear off his robes
and dress him in the white clothing of a layman. In contrast to his younger
brother, shamed at the hands of female temptresses, the older monk
achieves insight with the help of two very impure figures: a female cremation groundskeeper and a female corpse.

Mahākāla, declaring himself too old for scriptural study, adopts the ascetic practice of spending each night in the cremation ground. Kālī, the
groundskeeper, sees Mahākāla haunting the grounds late at night and instructs him to report to the proper authorities, lest he be taken for a thief
seeking refuge from the law.[50] She then indicates that if he attains Arhatship in her burning ground, she will cremate the next abandoned body
with honors; but if he fails to achieve this goal, she will drag, desecrate,
and mutilate the next body to come her way.[51] The elder answered her:
"Alright, ma'm. But if you see a suitable object for meditation on material
form, would you please tell me?" Conveniently, a remarkably good subject
dies that day.

> Now a certain young woman of social standing was attacked by a disease
> which overtook her quite suddenly. She died that evening, without a sign
> of withering or weariness. During the night, her family and servants brought
> her body to the burning-ground along with some wood and oil. Giving the
> keeper of the burning-ground a fee, they left the body with her and de-
> parted. When Kālī removed the cloth that covered this one who had died
> so suddenly and saw her delightfully pleasing, golden colored body, she
> thought to herself, "This corpse is a suitable object of meditation for him."

Kālī informs Mahākāla, who examines the body "from the soles of the
feet to the tips of the hair," then says: "Throw this extremely attractive,
golden-colored form into the fire, and as soon as the tongues of fire have
laid hold of it, please tell me." The keeper of the burning ground prepares
the pyre and calls the monk as instructed.

> When the flames had attacked the flesh, the color of the body was like
> that of a mottled cow; the feet were curled up and dangled curiously; the
> hands were bent back; the forehead was without skin. The Elder thought
> to himself, "This body, which only moments ago caused those who looked
> at it to forget the precepts, has now attained destruction, has now at-
> tained decay."

As a result of seeing the transformation of this enticing feminine form
into a thing of horror before his eyes, Mahākāla develops insight into impermanence and, that evening, attains Arhatship and supernatural powers.
Thus, whereas the younger brother is led astray by his wives, the older
brother attains liberation with the assistance of two very impure female
strangers. In this story, the wives of the younger brother are depicted as
temptresses, while the two liminal female figures who assist Mahākāla play
redemptive roles. In most other tales of insight achieved through aversion,
however, the same woman plays both roles. Casting one woman in the dual
role of temptress and redemptress neatly short-circuits desire by collapsing
the opposed forces of attraction and repulsion into one body.

In another instance of the theme of the cadaverous sleeping woman, the
wife of a lazy monk who cannot make up his mind about his true vocation
is the decisive factor in her husband's final determination to leave the world
once and for all.[52] The monk, who is ironically dubbed Thera Cittahattha
("Elder Thought-Controlled"), initially joins the sangha to ensure for himself a comfortable life and a plentiful supply of food. But, put to work as
an assistant to senior monks, Cittahattha returns home. After a few days
of tending the forest-fields at home, however, the man misses the relative
ease of the monastic life. Putting on his robes, he is again received into the
sangha. The same pattern recurs five times in succession until, on his seventh return to the householder's life, Cittahattha's wife appears visibly
pregnant.

> From his going back and forth, his wife became pregnant. On the seventh
> time, he returned from the forest with his ploughing implements, went to
> the house to put his yoke away, and entered the bedroom, saying to himself,
> "I'll put on my yellow robe again." Now his wife had laid down for a nap
> and was asleep at that moment. Her outer garment had fallen off, saliva
> was flowing from her mouth, snores resonated in her nasal passages, and
> her mouth was wide open. She looked like a bloated corpse. Thinking, "This
> is ephemeral and dissatisfying [*aniccam dukkham idam*]," he said to himself:
> "To think that because of her, all the time I have been a monk, I have been
> unable to stick to the monastic life!" Grabbing his yellow robe by the hem,
> he ran out of the house, tying the robe about his belly as he ran.

Attributing the wayward monk's failure to the siren song of the wife is
common in such stories (e.g., Nanda).[53] Apparently the preachers of
Dharma responsible for the form of this particular tale saw no incongruity
in blaming the wife of this lazy, indecisive monk for her husband's flighti-

The Hindu goddess Kālī wearing a string of decapitated
heads as a necklace and a pair of fetuses as earrings. She
is shown in a burning ground standing on Shiva, her
consort, who is represented in both an animated and an
unanimated form. From a private collection.

ness. Indeed, the unsteadiness of his mind must be attributed to her so
that the revolting sight of her swollen, cadaverous body can serve as a
remedy to Cittahattha's indecisiveness. For here, as in the case of Sirimā,
the song of the siren can be altered at the whim of the storyteller. Through
horrific transformation, the redactor of the *Dhammapada* commentary can
suddenly jam the transmission of sensuous messages and replace them with
the siren as we know it: a signal of danger.

   The erotic is easily transformed into the repulsive due to the widespread
idea of the duplicity of the female body. If one can only see through the
cosmetics and ornaments a woman wears, Hindu and Buddhist texts of the
post-Ashokan period frequently declare, one will find a walking cadaver, a
vessel of filth.[54] Thus the *Brahmavaivarta Purāṇa*, a medieval Vaishnavite

text, compares the female body to a jar of poison with honey smeared at the mouth.[55] Likewise, the *Lalitavistara* compares women to vases filled with vomit and razor blades smeared with honey.[56] Her charms intact, a woman is desire personified, the honey that draws flies and fools. As such, she wields the power of attraction, luring men "down the primrose path." But her power to repel is equally decisive. Her charms temporarily disfigured or permanently destroyed, she inspires disgust and thus leads men down the path of liberation.

Horrific representation unleashes the power of horror for the edification of the spectator by exposing what is normally hidden from the male gaze: the repulsive inner condition of the female body. Cadaverous and disfigured women are inversions of the duplicitous female body since their outer forms serve to reveal, not conceal, the horror within. Like the goddess Kālī decked out in human entrails, skull-necklaces, and fetus-earrings, these women display the inside of the body on the outside. The vile substances that the body contains spill out of their ruptured skin. Their bodies have become open, permeable forms accessible to the elements and to the life forms that feed on death.

Mikhail Bakhtin's contrast between the "grotesque body" valued in the premodern world and the "classical body" cherished by the modern bourgeoisie offers a convenient shorthand for describing the changes undergone by the women and men of these stories.[57] This well-known distinction between the canons of grotesque and classical representation hinges on the contrast between bodily openness and bodily closure. The grotesque body is not sealed off from material exchange with the world; it is an array of orifices through which matter constantly flows. Emphasis is laid on those parts of the body that are open to the outside world, such as the mouth, the nose, the genitals, and the anus, as well as other channels through which matter can enter the body or emerge from it.

Like the Rabelaisian hero Gargantua flooding the world with urine, semen, and excrement, the horrific "heroines" of Buddhist literature are not neatly and politely sealed off from the world. The inner recesses of their bodies are graphically exposed. Blood, pus, and worms flow out through their orifices and ruptured skin. Even the women who are not dead or mutilated but merely sleeping are described in accord with the canons of grotesque realism. Their mouths are wide open; saliva trickles from their parted lips. The integrity of outer form that comes with ornamentation and decorum dissolves in sleep-death.

The moral of these stories, however, is anything but Rabelaisian in spirit. The renewal of life through reproduction that Rabelais advocates in his celebration of the grotesque is precisely what the redactors of these texts wish to expose as a false ideal. These learned monks use grotesque figurations of the feminine to expose the illusion of reproductive immortality that drives men to marry and reproduce. This rhetorical strategy helps to keep monks chaste when threatened by intact female bodies and by the social pressure to reproduce. By inverting the female form through grotesque representation, the redactors of these texts promote a kind of x-ray vision by which monks can hold onto their reason and remember their vows.

Grotesque figurations of the feminine promote chastity in a very concrete way, inducing a corporeal experience of aversion in the body of the spectator or listener. This visceral kind of awakening enables monks to achieve the complete physical closure that is the hallmark of Bakhtin's "classical body." Modern etiquette and self-surveillance, Bakhtin suggests, produce a bounded, closed body that is classical in its discrete individuality. Whatever protrudes or bulges or opens out to the world is eliminated from the classical body. All apertures of the body are closed, presenting an impermeable façade to the world.

Like the hygiene-conscious Westerner, the purity-conscious Indian renouncer seeks to reinforce the boundaries of the body by carefully regulating bodily comportment and bodily flow. Buddhist monastic discipline produces a very finished, controlled body. Rules pertaining to outward conduct (especially dress and decorum) amount to roughly a third of the *Vinaya* regulations. Monks and nuns must exercise considerable self-control, always presenting a well composed public image.

Monastic regulations produce a body that is not only clearly bounded but also closed off from all adventitious material exchange with the world. Sexual activity has no place in the life of the sangha, and the ordination of those who knowingly indulge in intercourse is negated.[58] But physical chastity is only half the battle. Mental chastity is much more important to the life of the sangha and much more elusive than mere physical restraint. For this reason, wet dreams are of great concern. The involuntary emission of semen does not lead to censure, but it is considered to be indicative of an unchaste mental state. Wet dreams and passionate thoughts signal an incontinent mind, which is represented as something that leaks and drips in the liquid image of the *āsava*. These are four kinds of mental discharges (usually translated as "outflows") that are absent from the minds of Arhats, who are described as being *anāsava*. Before he became an Arhat, Nanda's mind was as porous as a sieve: *Dhammapada* 13 compares his mind to a leaky roof that lets in the rain of passion. But Arhats, *Dhammapada* 14 goes on to say, have minds like watertight roofs. Thus the ideal state that renouncers seek to achieve through monastic discipline seems to be one of total closure, symbolized by an impermeable, highly controlled body and a watertight mind.

In post-Ashokan horror stories, grotesque figurations of the female body are instrumental to men who seek total closure. Such closure is out of the question for the body that serves as a liberating spectacle. It is, by nature, an elevated mass of wounds, an array of openings that will not close. Peter Stallybrass has shown how the idea that women are naturally grotesque was used in Renaissance literature to ensure that women knew their place and behaved circumspectly.[59] But I don't think that Buddhist redactors were concerned so much with controlling women as with chastening and educating men. By constituting the female body as deceitful and dangerous, the redactors of these texts seek to reconstitute the male gaze and reconfigure the male body.

In a more recent book, Stallybrass takes a slightly different—and for the purposes of this essay, more helpful—tack, analyzing the grotesque body as a locus of class conflict. *The Politics and Poetics of Transgression,* co-authored with Allon White, shows how socially marginal groups play a symbolically central role in early modern and modern European literature as the primary means by which the emerging urban professional classes expressed and consolidated their moral world.[60] Using Bakhtin's contrast between the high and low aspects of the social body, represented by the head and the buttocks or genitals respectively, the authors show how those at the top of the social system rely on those at the bottom. Just as the dignity of the head depends on the humility of the buttocks, so the identity of those at the top of the social system is constituted by viewing those at the bottom in symbolically debased terms. Thus ethnic and religious minorities, women, the poor, and the physically abnormal are equated with excrement, pigs, and other symbols of degradation. Although the symbolic hierarchy places dominant social groups above debased ones, those at the top are psychologically dependent on those at the bottom. Without constantly degrading and excluding the other groups, those on top would be less secure in their self-definition, less bonded as a group, and the structures of their moral world would be much more obscure.

Those whose bodies are considered grotesque are profoundly ambivalent, both reviled by and necessary to those on high. This ambivalence is clearly documented in post-Ashokan literature. The very fact that women must be rendered grotesque at all attests to the extraordinary power attributed to women by the renunciant male psyche. Construed as powerful enticements to return to worldly life, women continually threaten the commitment of monks to their vocation. Grotesque figurations of the feminine allow renouncers to remain impervious to the power of seduction that women are thought to wield, thus maintaining their identity as chaste members of a renunciant counterculture. Through horrific transformation, "the snare of Māra" is exposed as a deadly trap and thereby rendered powerless.

But grotesque figurations of the feminine are symbolically central for another reason. Horrific "heroines" not only serve the renouncer by curbing his desire; they also serve to illustrate the fundamental truths of the Buddha's teaching. They reveal in a graphic and compelling manner the structures of the renouncer's moral world, especially its ephemeral and intrinsically dissatisfying nature. In this way, the grotesquely transfigured woman is put to work for, rather than against, the renouncer. Through horrific transformation, her power to seduce is converted into its opposite, and her transgressive body is simultaneously made into a display board for the Dharma. Horrific transformation converts the snare of Māra who holds men in carnal bondage into the servant of the Buddha who facilitates men's liberation from the world.

NOTES

1. From the *Carmen de Mundi Contemptu*, ascribed to Roger de Caen, an eleventh-century French monk. Quoted in *Not in God's Image*, ed. Julia O'Faolain and Laura Martines (Harper and Row, 1973), p. viii.

2. "Farewell to Love" from *The Works of Sir John Suckling*, ed. A. Hamilton Thompson (London: Routledge and Sons, 1910), p. 37.

3. The lust-ridden disciple of an anonymous desert father suggests the value of encountering desire in declining the old man's offer to relieve him of his battle with lust: "Abba, I see that I am afflicted; but I see that this affliction is producing fruit in me. Therefore ask God to give me endurance to bear it." *The Wisdom of the Desert Fathers: Apophthegmata Patrum*, The Anonymous Series, trans. Sister Benedicta Ward (Fairacres, Oxford: Fairacres Press, 1975), p. 9.

4. See Ved Mehta, "Profiles of Mahatma Gandhi and His Apostles," part 3: "The Company They Keep," *New Yorker* (May 1976): 46.

5. Cremation-ground dwelling is one of the ascetic practices *(dhutanga)* recommended by Buddhaghosa in the *Visuddhimagga*, where the benefits of this practice are given as follows: "He acquires mindfulness of death; he lives diligently; the sign of foulness [of the body] is available; greed for sense desires is removed; he constantly sees the body's true nature; he has a great sense of urgency; he abandons the vanity of health, etc.; he vanquishes fear and dread; nonhuman beings respect and honor him. . . . Even in sleep the dweller in a charnel ground shows naught of negligence, for death is ever present to his thought; he may be sure there is no lust after sense pleasure preys upon his mind, with many corpses present to his gaze." Translation by Bhikkhu Nyaṇamoli, in *The Path of Purification* (Berkeley: Shambala, 1976), p. 77. Contemporary Sri Lankan monks, especially those specializing in meditation, occasionally visit morgues for the purpose of contemplating the ravages of death. See Richard Gombrich, "Temporary Ordination in Sri Lanka," *Journal of the International Association of Buddhist Studies* 7 (1984): 41. In the lay context, one need not contemplate a decaying corpse in order to conjure up images of the foulness of the body. In Sri Lanka, where *asubha-bhāvanā* is a common form of meditation, the lay meditator goes to the temple on holy days and reflects on the bodies of oneself and others as excremental and repulsive. See Gananath Obeyesekere, "Despair and Recovery in Sinhala Medicine and Religion: An Anthropologist's Meditations," in *Healing and Restoring: Health and Medicine in the World's Religious Traditions*, ed. Lawrence E. Sullivan (New York: Macmillan, 1989).

6. Because I draw on literature belonging to more than one Buddhist canon here, I have found it convenient to use the term "post-Ashokan literature" as a catch-all for referring to Pali and Sanskrit texts of various scholastic affiliations. All of my sources were compiled after the reign of the Mauryan emperor Ashoka (third century B.C.E.); most were redacted around the fifth century of the Common Era. Even when dealing only with the scriptural tradition of a single school, such as the Theravāda, distinguishing between "canonical" and "noncanonical" materials can be a complicated and fruitless undertaking because of the way in which "canonical" materials are hermeneutically embedded in "noncanonical" commentaries. Moreover, much of the material cited here belongs to the controversial *Khuddhaka Nikāya* of the Pali Canon, and the canonical status of many of the texts of this fifth *Nikāya*

has been widely debated. On problems with the notion of a closed canon as applied to Buddhist scripture, see Steven Collins, "On the Very Idea of the Pali Canon," *Journal of the Pali Text Society* 15 (1981): 89-126. On some of the complexities of the *Khuddhaka Nikāya*, see K. R. Norman, *Pali Literature, Including the Canonical Literature in Prakrit and Sanskrit of all the Hīnayāna Schools of Buddhism*, vol. 7, fasc. 2, of *A History of Indian Literature*, ed. Jan Gonda (Wiesbaden: Harrassowitz, 1983), pp. 57-96.

7. Early students of Buddhist women's history such as Caroline Foley, Mabel Bode, and Isabelle Horner tended to view Buddhism as liberating for women because in their view it allowed women to leave their subordinate feminine social roles as wives and mothers and join with other men and women in a spiritual path that rendered gender largely insignificant. Contemporary students of Buddhist women's history such as Diana Paul and Karen Lang have challenged this view of Buddhism as egalitarian and gender-neutral. In *Women in Buddhism: Images of the Feminine in the Mahāyāna Tradition* (Berkeley: Asian Humanities Press, 1979; 2d ed., Berkeley: University of California Press, 1985), Diana Paul suggests that there is androcentrism in Buddhist scripture in arguing that her materials "reveal as much about men's self-concept in relation to women" as they do about what women might think of themselves. In "Lord Death's Snare: Gender-Related Imagery in the Theragāthā and Therīgāthā," *Journal of Feminist Studies in Religion* 2 (1986): 64, Karen Lang asserts that monks wrote and compiled virtually all of the texts included in the early Buddhist canon and that much of this material reflects their ambivalent attitudes toward women. Women were considered physically and spiritually weaker, less intellectual and more sensual, than men. The community of monks feared women as potential seducers. My findings challenge the conventional wisdom on the development of Buddhism in India in that I focus on a period of Buddhist history in which, according to many scholars, the rise of the Mahāyāna fostered a more egalitarian, gender-neutral mood among Indian Buddhists. My analysis of post-Ashokan materials suggests that the misogyny of the post-Ashokan period is just as pointed and just as prevalent as in the pre-Ashokan period. This is true of Mahāyāna as well as non-Mahāyāna texts.

8. The most elaborate accounts of the harem scene appear in the Sanskrit biographies, the *Mahāvastu, Lalitavistara*, and *Buddhacarita*. I quote here from E. B. Cowell's translation of the *Buddhacarita*, in *Buddhist Mahāyāna Texts* (Oxford, Clarendon Press, 1894). In Pali accounts of the Buddha's life, which have little to say about the bodhisattva's youth and the events leading up to his renunciation, a more condensed version of the harem scene is given. See the *Nidānakathā*, trans. T. W. Rhys Davids, *Buddhist Birth Stories* 1, (London: Trübner, 1880), pp. 80-81. The *Vinaya* tells of a similar experience of horror in the harem that leads the disciple Yasa to renounce the world. See I. B. Horner, trans., *The Book of Discipline*, vol. 5 (London: Oxford University Press, 1952), pp. 21-22.

9. Translated by Cowell, in *Buddhist Mahāyāna Texts*, p. 57.

10. Ibid., p. 58.

11. Ibid.

12. Ibid. Although the *Mahāvastu, Lalitavistara*, and *Buddhacarita* present virtually identical accounts of this scene, the *Lalitavistara* adds some pointedly misogynistic material not found in the other accounts. After the bodhisattva, at the prompting of the gods, announces "I really do dwell in the middle of a cemetery!" he offers thirty-two analogies for the predicament of men deluded by feminine charms, many of them scatological in nature. For example, "Fools delight here like boars wallowing in filth. . . . Fools sport with them [women] like little children playing with their excrement." See Gwendolyn Bay's translation, *The Voice of the Buddha*, vol. 1 (Berkeley: Dharma, 1983), pp. 310-13. Translations from Pali and Sanskrit sources are my own unless otherwise indicated.

13. The prince's father, determined to prevent his son from renouncing, provides all forms of indulgence for Gotama and also posts guards, in case the bonds of desire should fail to hold. See *Buddhacarita* 2.28-32 and 5.39.

14. At *Aṅguttara Nikāya* 3.67, the effect of women on men is described as follows: "Monks, even a woman who is going *(gacchantī)* remains captivating *(tiṭṭhati pariyā-dāya)* to a man's heart; whether standing, sitting, lying down, laughing, talking, singing, crying, stricken, or dead, a woman remains captivating to a man's heart. If anything can be called a snare of Māra, woman can truly be called a snare of Māra."

15. In Brahminical and Hindu texts, women who bear legitimate sons are said to offer their husbands the possibility of a reproductive "immortality" through perpetuation of the father in his son. Paul Mus describes the Brahminical context for this ritualized transfer of personality in his preface to *Barabudur* (Hanoi: Imprimerie d'Extrême-Orient, 1935), p. 12: "The son does not inherit from the father; the son inherits the father." See scriptural citations from classical Hindu sources in I. Julia Leslie, *The Perfect Wife: The Orthodox Hindu Woman according to the Strīdharma-paddhati of Tryambakayajvan* (Oxford: Oxford University Press, 1989), pp. 31-32.

16. When Ānanda inquires, shortly before the Master's death, about how one should behave toward women, the Buddha replies: "You must avoid their sight, Ānanda." "But what if we do see them, Blessed One? What are we to do then?" The Master replied: "Do not talk to them, Ānanda." "But what if we do talk to them, Blessed One?" "Then you must watch yourself, Ānanda." *Dīgha Nikāya* 2.141, trans. Mohan Wijayaratna, *Buddhist Monastic Life according to the Texts of the Theravāda Tradition,* trans. Claude Grangier and Steven Collins (New York: Cambridge University Press, 1990), p. 97.

17. I use the term *heroine* ironically. Few of these narratives include the female as a conscious agent or subject; the stories in which horrific women appear are generally not their stories but those of the monks who apprehend them as objects.

18. Michel Foucault, *Discipline and Punish: The Birth of the Prison* (Vintage Books, 1979), part 1.

19. The *Laws of Manu* and the *Daṇḍaviveka of Vardhamāna Upādhyāya* articulate a grammar of torture that is for the most part systematic. For example, the buttocks of a low-caste person who sits down next to a brahmin are to be branded or sliced open. If such a person spits on a brahmin, his or her lips are to be cut off. The grammar of punitive torture is less than systematic in those cases (like the cutting off of the hands and feet as punishment for theft and murder as well as sexual transgressions) where the same body parts are amputated as punishment for different crimes. For a detailed discussion of crimes and appropriate forms of punishment, see *The Laws of Manu,* trans. Wendy Doniger and Brian K. Smith (Harmondsworth: Penguin Books, 1991) esp. chap. 8; see also the *Daṇḍaviveka of Vardhamāna Upādhyāya,* trans. B. Bhattacharya (Calcutta: Asiatic Society, 1973).

20. On hair as an emblem of sexuality and shaving the head as symbolic of castration (owing to the unconscious device of the upward displacement of the genitals), see Charles Berg, *The Unconscious Significance of Hair* (London: Allen and Unwin, 1951). On the shaved head as indicative of general social status but not necessarily individual behavior, see E. R. Leach, "Magical Hair," *Journal of the Royal Anthropological Institute* 88 (1958): 147-68. For a discussion of Leach's argument in light of data gleaned from case studies of Indian women and men, see Gananath Obeyesekere, *Medusa's Hair: An Essay on Personal Symbols and Religious Experience* (Chicago: University of Chicago Press, 1981), pp. 33-40.

21. It is not possible to generalize about the punishment for male sexual transgression in Indic legal discourse because the punishment depends on the class identity of both the perpetrator and the person with whom he had sexual relations.

Lower class individuals may lose both their offending member and their life, while a brahmin may pay a fine and have his head shaved. See *The Laws of Manu* 8.359-79.

22. On nose-cutting as a symbol of fantasized clitoridectomy in Indian literature, see Sudhir Kakar, *The Inner World: A Psychoanalytic Study of Childhood and Society in India* (Delhi: Oxford University Press, 1981), p. 99. As Wendy Doniger pointed out to me, the cutting off of women's feet and hands may also be forms of symbolic clitoridectomy. Lévi-Strauss has argued (on the basis of Oedipus's story) that the foot can stand in for the transgressive phallus as a site of punishment. Likewise the removal of women's fingers may signify clitoridectomy. This is certainly the case when the fingers are the "offending members," as in *The Laws of Manu* 8.370, where one form of punishment specified for lesbians who have sex with virgins is the cutting off of their fingers. Alternatively, these women may have their heads shaved, another form of symbolic castration (see n. 20).

23. Māra is assisted in his administration of the realm of desire by his three daughters: Lust *(rāgā)*, Thirst *(taṇhā)*, and Discontent *(aratī)*. When they attempt to seduce the bodhisattva to return to the householder's life as he meditates under the bodhi tree, he uses horrific transformation to vanquish them, turning them into decrepit old women. Their father has no power to reverse the effects of impermanence now so graphically displayed by Lust, Thirst, and Discontent. Thus the daughters of Māra must take refuge in the Buddha, who is the overlord of Māra by virtue of his insight into the law of samsara. See *Buddhacarita*, book 15, verses 11-30 (Cowell, *Buddhist Mahāyāna Texts*, pp. 160-63).

24. John Strong's translation, from *The Legend of King Aśoka* (Princeton: Princeton University Press, 1983), p. 181.

25. In Rabindranath Tagore's retelling of this story, Upagupta goes to comfort Vasavadattā when she, abandoned by her friends and family, is dying of the plague. Instead of using her ulcerated body as an object lesson on impermanence, he bathes her sores with cool water while she dies in his arms; see *The Collected Poems and Plays of Rabindranath Tagore* (New York: Macmillan, 1937), pp. 154-55.

26. Strong, *Legend of King Aśoka*, p. 182.

27. Ibid.

28. Given the importance of punitive display in spiritual Upagupta's life, it may be significant that the young merchant goes on to become the adviser to king Ashoka, whose conversion to the Buddha-dharma occurred while the cruel king was engaged in torturing a monk.

29. I summarize and quote from the version of Nanda's story found in the commentary to the *Dhammapada (Dhammapadāṭṭhakathā)*, 1.9.b. *Dhammapadāṭṭhakathā*, ed. H. C. Norman, 4 vols. (London: Pali Text Society, 1906-14). See also the poetic rendering by Ashvaghosha: *The Saundarananda of Asvaghosa*, trans. E. H. Johnstone (Lahore, 1928; Delhi: Motilal Banarsidass, 1975).

30. This sort of spiritual jujitsu by which the Buddha overcomes resistance by apparent acquiescence is known as skill-in-means *(upāya-kaushalya)*.

31. In ensnaring Nanda by promising him five hundred nymphs, the Buddha mimics Māra, who frequently baits his traps with female flesh. K. C. Lang explores the androcentric ramifications of Māra's methods in "Lord Death's Snare: Gender-Related Imagery in the Theragāthā and the Therīgāthā," *Journal of Feminist Studies in Religion* 2 (1986): 59-79.

32. In *Sūtrālamkāra* no. 64, the bodhisattva in the form of King Shibi cuts off flesh from his thighs and other limbs in order to ransom a pigeon from a hungry hawk. The hawk is Indra in disguise, who describes this test of the bodhisattva as analogous to the process of testing a jewel to ensure that it is not artificial. See Edouard Huber, trans., *Sūtrālamkāra traduit en français sur la version chinoise de Kumarajiva* (Paris: E. Leroux, 1908).

33. The *Nikāya*s tend to speak generically of the impermanence and impurity of the body.

34. Male bodies ravaged by impermanence do figure prominently in the biography of the Buddha. According to the tradition of the Four Signs, the bodhisattva sees an old man, a sick man, a dead man, and a renouncer on four separate excursions from the palace. But although these sights turn his mind toward the possibility of renunciation, it is not until after seeing his harem transformed into a cremation ground that the young prince actually decides that the time to renounce is at hand.

35. *Dhammapadāṭṭhakathā* 11.2.

36. Sirimā pours boiling hot oil on a devoted lay follower named Uttara out of jealousy. But Uttara, rather than defending herself physically, suffuses herself with loving kindness and is therefore unaffected by the oil. Sirimā is so impressed by Uttara's serenity and kindness that she begs to be forgiven. Uttara directs Sirimā to ask the Buddha, as her spiritual father, for forgiveness. This encounter leads to Sirimā's adoption of new life of service to the sangha. See *Dhammapadāṭṭhakathā* 17.3b for an expanded account of Sirimā's conversion.

37. The *kahapana* was a copper coin in use during the post-Ashokan period.

38. Reflection on the foulness of the body often focuses on the body as an array of orifices emitting foul substances. In referring to the nine orifices as nine gaping wounds *(nava-vana-mukha)*, the text employs a standard trope. This comparison of orifices with wounds is used to describe the living body in *Aṅguttara Nikāya* 9.2.15: "Imagine, monks, a boil which has been gathering for many years. It might have nine gaping wounds, nine natural openings. Thence whatever might ooze out, foulness would certainly ooze out; stench would certainly ooze out, loathsomeness would certainly ooze out." Trans. E. M. Hare, *Gradual Sayings,* vol. 4 (London: Pali Text Society, 1935), p. 17.

39. Aversion therapy suppresses undesirable compulsive behaviors by pairing such behaviors with a noxious stimulus.

40. On the importance of eschewing diagnosis in favor of prompt therapeutic action, see the parable of the poisoned arrow *(Culamālunkyāsūtta)*, trans. I. B. Horner, *Middle Length Sayings,* vol. 2 (London: Pali Text Society, 1954), pp. 97-101.

41. See n. 5.

42. The Pali compound *āmaka-susāna* refers to a particular spot in a cremation ground *(susāna)* that I translate here as "charnel ground." In this place, the uncremated bodies *(āmaka* means "raw, uncooked") of paupers and criminals (like Vasavadattā of the *Ashokāvadāna*) are left to rot. The gradual consumption by carrion-eating animals and bacteria to which such bodies are subject makes the *āmaka-susāna* an ideal place to contemplate the impurity of the body.

43. Translation by Paula Richman, in *Women, Branch Stories, and Religious Rhetoric in a Tamil Buddhist Text* (Syracuse: Syracuse University Press, 1988), pp. 55-56.

44. For a discussion of this powerful subversion of Tamil poetic conventions for Buddhist rhetorical purposes, see ibid., pp. 63-77.

45. In the *Visuddhimagga*, Buddhaghosa asserts that monks should not contemplate female corpses when practicing *asubha bhāvanā*. The inappropriate excitement *(vipphandana)* a relatively undecayed female body might occasion could defeat the point of the meditation, which is to induce a perception of the foulness of the body. Nuns should likewise avoid using male bodies as objects of meditation. See *The Path of Purity,* trans. Pe Maung Tin (London: Pali Text Society, 1975), pp. 207, 212.

46. See Caroline Rhys Davids's translation of *Theragāthā* 198 and commentary, *Psalms of the Brethren* (London: Pali Text Society, 1913), pp. 189-90.

47. See ibid., pp. 211-12. Rhys Davids condenses the entire episode of magical transformation into this bromidic statement: "And when even this [*asubha bhāvanā*] sufficed not, he himself went with him and bade him to mark the process of putrefaction and dissolution. The Exalted One then sent out a glory, producing in him

such mindfulness that he discerned the lesson, attained the first jhana, and on that basis developed insight, won arahantship" (p. 211).

48. Peter Brown, *The Body and Society: Men, Women, and Sexual Renunciation in Early Christianity* (New York: Columbia University Press, 1988).

49. *Dhammapadaṭṭhakathā* 1.6.

50. The cremation groundskeeper's name may be significant. The earliest reference to Kālī, the fearsome goddess so popular in Bengal, appear within a century of the *Dhammapadaṭṭhakathā's* redaction.

51. This bloodthirsty threat strikes me as another clue to the latent divinity of the cremation groundskeeper (see previous note), since Kālī is often asked to trample, dismember, and mutilate the bodies of the enemy.

52. *Dhammapadaṭṭhakathā* 3.5.

53. The siren song of the former wife or beloved figures prominently in the narrative circumstances that lead the Buddha to tell several *Jataka* tales. The *Assakajātaka* and the *Valāhassajātaka*, for example, are cautionary tales told to lovesick monks who are dissatisfied (*ukkanthita*) with life in the sangha on account of their desire to be with the women they love. In the case of the *Assakajātaka*, it is a monk's former wife who troubles him. The Buddha tells the man how, in his former life, he was a king named Assaka who was unable to part with the body of his deceased wife due to his extreme attachment to her. Only when the love-stricken Assaka is shown that his former wife had become a dung-dwelling insect due to her vanity does the king relinquish the body of his dead wife. Hearing this scatological tale of the past, the lovelorn monk of the frame story is able to forget his former wife and recover his equanimity. See E. B. Cowell, trans., *The Jātaka, or Stories of the Buddha's Former Births*, vol. 2 (Cambridge: University Press, 1883), pp. 108-10. The *Valāhassajātaka* begins with another dissatisfied monk revealing his love-stricken condition to the Buddha. The Buddha warns this monk that women delight in seducing and then destroying men. He then tells a grisly tale about island-dwelling demonesses (*yakkinī*) who disguise themselves as human women in order to seduce and then devour the ship-wrecked sailors who land on their island. See ibid., pp. 89-91.

54. Lang discusses this emphasis on the artificiality of female beauty in "Lord Death's Snare," p. 71.

55. It is ironic that this and other caustic fulminations against women in the *Brahmavaivarta Purāna* are placed in the mouth of the Goddess; see Cheever Mackenzie Brown, *God as Mother: A Feminine Theology in India, an Historical and Theological Study of the Brahmavaivarta Purāna* (Vermont: Claude Stark, 1974), pp. 181ff.

56. The honey-coated razor analogy also appears in the *Lalitavistara's* harem transformation scene at *Theragāthā* 249; see Bays and Rhys Davids, p. 296.

57. Mikhail Bakhtin, *Rabelais and His World*, trans. Helene Iswolsky (Bloomington: Indiana University Press, 1984); see esp. chap. 5.

58. There is no penalty for nonconsensual sexual activity. For example, the monastic code warns monks to beware of female rapists who mount sleeping monks and otherwise force themselves on the unwary. But the code suggests that a monk who is thus violated is not considered guilty of a sexual offense. See Horner, *Book of Discipline*, vol. 1, pp. 58-63.

59. Peter Stallybrass, "Patriarchal Territories: The Body Enclosed," *Rewriting the Renaissance* (Chicago: University of Chicago Press, 1986).

60. Peter Stallybrass and Allon White, *The Politics and Poetics of Transgression* (Ithaca: Cornell University Press, 1986).

WOMAN AS SERPENT
THE DEMONIC FEMININE IN THE NOH PLAY
DŌJŌJI

Susan B. Klein

Dōjōji, one of the most popular plays in the Japanese Noh theater repertoire, presents us with a dramatically compelling vision of stark conflict:
the masculine forces of noble and pure spirituality battling the demonic
feminine, a monstrous embodiment of profane and bestial sexuality. In the
play the priests of Dōjōji temple attempt to exorcise a woman transformed
by lustful passion into a fire-breathing serpent who seeks revenge on the
temple bell which she associates with her betrayal by the man she loved.[1]
As such it provides a fascinating case study of the representation of the
embodied demonic feminine in medieval Japan.[2]

This essay takes a two-pronged approach to its subject. The first analytic
prong is universalizing: I consider how contemporary Western psychoanalytic theory might be productively brought to bear on a story developed
in a completely different temporal and cultural context. The second is
historicizing: I examine how the changing representation of the feminine
within the Dōjōji textual tradition might be homologous to historical
changes in attitudes toward gender and subjectivity in the wider social
context of medieval Japan. The two prongs are not to be kept isolated,
however, since I believe that by showing how psychoanalytic insights into
gender and subjectivity intersect with a particular historical context we can
make some important headway toward historicizing our understanding of
sexuality and the gendered body within medieval Japanese religion.[3]

A brief overview of the Noh theater is in order for the reader who is not
familiar with medieval Japanese theater. Noh, which attained something
approximating its present form in the mid- to late fourteenth century, combines music, dance, and text to portray subjects that vary greatly. A typical
subject might be the rage of a magnificent ghost warrior fated to reenact
his death eternally, the beneficent epiphany of a Shinto deity who brings
peace and harmony to the country, or the pathos of a mother driven mad

by the loss of her only child. These subjects are generally chosen for the opportunity they afford to present elegantly stylized dance sequences. The text, which is chanted in varying levels of melodic intensity, is highly poetic; as we shall see in the following analysis, Noh is quite complex rhetorically and heavily laden with allusions to the classical literary tradition, both Japanese and Chinese. The lines of the text are shared by the major character *(shite)*, the secondary character *(waki)*, and a chorus. The chorus, although seated along the side of the stage, is not considered a distinct persona; it occasionally presents third-person commentary but more often simply speaks for the principal characters, particularly during dance sequences. The musicians include a flute player and two or three drummers who sit at the back of the stage and provide accompaniment for the dancing as well as for the segments of melodic chanting. The *shite* actor nearly always wears a mask; and the costumes, made of sumptuous brocade richly decorated with embroidery, show to advantage during the dances. Although a few women are professional Noh actors today, in the medieval period all the parts were played by men.

Dōjōji involves two of the most exciting and difficult performance elements in Noh: the *ranbyōshi* "disordered rhythm" dance and the *kaneiri* "bell entering" scene. In the eerie *ranbyōshi*, the serpent-woman, disguised as a beautiful *shirabyōshi* (dancer and entertainer) entrances the low-ranking temple workers who guard the temple bell that is the object of her passionate resentment. As the *shirabyōshi*, the *shite* actor circles slowly and continuously, stamping out a rhythm accented by a single shoulder drum *(kotsuzumi)* and embellished by occasional flute melody. Long drawn-out silences, abruptly pierced by the drummer's high-pitched cries, add to the atmosphere of unbearable tension, which builds inexorably to the climax of the play, the show-stopping *kaneiri*. The woman, having lulled everyone to sleep with her hypnotic dance, seizes her chance to attack the huge bell, which hangs suspended over the stage. Moving directly beneath it, she suddenly leaps up into the bell as it comes crashing to the ground. If done correctly, this dangerous leap gives the impression that the dancer has vanished right before one's very eyes.[4] Because of the physical and mental demands made on the actor by these two scenes, performing *Dōjōji* is considered a kind of test which actors in their early thirties must pass in order to take their places as fully qualified master actors.

Despite its great appeal as a theatrical set piece, however, and its importance within the Noh repertoire as a test of the *shite* actor's skill, *Dōjōji* is not generally considered especially interesting as literature. One attraction of Noh for a literary critic lies in the way a relatively simple poetic image introduced at the start of a play takes on new associations as it reappears in later contexts, developing a polysemous texture of interrelated imagery. This imagery tends to cohere around a few essential themes, creating a sense of "mysterious depth" that entices the critic to unravel its complexly interwoven strands.[5] *Dōjōji*'s poetic images, however, are peculiarly resistant to efforts to relate them meaningfully to a thematic context, or even to find satisfying links with images that come before and after. The poetic allusions in particular seem disconnected, arbitrary, a clichéd varnish applied to the action merely to give it a poetic sheen. The imagery of *Dōjōji* seems to be as superficial as its plot line is simple and its theatrics streamlined.

Some critics claim that such imagistic discontinuity mirrors the temporal rift created by the *shite*'s leap into the bell, a radically disruptive moment (everything changes, nothing is as it seemed before) that tears the conventional ideal of *mugen* "dream vision" to shreds.[6] This may well be so, but still the strange incoherencies remain, a nagging, albeit niggling, thorn in the side of the literary critic. A much larger thorn, at least for any feminist critic, is *Dōjōji*'s extremely negative view of women. Granted, the play is based on a Buddhist *setsuwa* (didactic tale) whose moral cautions monks to avoid women because of "the strength of evil in the female heart."[7] Still, at the end of the *setsuwa* the evil serpent-woman does achieve enlightenment; even as the *setsuwa* stresses that it is the inescapable fate of women to be the embodiment of desire, it also holds out the possibility for an individual woman to find redemption through the *Lotus Sutra*.[8] In *Dōjōji* as we know it today, when the serpent-woman is exorcised and driven back to the Hidaka River from whence she came, there is no hint that she has achieved enlightenment. In *Dōjōji* the triumphant exorcism of the woman from the temple is thus simultaneously an exclusion of the woman from Buddhist salvation.

Actually, the serpent-woman's failure to achieve enlightenment is quite unusual in Noh; although a number of plays center on a demonic woman driven mad by jealousy and a passion for revenge, only a very few deny her the solace of enlightenment in the end. *Kanawa* (The iron crown) is one such play: a woman who has turned herself into a demon to gain revenge on a faithless husband is defeated by esoteric Buddhist deities; but, unrepentant, she vows to return again. In *Kanawa*, however, there is never any suggestion that the woman is searching for escape from her passion; from first to last she is driven by an unambivalent thirst for revenge. In *Aoi no Ue*, on the other hand, the vengeful ghost of Lady Rokujō has very mixed feelings toward Prince Genji, and the process of exorcising her is inextricably bound up with the process of bringing about her release from blind anger and passion.

In *Dōjōji* there are clear indications that the spiteful and destructive serpent-woman disguised as a *shirabyōshi* dancer is, like Lady Rokujō, simultaneously searching for release from the karmic bonds of her "original sin."[9] For example, when the *shirabyōshi* first appears on stage, she enters to a *shidai* couplet, "My sin, my guilt, will melt away, I will go to the service for the bell."[10] This line signals her belief that if she dances at the dedication service for the Dōjōji temple bell, her sins will vanish, a belief given additional emphasis in the Komparu school version of the play, where she explicitly tells us that by attending the service, she hopes to get a "karmic link" *(kechien)* to salvation.[11] Later, at the height of the exorcism scene, the priests quote the compassionate vow of Fudō (one of the five Myō-ō, or Wisdom Kings),[12] "He who hearkens to My Law shall gain enlightenment, he who knows My Heart will be a Buddha in this flesh," and tell us, "Now that we have prayed for the serpent's salvation, what rancor could it bear us?"[13] These lines hint that the woman will ultimately gain release from her passion; and yet the serpent-woman's rancor is unabated as she hurls herself back into the depths of the Hidaka River at the end of the play.

That the woman fails to benefit from the compassionate vow of Fudō is even more puzzling when one considers that the play was probably originally written under the auspices of the Dōjōji temple. One would think that if the woman evinced any signs of desiring enlightenment, didactic motives alone would necessitate her ultimate salvation, since a Buddhism that has the power to transform evil into good, saving even the most miserable of sinners, is much more impressive than a Buddhism that has only the negative power to temporarily hold evil at bay.

Given the hints in the poetic text as well as didactic motives, it should not be surprising, then, to find that an earlier version of *Dōjōji does* conclude with the enlightenment of the serpent-woman. *Dōjōji* began as a much longer play called *Kanemaki* (literally, "bell-enwrapping"), tentatively attributed to Kanze Kojirō Nobumitsu (1435–1516).[14] All it took to deprive the woman of salvation was the deletion of a single line at the end of *Kanemaki;* but as it turns out, this simple cut had a disproportionate effect, since it in turn necessitated a whole series of other cuts, disrupting and unraveling the complex polysemic texture, both thematic and imagistic, of the play as a whole.

Dōjōji is thus a drastically cut—Donald Keene has gone so far as to say "mangled"[15]—version of *Kanemaki,* and much of what was eliminated from *Kanemaki* actually posited a positive alternative to women viewed as embodied animal lust. The historical process of selective cutting which produced *Dōjōji* out of *Kanemaki* can be understood as the narrative, thematic, and performative production of a symbolic feminine that was purely negative and so appropriate for exclusion from the temple, and ultimately from Buddhism. And although I cannot attempt to substantiate this point fully here, I would like to suggest that this production of the feminine as univocally evil may well be symptomatic of ideological changes occuring at the end of the Muromachi/Momoyama period.

Dōjōji's exclusion of any positive image of the feminine is not total, however; as I have pointed out, some positive ambivalence remains, especially in fragments of poetry retained from *Kanemaki.* One likely reason this poetry was retained is that unlike prose, which is easily altered, the characteristically condensed imagistic word play of Japanese poetry makes it particularly resistant to change. The poetic imagery thus had at least some subversive potential; in practice, however, once the imagery was cut loose from its anchoring prose context in *Kanemaki,* annotators and critics have tended to write off any imagery that does not quite seem to "fit" as mere rhetorical ornament (and therefore meaningless), or have done their best to minimize or normalize it via interpretive translation. My interest in *Dōjōji* thus lies precisely in those elusive fragments of poetry, in those enigmatic gaps and striking absences—most important, the absence of the woman's enlightenment at the end—that have both incited and resisted the initial revision process, as well as various secondary revisions in the form of normative interpretations, both critical and performative. I do not expect or even want to be able to completely resolve those imagistic and thematic aporias here, but I believe that by supplementing a close textual reading with feminist psychoanalytic interpretation, at least some of the blanks can be filled in. At the same time, perhaps some headway can be made toward an historicized understanding of the cultural construction of gender in late medieval Japan.

Given my interest in what has been left out or cut out of *Dōjōji*, a good part of my analysis will be devoted to looking at other texts, texts that were used to create the *Dōjōji* we know today. I begin by giving a brief synopsis of the Buddhist *setsuwa* which narrates the original events that set the plot of the Noh play in motion, followed by a synopsis of the play itself. Next I explore possible historical as well as psychoanalytic explanations for the negative view of women that is presented in the *setsuwa*, a strain of misogyny that is actually intensified in the later Noh versions of the story. I then use these insights to examine the Noh *Dōjōji*'s textual development, focusing particularly on the transformations of two important symbolic loci in the Dōjōji story: the woman as snake and the temple bell. Finally, I try to draw all these strands together as I do a close comparative reading of *Kanemaki* and *Dōjōji* in the hope that a look at *Kanemaki*'s excluded portions will yield some light on the narrative and thematic exclusion of women from Buddhism, which lies at the heart of *Dōjōji*.

Variations of the Dōjōji Story in the Setsuwa and Noh

The Dōjōji story appears initially in two *setsuwa* collections: *Dai Nihonkoku Hokekyōkenki*[16] (commonly known as the *Hokkegenki*), attributed to the priest Chingen and dated 1040–43, and *Konjaku monogatarishū*,[17] traditionally attributed to Minamoto Takakuni (1004–77) but now tentatively dated around 1120. These two versions tell basically the same story. Two monks are on a pilgrimage to the Kumano *Shugendō* complex. One is rather elderly, the other young and quite good-looking. The two stop for the night at the home of a young widow, whose lustful desires are deeply aroused by the handsome young monk. In the middle of the night she sneaks into his room and tries to get him to sleep with her by embracing, teasing, and fondling him. The monk, at his wits' end as to how to placate her, tells her that although he cannot sleep with her now because he must remain pure for his pilgrimage, he will come back for her on his return from Kumano. Of course the monk is lying, and on his return trip he takes a different route to avoid her house.

The woman, deeply chagrined when she discovers his duplicity, goes into her bedchamber and dies. As the maidservants are weeping and wailing, a forty-foot snake suddenly emerges from her chamber. It slithers out of the house and down the road in pursuit of the man who has betrayed her. The young monk, realizing that he is being pursued, races to Dōjōji temple, where the priests hide him under the large temple bell. When the snake reaches the temple she quickly realizes where the monk is. Wrapping herself tightly around the bell, she sheds tears of blood as she beats her tail upon its dragon-headed boss.[18] When she at last slithers away, five or six hours later, the bell is blazing hot to the touch. Raising the bell, the priests find that only a few blackened bones remain of the young monk.

Some time later, a senior priest of the temple has a dream in which the monk appears as a serpent, explaining that he has been reborn into this vile, filthy body as the husband of the evil widow-serpent. He begs the priest to copy out the *Lotus Sutra* chapter "The Limitless Life of the Tathā-gata" to release both of them from their suffering. After the priest does so, the man and woman appear and thank him, explaining that due to his intercession they have been reborn in separate heavens. The *Konjaku Monogatari* version of the *setsuwa* ends with the moral "You see, therefore, the strength of evil in the female heart. It is for this reason that the Buddha strictly forbids approaching women. Know this and avoid them."[19]

A Muromachi version of the Dōjōji story, *Dōjōji engi emaki* (Picture scroll of the founding of Dōjōji),[20] which strongly influenced the Noh version, replaces the "lustful widow" with an innocent young daughter of a local innkeeper. More important for the Noh, in the *emaki* (picture scroll) version of the story the woman is no longer transformed into a snake in the privacy of her own bedchamber; instead she completes her metamorphosis when she dives into the Hidaka River in her relentless pursuit of the monk. The transformation is graphically illustrated in the *emaki:* as the young woman runs along the road, her clothing and hair become increasingly disheveled, she begins to breath fire, and her neck, stretching forward in her anxiety to catch the man, becomes elongated and snakelike. The final definitive transformation comes when she reaches the river, which has suddenly swollen to flood stage. When the local boatman refuses to take her across, she strips off her clothing and dives in, becoming a full-fledged serpent in the process. The rest of the story basically follows the *Konjaku Monogatari* version.

The setting of the Noh *Dōjōji* is at the Dōjōji temple; the time is many years after the events narrated in the *setsuwa*—in *Dōjōji* the exact date is left unspecified, but it seems clear that the original events are no longer within anyone's living memory, since only the head priest knows the story. The plan is to reinstate the bell with a reading of the *Lotus Sutra,* and the head priest (for "reasons best known to himself") has forbidden women entrance to the service. Along comes a *shirabyōshi* who requests admittance so that she can perform a purification dance for the bell. *Shirabyōshi* were popular entertainers and occasional religious specialists of the late Heian and early Kamakura periods. They were known for dancing in male attire: they took their name, "white rhythmic stamping," from the fact that they wore the white silk robe of a court aristocrat, along with his black lacquered court cap and short sword.[21] Although *shirabyōshi* heroines are common enough in Noh (Shizuka Gozen in *Funa Benkei* and *Futari Shizuka*, Hyaku-man Yamamba in *Yamamba* spring to mind), it is particularly significant here that the *shite* appears dressed as a man, for she uses it to support her claim that as a *shirabyōshi* she is not an "ordinary" woman and so should be allowed to enter the temple grounds.[22]

The low-ranking temple worker is charmed by the *shirabyōshi*'s beauty, disarmed by her argument, and most of all desirous of seeing her dance. He therefore takes it upon himself to let her enter and offers her the courtier's dancing cap. She performs the famous *ranbyōshi*, which entrances everyone on stage into deep sleep, followed by a frenzied *kyū no mai* dance. At the height of the dance the *shirabyōshi* seizes her opportunity. Hinting at her true nature as the ghost of the serpent ("This loathsome bell, now I remember it!"),[23] she moves to strike the bell, but then leaps upward into the bell instead, figuratively wrapping it around her as it falls. The temple servants, awakened by the sound of the bell crashing down, reluctantly inform the head priest, who immediately realizes what has happened. He gathers everyone together and recounts the Dōjōji *setsuwa*, basically following the *Dōjōji engi emaki* version.[24] When the head priest has finished narrating the story, he calls upon his fellow priests to unite in chanting prayers to raise the bell. Their prayers are successful, and the serpent soon emerges to do battle with them. A violent exorcism follows, and in the end the serpent, burned by the flames of her own passion, is driven back to the depths of the Hidaka River.

The earlier version of the Noh *Dōjōji*, *Kanemaki*, differs from *Dōjōji* in a number of ways, small and large; here I will just list the points that are important for my argument.[25] In the opening of the play, *Kanemaki* contains two important explanatory sections missing from *Dōjōji*. The first is a *sashi/ageuta* in which the head priest explains more fully the reasons for the dedicatory service. He mentions that it has been seven hundred years since the temple was established and compares the sound of the temple bell to the *Lotus Sutra:* because the bell, like the *Lotus Sutra*, is only rarely heard, as the moon sets to the west, a multitude of people have gathered for the evening service. The second section in *Kanemaki* which provides us with information deleted from *Dōjōji* occurs when the *shite* enters. In a variant *nanori* (name-announcing scene) and a deleted *sashi/sageuta*, the *shite* announces that she is a *shirabyōshi* living along the coast at Komatsubara and explains her ambivalence about going to hear the bell, whose sound may bring back unwanted memories of the distant past.

When she reaches Dōjōji, she asks to be admitted. The process by which she accomplishes this is quite different than in *Dōjōji*, since it involves a long *mondō* (debate) with the head priest himself, rather than with the low-ranking temple servant. At the end of their discussion the head priest (not the servant) decides to let her in. In *Dōjōji* the *shirabyōshi* immediately begins the *ranbyōshi* dance, but in *Kanemaki* there is first a *kusemai* danced to the story of the founding of Dōjōji by an impoverished woman diver *(ama)*. Another important deletion occurs in the final exorcism scene, after the bell is raised: in *Kanemaki* the priests directly address the serpent-woman, telling her to return from whence she came; she replies that she won't leave until she has exhausted her resentment by striking the bell. Finally, as mentioned previously, the endings are completely different; whereas in *Dōjōji* the serpent-woman is driven off, to plunge headlong into the Hidaka River, in *Kanemaki* the woman achieves enlightenment and vanishes.

The Demonic Feminine in the Dōjōji Story

The view of women that pervades the *setsuwa* versions of the Dōjōji story, particularly the *Konjaku monogatari*, is profoundly negative. Women are psychologically and biologically determined to a weakness of will that keeps them from being able to control their passions; women by their very existence are an inevitable obstacle to men's spiritual progress. They must therefore be avoided in daily life and excluded from participation with men in the soteriological path to enlightenment. Given that the popular Buddhist sects of the Kamakura-Muromachi period held relatively "enlightened" views on women's spirituality, the explicitly misogynist tone of this *setsuwa* is rather puzzling. And since this misogynist attitude is, if anything, intensified in the Noh *Dōjōji*, it raises the question of where the view of woman as powerful demonic force that must be excluded comes from.

According to theorists such as Melanie Klein, Karen Horney, and Nancy Chodorow, the fantasy image of the all-powerful demonic woman goes back to the young boy's earliest relationship with an all-powerful mother and the frightful difficulty of establishing his autonomous identity from her, both as subject and as engendered male. Lurking in the unconscious of every grown man's mind is a vision of a mother who holds out the promise of a pleasurable, mindless union in which all needs are satisfied, but simultaneously, by that very promise of union, threatens to overwhelm the young boy's precarious subject and gender identity. By a process of metonymic contagion, the simultaneous fear and attraction that the young boy feels for his mother infects his attitudes toward all women.[26]

Freudian/Lacanian analysts locate the genesis of the demonic feminine in the child's discovery of his mother's "castration": since in patriarchal culture (in the realm of the symbolic) to have power is to possess the phallus, the all-powerful mother is retroactively believed by the child to be phallic. Even though on some level the boy comes to realize the "reality" of his mother's "castration"—i.e., that she is virtually powerless within a patriarchal society that suppresses and marginalizes women—the primordial vision of an uncontrollably powerful, phallic woman, a veritable force of nature, periodically erupts in popular narrative forms as the demonic woman.[27]

Julia Kristeva, in *The Powers of Horror: An Essay on Abjection,* combines elements of both theories. She posits the pre-Oedipal ("archaic") maternal body as the "abject": the impure, defiled "Other" which threatens the unity of the subject within language and which must therefore be radically excluded. Kristeva argues that religious rituals of purification and exorcism are based on a feeling of abjection (defilement) that, "converging on the maternal, attempt to symbolize the other threat to the subject: that of being swamped by the dual [i.e., pre-Oedipal mother-child] relationship, thereby risking the loss not of a part (castration) but of the totality of his living being. The function of these religious rituals is to ward off the subject's fear of his own identity sinking irretrievably into the mother."[28] The priests' successful exorcism of the serpent-woman in *Dōjōji* would seem to bear out Kristeva's characterization that "the masculine, apparently victorious, confesses through its very relentlessness against the other, the feminine, that it is threatened by an asymmetrical, irrational, wily, uncontrollable power. . . . That other sex, the feminine, becomes synonymous with a radical evil that is to be suppressed."[29]

Psychoanalytic explanations such as these can point us toward the unconscious sources of certain symbolic gender constructions, such as the demonic feminine, that seem to appear in a number of different historical periods and cultures. However, such psychoanalytic explanations are meaningless, except as a confirmation of the universal validity of psychoanalysis, unless at the same time that gender construction is historicized to show how it actually functions symptomatically within a specific cultural context. As Laura Mulvey has put it, we need to look for the ways that the "problems, contradictions and irreconcilable demands made by the acquisition of sexual identity, family structures and historical conditions surface in collectively held desires, obsessions and anxieties. This is the shared, social dimension of the unconscious, of the kind that Freud referred to in *Jokes and the Unconscious,* which erupts symptomatically in popular culture, whether folk-tales, carnival or movies. These are temporal forms, narrative forms."[30] Although it is beyond the scope of this essay, it may be the case that by historicizing the construction of gender within different periods and cultures some of the blind spots and limitations of contemporary psychoanalytic theory can be revealed, allowing for a historicization of psychoanalysis itself.

In the case of the *setsuwa,* the ideological motivation for the story and the material conditions under which the text was produced certainly need to be taken into account. *Setsuwa* collections were often used as source books for Buddhist sermons, and so the didactic moral was likely to depend on the intended audience. It seems probable that the *Konjaku monogatari* version of the Dōjōji story was used as a cautionary tale meant to keep itinerant young monks and *yamabushi* mountain priests in line by warning them of the horrible dangers awaiting them if they gave in to the ever-present temptations inherent in daily contact with women. The setting of the story at Dōjōji, a gateway temple to the Kumano Shugendō complex, and the fact that the young monk offers the excuse that he must remain ritually pure for his pilgrimage both support this interpretation. (Shugendō, which mixed elements of Shinto and Taoism with esoteric Buddhism, was particularly antagonistic toward women, considering them ritually impure and therefore excluding them from their sacred mountains.) It seems likely that the *setsuwa* was developed at Dōjōji or Kumano to combat a pervasive problem of moral laxity, and so it is perhaps not surprising that the story strongly stresses the evil consequences of too close an association with women. In this sense, the story plays much the same function as the post-Ashokan texts that Elizabeth Wilson analyzes in her essay in this volume.

As wives and lovers, women tempted the Buddhist monks to return to the world of suffering and thus had to be excluded from male monastic enclaves as potential obstacles to male spiritual growth. However, although absolute avoidance was the ideal, in practice traveling monks had to interact with laywomen when they begged for alms or asked for shelter for the night. Thus exclusion and avoidance was not enough: monastic authority had to instill fear of the woman's appeal as a way to control their members and ensure their chastity. The post-Ashokan tales of tempting female bodies transformed into horrific corpses provided a salutary lesson in the useless suffering caused by passion. The Dōjōji *setsuwa* would seem to have served a very similar goal of what Wilson calls "behavior modification through aversive stimulation."[31]

There are some important differences in the strategies taken by the two cultures. As Wilson makes clear, in most of the post-Ashokan redactions, the woman, who generally appears as little more than the object of the man's sexual desire, is rarely allowed to attain subjecthood; her transformation into a "charming cadaver" reduces her even further to the level of the abject. In the Dōjōji *setsuwa*, the woman is no passive spectacle; quite the contrary, she is endowed with horrific agency. To begin with, it is *her* sexual desire, not the man's, that precipitates the tragic events. The point of the tale is that women's desire could change at any moment into ungovernable rage; it was for this reason that they were to be avoided at all costs. Nevertheless, in the end, both the man and the woman attain enlightenment; the lesson is salutary for both of them. It would seem that in the context of medieval Japanese Buddhism, women had enough cultural power to warrant representation as subjects in their own right.

To clarify how the historical context as well as the intended audience of a *setsuwa* text might have affected its representation of women, it is useful to compare the *Konjaku Monogatari* version of the Dōjōji story with a *setsuwa* found in the *Kegonshū soshi eden* (commonly referred to as the *Kegon engi*).³² The *Kegon engi* tells the story of the Korean monk Gishō's relationship with a beautiful Chinese maiden named Zenmyō. The narrative structure is very similar to that of the Dōjōji *setsuwa:* Zenmyō, a young T'ang woman, falls in love with Gishō, a handsome priest from Silla on his way to study at the T'ang capital, when he stops at her father's house to beg for alms. She approaches him seductively, but he refuses her advances. Whereas in the Dōjōji *setsuwa* the priest's deceit causes the woman to change into a serpent out of rage and jealousy, in the *Kegon engi* his steadfast refusal causes Zenmyō to have a sudden religious awakening. Confessing her shame at her blind attachment to passion, Zenmyō vows to entrust her fate to her teacher: she will follow him like a shadow throughout all their future lives and provide for his daily needs as he benefits sentient beings in the Dharma realm. Later, when Gishō returns from the T'ang capital on his way home to Silla, he takes another route to avoid coming by Zenmyō's house to bid her a final farewell (perhaps because he still does not trust the sincerity of her intentions). Realizing that she may never see him again, Zenmyō hurries to the harbor; however, his ship is already far out to sea. Calling on the Buddhas, bodhisattvas, and *nāga* (dragon) kings, she vows that she will protect her teacher on his trip home with her very body. Throwing herself into the ocean, she is transformed into a huge dragon that carries Gishō's ship safely back to Silla.

It seems likely that the fact that the Dōjōji and *Kegon engi setsuwa* have such similar narrative structures and yet were given nearly antithetical endings and morals has much to do with their prospective audiences. Karen Brock, in her analysis of the production and reception of the *Kegon engi*, suggests that the Gishō story was directed at a primarily female audience of wealthy laywomen (Brock in fact names a specific patroness who she believes may have supported the project).³³ It seems to me that Brock's analysis is borne out by the moral of *Kegon engi*, which encourages the idea that feminine desire can be a power for good in Buddhism, and which also (not incidentally) encourages wealthy laywomen's monetary support for Buddhism via its description of how Zenmyō uses up all her wealth to support Gishō. That the compiler of the *Kegon engi* was fully aware of the negative view of women presented in the Dōjōji *setsuwa* is evident from an explicit comparison made toward the end of the tale:

> We have heard of another instance where [a woman] caught in the raging flames of angry jealousy, along the road of attachment between men and women, became a snake and chased after a man. The [two] cases are not

the same. That [Dōjōji woman] was caught in the power of passionate desire and actually became a snake. Her sin of attachment was deep. In this case, [Zenmyō] received the blessings of the Buddhas and Bodhisattvas because of her earnest vow, and instead became a dragon. This was because of her belief in the Buddhist teachings and respect for the virtue of a profound teacher.[34]

Given the self-conscious reference to the Dōjōji *setsuwa*, it seems clear that the compiler of the *Kegon engi* was purposely trying to counter the Dōjōji *setsuwa*'s negative image of women by showing how women can play an important positive role supporting the Buddhist clergy. The moral of the *Kegon engi setsuwa* demonstrates that the power of feminine desire, even in the monstrous form of a dragon, can be transformed by the teaching of Buddhism into a power for good. Here we see the phallic mother's symbolic opposite: the compassionate and self-sacrificing mother whose selfless (and sexless) desire is only to protect and serve those she loves.

Set in opposition to the positive representation in *Kegon engi*, the Dōjōji *setsuwa*'s negative representation of the feminine can be historicized to show how a pragmatic hostility toward women (who as sexual temptation were considered obstacles to spiritual progress) might be supplemented by unconscious fears of women as uncontrollably powerful, to create the monstrous phallic serpent-woman. The Dōjōji *setsuwa*'s fantasy of the demonic feminine easily lends itself to analysis via an interpretative grid shared by contemporary deconstructive and/or psychoanalytic feminists: the paradigm of a gendered binary opposition that identifies the masculine with a transcendent nonmaterial spirituality and the feminine with a material body mired in profane sexuality.[35] The two terms are, of course, asymmetrical: the feminine is clearly subordinate to the masculine. And although the feminine is actually constitutive of its opposite term, that constitutive moment must get suppressed for the masculine ideal to function as natural and self-evident. However, because the centralized masculine can only maintain its idealized character through the exclusion of the feminine (a feminine which is nevertheless ontologically constitutive of the masculine), their relationship is inherently unstable. Perhaps it is not surprising that the phantasmatic demonic feminine rises up again and again to overthrow her spiritual counterpart.

Two points need to be noted, however. Given that the *Kegon engi* story takes an almost identical narrative structure and yet manages to invert the representation of monstrous feminine power into a positive image, it would seem that in early medieval Japan the construction of the feminine positively or negatively depended to a great extent on when and for whom the text was being produced. In addition, the fact that even in the Dōjōji *setsuwa* the woman and the man achieve salvation in the end undercuts any simple reading of the *setsuwa* in terms of a binary logic of exclusion, since ultimately the feminine is recuperated. This recuperation depends on the

specifically Buddhist logic of *gyakuen*, that sin itself may paradoxically form
the ladder or link to salvation, a "paradoxical" logic that retroactively rein-
terprets the woman's passion positively, since in the last analysis it allows
both the man and the woman to achieve rebirth in one of Buddha's para-
dises.[36] In this way, *gyakuen* actually subverts the main ideological thrust of
the narrative (women are evil incarnate and must be avoided at all costs)
and thus keeps the *setsuwa*'s narrative logic from fitting comfortably into a
contemporary Western critical analysis of the structure of gendered binary
oppositions. At the same time, on a pragmatic level, the narrative still
manages to retain its suasive moral force, since it is unlikely that anyone
would ever actively attempt to reach salvation via a process that entails
being burned alive and then being reincarnated as a snake.

What is interesting about the Noh *Dōjōji* is that once the woman's salvation is eliminated, the logic of *gyakuen* disappears as well, and the narrative
structure of the story becomes fully congruent with the binary logic of
exclusion; in fact, it takes that fantasy of asymmetrical dualism to a new
level of psychosexual intensity. As such it may be symptomatic of a
disturbing historical trajectory whereby a specifically feminine desire for
enlightenment becomes increasingly unrepresentable, increasingly unre-
cuperable, within elite Japanese religious and aesthetic discourses.

The Historical Development of the Noh *Dōjōji*

The plot of the Noh *Dōjōji* was generated in two stages. The first stage
was the creation of the play *Kanemaki* by a process of condensation and
displacement; that is, symbolically charged narrative elements of the original *setsuwa* were condensed and displaced in the Noh version, yielding
imagery that was much more psychosexually potent. I am using the terms
condensation and displacement, familiar from Freud's *Interpretation of
Dreams*, in the Lacanian sense, that symbolically charged narrative elements
which function autonomously in the *setsuwa* are displaced metonymically
and condensed metaphorically with other images to form new highly reso-
nant symbolic loci of affect.[37] The second stage was the creation of the Noh
play *Dōjōji* out of *Kanemaki* through a series of selective cuts.

It is important to recognize the theatrical and historical context in which
this second stage of textual revision took place. One completely pragmatic
theatrical reason for the revision of *Kanemaki* was the need to make room
for the *ranbyōshi* dance and *kaneiri* bell-entering scene, which were not included in early versions of the play. It seems that in *Kanemaki* the *shite*,
rather than leap up into the bell, simply raised his sleeve, wrapping it
around his body as he sank to the floor.[38] The *kaneiri* is thought to have
been added sometime in the 1580s;[39] the *ranbyōshi* is thought to have been
added about sixty years earlier by a Komparu School actor.[40] Both the
kaneiri and *ranbyōshi* take up a considerable amount of stage time, and

given that performing them makes tremendous physical demands on the *shite,* practical considerations alone necessitated cuts in the *Kanemaki* libretto.

In a similar fashion, we can identify a specific theatrically pragmatic motivation for the elimination of the woman's salvation from *Dōjōji* by comparing how the conclusion for each play is staged. In *Dōjōji,* removing the reference to the serpent-woman's salvation and ending with the serpent-woman hurling herself into the Hidaka River acts as the pretext for the *Dōjōji shite*'s exciting final running leap through the curtains at the end of the *hashigakari* bridge. In theatrical terms this flying exit provides a far more satisfyingly dramatic ending than if the *shite* left the stage quietly, as the actor certainly would have if he were representing a woman who had just achieved enlightenment.

Within the context of Japanese theater history, the *kaneiri* scene, the *ranbyōshi,* and the final flying leap all represent a general trend toward a more "literal" representation of the dramatic events (I would not want to go so far as to say "realistic"), which is in line with changes of theatrical emphasis in the late sixteenth century that would lead to the development of Kabuki. I do not believe, however, that these changes in theatrical emphasis are enough to explain the elimination not only of the woman's salvation, a move that has serious ideological implications, but also just about every line that unequivocally indicates her desire for enlightenment. I would argue that when *Kanemaki* was first written, the ultimate salvation of any *shite* character (whether a man or a woman) was still considered a necessary and integral part of Noh. In medieval Japan, Buddhism's persuasive power lay in its ability to ultimately recuperate every living being, no matter how evil or abject. In fact, it was precisely to the extent that the female *shite* in Noh was impeded by her carnal desires from attaining enlightenment that she achieved symbolic power as a figuration of the universality of Buddhism's promised salvation. In addition, in the medieval period, women still had enough economic power to play important roles in terms of patronage, as evidenced in the description already given of how the *Kegon engi setsuwa* was created. How do we explain, then, *Dōjōji*'s loss of a didactic Buddhist moral?

It seems likely that one explanation lies in changes in late Muromachi-Momoyama Buddhism. As William LaFleur points out in *The Karma of Words,* the late sixteenth century saw a gradual lessening of the importance of the Buddhist episteme as a more pragmatic, "secularized" Confucianism began to take hold in elite aesthetic discourses—and Confucianism's attitude toward women was certainly decidedly negative.[41] In addition, we need to take into account changes in patterns of patronage. Early Noh was dependent on temple-shrine complexes for support and was used to propagate religious teachings in an easily understood and appealing form that would attract people. Given that the story of *Kanemaki* is a popular *setsuwa* associated with the Dōjōji temple and that the *kusemai* in *Kanemaki* is the story of the temple's founding, it seems likely that *Kanemaki* was originally written specifically for the Dōjōji temple. As it happens, there is on record a dedication ceremony for a new temple bell at Dōjōji in 1359, a data that corresponds fairly well with the opening *sashi* in *Kanemaki*, which explicitly dates the play at seven hundred years after the founding (701).[42] So one might speculate that some form of the play was originally written for the dedication ceremony itself and later extensively rewritten by Kanze Nobumitsu or (more likely) was written for a later memorial celebration of that dedication ceremony. Of course, we have no proof of any of this.

At any rate, by the late Muromachi-Momoyama period, Noh's primary base of support had shifted from temple-shrine complexes to the patronage of high-ranking samurai, such as Hideyoshi and Tokugawa Ieyasu, whose taste ran to warrior tales and powerful conflicts between the *shite* and *waki*.[43] It was only in this relatively secularized context that theatrical spectacle could be valued above subtle religious argument or even simple didactic moralizing. By the late Muromachi period, producing dramatically satisfying theater more than justified depriving the woman of release from the pain of her passionate anger.

However, the moral code of the Buddhist episteme still held to the extent that a narrative structure in which the woman clearly pronounced her desire for enlightenment but failed to receive it in the end was simply not culturally intelligible. I would argue that it was this lingering Buddhist morality that necessitated the retroactive deletion of nearly every line in *Kanemaki* that suggested the serpent-woman's desire for enlightenment.

The Textual Development of the Noh *Dōjōji*

To analyze the Noh text, I concentrate on how the two most important symbolic loci, the image of the woman as snake and the temple bell, were transformed in the development of the Noh. The original version of *Dōjōji*, *Kanemaki*, incorporated and transformed these symbolic elements of the *setsuwa* through a process of condensation and displacement. This process enabled the Noh to symbolically resolve medieval Buddhism's problem of masculine desire through its fetishization of the young woman's body.

In examining the role of the woman in both the Noh play and the *setsuwa*, the first thing we confront is the obvious fact (obvious to post-Freudians, at least) that the woman's body, the embodiment of lust, is transformed into a living phallus. In the *setsuwa*, we can see masculine desire being projected onto the female body, a projection that enabled men to deny those negative aspects of their own sexual nature which had to be eliminated for enlightenment to occur: the woman as female snake (that is, simultaneously phallic and female) embodies the animal nature of both masculine and feminine sexuality. The "pure" monk is a passive victim of feminine passion: the danger of a sexuality associated exclusively with the feminine is reinforced by the moral of *Konjaku Monogatari* which implies that it is the woman's blind passion alone that causes the tragedy.

In the move from the *setsuwa* to the Noh, the symbolic union of feminine and masculine in the body of the serpent-woman is strengthened by a further condensation. In the Noh the young monk does not appear as a separate character; the Noh combines the roles of both the monk and the woman into that of the *shirabyōshi* dancer, who although a woman, appears dressed as a man. That she is "standing in" for the monk becomes clear when, instead of wrapping herself around the bell, she takes the monk's place under it.[44] In this way the role of the monk, who at first might appear to have been left out of the Noh, continues in a new, "disguised" form. In the Noh's symbolic economy, desire is no longer the outcome of a "natural" attraction between the sexes because masculine desire does not exist; desire is instead produced "spontaneously" in a woman who is at the same time symbolically a man.[45]

However, although *Kanemaki* intensifies the *setsuwa*'s projection of desire onto the feminine, in the end this fusion of male and female in the *shirabyōshi* figure symbolically enables the monk as well as the serpent-woman to gain salvation. In this sense, *Kanemaki*, like the original *setsuwa*, follows the Buddhist logic of *gyakuen*. In both *Kanemaki* and the *setsuwa*, although the serpent-woman's passion appears at first to be purely negative, it can ultimately be interpreted positively because it results in salvation. In *Dōjōji*, on the other hand, this positive interpretation is blocked because the *shirabyōshi* fails to achieve enlightenment in the end. *Dōjōji* merely intensifies the *setsuwa*'s misogynistic projection of male desire onto the female, a desire that in *Dōjōji* can have only tragic consequences.

Of course, as we have seen in the *Kegon engi setsuwa*, female power associated with animal nature in the form of a snake does not necessarily have to be viewed as negatively as it is in *Dōjōji*. Probably the most famous Buddhist story of a woman associated with a snake is the story of the Nāga King's Daughter found in the "Devadatta" chapter of the *Lotus Sutra*.[46] The word *nāga* is translated as "dragon" in Chinese and Japanese, but in India *nāga* were usually portrayed as half-snake, half-human. In the *Lotus Sutra*, the Nāga King's Daughter achieves Buddahood with amazing speed, despite her five hindrances as a woman (not to mention being eight years old and a snake).[47] Of course, she cannot become a Buddha directly—she goes through an intermediate (nearly instantaneous) stage as a man first.[48] Nevertheless, she is held up as a positive role model for women in a number of Noh plays that relate to women's spirituality. In *Genzai Shichimen* an old serpent who lives in Shichimen pond on Mt. Minobu appears as a woman to hear Nichiren Shōnin's daily sermons on the *Lotus Sutra*. When she hears the story of the Nāga King's Daughter, she realizes that women too can achieve Buddahood. Whereas before she resented Buddhism because it seemed to exclude women, now she eagerly embraces this truly marvelous faith which promises enlightenment equally to all. By the power of Nichiren and the *Lotus Sutra* she is transformed into a dragon and vows to protect Buddhism as a mountain *kami* (Shinto deity).

The Nāga King's Daughter also plays a prominent role in *Miidera,* a play whose plot structure may sound rather familiar: as in *Dōjōji,* a woman obsessed with ringing the temple bell is told that she cannot enter the temple grounds, but she gets in because a temple worker wants to see her dance. The *shite* character in *Miidera* is a mother who has lost her child, and she believes that because the temple bell is said to come from the Nāga King's palace, if she rings the bell it will create a karmic link *(kechien)* with the Nāga King's Daughter, who will then cause her five hindrances as a woman to vanish, as well as bring about the return of her child. Another variation on this theme occurs in the Noh play *Ama* (The diver), the story of a woman diver who, in exchange for a promise that her son will be made her lord's heir, sacrifices her life to retrieve a Buddhist jewel from the Nāga King's palace. In the second half of the play, the ghost of the woman diver appears as the Nāga King's Daughter to dance in celebration of the *Lotus Sutra.*

The self-sacrificing mother in *Ama* and the mother driven to madness by the loss of her child in *Miidera* can both be interpreted as symbolic figurations of the "good mother." In *The Powers of Horror,* Julia Kristeva characterizes this "other face" of the maternal as an image "tied to suffering, illness, sacrifice and a downfall," an "archaizing idealization" whose precondition is "the devalorization of sex."[49] As mentioned earlier, in *The Powers of Horror,* Kristeva describes how the horror of the maternal lies in its negative power to disrupt the symbolic, to overwhelm the subject with an archaic chaos of abject undifferentiation. It seems to me that Kristeva's characterization of the maternal as essentially abject fails to encompass the active agency of the serpent-women of *Genzai Shichimen, Kegon engi,* and the *Lotus Sutra.* These phallic women are presented not merely as having the negative capacity to disrupt but as having the positive power to fundamentally rearticulate the patriarchal symbolic in which they "exist." As such, they are very different from Kristeva's "phallic idealizations," who although idealized, continue to be understood as essentially abject and powerless: "dissociated, parcelized, marginalized, and in the final analysis degraded."[50] Part of the problem here is, I think, that when Kristeva refers to this idealization of the maternal feminine as "phallic," she does not mean the "phallic mother" but only "woman as phallus." Within Lacanian psychoanalysis, when one assumes the feminine position of "being the phallus" by definition one can have no positive agency, since only by "having" the phallus (that is, assuming the masculine position) can one have power. The "phallic mother," however, gets to both be the phallus (the feminine position) and to have it. As a woman who nevertheless has the power to rearticulate the patriarchal symbolic, the phallic woman in her demonic guise is understandably threatening to that patriarchy.[51]

However, in the various narratives outlined above of women associated with the power of snakes, what we see is the demonic power of the phallic mother transformed into a purely beneficent power placed completely at the service of whomever or whatever she loves, including (most especially) Buddhism. This positive fantasy of a maternal that is both phallic (i.e., powerful) and yet beneficent seems to have no place within contemporary psychoanalysis. As Judith Butler has pointed out,

> [the] figure of excessive phallicism, typified by the phallic mother, is de-vouring and destructive, the negative fate of the phallus when attached to the feminine position. Significant in its misogyny, this construction suggests that "having the phallus" is much more destructive as a feminine operation that as a masculine one, a claim that symptomatizes the displacement of phallic destructiveness and implies that there is no other way for women to assume the phallus except in its most killing modalities.[52]

It is possible that the greater the repression of women within a particular society, the more terrifying this idea of the phallic mother becomes as a potential return of the repressed seeking to exact vengeance and the less likelihood there is of a positive recuperation within fantasy. One might speculate, then, that *Dōjōji's* reduction of the phallic serpent-woman to a purely demonic figure is symptomatic of the fact that the position of women at elite levels of Japanese society was taking a distinct downward turn at the end of the Muromachi period.[53]

Returning once again to my analysis of the textual development of *Dōjōji*, it turns out that in *Kanemaki* itself we have a positive image of the feminine similar to that represented in the Noh play *Ama:* according to the *engi* (founding legend) of Dōjōji, the temple was founded by a young woman diver who lived along the shore at Komatsubara, and the *kusemai* is danced to a retelling of that legend. As the sole support for her aging parents, this *ama* spent her days diving in the cold sea water or gathering wood in the mountains to burn as fuel for salt-making. One day when she was diving, she found a small Buddhist icon (perhaps Kannon) glowing beneath the waves. It was this image, a reward for her faith and filial piety, that was enshrined at the establishment of Dōjōji temple. It is not, I think, accidental that within *Kanemaki* we find two women diving into the water but with such completely different results; or that we find, ironically enough, that a temple famous for its successful exorcism of the demonic feminine was actually founded through the faith of a poor young *ama*.[54]

I would argue that in *Kanemaki* the *shirabyōshi* is meant to represent both the *ama* and the serpent-woman in the performance. In *Kanemaki's kusemai* dance, the *shirabyōshi* is reenacting the founding of the temple by the *ama;* in the *ranbyōshi* she reenacts the serpent-woman's attack on the bell. This idea that the *shirabyōshi* in *Kanemaki* is a double reincarnation is supported by the opening line *(sageuta)* of the travel poem the *shirabyōshi* recites when she first sets out for Dōjōji. In it the *shirabyōshi* states explicitly that she has been living in Komatsubara (the home of the *ama*).[55]

The *shirabyōshi* in *Kanemaki* thus enacts a complex double masquerade of both masculine and feminine (a feminine which is itself doubled given that she is the reincarnation of both the good *ama* and the evil serpent-woman). I would hypothesize that the process that reduced this complex gender ambiguity to a univocal reading of the *shirabyōshi* as a treacherous feminine masquerade with malevolent intent took place in at least two stages, one textual and one performative. First, the *ama* was removed from her character through the deletion of the *kusemai* and the line in the *sageuta*. This textual revision took place sometime in the sixteenth century. Second, a performative reinterpretation of the *shirabyōshi*'s character occurred probably sometime in the early Edo period, when a performance convention developed whereby the *shirabyōshi*, who "realistically" ought to be dressed as a man, began to be costumed as a woman. This means that although the woman's claim that as a *shirabyōshi* she is not an "ordinary" woman remains in the text, in performance her symbolic union with the man is suppressed. In addition, at some point certain signifying marks became conventional parts of her costume: the triangular scales on her inner robe reveal her "true" nature as a serpent; the "karmic wheels" on her outer brocade robe indicate her karmic destiny to compulsively reenact the past. Her costume thus emphasizes her duplicitous masquerade as a "good" woman: for the knowledgeable Noh audience today, these signifying marks help foreclose any ambiguity about her motive in wanting to enter the temple compound and ring the bell.[56]

The temple bell functions as a second important locus of condensation and displacement. In Japanese esoteric Buddhism, bells function as symbolic wombs, particularly associated with the Womb *(Taizō)* Mandala, and the temple bell certainly retains those associations in *Kanemaki* and *Dōjōji*. Whereas in the *setsuwa*, the snake wrapped herself around the bell, in the Noh the woman's aggression becomes even more overtly masculine, when as a phallic snake she leaps into the womb of the bell. Here we can see another displacement from the *setsuwa* at work: the Noh takes the earlier *setsuwa*'s narrative element of the woman changing into a snake in her private bedchamber and condenses it with the bell whose secret interior space now provides the "womb" for the woman's rebirth/transformation into a snake.[57] Both *Kanemaki* and *Dōjōji* reinforce this symbolic interpretation by suggesting in the last lines of the play an analogical relation of identity between the woman's body and the bell: when the serpent-woman vomits raging flames at the bell, she only manages to burn herself.[58]

This relation of identity between women's bodies and sacred icons shows up in other Noh plays as well. In *Miidera* it serves to reinforce the logic of the mother who believes that if she rings the temple bell, her son will be returned to her. And in *Sotoba Komachi*, when priests from Mount Koya catch the aged Komachi sitting on a stupa and sharply reprimand her, she argues that a relation of identity holds between her body and the old wooden stupa: "I, too, am a fallen tree, decaying in the earth, yet in my heart flowers burst in poetic bloom which I might offer to my holy Lord."[59] Komachi wins her duel of wits with the priests by skillfully using the Mahāyāna doctrine of emptiness to prove that since there can be no essential difference between her body and mind and the stupa as the Buddha Body and Buddha Mind, she has a perfect right to rest on it.[60]

There are at least two ways to interpret the *shirabyōshi*'s relation to the bell in *Dōjōji*. One interpretation hinges on the argument that the *shirabyōshi* is simply the serpent-woman in disguise, and justifies her failure to achieve enlightenment by interpreting her professed desire to absolve her sins by performing a purification dance for the bell as a cunning deceit used to gain entrance to the temple. This treacherous masquerade of faith, like her *shirabyōshi* costume, helps disguise her true nature as evil incarnate and conceals her true goal, the destruction of the bell.

A second interpretation would be that the *shirabyōshi* is not actually the *onryō* (vengeful spirit) of the serpent-woman but merely her possessed vehicle. *Shirabyōshi* were religious performance specialists of a sort; they were often called upon to perform dances of purification at temple-shrine complexes. The *ranbyōshi* is generally considered to be a secularized version of such a purification dance: a *fumi-shizume* ("ground quieting") dance ritual through which malevolent spirits dwelling in the earth were subdued.[61] Thus the *shirabyōshi*'s offer to dance for the dedication ceremony would be perfectly ordinary; it may even be sincerely meant. It is possible to think of the *shirabyōshi* as an innocent young girl who is drawn to the temple by a compulsion whose source she herself is not consciously aware of. The interpretation that the *shirabyōshi* is suddenly possessed is supported by the very abrupt shift in tone at the height of the *kyū no mai:* "The peaceful fishers will show their lights in villages along the banks—and if the watchers sleep when danger threatens, I'll not let this opportunity pass me by!"[62] It might be that the *onryō* is simply too powerful for the dancer to subdue through her dance; or it might be that this was the goal of the *fumi-shizume* dance all along: to make the *onryō* appear so that she could be exorcised.[63] This second interpretation creates a binary split that places all the good intentions on the side of the *shirabyōshi* and all the bad intentions on the side of the serpent-woman; such a clean "splitting off" of character accords well with *Dōjōji*'s overall tendency toward starkly contrasting dualisms. By making the dancer an innocent victim of a kind of karmic repetition compulsion, it simultaneously paints the serpent-woman as so univocally evil that her failure to achieve enlightenment at the end can be justified.

In *Kanemaki*, however, the fact that the woman ultimately achieves release from her passionate resentment makes it seem more likely that the serpent-woman herself is extremely ambivalent in her feelings toward the bell. This interpretation is supported by intimations in the *Kanemaki* text that the *shirabyōshi* wishes to strike the bell because she believes that ringing it is the soteriological equivalent of chanting the *Lotus Sutra*. In other words, striking the bell and chanting the *Lotus Sutra* both have the power to absolve her sins (that is, rid her of the negative feminine sexuality that caused her past bad karma), a first step toward enlightenment. She is simultaneously drawn to the bell by her desire for enlightenment and by her desire to take revenge on the displaced object of her resentment toward the monk.

The bell in *Kanemaki* thus functions in much the same way as the fulling block in the Noh play *Kinuta*. In *Kinuta*, a woman who is angry at her husband's neglect takes out her grief and resentment by beating kimono on a fulling block. Succumbing to her grief, she falls ill and dies. In the second half of the play, when her husband returns home for her funeral service she appears before him as a ghost and explains that she has been condemned to hell for her passionate attachment. She then goes on to vividly describe how the fulling block, which in life had been the displaced object of her furious resentment over her husband's neglect, has now in death become the instrument of her torture in hell. And yet in the end when the sounds of the fulling block are equated with the sounds of the chanting of the *Lotus Sutra*, it becomes, paradoxically, the instrument of her salvation. In much the same way, the bell in *Kanemaki* functions as the object of the woman's displaced anger and resentment over her rejection by the monk, but in the end it also functions as the instrument of her salvation by the equation of its sound with the chanting of the *Lotus Sutra*. In fact, the salvation that comes at the end of *Kanemaki* could be seen as simply a displaced deferral of the ending of the *setsuwa*. In *Konjaku Monogatari* the monk, himself transformed into a snake, appeared to a senior priest of Dōjōji and begged him to chant a chapter of the *Lotus Sutra*; in *Kanemaki* the *shirabyōshi*/serpent who symbolically fuses in her body both the monk and passionate woman of the *setsuwa*, achieves salvation for both of them by ringing the temple bell, which is the soteriological equivalent of chanting the *Lotus Sutra*. As we shall see, however, this soteriological function of the bell is for the most part eliminated in *Dōjōji*.

An Analysis of the Cuts in *Kanemaki* Which Produced *Dōjōji*

A systematic analysis of the cuts made in the *Kanemaki* text will show those cuts' imagistic and thematic effects. The first cut in *Kanemaki* is of an opening *sashi/ageuta* in which the head priest explains that it is because the "marvelous" sound of the bell is so "rarely heard" that such a multitude of people have gathered for the service of the reinstatement of the bell. The phrases "marvelous" and "rarely heard" are two of the most common descriptive predicates for the *Lotus Sutra*, used especially in arguing its effectiveness for bringing people to enlightenment; this sets up the initial identification between the bell and the *Lotus Sutra*. The head priest also indicates that the service is to be performed at an unusual time. Although it is evening, the dawn moon *(ariake no tsuki)* will soon be setting to the west in the direction of the "Sun-High Temple" (Hidakadera, another name for Dōjōji): "ariake no tsuki wa hodonaku irigata no Hidaka no tera."[64] The phrase *ariake no tsuki* is usually understood to refer to a moon that lingers on in the sky even as the day dawns, and so its appearance here in the evening is highly unusual.[65] Although it is possible to normalize this unusual image as a cyclical lunar phenomenon (at about the twentieth day in the lunar cycle, the moon rises in the early morning hours and sets in the late afternoon), it is not possible to normalize it in terms of the standard Japanese literary conventions for the use of "dawn moon" as a poetic image.

In the next scene, this same strange image of a dawn moon in the evening reappears in the *shirabyōshi*'s self-introduction, or *nanori*. As mentioned previously, *Kanemaki* has a slightly different *nanori* that includes an explanatory *sashi/sageuta* that is omitted from *Dōjōji*. In this *sashi/sageuta* the *shirabyōshi* tells us that she lives along the shore at Komatsubara and comments on her ambivalence toward the bell. She wants to go to hear the service but is afraid of what will happen if she sees/hears the bell being struck by the dawn moon again: "If I go today to hear the service of the Dōjōji bell which has been silent for so long, hearing it, my heart will return to the past, that time when the dawn moon struck the bell in the lingering twilight, as it must be doing even now; I shall go pay my respects."[66] In other words, the *shirabyōshi* is telling us that those events of the past, which she would prefer to forget, are somehow associated with a singular moment when the dawn moon struck the evening bell. As the same strange astronomical phenomenon is about to take place again, the *shirabyōshi* feels an irresistible compulsion to return to the scene of "origin."

The phrase "mukashi ni kaeru ariake no tsukigane nokoru iriyai no koro" (returning to that past time when the dawn moon struck the bell in the lingering twilight) puns on *tsuki* (moon) and *tsuku* (to strike). These puns, cohering around the dawn moon and the evening bell, recur again and again throughout the rest of the *Kanemaki*. One result of this nearly obsessive repetition is that although *Kanemaki* is ostensibly a *genzai* (present time) Noh there is no "normal" progression of time corresponding to the unfolding of events onstage. Instead, from the head priest's opening speech to the climactic exorcism scene, everyone seems caught in the lingering twilight, trapped in those last few moments before the dawn moon strikes and the sunset bell rings out. Within this other, psychological, kind of temporality the past is indistinguishable from the present and so must be compulsively reenacted.[67]

It may very well be precisely because the image of a dawn moon striking the evening bell is so inexplicable in terms of both the standard poetic conventions and the standard temporal progression for a *genzai* Noh that the playwright who created *Dōjōji* from *Kanemaki* attempted to normalize the time sequence as much as possible. He did so by deleting any lines of prose that clearly specified the time as early evening with both the sun and moon about to set in the west. The mysterious image of the "dawn moon striking the evening bell" was allowed to remain only in the poetry, where it could easily be dismissed as odd but essentially meaningless. Given those deletions, it makes sense that most modern commentators, annotators, and translators of *Dōjōji* have either ignored (and thereby repressed) the strangeness of this image or have actively attempted to normalize it.

Nevertheless, it seems to me that the ambiguous punning grammar of "ariake no tsukigane nokoru iriyai no koro," a grammar that disrupts the conventional linear flow of rhetoric, time, and narrative, is not unmotivated. The power of this image of the dawn moon striking the evening bell rests on its ability to condense a number of binary oppositions into a single symbolic locus. To begin with, it blends the visual and aural through the synesthesia of moonlight "striking" the bell. Second, it rhetorically combines two antithetical periods of the day: dawn and sunset. Third, it condenses the past and the present into one "uncanny" moment, a moment when the horrific events of the past erupt suddenly and violently into the present.

The adroit blending of the aural and visual through the word play on "striking" has specific thematic ramifications. Given that the moon is often a symbol of enlightenment, it is significant that at several points in *Kanemaki* the *shirabyōshi* clearly expresses her desire to "hear" the moon strike the bell. It seems to me that one possible explanation for this desire might be found in the Noh play *Miidera* (which some scholars believe was used as a model for the writing of *Dōjōji*).[68] *Miidera* quotes a popular song that associates the tolling of the temple bell at set hours with four lines of poetry (*gāthā*) from the *Nirvana Sutra*. The lines from *Miidera* read: "The early morning bell tolls 'Nothing that is, remains.' When the late night bell resounds, it echoes, 'All that is born must die.' What echo does the bell at dawn make? 'When what has passed has ceased to be. . . .' And what does the sunset bell toll? '. . . Nirvana's bliss is then attained.'"[69] Thus, at the moment when the dawn moon strikes the evening bell, the union of dawn and sunset form a couplet that by association indicates the achievement of enlightenment: "when what has passed [that is, the past karma that attaches the woman] has ceased to be, Nirvana's bliss is then attained." This couplet provides a likely motivation for the *shirabyōshi*'s expressed desire to hear and see the dawn moon strike the bell at Dōjōji. And when she finally gets her wish at the climax of the exorcism scene, the moment is given added punch by the literalization of the synesthesia: the bell actually rings out although nothing but the moonlight has touched it.

In *Kanemaki*, on one level the recurrence of the dawn moon striking the evening bell can be seen as a physical manifestation of the powerful karmic law that has all participants in its grip, the karmic bond that has led inexorably to a repetition of the awful events of the distant past; yet on another level it helps make possible the ultimate release of the serpent-woman when she herself strikes the bell. In *Dōjōji,* on the other hand, because the initial association made in *Kanemaki* between the dawn moon, evening bell, and past events has been eliminated along with the final salvation of the woman, when the image suddenly appears at the climax of the play, it seems little more than an elegant rhetorical flourish, given a puzzling amount of stress in performance by being sung with heightened lyric intensity by the *waki*/ head priest alone. One could still, of course, link it with the lines from the *Nirvana Sutra* quoted in *Miidera,* but if the woman does not achieve salvation in the end, what would be the point?

The next section that is cut from *Kanemaki* is the *mondō* between the *shirabyōshi* and the head priest of the temple. In it the *shirabyōshi* argues that she should be allowed to enter the temple, since by dancing as part of the Buddhist service her past karma will be absolved. When the head priest refuses to admit her she responds with a rather sophisticated philosophical argument. Her position, grounded in the Mahāyāna doctrine of emptiness and radical nondualism, is argued via an analogy with the *honji-suijaku* theory of assimilation between Buddhas and *kami.*[70] Stating that the relation between the Buddhas and *kami* is like that of waves and water—although the names are different the substance is the same (*ittai,* literally "one body")—she implies that the distinction between men and women is merely nominal, and thus the priest has no grounds for excluding her from the salvation promised by Buddha.[71]

The *Kanemaki mondō* continues with the *shirabyōshi* weeping at the head priest's heartlessness. She then describes the surrounding scene in a speech that manages to pun on two of the eight famous views of the area: the bell at Enji and the moon at Dōtei. Both the moon and the sun are setting to the west, and although the evening bell at distant Enji temple has tolled already, the bell at Dōjōji has still not tolled. The *shirabyōshi* suggests that if she were allowed to ring the bell, it might finally be heard.[72] The head priest, impressed as much by her ability with literary allusions as with her religious understanding, consults with the other priests, who ask him to let her dance for them as a special reward for having gone through so much hardship getting the bell up. He cannot refuse their request, and so, although he still has qualms, the woman is allowed to enter.

When the *mondō* debate was eliminated from *Dōjōji,* the *shirabyōshi*'s sophisticated argument that the head priest has no right to deny her entrance to the temple was eliminated as well. The *Dōjōji* version of how the woman gains entrance is completely different: as mentioned previously, instead of demonstrating her philosophical and literary understanding to the head priest, the *shirabyōshi* employs her seductive arts on a rather simple-minded, low-ranking temple worker. Using the deceptive argument that as a *shirabyōshi* she is no "ordinary" woman, she tempts him with her beauty and the lure of her dance into letting her enter the temple precincts despite the head priest's strict prohibition. Once again, in *Dōjōji* the woman is reduced to nothing more than her dangerously seductive feminine sexuality.[73]

Continuing with the story, the *shirabyōshi* expresses her delight at being allowed to enter the temple and prepares for the dance. In both *Kanemaki* and *Dōjōji*, the opening lines for the dance are "Apart from the cherry blossoms, there are only the pines; when darkness falls, will the bell ring out?" (hana no hoka ni wa matsu bakari, kure somete kane ya hibikuran).[74] Whereas in *Dōjōji* this line is simply repeated, as is normal for a *shidai*, in *Kanemaki* the second repetition is altered to "as darkness falls I do not hear the bell" (kure somete kane wa kikoezu). Once again, in the *Kanemaki* version, the *shirabyōshi*'s desire to hear the bell is given quite explicit emphasis.

This desire to hear the bell is given further reinforcement just a few lines later in the poem that comes at the climactic point just before the *kaneiri* (that is, at the climax of the *kyū no mai*): "Visiting a mountain temple on a spring evening, when the evening bell tolls, the blossoms fall."[75] In the Komparu version of *Dōjōji* the last line, "hana zo chirikeru" (the blossoms fall), is changed to "hana ya chiruran." The altered poem now reads, "when the evening bell rings, *will* the flowers fall?" echoing the *shidai* couplet of a few lines before ("when darkness falls, will the bell ring out?"). It also poses an implicit question: "do the flowers fall *because* the evening bell tolls?"[76] This question, which indicates a causal link between the bell's tolling of the fleeting hours and the flowers' evanescence, lends a slightly more ominous cast to the bell; while the image of flowers falling foreshadows the imminent fall of the bell itself.

At this point in the story the *shirabyōshi* has managed to entrance everyone onstage through her *ranbyōshi* dance. Seeing them all asleep, she seizes her chance to strike the bell, but at the very last moment she remembers her resentment, and instead of striking it, she flies upward into the bell, wrapping it around her as it crashes to the ground. If we were only discussing *Dōjōji* here, without reference to *Kanemaki*, at this point we would be under the impression that the *shirabyōshi*'s desire to strike the bell is motivated only by malicious spite. The obvious question then would be, why did the *shirabyōshi* not strike the bell when she had the chance? Taking the eliminated sections of *Kanemaki* into account, however, we can see that her desire to strike the bell is not motivated solely by resentment but also by her desire for enlightenment. As she goes to strike the bell, and really sees it for the first time, suddenly all the old memories come surging back, and her furious anger and resentment reassert themselves. It is the refusal to give up her attachment to her rancor that keeps her from striking the bell and gaining release.

The argument that the *shirabyōshi* would gain release from her attachment if she struck the bell is given strong support in the next section of *Kanemaki*, when a pun on *tsuku/tsukusu* (to be exhausted/to exhaust, as in "the exhaustion of resentment") is added to the cluster of images that cohere around puns on *tsuki* (moon) and *tsuku* (to strike). When the priests are praying to raise up the bell, the head priest gives them a little pep talk, telling them that their power will never be exhausted (*tsuku*) even if the Hidaka River runs dry and all its sands run out (again, *tsuku*).[77] The priests begin their exorcism with a *dhāraṇī* spell (the same one used in *Aoi no Ue* and *Funa Benkei*), a terrifying invocation of the awesome power of the five Wisdom Kings (Myō-ō). They seem to get better results, however, when they pray for the salvation of the serpent by invoking Fudō's compassionate vow,[78] since it is immediately after they chant, "He who hearkens to My Law shall gain enlightenment, he who knows My Heart will be a Buddha in this flesh," that the dawn moon strikes the bell (*ariake no tsukigane*), the bell rings out although no one has touched it, and it appears to dance.[79]

With the bell finally raised, the priests at last confront the serpent. At this point in *Kanemaki*, when the priests order the serpent to return from whence she came, she tauntingly echoes their use of *tsuku*: "How angry/resentful I am! How can you tell me to depart when I haven't exhausted (*tsukusu*) my resentment by striking (*tsuku*) the bell?"[80] Here, through the pun on *tsukusu* (to exhaust) and *tsuku* (to strike), the essential identity between striking the bell and exhausting one's resentment is most clearly expressed. But of course, as could be predicted by now, this line has been cut from *Dōjōji*.

In the dramatic close to *Dōjōji*, the priests call on, appropriately enough, the Nāga Kings to fight off the serpent-woman. She is forced to her knees by their power but then springs back up and, turning on the bell the full force of her fury, vomits raging flames. In so doing, however, she only succeeds in burning herself: "kane ni mukatte tsuku iki wa myōka to natte mi o yaku."[81] In this penultimate line we find our last pun on *tsuku*: to vomit, or give vent to. In *Dōjōji* the serpent-woman attempts to vent (*tsuku*) her burning anger against the bell, but because she does so with malevolent intent, she is unable to strike the bell; she ends up only harming herself. Completely vanquished by the power of the priests, she leaps into the Hidaka River, and the priests, their prayers granted, go happily home. *Kanemaki*, however, ends quite differently. Choked in flames, her body burning with passionate despair, the serpent-woman is about to throw herself into the river when she suddenly returns to the main stage. As the chorus describes her action ("mata kono kane o tsukuzuku") and repeats it for emphasis, she strikes the bell (*tsuku*) again and again, thereby completely exhausting (*tsukuzuku*) her resentment. As her attachment to her hatred for the bell vanishes, she herself fades slowly from view.[82]

Kanemaki is not somehow better theater than *Dōjōji* simply because it espouses a more enlightened view of women. It seems clear that the cuts made in *Kanemaki* allow *Dōjōji* to attain much greater intensity as a theatrical experience for contemporary audiences. Both *Kanemaki* and the *setsuwa* name names and cite specific dates; more important, they provide an absolute temporal closure to the story when, in their different ways, they indicate that the monk and the woman have achieved salvation and vanish forever. *Dōjōji*, which eliminates those specific names and dates, is vaguely set at "some time after the original events"; it could be four hundred years ago, it could be yesterday. And by eliminating the woman's final salvation, *Dōjōji* leaves open the possibility that the serpent-woman will rise again from the depths of the Hidaka River to attack the bell, an eternal return in which the past is compulsively replayed before us each time the play is reenacted.

Dōjōji thus seems literally to "act out" the binary logic whereby a disembodied universal masculine maintains its idealized identity through the exclusion of a feminine constructed as disavowed corporeality in the form of the serpent-woman. That in *Dōjōji* the *ama* who actually founded the Dōjōji temple is eliminated from the character of the *shirabyōshi* would also seem to be a "staging" of the deconstructive logic by which a dominant term in a binary opposition seeks to suppress the fact that its subordinate opposite is actually constitutive of its very identity. In addition, the fact that *Dōjōji* is one of the most popular plays in the Noh repertoire today in and of itself attests to how closely it approaches a modern construction of gender relations: a construction simultaneously motivated by our deepest psychological desires and fears and yet at the same time historically sited at the convergence of modern social, political, and economic relations. However, if, as I've argued here, the construction of a symbolic feminine is a historicized phenomenon, the more interesting question for the future is how the representation of the feminine in both the *setsuwa* and *Kanemaki* resists being fit into deconstructive and psychoanalytic conceptual grids. Analyzing material from other cultural and temporal contexts provides one way that we can begin to reveal the limits and aporias of contemporary Western theory, a project that is long overdue.

NOTES

1. This essay is a revised version of an article published in the *Journal of Japanese Studies* (Summer 1991); "When the Moon Strikes the Bell: Desire and Enlightenment in the Noh Play *Dōjōji*." I would like to express my gratitude to the many people who carefully read and offered comments on the earlier version, most especially Karen Brazell and John McRae at Cornell University and Tom Looser at the University of Chicago. With regard to the revised version, I would especially like to thank Terashima Shoichi and Judith Butler, both of whom helped me to rethink my argument substantially.

2. In this essay I am using a working definition of "medieval Japan" as equated primarily with the Kamakura (1185–1333) and Muromachi (1338–1573) periods. The Momoyama period (1573–98) is considered "transitional" and the Edo period (1603–1867) "early modern." The assigning of such precise dates and designations is of course provisional, given that they are still the topic of much debate in Japanese scholarship.

3. In making this argument, I am taking up a critical position in line with what Judith Butler, in *Gender Trouble: Feminism and the Subversion of Identity* (New York:

Routledge, 1990), p.10, characterized as "those historical and anthropological positions that understand gender as a *relation* among socially constituted subjects in specifiable contexts." From this point of view, gender is considered "a shifting and contextual phenomenon, [which] does not denote a substantive being, but a relative point of convergence among culturally and historically specific sets of relations."

4. This flamboyant maneuver is so unusual in Noh that audiences have been known to burst into applause when it is done particularly successfully—a unique response in a Noh audience, where sedate, although usually rapt, attention is the norm.

5. See Karen Brazell's discussion of this point in "Unity of Image: An Aspect of the Art of Noh," in *Japanese Tradition: Search and Research* (Los Angeles: Asian Performing Arts Summer Institute, UCLA, 1981), pp. 25-42.

6. Matsuoka Shinbei and Yamanaka Reiko, "*Dōjōji*," *Kokubungaku*, vol. 31, no. 10 (September 1986), p. 92. In *mugen* Noh, dream and reality are so fluidly intertwined that they can hardly be distinguished. *Dōjōji* is ostensibly a *genzai* (present time) Noh, with no dream elements, and yet its plot and thematic structure pivot on certain "uncanny" moments (such as the *shite*'s leap into the bell) when the past suddenly comes alive in the present. These moments (which cannot be written off simply as dreams or déjà vu) radically disrupt the linear flow of time and in so doing put into question the whole idea of "past" and "present."

7. "Shikareba, nyonin no ashikikokoro no takeki koto, sude ni kaku no gotoshi." Marubuchi Kazuo, Kunisaki Fumimarō, and Konno Tōru, eds., *Konjaku monogatarishū (1)*, vol. 21 of *Nihon koten bungaku zenshū* (Tokyo: Shōgakkan, 1971), p. 487; translation taken from Marian Ury, trans., *Tales of Times Now Past* (Berkeley: University of California Press, 1985), p. 96.

8. Mark Oshima makes this point in an unpublished paper, "Snake in the Grass: Femininity on the Kabuki Stage," presented at the Harvard University *Fukiyose* Conference, Cambridge, 1986, p. 12.

9. *Kanawa, Aoi no Ue*, and *Dōjōji* form a group called the "three demoness plays." Erika Bainbridge has pointed out how the masks appropriate to each of these plays reflect the traditional perceptions of the quality and degree of each woman's anger. The mask worn by the woman in *Kanawa* is called *namanari* (incomplete transformation) because she requires aid to change into a demon; the mask is the face of an angry woman with mere "buds" of horns. The mask worn by Lady Rokujō in *Aoi no Ue* is called *hannya* (half-serpent); only half transformed (*chūnari*), the mask reflects Rokujō's deeply ambivalent feelings of love and anger. The woman in *Dōjōji*, however, is often played wearing the *ja* (serpent) mask; it represents her full transformation (*honnari*) into a snake. The fact that the *ja* mask is generally used in *Dōjōji* today corroborates a point that I make later in this essay, that the strong ambivalence voiced by the serpent-woman in an earlier version of the Noh play has mostly been lost from *Dōjōji*. See Bainbridge, "Deranged Women's Role in Japanese Drama," paper presented at the annual meeting of the Association for Asian Studies, Chicago, 1990, pp. 5–6: See also Koyama Hiroshi, Satō Kikuo, and Satō Ken-'ichirō, eds., *Yōkyokushū (2)*, vol. 34 of *Nihon koten bungaku zenshū* (Tokyo: Shōgakkan, 1975), p. 5, and Baba Akiko, *Oni no kenkyū* (Tokyo: Chikuma Shobō, 1988), p. 252.

10. "Tsukuri tsumi mo kienubeki kane no kuyō ni mairan." Yokomichi Mario and Omote Akira, eds., *Yōkyokushū (ge)*, vol. 41 of *Nihon koten bungaku taikei* (Tokyo: Iwanami Shoten, 1963), p. 131. For the most part, quotations from the Japanese text are taken from this volume, which is based on a Kanze school text. However, because there are significant textual variations, particularly between the Kanze and Komparu versions, other editions are cited as well. The English renderings follow Donald Keene's elegant translation in Keene, ed., *Twenty Plays of the Noh Theater* (New York: Columbia University Press, 1970), pp. 238–63. I have modified or retranslated only where it seemed necessary for the clarity of my argument.

11. "Sate mo atari chikaki Hidakadera ni kane no okuyō no yoshi moshi sorofu hodo ni kechien no tame mairaba ya to omohi soro" (I understand that in nearby Hidakadera [another name for Dōjōji] there is to be a dedication service for the bell, and so I am minded to go there to get a "link" to my salvation). Koyama, *Yōkyokushū* (2), p. 238. This *yōkyokushū* is based on a Komparu text. The corresponding line in the Kanze text is "sate mo Dōjōji to mōsu ontera ni kane no kuyō no onhairi sorofu yoshi moshi sorofu hodo ni tada ima mairaba ya to omohi soro" (I understand there is to be a dedication service for the bell at Dōjōji, so I am minded to go there now); Yokomichi and Omote, *Yōkyokushū (ge)*, p. 132. Donald Keene explains in his introduction that his translation makes use of both the Kanze and Komparu texts in order to provide the most effective version of the story. He combines the two texts as "I have heard that a bell is to be dedicated at the Dōjōji, and so I am hurrying there now, in the hopes of improving my chances of salvation." Keene, *Twenty Plays*, p. 243.

12. The five Myō-ō (Vidyā-rāja) are messengers of Dainichi-nyorai; as manifestations of the Dharma Body they assume terrifying forms to quell beings of stubbornly evil nature.

13. "Chō ga sessha tokudai chie, chi ga shinsha sokkushin jōbutsu to, ima no jashin o inoru ue wa nani no urami ka." Yokomichi and Omote, *Yōkyokushū (ge)*, p. 141; Keene, *Twenty Plays*, p. 245.

14. *Kanemaki/Dōjōji* generally adheres to Nobumitsu's style: like other plays by Nobumitsu, such as *Momijigari* and *Funa Benkei*, *Dōjōji* is set in the dramatic present with a corresponding emphasis on the literal level of the dramatic working out of the plot, rather than on the metaphorical level of literary allusions and complex imagery. In line with this greater emphasis on dramatic plot, we also see a greater emphasis on the roles played by the *waki* and *kyōgen* actors (Nobumitsu was himself a *waki* actor).

15. Keene, *Twenty Plays*, p. 238.

16. See Inoue Mitsusada and Ōsone Shōsuke, eds., *Ojōden hokkegenki*, vol. 7 of *Nihon shisō taikei* (Tokyo: Iwanami Shoten, 1974), pp. 217–19. There is a translation of the *Hokkegenki* version of the Dōjōji story in Yoshiko Dykstra, trans., *Miraculous Tales of the Lotus Sutra from Ancient Japan: The Dainihonkoku hokekyōkenki of Priest Chingen* (Hirakata: Kansai University of Foreign Studies, 1983), pp. 145–46.

17. Marubuchi, *Konjaku monogatarishū (1)*, pp. 481–87; Ury, *Tales of Times Now Past*, pp. 93–96.

18. The boss is a loop at the top of the bell, which is used to suspend it. It often takes the form of a serpent or dragon's head and suggests the traditional association of fire-breathing dragons with the fiery furnace used to cast the bell.

19. "Shikareba, nyonin no ashikikokoro no takeki koto, sude ni kakugotoshi. Kore ni yorite, onna ni chikazuke koto o hotoke anāgachi ni imashimetamau. Kore o shirite todomubekinari to namu kataritsutahetaru toya." Marubuchi, *Konjaku monogatarishū (1)*, p. 487; Ury, *Tales of Times Now Past*, p. 96.

20. It is traditionally attributed to the Emperor Go-Komatsu (reign: 1382–92 [Southern Court] and 1393–1412). A fold-out reproduction can be found inserted at the beginning of Sōga Tetsuo, ed., *Dōjōji* (Tokyo: Shōgakkan, 1982).

21. At the time this cross-dressing was considered quite erotic; *shirabyōshi* were often mistresses of the highest-ranking samurai. See, for example, the *Heike monogatari* chapter about the *shirabyōshi* dancers Giō and Hotoke, who were mistresses of Taira no Kiyomori. Helen McCullough, trans., *The Tale of the Heike* (Stanford: Stanford University Press, 1988), pp. 30–37.

22. I am indebted to Mark Oshima for this observation.

23. "Omoheba kono kane, urameshiya tote." Yokomichi and Omote, *Yōkyokushū (ge)*, p. 137; Keene, *Twenty Plays*, p. 245.

24. He adds some details not found in the other versions. The innocent young

girl has been misled by her father's teasing into believing that the monk who stays with her family every year and always remembers to bring her a pretty toy will one day be her husband. One year, when she has reached marriageable age, she sneaks into the monk's room and reproaches him, asking when he is going to make her his wife. Horrified, he placates her by promising to return for her on the way back from his pilgrimage to Kumano. The rest of the story continues as in the *Dōjōji engi emaki*. At first glance, replacing the lustful widow with an innocent young maiden would seem to make the audience more sympathetic toward the serpent-woman. On another level, however, this change demonstrates that all women, no matter how young and innocent they may appear, are capable of truly monstrous passion and rage, and thus justifies the exclusion of all women.

25. For the text of *Kanemaki* I have referred to the version contained within the *Dōjōji* text in Yokomichi and Omote, *Yōkyokushū (ge)*, pp. 128–42. For purposes of comparison I have also referred to the versions in Itō Masayoshi, ed., *Yōkyokushū (chū)*, vol. 78 of *Shinchō Nihon koten shūsei* (Tokyo: Shinchōsha, 1988), pp. 491–93, and the Kurokawa Noh version reprinted in Sōga, *Dōjōji*, pp. 265–72. All translations are my own.

26. Nancy Chodorow uses Karen Horney's 1932 paper, "The Dread of Women," to support her point that the dread of women, unlike the fear of the father, is "uncanny" in quality, because its formation occurs at a time when the child has no reflective capacities for understanding. This "uncanny" quality certainly seems to inhere in the *shirabyōshi*'s *ranbyōshi* dance—a return of the repressed in a new guise, simultaneously fascinating and dangerous, seductive and repelling. See Chodorow, *The Reproduction of Mothering* (Berkeley: University of California Press, 1978), p. 183.

27. I am indebted here to Mark Oshima's "Snake in the Grass," where he sets out some of the initial Freudian-Lacanian implications of both the *setsuwa* and the Noh. Oshima bases his analysis on Laura Mulvey's "Visual Pleasure and Narrative Cinema," *Visual and Other Pleasures* (Bloomington: Indiana University Press, 1989). See also Freud's brief essays "Fetishism" (1927) and "Medusa's Head" (1922), in Philip Rieff, ed., *Sexuality and the Psychology of Love* (New York: Collier Books, 1963).

28. Julia Kristeva, *The Powers of Horror: An Essay on Abjection*, trans. Leon S. Roudiez (New York: Columbia University Press, 1982), p. 64.

29. Kristeva, *The Powers of Horror*, p. 70.

30. Laura Mulvey, "Myth, Narrative and Historical Experience," *Visual and Other Pleasures*, p. 175.

31. Diana Paul enumerates a number of reasons for misogynist attitudes in Buddhism. According to Paul, it was the monks' resentment at being dependent on and tempted by laywomen, together with the monastic order's need to instill fear of women as a means of control, that led to a strongly negative view of the feminine within some areas of Buddhism. The Dōjōji *setsuwa*'s misogyny certainly seems to fit this pattern. See Paul, *Women in Buddhism: Images of the Feminine in Mahāyāna Tradition* (Berkeley: Asian Humanities Press, 1979), pp. 6–9. See also William LaFleur's "Women and the Dharma," *Buddhism: A Cultural Perspective* (Englewood Cliffs: Prentice Hall, 1988), pp. 49–56.

32. *Lives of the Founders of the Kegon Sect* or *Founding Legends of the Kegon Sect* (dated somewhere between 1219 and 1225). The six scrolls are reproduced and discussed in Tanaka Ichimatsu, ed., *Kegon engi*, vol. 7 of *Nihon emakimono zenshū* (Tokyo: Kadokawa Shoten, 1959); the text is reprinted on pp. 46–59. The sections of the text that directly refer to the *Dōjōji* story are also quoted in Matsuoka and Yamanaka, "*Dōjōji*," pp. 91–92. My description of the plot structure of *Kegon engi* and its intended audience is based on the synopsis and translation of the *Kegon engi* in Karen L. Brock's "Chinese Maiden, Silla Monk: Zenmyō and Her Thirteenth-Century Japanese Audience," in *Flowering in the Shadows: Women in the History of*

Chinese and Japanese Painting, ed. Marsha Weidner (Honolulu: University of Hawaii Press, 1990). I am grateful to Brock for letting me read her manuscript before it was published. See also her abbreviated version, "Gishō-e ni okeru Zenmyō no byōsha: sono igi to juyō" (The portrayal of Zenmyō in the *Gishō-e:* Its meaning and reception), *Bukkyō Geijutsu,* no. 176 (1988), pp. 11–36.

33. See Brock, "Chinese Maiden, Silla Monk," pp. 205–10. She identifies the patron as "Lady Sanmi" or Tokiko, the daughter of an adopted son of Taira no Kiyomori.

34. Tanaka, *Kegon engi,* p. 52; Matsuoka and Yamanaka, "*Dōjōji,*" p. 91 (translation mine). The *Kegon engi* is interesting not only because it shows how the representation of the role of women in Buddhism changed when the audience changed, but also because its narrative element of the woman throwing herself into the sea and becoming a dragon seems, in turn, to have influenced the development of the Dōjōji story. Matsuoka and Yamanaka suggest that the *Dōjōji engi emaki's* narrative variation of the woman throwing herself into the Hidaka River was influenced by the *Kegon engi,* infiltrating into the popular dissemination of the Dōjōji legend in the Kamakura period, and from there eventually into the Noh.

35. This interpretation was first set forth in Simone de Beauvoir's *Second Sex,* trans. E. M. Parshley (New York: Vintage Press, 1973). For a discussion of the various ways the assymetry of this binary opposition has been articulated in feminist theory since then, see Judith Butler's *Gender Trouble,* esp. pp. 9–13.

36. Arthur Thornhill makes a similar point. He calls the relation of suffering and anger between the woman and the monk "codependent" suffering and points out that in the Dōjōji *setsuwa,* although this "codependent" suffering initially causes the woman and monk both to be reborn as snakes, through the power of the *Lotus Sutra* (and the logic of *gyakuen*) it ultimately leads to their mutual, or codependent, salvation. See Thornhill, "The Dōjōji Tale: Codependent Salvation in *Konjaku Monogatari,*" paper presented at the annual meeting of the Association for Asian Studies, Chicago, 1990, pp. 8–9.

37. See Sigmund Freud's "Dream Work" chapter in *The Interpretation of Dreams* (New York: Avon Books, 1965), pp. 312–44, and Jaques Lacan, "The Agency of the Letter in the Unconscious or Reason since Freud," *Écrits: A Selection,* trans. Alan Sheridan (New York: Norton, 1977), pp. 146–78. See also Kaja Silverman's lucid discussion of these processes and their importance for literary theory in *The Subject of Semiotics* (New York: Oxford University Press, 1983). In using the terms *condensation* and *displacement* I am, in some sense, treating the play as a conscious fantasy whose structure is nevertheless guided by unconscious processes. One does not have to make a decision, however, about the relative degree of self-consciousness or unconsciousness with which the play was created; Freud himself refused to make any absolute distinction between the two. For a discussion of the use of psychoanalysis to interpret conscious fantasies, see Elizabeth Cowie, "Fantasia," in *The Woman in Question: m/f,* ed. Parveen Adams and Elizabeth Cowie (Cambridge, MIT Press, 1990), pp. 148–95.

38. For proof, Itō Masayoshi points to a phrase in *Kanemaki,* "hikikazukite zo, fushitarikeru" (wrapping [the bell] around her, she prostrates herself). In *Dōjōji* the line has been altered to "hikikazukite zo, usenikari" (wrapping [the bell] around herself, she disappears). Itō, *Yōkyokushū (chū),* n. 8, p. 379. Matsuoka and Yamanaka, "*Dōjōji,*" p. 92, add the evidence of an actor's handbook (*Dōbushō*) dated 1596: "In the past the actor wrapped his sleeve around himself. In recent years [this practice] has disappeared."

39. Itō dates the practice to the end of the Muromachi period on the basis of an entry dated 1591 in a personal diary *(Haretoyoki)* of a high-ranking nobleman, Kajūji Haretoyo (1544–1602): "There was a Noh performance at the temple. . . . *Dōjōji*

was the fourth piece performed. The rope of the hanging bell broke. Often before there have been injuries performing *Dōjōji.*" Itō, *Yōkyokushū (chū)*, n. 8, p. 379.

40. Matsuoka and Yamanaka, *"Dōjōji,"* p. 92. Itō, *Yōkyokushū (chū)*, p. 490, suggests that Komparu Zenpō (Zenchiku's grandson) might have inserted it into the play sometime between 1504 and 1520. It seems that for a while at least, both versions of the play were performed: there is a record of a performance of *Dōjōji* in 1536, but there are also records of *Kanemaki* performances in 1554 and 1586.

41. William LaFleur, *The Karma of Words* (Berkeley: University of California Press, 1983), p. 13.

42. Yokomichi and Omote, *Yōkyokushū (ge)*, p. 130, n. 22.

43. See Jacob Raz's extended discussion of this point in *Audience and Actors: A Study of Their Interaction in the Japanese Traditional Theater* (Leiden: E. J. Brill, 1983), pp. 131–36.

44. Note that the title, *Kanemaki*, would normally be read as "enwrapping the bell," and thus the medieval Japanese audience would have been led to expect from the title that the play would be a simple reenactment of the events of the *setsuwa*. When the serpent-woman wraps the bell around herself instead, the fact that the audience's expectations are controverted would have given dramatic emphasis to this thematic inversion.

45. To add to the complexity, in performance the *shirabyōshi* is literally a man as well: on stage we are faced with a male actor playing the role of a female *shirabyōshi* who dances dressed as a male aristocrat.

46. See Katō Bunnō et al., trans., *The Threefold Lotus Sutra* (Tokyo: Kosei, 1975), pp. 210–14.

47. Śāriputra argues against the possibility of the Nāga King's Daughter gaining speedy enlightenment: "the body of a woman is filthy and not a vessel of the Law. How can she attain the supreme Bodhi? . . . Moreover, a woman by her body still has five hindrances: she cannot become first, king of the Brahma-heaven; second, Śakra; third, a Māra-king; fourth, a holy wheel-rolling king; and fifth, a buddha. How then could a woman's body so speedily become a buddha?" Katō, *The Threefold Lotus Sutra*, p. 213.

48. If we keep in mind that in *Kanemaki* the woman is granted salvation in the end, her symbolic masquerade as a man in the first half of the play, and her transformation inside the womb of the bell into the phallic snake in the second half, might be compared to the instantaneous transformation by the Nāga King's Daughter into a man; in other words, as preparation for her final enlightenment.

49. Kristeva, *The Powers of Horror*, pp. 158, 162

50. Ibid., p. 162.

51. Of course, in Lacanian psychoanalysis ultimately no one "really" has the power to rearticulate the symbolic, but since I am dealing with fantasy here, I am going to set aside that (admittedly serious) problem for now.

52. Judith Butler, "Crossing the Divide: Phantasmatic Identification and the Question of Sex," paper presented as part of the Gay, Lesbian, and Bisexual Speakers Forum at Cornell University, Ithaca, N.Y., November 6, 1991.

53. For discussion of the decline of women's economic and political power in the Muromachi period, see Wakita Haruko, "Marriage and Property in Premodern History," trans. Suzanne Gay, *Journal of Japanese Studies*, 10, no. 1 (1984), pp. 73–99, and Hitomi Tonomura, "Women and Inheritance in Japan's Early Warrior Society," *Society for Comparative Study of Society and History*, 32, no. 3 (1990), pp. 592–623.

54. I suspect that the fact that *ama* can also mean "nun" is pertinent here as well.

55. "Suminareshi Komatsubara oba tachiidete" (setting out from my familiar dwelling place, Komatsubara). Yokomichi and Omote, *Yōkyokushū (ge)*, p. 132. A reference to Komatsubara does linger on in the *Dōjōji* version of the *shirabyōshi's* travel poem ("the moon will shortly set in the swelling tide whose mists rise along

[the shore at] Komatsubara"), but since the grounds for connecting the *shirabyōshi* with the *ama* have been eliminated, the allusion to Komatsubara is rendered meaningless.

56. Given that the *shirabyōshi* figure in *Kanemaki* is quite typical of how fluid and complex the gender and subject positions can be in Noh, and given that in Kabuki this kind of fluidity is largely absent, I suspect that the suppression in performance of the *shirabyōshi*'s masquerade as a man might also be symptomatic of an increasing rigidity in the theatrical representation of gender roles in the Edo period, a rigidity which itself would be symptomatic of women's decreasing economic and social importance at elite levels.

57. The notion that the bell is a displacement of the bedchamber in the early *setsuwa* is suggested in Matsuoka and Yamanaka's discussion of the relation of the *setsuwa* to the Noh; however, the notion of the bell as a womb is my own interpretation. Matsuoka and Yamanaka, *"Dōjōji,"* p. 91.

58. "Kane ni mukatte tsuku iki wa myōka to natte sono mi o yaku." Yokomichi and Omote, *Yōkyokushū (ge)*, p. 142; Keene, *Twenty Plays*, 251.

59. Itō, *Yōkyokushū (chū)*, pp. 115–56; translation taken from *Japanese Noh Drama: Ten Plays*, vol. 3 (Tokyo: Nippon Gakujutsu Shinkōkai, 1960), p. 86. For an indepth analysis of this point, see Etsuko Terasaki, "Images and Symbols in *Sotoba Komachi:* A Critical Analysis of a Nō Play," *Harvard Journal of Asiatic Studies*, 44, no. 1 (June 1984), esp. pp. 171–76.

60. The doctrine of emptiness *(sūnyata)* and interdependent origination was first rigorously laid out by the Mahāyāna philosopher Nāgārjuna in his treatise *Mūlamadhyamakārikā*. The T'ien-T'ai patriarch Chih-i incorporated it into his doctrine of the Three-fold Truth *(kū, ke,* and *chū)* which leads to the Middle Way: the simultaneous affirmation of both emptiness and conventional existence as aspects of a single integrated reality. This logic, which calls into question the subjective discrimination of reason, necessarily negates discrimination between all dualistic categories, including mind–body and male–female. It thus forms the basis for the Mahāyāna proposition often cited in Noh that "the passions are none other than enlightenment" *(bonnō soku bodai)*, since according to the doctrine of emptiness, there is no essential difference between samsāra and nirvana. See Paul L. Swanson's discussion in *Foundations of T'ien-T'ai Philosophy* (Berkeley: Asian Humanities Press, 1989), pp. 3–10.

61. The circling *(mai)* and stamping *(byōshi)* patterns present in Noh are said to have two main purposes: to purify the space of evil spirits and to invoke the *kami* through shamanic possession. In *Okina* (the Noh purification ritual still performed at New Year's), the initial stamping dance by the unmasked Senzai is meant to purify the space, while the dancing by the masked Okina is meant to invoke the *kami*. Unlike most other Noh dance, Okina's stamping is synchronized with the calls *(kakegoe)* and beats of the *kotsuzumi* drum. The *ranbyōshi* performed in *Dōjōji* is the only other dance performed in Noh today that has this kind of synchronization with the *kotsuzumi* drum; this is one of the strongest reasons that the *ranbyōshi* is thought to have been originally developed by *shirabyōshi* dancers as a ritual purification dance. For more on the relationship between shamanistic dance ritual and the development of Noh, see Monica Bethe, "Okina: An Interview with Takabayashi Kōji" in *Mime Journal: Nō/Kyōgen Masks and Performance* (Claremont: Pomona College Theater Department, 1984); Honda Yasuji, "Yamabushi *kagura* and *bangaku:* Performance in the Japanese Middle Ages and Contemporary Folk Performance," trans. Frank Hoff, *Educational Theatre Journal* 26, no. 1 (May 1974), pp. 192–208; and Jacob Raz, "Chinkon—From Folk Beliefs to Stage Conventions," *Maske und Kothurn*, 27, no. 1 (1981), pp. 5–18.

62. Yokomichi and Omote, *Yōkyokushū (ge)*, p. 137; Keene, *Twenty Plays*, p. 245 (translation modified).

63. Reinier Hesselink has pointed out that there is another pre-Buddhist motive

for the exclusion of women from the dedication ceremony: in ancient bell-casting ceremonies the only woman that was allowed near the casting site was the virgin who was to be sacrificed (married) to the fire-breathing dragon of the furnace. Hesselink, "The Dōjōji Tale and Ancient Metallurgical Traditions," paper presented at the annual meeting of the Association for Asian Studies, Chicago, 1990, pp. 12–13. One might therefore hypothesize that lurking beneath the Buddhist surface of the Dōjōji tale is another pre-Buddhist layer, the story of a woman transformed into a dragon when she was thrown into the fiery crucible during the casting of the bell, and who in the Noh *Dōjōji* seeks revenge on the bell as the cause of her violent death. This would give added impetus to the head priest's anxiety about a vengeful female *onryō* attacking the bell and reinforce the logic of having an exorcism rite be performed by a *shirabyōshi* to quell the angry spirit.

64. Yokomichi and Omote, *Yōkyokushū (ge)*, p. 131.

65. See, for example, the entry under *ariake* in Katagiri Yōichi's *Utamakura utakotoba jiten* (Tokyo: Kadokawa shoten, 1983), p. 40.

66. "Sate mo Dōjōji ni taete hisashiki kane no kuyō kefu to kiku yori waga kokoro mukashi ni kaheru ariake no tsukigane nokoru iriyai no koro mo ima ya narinubeshi mairite ogami mosubeshi." Yokomichi and Omote, *Yōkyokushū (ge)*, p. 132.

67. This might explain why the poetry quoted in *Dōjōji/Kanemaki* often seems to disregard the season (a point which most commentators consider a criticism of the play). For example, during the *kyū no mai* a spring poem is immediately followed by a winter one. It seems to me, however, that these poems were chosen because each contains an image of the evening bell being struck. In *Dōjōji/Kanemaki* the reiteration of this particular image is simply more important than consistency of season (and in fact, the confusion of seasons contributes to our sense that the play takes place in some other "psychological" time rather than any "real" time).

68. Itō Masayoshi suggests that at least parts of *Dōjōji* were based on *Miidera*. The two plays not only share three poems (which happen to be the most important poems in *Dōjōji*); their poetic variations are identical too. And as I mentioned previously, there is a striking similarity on the level of narrative structure as well. Itō, *Yōkyokushū (chū)*, p. 378, n. 5. Most Kabuki treatments of *Dōjōji* depend on *Miidera*'s bell imagery rather than on *Dōjōji*'s. For a discussion of the relation between *Miidera* and Kabuki versions of *Dōjōji*, see Hirano Kenji, "Yōkyoku no *Dōjōji* to *Miidera*" in Sōga, *Dōjōji*, pp. 149–51.

69. "Mazu shoya no kane o tsuku toki wa, shogyō mujō to hibikunari; goya no kane o tsuku toki wa, zeshō meppō to hibikunari; jinjō no hibiki wa, shōmetsumetsu ni; iriyai wa jakumetsu iraku to hibikite." Itō, *Yōkyokushū (ge)*, p. 273; *Japanese Noh Drama: Ten Plays*, p. 69. My translation is based in part on an unpublished translation of *Miidera* by Eileen Katō.

70. There are a number of other plays where a focal point of the plot is a debate between a woman/*shite* and a priest/*waki* over some point of religious philosophy: *Sotoba Komachi, Eguchi, Yamamba,* and *Miidera,* to name a few. Although the goals of their arguments differ according to the demands of each play's plot, each of the women wins her argument by employing the sophisticated dialectical analysis of emptiness and radical nondualism. In other words, for a woman to prove that she is worth salvation, she has to be extraordinarily gifted in religious understanding, defending her position by resorting to subtle philosophical insights that transcend the popular understanding of Buddhism. One should keep in mind, then, that by being exceptional these *shite* actually reinforce the idea that "ordinary" women deserve to be excluded.

71. Yokomichi and Omote, *Yōkyokushū (ge)*, pp. 133–34. This passage in *Kanemaki* is rather obscure. It may be that I am reading too much into it when I explicitly link the "waves/water: *kami*/Buddha" analogy with "female/male," although the context—the *shirabyōshi* arguing that even though she is a woman she should be admit-

ted—seems to suggest it. In fact, the lines in *Kanemaki* could also be interpreted in a more equivocal way. *Shirabyōshi* were liminal figures: women dressed as men, prostitutes who performed religious dance rituals, *miko*/shamans whose place within Buddhism was hard to define. It could be that here she is asserting not so much her identity as female as her identification as a *shirabyōshi* who, like the *kami*, had a very ambiguous position in Buddhism. The lines which immediately follow her waves/water analogy seem to bear this out: "urameshi no myōjin ya nadoshimonaku wa tsuge no ogushi urami kakoteba toki utsuri sekiyō nishi ni iriyai." A translation might be: "How resentful I am! Bitterly cursing the *myōjin* [the shrine's main *kami*] for this heartless oracle in the form of a boxwood comb, the time passes and both moon and sun begin to set in the west. . . ." The reference to the *myōjin*'s boxwood comb-oracle seems to indicate that the resident *kami* has given an oracle supporting the exclusion of the *shirabyōshi*. She is so resentful of this (after all, as a *kami* he should be on her side) that she threatens to call down a curse. Significantly, the curse is that the time has come once again for that uncanny conjunction of sun and moon setting together in the west; an ominous omen of dire events soon to follow. (I am indebted to Tom Looser for directing me toward this alternative interpretation of the link between the *kami* and *shirabyōshi*.)

72. "Enji no banshō wa hibikedomo kono kane wa Dōtei no tsukitaraba koso kikoeme." Yokomichi and Omote, *Yōkyokushū (ge)*, p. 134. This line could also be interpreted as "although the evening bell at Enji has rung out, the [Dōjōji] bell [still has not]: if the moon at Dōtei strikes the bell [here at Dōjōji], will I then hear it?" Here the ambiguity of subject with regard to the pun on *tsuki* (the moon, to strike) implicitly identifies and equates the *shirabyōshi*'s desire to hear the moon strike the bell with her desire to strike the bell herself.

73. Actually there is a problem here that I have not quite resolved. It is clear that the *shirabyōshi*'s masquerade as a man is meant, at least on one level, to help her get into the temple grounds despite the order prohibiting women. But it is also quite clearly perceived by the temple-worker as erotic in and of itself. Is it then the *shirabyōshi*'s feminine sexuality that is being used seductively? Or is it the gender ambiguity of her masculine masquerade that is being eroticized here? Given the widespread practice of homosexuality within medieval Japanese monasteries, this latter possibility cannot be ruled out simply because it does not fit contemporary normative stereotypes. I am not sure, however, how a possible eroticization of the *shirabyōshi*'s masculine masquerade would fit into the symbolic sexual economy that I have outlined.

74. Yokomichi and Omote, *Yōkyokushū (ge)*, p. 134; Keene, *Twenty Plays*, p. 244 (translation modified).

75. "Yamadera ya haru no yūgure kite mireba iriyai no kane ni hana zo chirikeru." Yokomichi and Omote, *Yōkyokushū (ge)*, pp. 136–37; Keene, *Twenty Plays*, pp. 144–45 (translation mine). This line is a slightly altered version of *Shinkokinshū* poem 116: "Yama sato no haru yūgure kite mireba iriahi no kane ni hana zo chirikeru."

76. See Koyama, *Yōkyokushū (2)*, p. 240. One justification for using this minor variation is that it indicates that *someone* was interpreting the play the way that I am. In fact, however, it seems that the poem does not need to be changed for this interpretation to be valid: although the grammar of "hana zo chirikeru" would not normally indicate a causal relation between the tolling of the bell and the falling of the flowers, Yokomichi and Omote gloss this line, "As though invited/seduced by the evening bell, the flowers quietly fall." Yokomichi and Omote, *Yōkyokushū (ge)*, p. 137, n. 14. On the other hand the modern commentary attached to the poem in the Iwanami edition of the *Shinkokinshū* states quite specifically that the poem should not be understood to mean that the bell causes the flowers to fall: "The flowers do not fall because the evening bell invites them. It is that the pathos

[*awaresa*] of the evening bell resonates with the pathos of the falling flowers." The fact that the editor finds it necessary to make this comment at all indicates that this poem has a long history of "creative misreading." Hisamatsu Sen'ichi, Yamazaki Toshio and Gotō Shigeo, eds., *Shinkokinwakashū*, vol. 28 of *Nihon koten bungaku taikei* (Tokyo: Iwanami Shoten, 1958), p. 59.

77. "Mizu kahetsute Hidakagawara no masago no kazu wa tsukuru tomo, gyōja no hōriki tsukubeki ka." Yokomichi and Omote, *Yōkyokushū (ge)*, p. 140; Keene, *Twenty Plays*, p. 248.

78. Fudō, the most important of the five Myō-ō, is especially venerated in Shu-gendō. He is usually represented holding a sword of wisdom to cut down the wicked and a rope of mercy to bind them. Fudō, the "Immovable One," is surrounded by a constantly raging fire that consumes all evil passions, and is therefore particularly appropriate here as the righteous mirror of the serpent who burns with the flames of passion.

79. "Tsukanedo kono kane hibikiide, hikanedo kono kane odoru tozo mieshi." Yokomichi and Omote, *Yōkyokushū (ge)*, p. 141; Keene, *Twenty Plays*, p. 250. The use of *odoru* (dance) to describe the movement of the bell is another hint that the bell and the *shirabyōshi* have a deeper relation of identity and provides another reason why the serpent-woman did not strike the bell earlier when she had the chance. Because she leapt into the bell instead, now when the dawn moon strikes the bell the serpent-woman is struck by it as well, and together they "dance" in response.

80. "Urameshi ya sashi mo omohishi kane no ne o tsukusade ware mi kahere to ya." Yokomichi and Omote, *Yōkyokushū (ge)*, p. 141. There is a pun on *tsukusu* (to exhaust) and *tsuku* (to strike) in *tsukusade* (have not exhausted/rung).

81. Yokomichi and Omote, *Yōkyokushū (ge)*, p. 142; Keene, *Twenty Plays*, p. 251.

82. "Honō ni musebeba, mi o kogasu kanashisa ni Hidaka no kawa nami shinnen ni kaheru to mietsuru ga, mata kono kane o tsukuzuku to, mata kono kane o tsukuzuku to kaheri mi, shushin wa kiete zo usenikeri." Yokomichi and Omote, *Yōkyokushū (ge)*, p. 142.

GLOSSARY

Ama 海士

Dai Nihonkoku Hokekyōkenki 大日本国法革経験記

Dōjōji 道成寺

Dōjōji engi emaki 道成寺縁起絵巻

fumi-shizume 踏み静め

gyakuen 逆縁

ittai 一体

kami 神

kaneiri 鐘入り
Kanemaki 鐘巻
kechien 結縁
Kegon engi 華厳縁起
Kegonshū soshi eden 華厳宗祖師絵伝
Kinuta 砧
Konjaku monogatarishū 今昔物語集
kotsuzumi 小鼓
kusemai 曲舞
kyū no mai 急舞
Miidera 三井寺
mondō 問答
nanori 名のり
onryō 怨霊
ranbyōshi 乱拍子
sashi/ageuta さし／上歌
setsuwa 説話
shirabyōshi 白拍子
shite 仕手
waki 脇
yamabushi 山伏

GOD'S BODY
THE DIVINE COVER-UP

Howard Eilberg-Schwartz

Like other interpreters of religion who have taken feminist criticism seriously, I no longer see things as I once did. Gender is no longer simply one subject among many that intersect with the study of religion. On the contrary, the consideration of gender and the related topics of sexuality, desire, and the body are indispensable in understanding religion. That, at any rate, has been the result of my own encounter with feminist criticism and gender theory. Nothing in the landscape of religious studies remains quite the same. The old questions, if they make sense at all anymore, require radically different answers.

Gender theory centers on a loosely related set of concerns. At the most basic level there is of course a concern with gender—with the images of men and women and the representations of masculinity and femininity. But that hardly says it all. Almost invariably and necessarily, these subjects turn into questions of sexuality, desire, and the body which are inseparable from the basic concern about gender. But gender is not simply a subject to be studied; it is also a theoretical lens, a way of looking at things, a set of questions to ask and certain kinds of answers that are deemed reasonable. It is not just that religion is an opportunity for studying gender but that a gendered analysis of religion is theoretically illuminating. Indeed, religion cannot be fully comprehended without gender as a component of its analysis.

The problem of God's body is one such religious issue whose solution is transformed by a gendered analysis. The question, as old as monotheism itself, is why Jews were ambivalent about imagining their God in human form. Why did they feel the need to prohibit the making of images of this deity, and why did they veil the body of this God in myth? In approaching this problem afresh, it is important to tentatively bracket our most cherished assumptions about monotheism and be willing to entertain a new way of thinking about an age-old problem. What I hope to show is how the standard answer to a very basic question—a question that goes to the heart of what religion is and how it works—can be radically revised by taking account of gender, sex, and desire.

The Invisible God

The question of why Jews prohibited the making of images of their God has preoccupied interpreters of Judaism since the first Greek contact with the Jews, at least as early as the second century C.E.[1] The Greeks were intrigued by these people who prohibited divine images. They believed they had discovered a people who independently had come to the great insights of Greek philosophy.

The prohibition on making divine images testified, so the Greeks thought, to the Jewish belief that God did not have a human form. Jews were admired for this abstract and philosophical conception of God and explicitly contrasted with Egyptians, who imagined their gods in animal forms. It is not surprising that Greek writers regarded Moses as a great philosopher for having instituted this prohibition on images. Nor is it surprising that Greek writers, and perhaps their Jewish informants, singled out the Jewish prohibition on images as one of the most distinctive qualities of Jewish monotheism. This religious practice seemed to embody the most basic philosophical assumptions of Greek philosophy. After all, the Greek philosophers themselves had criticized what they regarded as the naïveté of Greek myths, which told stories of gods who were imagined in human form and performed a variety of humanlike activities. The Greek philosophers, however, found these conceptions of the gods philosophically primitive. If God was perfect, God could not be embodied, for the body was full of imperfections. The Jewish prohibition on divine images suggested that the Jews had come to similar conclusions.

Whether it was Greek writers or Jews themselves who were first to propose this interpretation of the Jewish prohibition on images, we cannot be certain. In any case, Jews found this interpretation of their religious tradition persuasive. Interpreters such as Philo and Maimonides, to name only the most notable, explained the ancient tradition in the same way.[2] And this understanding of Jewish monotheism came to dominate the understanding of Judaism for well over a thousand years and continues in one form or another to dominate today.

But at the outset there are reasons to assume that this story serves very strong apologetic and theological interests. That modern interpreters keep repeating an interpretation with a thousand-year history is grounds enough for raising our suspicions. Moreover, the older interpretation is a classic example of the tendency to spiritualize monotheism. By spiritualization, I refer to a host of techniques that interpreters have used to make monotheism appear sublime. In part this involves the tendency to explain the conceptions and practices of ancient Jews predominantly in theological terms, such as ideas about God, the good life, ethics, the covenant, and so forth. Ideas about the body, sexuality, desire, and gender have tended to be systematically excluded in the modern interpretation of Judaism to prevent it from seeming primitive, as I have argued elsewhere.[3]

The reason for this spiritualization of monotheism is self-evident. Initially, it helped interpret Judaism to a Greek world in which certain philosophical conceptions of God were admired. To package Judaism in such terms made it not only more comprehensible to Greeks but also more palatable to Jews who lived in a Hellenized world. As long as these philosophical ideas about God retained their appeal, as they have off and on until the present day, Jews found this interpretation of monotheism compelling. Modern interpreters are no exception.

This spiritualization of monotheism contrasts with the ways in which religious traditions other than Judaism and Christianity have been treated in Western discourses. A completely different set of questions and interpretive techniques emerged to deal with these traditions. Since interpreters do not have the same investment in discovering deep intellectual, moral, or ethical insights in these traditions, they are far more willing to explore other kinds of meanings in these myths and rituals.

The assumption that Jews found a notion of an embodied God problematic is a prime example of a spiritual interpretation. It assumes that the Jews somehow came to believe in a notion of God superior to that of their neighbors. Not only did they abandon the primitive belief in many gods, but they also realized the folly of thinking of God as a big person. This revolution in religious thinking becomes one of the hallmarks of monotheism that makes it superior to other religions. But there is in fact no statement anywhere in ancient Israelite literature that explicitly criticizes the notion of God having a body. This interpretation of ancient Judaism is therefore just that: an interpretation. There is no unequivocal evidence that proves it is true.

This revolution in religious perspective which Israel is said to have undergone is imagined as an almost organic and natural process. Interpreters take this process so much for granted that they do not feel any need to explain why it happened. They have grown so accustomed to thinking of monotheism as a moral and intellectual breakthrough that it requires no explanation.

It is not an easy task to think one's way out of this spiritual mode of interpretation. Even interpreters who are not committed to the superiority of monotheism have uncritically inherited these biases from their predecessors and teachers. What is required is a willingness to temporarily bracket all one's cherished assumptions and to encounter monotheism afresh. What might we say about it if it were just another religious tradition that had been discovered among some newly found people?

God Sightings

The argument that Jews believed in a noncorporeal image of God always had to contend with one major difficulty: there are several Jewish myths that imagine God in what appears to be a human form. In these theophanies, or God sightings, Israelites are said to have gazed on the deity. These God sightings are generally the privilege of Israelite leaders or religious virtuosi. In the words of one early Israelite myth,

> Moses, Aaron, Nadab, Abihu and seventy elders of Israel ascended and they saw the God of Israel: under His feet there was the likeness of a pavement of sapphire, like the very sky for purity; Yet he did not raise His hand against the leaders of the Israelites; they beheld God and they ate and drank. (Exod. 24:9–11).[4]

There is a second early myth in which Moses is given permission to gaze on the deity from behind. This incident occurs after the Israelites have worshiped the golden calf. In anger God declares that "if I were to go in your midst for one moment, I would destroy you." Moses is particularly worried about the implications of this declaration. "You have not made known to me whom You will send with me," Moses says. "Now if I have truly gained Your favor, pray let me know Your ways that I may know you and continue in your favor." God promises that "I [literally, my face] will go in the lead." Yet Moses still remains ill at ease: "Unless You [literally, your face] go in the lead, do not make us leave this place for how would it be known that I have gained Your favor, I and your people. . . ." Once more God reassures Moses that he does indeed have divine favor, at which point Moses unexpectedly says, "Oh let me behold Your Glory *(Kavod)*!" And God answers, "I will make all My goodness pass before you [literally, before your face] as I proclaim the name Lord before you. . . . But you cannot see My face, for man may not see Me and live."

> And the Lord said, "See, there is a place near Me. Station yourself on the rock and, as My presence passes by, I will put you in a cleft of the rock and shield you with My hand until I have passed by. Then I will take My hand away and you will see My back; but My face must not be seen. (Exod. 33:23)

In addition to these two early myths about Israel's period of wandering, myths to which I will return, various prophets are reported to have sighted the deity in dreams or visions. The prophet Amos sees God standing by the altar (9:1); Job sees God at the end of his long ordeal (42:5), and the prophets Micaiah (1 Kgs. 22:19), Isaiah (6:1–2), Ezekiel (Ezek. 1:26–28, 8:3) and Daniel (7:9–10) see God seated on a throne. The visual content of these God sightings is either not reported at all, which suggests that the appearance is not at all extraordinary or surprising, or reported in an apparently censored version. But enough information is conveyed to make it clear that the deity is imagined in the form of a human figure. Isaiah, for example, sees that "the skirts of His robe filled the Temple. Seraphs stood in attendance on Him. Each of them had six wings; with two it covered its face, with two it covered its legs and with two it would fly. . . ."

Ezekiel and Daniel are the most explicit about what they saw. Ezekiel reports that the heavens opened and he saw four creatures of strange configuration. For twenty-five verses he describes these creatures until, in what is undoubtedly the climax of the passage, he describes what is above these creatures.

> Above the expanse over their heads was the semblance of a throne, in appearance like sapphire; and on top, upon this semblance of a throne, there was the semblance of a human form. From what appeared as his loins up, I saw a gleam as of amber—what looked like fire encased in a frame;[5] and from what appeared as his loins down, I saw what looked like fire. There was a radiance all about him. Like the appearance of the bow which shines in the clouds on a day of rain, such was the appearance of the semblance of the Presence of the Lord. When I beheld it, I flung myself down on my face. And I heard the voice of someone speaking. (Ezek. 1:26–28)

A similar scene appears to Daniel in a dream, an image that is influenced by the earlier visions of Isaiah and Ezekiel. In this extraordinary dream, Daniel first sees four beasts and then the figure of the deity:

> Thrones were set in place, and the Ancient of Days took His seat. His garment was like white snow, and the hair of His head was like lamb's [or clean] wool. His throne was tongues of flame; Its wheels were blazing fire. A river of fire streamed forth before Him; Thousands upon thousands served Him: Myriads upon myriads served Him; The court sat and the books were opened. (7:9–10)

There are traditionally three basic ways of accounting for these representations of God: the metaphorical, the literalist, and the developmental. The first construes references to God's form as simply metaphors, as religious language that is to be taken figuratively. Interpreters who follow this construction point out that Israelites used various metaphors to talk about God. For example, God is described as "a lion" (e.g., Hos. 13:8) and "a rock" (Deut. 32:4, 15, 18, 30, 31) and "a mother bear" (Hos. 13:8), among other things. References to God's human form are also just literary tropes or figures. Israelites did not actually think of God in human form but simply drew on the human body, as they did on rocks and lions, to conceptualize the deity. No one would say that Israelites actually thought of God as a lion or a rock or a mother bear, so why should we believe that they actually thought of God in human form? Thus when God leads the children out of Egypt with "a strong arm" the reference is to the power of the deity which is symbolized by the outstretched arm. On this view, references to God's body are metaphors which describe God's qualities, not the actual form or appearance of the deity. While God is sometimes said to have become visible, God's appearance and essence are in fact beyond human description and comprehension. The references to the deity's body parts are simply metaphors used to conceptualize what otherwise cannot be communicated. This metaphoric line of interpretation, however, refuses to allow for a vast historical distance between ancient Jews and Westerners of modern sensibilities. It thus imposes on Israelites and ancient Jews a set of commitments that they may not have had.

Some interpreters therefore prefer a literal reading. They argue that many Israelites and Jews believed that God actually had a humanlike form. The restraint about representing the deity stems not from a desire to avoid anthropomorphism, as the advocates of the metaphoric interpretation suggest, but from the transcendence or otherness of the deity.[6] Awe and fear of the deity's numinosity are responsible for this hesitation about describing its form.

If the metaphorical and literalist strategies of interpretation define the ends of a spectrum, the developmental perspective falls somewhere between and attempts to reconcile them. From this perspective, the earliest sources reflect primitive or naïve notions of a God in human form. But these naïve conceptions of God were eventually outgrown as Israelite religion developed.

These three positions define the framework in which sources describing God's form are interpreted. They define the kinds of questions that are posed, and they limit the kinds of answers that are imaginable. But these three positions are too constrictive and do not allow for other kinds of questions to be asked.

Those who prefer a metaphoric reading are mistakenly importing certain Greek (and later popular Western) ideas into their reading of ancient Jewish sources. Specifically, they are assuming that Israelites and Jews shared the Greek philosophical commitment to a disembodied incorporeal God. Because of this anachronism, they fail to consider other possible sources of the ambivalence which they detect. The literalist interpretation obviously avoids many of these problems. After all, it represents a break with the Greek paradigm of reading. It recognizes the difficulty of importing Greek ideas into ancient Israelite sources and therefore construes the earliest sources literally. But taking them literally does not by itself advance the discussion very far. For the real question, which the literalist perspective also does not engage deeply enough, is why this divine body is veiled. In other words, interpreters have been so caught up in the debate over whether references to God's body are metaphorical or literal that they have not considered other possible sources of the ambivalence they detect. They have assumed, as noted above, that God's transcendence or sacrality is responsible for the reticence in describing God's body. But because they have been sidetracked into arguing with the metaphorical perspective, they have not freed themselves enough from that debate to consider other possible reasons why this body of God might need to be veiled. The developmental perspective, since it shares features of the literalist and metaphoric interpretations, falls subject to criticisms of both.

This debate, as now formulated, thus is not very useful. Asking whether Jews really believed God had a body is not in the end a very productive question. It leads down a road that has already been much traveled and whose alleys and detours are already well explored. But even more problematical is that to ask this question is to get drawn into a set of questions in which the ancient texts seemingly wish to entangle us. I suggest that the sources themselves are evasive about whether references to God's form are to be taken literally or not. And that is one of the ways in which these sources successfully divert attention from a deeper question that cannot be imagined. In other words, the very ambiguity of these sources on the question of whether God really has a body is a symptom of the very ambivalence that needs to be explained. What I wish to do, then, is reject the age-old question of whether these images are literal or metaphorical. In setting this question aside, we can gain a new ground and formulate a new set of questions.

To reformulate the matter, the important issue is not whether Jews really believed God had a body but why, when they imagined God in a human form, that form was so carefully veiled and why it was veiled in the particular way it was. This question remains relevant whether the images are taken literally or figuratively. In other words, it shifts the focus of discussion away from the nature of the belief to the use of the images. How are images of the body drawn upon to represent God and what kinds of limitations are imposed on their use? As I hope to show, the standard answers provide only part of the picture.

God's Body and Other Private Matters

Averting one's gaze from God's figure, in addition to reflecting a fear of and deference to the holy, reflects an ambivalence about the deity's sex. Specifically, the gaze is averted from precisely those parts of the deity's body that would indicate a human figure's sexual identity, the front and the face. It is the front of the body—the genitals and breasts—and the face, with or without hair, that reveal this identity. It is as if the whole question of this being's sex posed a fundamental danger that could not be faced. The turning of the divine figure and the diversion of the viewer's gaze from the midsection to the feet represent acts of modesty, on the part of the deity who turns away and on the part of those Israelites who avert their eyes.

That is not to say that the divine genitals would actually have been exposed if God had not turned away or the gaze not been diverted to the deity's feet. In Israelite imagination, God presumably was clothed, as is suggested by the robes in the theophany of Isaiah. But because the front of the body, particularly the groin area, is ultimately the most important part of the body in determining a person's sex, the turning of the back, whether or not the being is clothed, symbolically represents a hiding of the very spot where sexual identification can be confirmed once and for all.[7]

This interpretation makes the most sense of the fact that the deity is represented as turning away from Moses. Surely there are easier ways to hide the face than by turning the whole body around? Why, then, this elaborate choreography, if not to hide something else? In fact, upon closer inspection the text not only allows but actually encourages this understanding. The word that is rendered as "my face" *(panai)* is more equivocal than translations suggest. *Panai* can also mean "my front side."[8] When God says to Moses, "I will take My hand away and you will see My back *(ahorai);* but *panai* must not be seen," it is certainly plausible to understand the deity to be presenting the backside in order to hide the divine front side.

Indeed, it is significant that Ezekiel, who has a direct frontal view of the deity, rivets his gaze on God's loins. His description of the deity proceeds from the loins up and from the loins down, rather than from one end to another, as if his eyesight is irresistibly drawn back to the mid-section of the deity's body. If Ezekiel's description is any indication of what other more circumspect texts dared not imagine, it is the deity's midsection that becomes most prominent on a frontal view. Significantly, this vision of Ezekiel is subsequently treated as esoteric doctrine that must not be studied publicly.[9]

The hiding of the face then serves a double purpose. It is itself a veiling of God's sexual identity, since the face itself is one of the prominent places in which this identity can be displayed. Indeed, it is significant that in none of the God sightings, even those that are graphic about the divine figure, is God explicitly represented with a long flowing beard, even though we learn the nature of the hair on the deity's head (Dan. 7:9). We have no indication, then, that God has facial hair, a prominent characteristic of males in general and in the ancient Near East in particular. Indeed, the God El, on whom Yahweh is so closely modeled, is normally described and represented in art with a long flowing beard.[10] So it is curious that the face of Israel's God cannot be seen and no mention is made of a beard. The hiding of the face therefore does not just signify respect. It also hides a part of the body which is a marker of sexual identity.

At the same time, the hiding of the face is also a diversion from a more explicit version of the same problem. In other words, the whole question of God's genitals has been deflected to the extremities of the body and replayed there. In serving this double purpose, the hiding of the deity's face is thus a screen. It diverts attention from the question of God's genitals, even as it veils the sexual features of God's face. The diversion of the gaze to the feet reflects an analogous process. The feet, being at the other extremity of the body, also draw attention away from the deity's midsection. Significantly, the term *feet* is in fact an occasional Biblical euphemism for penis (Ruth 3:7, Isa. 7:20).[11] I am not suggesting that the reference to the feet of God is meant euphemistically in this text, although it comes to have this meaning in later sources.[12] But it does provide evidence from ancient Israel of how the desire to avoid referring to the genitals is deflected onto the body's extremities.

It is also significant that in one of these myths (Exod. 33:13) Moses desires "to know" God: "Now if I have truly gained Your favor, pray let me know Your ways that I may know You and continue in Your favor." As is well known, the term for "knowledge" in Biblical Hebrew is sometimes used to describe sexual intimacy. Moses' desire to know God is deeply connected with his desire to see God's glory, to know God in a way that he has not known the deity before. The possible allusion to sexual intimacy cannot be dismissed. To really know God is more than knowing God's name or the divine nature. Moses has long ago learned the personal name of God, "I will be Who I will be" (Exod. 3:14). Now Moses wants something more. For now the point is simply to note how Moses' desire to know God leads to a veiling of God's body, to a covering of the divine face and a presentation of the divine back. God will not entirely satisfy Moses' desire.

At this point the question naturally arises as to what precisely is being veiled and why. I suggest that what is being veiled is a divine phallus. The ambivalence interpreters have detected about God's body stems from the dilemmas that are generated by the body of a male father God. Specifically, the image of a male God—in particular the thought of a divine phallus—potentially poses a problem for Israelite men. Israel is frequently personified collectively as the female lover or wife of God who strays from God and commits adultery with other gods (e.g., Hos. 1–3; Ezek. 16:23; Jer. 2:1–2, 2:23–25, 3:1–11). But this image of Israel as the wife of God actually hides the fact that the primary relationships in Israelite religion are those between God and individual Israelite men, and it is the men who are to imagine themselves as lovers of God.

The body of a God who is male thus potentially evokes homoeroticism, that is, erotic love of a human male for a divine father. Homoeroticism is a problem only because it comes into conflict with the dominant image of masculinity in ancient Judaism. To be a man in Israelite culture involved first and foremost the ability to father children and to reproduce the lineage of one's fathers.[13] Homoeroticism between Israelite men and a male God, if it were fully expressed, would prove an embarrassing problem, for it would undermine the basic assumptions about masculinity as it was symbolized in Israelite culture. The veiling of God's body, in both myths and ritual, is one of the ways in which this embarrassing tension is eliminated in Israelite religion. For a father whose image cannot be represented does

not evoke the issue of homoeroticism. The prohibition on images is part
of this attempt to avoid thinking about the father's body.

As is obvious, my interpretation of this ambivalence assumes that it is a
male body and a phallus in particular that is being veiled. But what is the
basis of this assumption? Ultimately, of course, there is no way of knowing,
because the sources never imagine God's sex. It must be inferred from
God's gender. There have been two strands of feminist thought on this
subject. One strand, represented by Daly, Gross, and Plaskow among
others, argues that God's maleness is implied by the masculine gendering
of God.[14] A second strand, represented by Trible and Mollenkott, notes
the occasions on which God is gendered feminine.[15] This suggests a basic
androgyny of God. Both male and female are in God's image. My own
analysis follows the lead of Daly, Gross, and Plaskow in assuming that because God is most often imagined as masculine, what is being veiled is a
male body. There are good reasons to work with this assumption. God is
often called a father. Moreover, as Trible herself notes, statistically speaking,
God is more often gendered masculine than feminine.

The interpretation I have offered may initially sound implausible. After
all, it contests a theory of interpretation that has been repeated for two
thousand years. But it is important to separate the issue of plausibility from
the issue of familiarity. The unfamiliarity of an interpretation does not
mean it is necessarily implausible. Plausibility of an interpretation must be
judged against the evidence. And as this analysis tries to show, much of
what we have accepted as true about Jewish monotheism has no more
evidence to support it than the alternative I am proposing.

The question at this point is how to give what is a highly speculative
reading of these myths some further grounding. In other words, what
can make what is obviously a radically different reading of these stories
seem sensible?

Another myth dealing with fathers and sons further strengthens the
interpretation of the myths about God. Indeed, it is reminiscent of the
myth of God turning his back to Moses. In the Biblical tale of Noah's
indecent exposure (Gen. 9:18–27), Noah and his wife, sons, and their
spouses leave the ark once the waters of the flood have subsided. Noah
immediately plants a vineyard and becomes drunk; it is during his drunken
stupor that he becomes indecently exposed in front of his sons. At this
point, Noah's son Ham, "the father of Canaan, saw his father's nakedness
and told his two brothers outside."

> But Shem and Japheth took a cloth, placed it against both their backs and
> walking backwards, they covered their father's nakedness; their faces were
> turned the other way, so that they did not see their father's nakedness.
> When Noah woke up from his wine and learned what his youngest son had
> done to him, he said, "Cursed be [Ham's son] Canaan; the lowest of slaves
> shall he be to his brothers." And he said, "Blessed be the Lord, the God of
> Shem; let Canaan be a slave to them. . . . (Gen. 9:20–25)

The similarities between this story and the story of God turning the divine back (Exod. 33:12ff) are striking indeed. God turns away so that Moses cannot see what should not be exposed. For their part, Noah's virtuous sons turn their backs and divert their gaze lest they see their father's genitals. The myth of Noah's indecent exposure is crucial in making sense of why God's body must be veiled. It supports, in fact, the latter's sexual interpretation: by turning away, God protects Moses from being like Ham and improperly feasting his eyes on his father. The parallelism of these two myths, moreover, suggests that Moses may not see God for the same reasons that a son may not see his father's nakedness.

Unfortunately, the myth of Noah's nakedness does not say why it is so problematic for sons to gaze on their father's genitals. It takes this prohibition as a given that needs no explanation. Ancient and modern commentators speculate that Ham has committed a homosexual act.[16] But I suggest that it is the very act of gazing at the father's nakedness that is considered so problematic. For why would Ham's brothers walk backward when covering their father if gazing at their father's nakedness were not problematic? In a culture in which masculinity is defined by procreation, by the fathering of children, the son's erotic gaze should not be directed at his father. Thus gazing and desiring are linked. And the prohibition on Ham seeing his father is intended to direct the male gaze away from the male body. It is part of the mechanism for inscribing the heterosexual gaze. Furthermore, it is Noah's passivity, his position in the what normally is regarded as the female position, that makes the viewing of his nakedness so problematic. The same eroticism of the gaze is involved in the covering of God's body. For a man to gaze at God is like Ham looking at his father. It is no accident, in my view, that modern interpreters have seen ancient Judaism as embracing a disembodied incorporeal God. In accepting this Greek reading of the tradition, they can safely ignore the same question their ancient predecessors ignored: what does it mean for a man to love a male God?

Constraints of space make it impossible to offer all the evidence that supports this interpretation.[17] But I think I have offered enough evidence to make convincing the importance of a gendered analysis for a theory of religion. Our understanding of monotheism—and indeed, our understanding of what effects the symbol of God has on masculinity—are radically transformed when we make the problem of God's sex and gender central to the analysis. The old myths no longer seem the same.

NOTES

This essay is adapted from Howard Eilberg-Schwartz, *God's Phallus and Other Problems for Men and Monotheism* (Boston: Beacon Press, 1994).

1. For treatments of this initial contact between Greeks and Jews and the way

in which Greeks interpreted the Jewish prohibition against images, see John G. Gager, *Moses in Greco-Roman Paganism* (Nashville: Abingdon Press, 1972), and Menahem Stern, *Greek and Latin Authors on Jews and Judaism,* 3 vols. (Jerusalem: Israel Academy of Sciences and Humanities, 1974).

2. On Philo's view of anthropomorphic images of God, see Ronald Williamson, *Jews in the Hellenistic World: Philo* (Cambridge: Cambridge University Press, 1989), pp. 28–85.

3. Howard Eilberg-Schwartz, *The Savage in Judaism: An Anthropology of Israelite Religion and Ancient Judaism* (Bloomington: Indiana University Press, 1990).

4. I follow the translations of the Jewish Publication Society in *Tanakh* (New York: Jewish Publication Society, 1985).

5. The meaning of the Hebrew is uncertain.

6. See James Barr, "Theophany and Anthropomorphism in the Old Testament," *Vetus Testamentum, Supplements* 7 (1959): 31–38.

7. On several occasions, I have had the experience of seeing a person from the back and being unsure whether the person was male or female. Seeing a person from the front generally, although not always, reveals his or her gender.

8. Martin Noth, *A History of Pentateuchal Tradition,* trans. Bernhard Anderson (Chico: Scholars Press, 1981), p. 258, suggests that "front side" is the primary meaning in verse 23; the suggestion of God hiding the face in verse 20 was added by a later writer to imply that no one may see Yahweh's face.

9. In a forthcoming book, I explore the way in which early Jewish "chariot" mysticism is entangled in issues of eroticism with God.

10. See Frank Moore Cross, *Canaanite Myth and Hebrew Epic* (Cambridge, Harvard University Press, 1973), 16, 35.

11. It may also have this euphemistic meaning in Exod. 4:25.

12. See esp. Elliot Wolfson, "Images of God's Feet: Some Observations on the Divine Body in Judaism," in Howard Eilberg-Schwartz, ed., *People of the Body: Jews and Judaism from an Embodied Perspective* (Albany: SUNY Press, 1992), 143–83.

13. I partially develop this point in Eilberg-Schwartz, *Savage,* pp. 141–76, and in "The Problem of the Body for the People of the Book," *People of the Body,* pp. 17–46.

14. See, for example, Mary Daly, *Beyond God the Father* (Boston: Beacon, 1973); Rita Gross, "Steps toward Feminine Imagery of Deity in Jewish Theology," in Susannah Heschel, ed., *On Being a Jewish Feminist* (New York: Schocken, 1983), pp. 234–47, and Judith Plaskow, *Standing Again at Sinai* (San Francisco: Harper and Row, 1990).

15. Phyllis Trible, *God and the Rhetoric of Sexuality* (Philadelphia: Fortress, 1983), and Virginia Mollenkott, *The Divine Feminine* (New York: Crossroad, 1986).

16. See, for example, Rashi ad loc and Edmund Leach, *Genesis as Myth* (London: Jonathan Cape, 1969), p. 9.

17. I develop this argument at greater length in my forthcoming book.

III.

Transformations of the Body and Spirit in Ritual Practice

ON TRANCE AND TEMPTATION
IMAGES OF THE BODY IN MALAYSIAN
CHINESE POPULAR RELIGION

Jean DeBernardi

In Chinese popular religious culture, the social body of rich and poor, educated and illiterate, is mirrored in a cosmology that ranks spiritual difference as if it were a difference in social class. Many deities with high rank in the spiritual world are humans who earned that rank through self-control and the transcendence of desire. By contrast, lower deities (and ghosts) feel desire and attachment, and for this reason may be tempted to possess spirit mediums in order to enjoy life's pleasures. These images find vivid expression in two major festivals, the first celebrating the principle of heaven (associated with *yang*), the second celebrating the principle of earth (associated with *yin*). This cosmology also informs the trance performance of spirit mediums.[1]

Though I speak of Chinese popular religious culture, the analysis presented here draws primarily on data collected during two years of field research with the Hokkien Chinese community of Pinang, Malaysia.[2] The Pinang Chinese, though long resident in Malaysia, celebrate popular religious events lavishly. I have argued elsewhere that in the Malaysian context, where Chinese are an economically successful but politically disadvantaged minority, the symbols of Chinese popular religious culture express ethnic pride.[3] This interpretation places religious practice within the social field of ethnic politics but does not fully explore the meaning of that practice for participants.

My fieldwork methodology drew on that proposed by Victor Turner, who recommended that an understanding of the meaning of ritual symbols be based on an investigation of (1) the meanings cultural virtuosi provide in exegesis, (2) their meanings in use within a ritual performance (operational meaning), and (3) their meanings in relation to other symbols within a totality, which Turner termed "positional meaning."[4]

As Poul Andersen notes in his essay in this volume, in the study of ritual, description and interpretation cannot be separated. In Chinese popular religious culture, the complementary dualisms that inform cosmological images of the body (yang/yin, pure/impure, gods/ghosts, male/female) are given colorful, tangible expression in ritual performances. However, religious specialists complete the meanings of these images with their interpretations. Thus my discussion draws equally on (1) interviews with a number of religious specialists, including most importantly spirit mediums (who sometimes taught doctrine while possessed by their gods), (2) the observation of specific ritual events, and (3) interpretation of the meaning of symbols in the total field of the festival cycle.

In his later work, Turner emphasized the importance of studying cultural performances, and indeed argued that "experience always seeks its 'best,' i.e. most aesthetic expression in performance—the vital communication of its present essence. . . . Cultures, I hold, are better compared through their rituals, theaters, tales, ballads, epics, operas than through their *habits*."[5] He noted as well that every type of cultural performance (including ritual) was "explanation and explication of life itself."[6]

Ritual is a theatrical medium, but sacred theater, unlike secular theater, is powerful and transformative. In trance performance, for example, the personality of a god replaces that of the human spirit medium. Chinese regard the act of impersonation not as an art (acting) but as a real transformation that establishes contact with the spiritual domain. In a similar fashion, Japanese regard puppet performances as the transformation of inert matter (a sum of body parts) into a "living, moving, and even ecstatic being."[7] Ritual performance reminds the audience that it is spirit that infuses matter with life force and makes contact possible with that vitalizing force.

On Spiritual Rank

Chinese deities are ranked as high or low, big or small. Pinang Chinese regard lower deities as closer to humans than are higher deities, more approachable and willing to help people. These lower deities therefore are more often the recipients of regular acts of devotion and are appealed to for advice and aid through divination or directly approached through the spirit medium.

The most highly ranked spiritual beings in the Chinese pantheon are deities who have never gone through the cycle of life, death, and rebirth. These gods are especially pure, since they have not undergone the polluting experiences of birth and death. They often have little to do directly with the lives of ordinary humans, and for most worshipers they remain abstract and distant.

Unlike these highly ranked beings, most of the deities who are worshiped in popular religion are like Christian saints. They are deceased persons who have distinguished themselves in their lives and are remembered and honored after death. Some have achieved immortality through a life of self-cultivation following the *tao,* and these deities often possess spirit mediums. The gods are placed in rank order on family or temple altars, their rank determined by the achievement of control and enlightenment. In the words of a retired spirit medium, "We argue about high or low. But stages of enlightenment determine respect in the upper realm. . . . Tai Shang Lao Jun [Lao Tse] has reached the stage where he has overcome all passions or emotions. The Goddess of Mercy [Guan Yin] also has no passions or emotions. Her assistants do have passions."[8] Self-control and self-transcendence thus are translated into high spiritual status, while passion marks those ranked lower.

The contrast between high and low gods is expressed in the form taken by the trance performance. In general, a contrast exists between the simplicity and lack of emotion in the behavior of higher gods and the expressiveness of lower gods. In the words of a spirit medium who taught a Taoist doctrine of simplicity, "When the god returns, the medium slumps and the people are called to look after him. If it is a real, 'large' god then there is no slump, the medium simply returns to himself. The more simple it is, the greater the spiritual power. Power is high if it is like this. The lower gods are more violent."[9] Thus the self-control of the high gods contrasts with the fierceness of lower gods. Those turning for aid to the gods who possess spirit mediums often are turning to these fierce lower gods, for these gods most often allow themselves to be persuaded to help suppliants. In return for this help, their devotees fete them with Chinese wine or Martell brandy, provide them with opium or tobacco, and conduct lively temple fairs for their pleasure and amusement.

According to spirit mediums, self-cultivation and following the *tao* was the human path that led to escape from the cycles of death and rebirth. In a discussion of the failure of contemporary persons to follow this path, a spirit medium who taught a syncretic doctrine made these comments:

> You must keep the *tao.* Human beings can come [to earth], and they must return. But today, there are no longer any people who want to return. Those who meditate and go to heaven are no more.
>
> Why is this? It is because people today are greedy for office, greedy for "color" [sex], greedy for money, greedy for power. . . . People cannot return—they go instead to hell. When you are born, you come to earth. When you die, it's not definite that you will return to heaven. These days, all people go to hell.
>
> What is it like to return? You meditate, and you can take soul and matter and return to heaven. If you go to hell, your flesh and bones are lost to you. It's not that you can't return, but you must know how to go back.[10]

This medium also offered observations on desire:

> When men come to be born, they have sin, and we repay our sins. We have sin, and we have desire. This word "desire" is very deep. If there were no

desire, no one would come down [from heaven], no one would desire the world. Heaven gives you the choice of how to make up for your sins. You decide where you want to go, and what you want to link up with. You look and say: "Wa! The world is so pretty!" and you want to be reborn in the world. Good. So heaven lets you link up with a womb to be reborn. Once you have been reborn, you arrive in the world and know the bitterness. This is called "taking the sins." It is the same for everyone. This is called *taoli*. *Taoli* is very deep. I will tell you about it.[11]

Then he described the period of dependency of the child, during which the parents taught the child to distinguish between pure and impure substances (in his example, food and excrement), and took responsibility for the child's sins.

In contrast with gods, ghosts are below, on earth, or in the prisons of hell. Ghosts still have human desires, and many of the offerings Chinese make to them are intended to fill needs similar to those of human beings: they are offered food and wine, paper clothing, and hell money. Still attached to their families on earth, they sometimes disrupt the lives of those who are living and make demands on them for offerings to make their lives more comfortable.

The contrast between gods and ghosts parallels a social class distinction. God images represent deities as bureaucrats, generals, and kings—persons of high rank—while ghosts, rarely represented with images, are compared to beggars and thieves in conversation. The difference also is imagined in terms of a contrast between the purity of the gods and the impurity of ghosts, who sometimes are called "dirt" (in the Southern Min language, *lasam*).

In society, social hierarchy and spiritual hierarchy are also mutually confirming. Chinese may interpret high social status as a reward for actions done in a past life, actions that determined the individual's fate in this life. Ironically, a bad life or fate often leads poor Chinese to "do bad," i.e., to throw in their lot with the dark side of society in order to enjoy some of life's goods. Thus morality and social status appear to be inextricably related.[12] In the Chinese popular religious ethic, nobility of spirit is an expression of the transcendence of desire; plebeian souls by contrast are passionate beings.[13]

The status difference of women and men is considered to be rooted in bodily difference. Women are deemed impure because they menstruate and suffer the pollution of childbirth, and rebirth as a woman is considered to be lower on the karmic scale than rebirth as a man. A section of the *Blood Bowl Sutra* performed by Taoist priests at a woman's funeral expresses the theme of the impurity of the body:

> What are the five unclean things?
> Birth is unclean.
> Intercourse is unclean.

>The body is unclean.
>The ego is unclean.
>Death is unclean.[14]

The text describes the womb that the child must pass through as "an unclean collection of worms, pus and filth," concluding that "this body is not the Pure Land." In the texts of the Taiwanese funeral rites, an implicit connection is also made between the grave and the womb: while hell is the "earth prison," the womb is a "female prison."[15] And as Seaman notes, "[i]t is almost irresistible to associate the ten courts of Hell [through which the soul travels after death] with the ten months of pregnancy."[16] In Chinese religious culture, birth and death are symbolically parallel processes.

When women are impure (during menstruation, for example, or after childbirth), they must avoid contact with the sacred. Hokkien women who have "impurity" (in Southern Min, *lasam,* the same term that is translated "dirt") risk offending the gods if they pray at the family altar, enter a temple, or watch a possessed spirit medium, and such an offense invites retaliation in the form of illness. Because of their impurity, premenopausal women rarely are possessed by gods. Thus the spiritual inferiority of women finds expression in the exclusions of ritual practice.

Festivals of Heaven and Earth

The relationship between status and spirituality also is expressed in the ritual events of the festival cycle. Inscribed in the structure of the lunar year is celebration of the fundamental cosmological principles of *yang* and *yin.* The conjoined dualism of *yang* and *yin* is an abstraction that represents totality in complementarity, and this dualism is often explained in light of the complementary dualisms of male and female, light and darkness, heaven and earth. Appropriately, Chinese popular religion associates *yang* with the gods (who are in heaven) and *yin* with ghosts (trapped in the prisons of earth). Thus the two principles are linked with the metaphor of above and below.

In the festival cycle the dualistic spatial symbolism of above and below is temporalized, and these two principles are celebrated at pivotal junctures in the beginning and middle of the cycle. The first of these celebrations is worship of the Lord of Heaven on the ninth day of the first lunar month, while the second, feasting of the hungry ghosts, occurs throughout the seventh lunar month.[17] While the festival cycle is lunar rather than solar, it would seem that heaven is celebrated at the beginning of the year, when the *yang* sun begins to increase, and earth at the midpoint of the year, when *yin* again becomes ascendant. At the same time, the histories told of the human community's interactions with the Lord of Heaven and the residents of the "prisons of earth" give image to *yang* and *yin* forces.

The symbolism of heaven and earth expresses two fundamental aspects of time. The cycles of heaven represent the enduring, repetitive structures of nature (for example, lunar and solar cycles). Earth, by contrast, is associated with the repetitive (but at the same time historical) cycle of human life and death. Taken together, heaven and earth represent two aspects of human experience: social unity and social (unity in) division. Finally, heaven and earth represent the ethereal and the material.[18]

The Pinang Chinese offer worship to the Lord of Heaven on the ninth day of the first lunar month in a ritual that some regard as the most important of the calendrical year. Families set up three-level altars in front of their residences or businesses, and Hokkien Chinese decorate these altars with tall stalks of sugarcane. In the home ceremony, the Lord of Heaven is not represented with an image. Instead, worshipers face the evening sky, an image of overarching unity in a ceremony which unites the Hokkien Chinese in their memory of salvation from their enemies. In his Taoist guise, the Lord of Heaven is imagined as an emperor, and many Chinese also worship at the temple of the Jade Emperor on this night. Appropriately, in Pinang there is only one temple to the Jade Emperor, who is a symbol of community wholeness.

Pinang Chinese commonly invoke an historical myth to explain the Hokkien use of sugarcane in the worship of the Lord of Heaven. A temple committee member who at one time had been a spirit medium offered this account:

> In the old days, the people were praying to all sorts of deities. The Minister of the Emperor thought of an innovation. There was an Emperor on earth, so there must be one in Heaven. He suggested that they must start praying to him with a tall table. All the other Emperors followed him in doing so. . . .
>
> In the Hokkien community, the province was raided and there was no place to go. The people ran to a sugarcane plantation and prayed to heaven for their lives to be saved. The enemy passed by without discovering them, on the ninth day of the first lunar month. Now there is a thanksgiving ceremony on this day.[19]

In this story, heaven is a savior but has no material being, though another spirit medium in recounting this historical myth added that "the Jade Emperor had greater power than the Emperor: it was he who saved them." Thus worship of an abstract and immaterial god represents the abstract social body of this dialect group.[20]

The hungry ghosts festival celebrates the residents of the prisons of earth, whom Chinese describe as enjoying a vacation on earth during the seventh lunar month. In contrast with the symbolism of community unity and thanksgiving in worship of the Lord of Heaven, the organization of the hungry ghosts festival expresses territorial division.

During this festival, celebrants worship the hungry ghosts both at home and in the marketplace. At home, they make special offerings, and ghosts are distinguished from the Lord of Heaven in a spatial symbolism that represents their marginality and low status. Their offerings are placed either on a table in the kitchen facing the back door or on the ground at the perimeter of the front yard. The ghosts are normally referred to insultingly as "dirty things" (Southern Min: *lasam e mihkia*), and their impurity is described with the same Southern Min term that describes dirt and the ritual impurity of women. During the period of the festival, however, the ghosts are respectfully called "the good brothers" or "the backdoor god." In an elaboration of a spatial metaphor of inferiority, their worship is described as "worshipping at the foot of the door" (Southern Min, *bai muikha*).

In Pinang the festivities rotate from marketplace to street throughout the entire seventh month. Each market area raises money through subscription to pay for the erection of a temporary altar area and stage, and the organizers arrange for ritual performances, a stage show, and a collective banquet in which up to a thousand persons participate. The Chinese offer food and drink to the vacationing ghosts, though these offerings are not made directly to the ghosts lest they should fight. Rather, they are divided among the ghosts by the King of Hell and his four assistants. A larger-than-life paper image (burned at the end of the festival) represents the King of Hell as a fierce general. However, on his headdress stands a tiny image of the Goddess of Mercy, Guan Yin. Chinese explain that the King of Hell is a transformation of Guan Yin, who as a woman is not considered intimidating enough to control the ghosts.

The offerings made to the hungry ghosts through the King of Hell and his sidekicks express the earthiness of the ghosts. In the collective worship of market areas, enormous tables are heaped with a variety of foods, and the ghosts are also offered brandy and cigarettes, opium, and decks of cards. These are all pleasures enjoyed by society's ghosts, the "gambling ghost" and "the opium immortal." The King of Hell, though a transformation of the Goddess of Mercy, is himself regarded as particularly dangerous in his desires.

One Chinese described the King of Hell in terms that might be easily applied to a gangster demanding protection money: "this King of Hell, you thank him, there's peace; you disturb him, then there's no rescue." In 1980, residents in my community were abuzz with the rumor that a baby left briefly on an offering table at the festival had died a sudden death. Many were certain that the King of Hell had taken the child as an offering. At this time, my landlady recalled the story of a beautiful girl who had caught the fancy of the King of Hell when she went to pray during the festival. Soon after, she fell from the ferryboat, was lacerated by the boat's rudder, and died. Her spirit returned, and through a spirit medium she explained her violent death. On learning that the King of Hell had taken their daughter as his wife, her parents deified her on the family altar.

Mikhail Bakhtin, in his discussion of the roots of Rabelais's satire in the

humor of the medieval carnival, discerns a cosmological division not unlike
what I am describing for the Pinang Chinese worship of heaven and earth:

> "Upward" and "downward" have here an absolute and strictly topographical
> meaning. "Downward" is earth, "upward" is heaven. Earth is an element
> that devours, swallows up (the grave, the womb) and at the same time an
> element of birth, renascence (the maternal breasts). Such is the meaning of
> "upward" and "downward" in their cosmic aspect, while in their purely
> bodily aspect, which is not clearly distinct from the cosmic, the upper part
> is the face or the head and the lower part is the genital organs, the belly,
> and the buttocks.[21]

In Chinese cosmology, "upward" and "downward" also express social hierarchy and relative rank: the aristocratic detachment and purity of the
higher deities contrasts with the passionate desires found in the *yin* world
of ghosts. However, there is no doubt that in this cosmological scheme both
yin and *yang* have their place.

Personality and Desire in the Trance Performance

In popular religion, Chinese pay respect to the ethereal and transcendent, but they celebrate the material. This is especially true in the trance
performance, in which low-ranking gods are the ones most likely to possess
spirit mediums. Thus one finds martial-artist gods and bureaucrats in hell
as possessing deities far more frequently than high and pure deities such
as the Goddess of Mercy.

In general, it is lower gods who are invited to possess spirit mediums,
though occasional exceptions exist. For example, in Singapore there is a
spirit medium who "dances" Shakyamuni Buddha, a very high deity who
does not normally involve himself in the lives of ordinary men and women.
Members of the temple committee say, however, that they succeed in enticing him to possess the spirit medium by offering him a pacifier, which
represents a woman's breast. They explain that Buddha was married before
he left the palace to seek enlightenment and that he very much enjoyed
caressing his wife's breasts. Therefore they are able to entice him back
to earth with a symbolic taste of that which he enjoyed most before he
reached nirvana.[22]

While potentially dangerous, beings associated with hell are considered
likely to aid human beings in achieving their desires. As I have discussed,
the spiritual world linked to hell is much like the human realm. Chinese
imagine ghosts as passionate, as filled with desire, anger, and resentment
of those still living. Human beings can tempt these spirits to embody spirit
mediums in order to enjoy earthly pleasures once again. The spirits repay
the favor by responding to requests from those humans who have courted

their company; in turn, they expect gratitude from the persons they assist in the form of further gifts and offerings.

The trance performance thus gives the disembodied spirit a local habitation in the body of the spirit medium. Spirit mediums commonly state that they prepare for the trance performance by fasting and self-purification. To quote one spirit medium: "If you go into trance, you must be clean. You cannot mix with women for three days before, or during the period of the festival."[23] When the god possesses the medium, the medium's soul is said to be "covered" and the personality of the medium no longer conscious. Thus spirit mediums frequently claim that they have no memory of their actions during the trance.

For members of the community, two proofs demonstrate the genuineness of the trance state, and both involve a transformation of the body of the medium. The first proof is that the spirit medium's body becomes invulnerable to pain, and this invulnerability is demonstrated in a variety of forms, including, for example, being struck on the back with a sword or walking on hot coals with no ill effect. The second proof is that their manner (Southern Min, *kuan*) changes when they go into trance. The Hokkien idea of manner is similar to our notion of personality. A person's manner might be coarse or refined, crazy or dignified, and manner refers to such aspects of the person as characteristic ways of speaking, movements (the acrobatics of the Monkey God, the dignity of a magistrate), personal taste in food and intoxicants (cooling tea or opium, Guinness or brandy), an insistence on purity (the Holy Mother) or an aversion to baths (the Vagabond Buddha).

Three examples of manner will illustrate the concept. The Holy Mother, as performed in a trance, was autocratic, demanding, and easily offended. On her arrival at a temple celebrating Lao Tse's birthday, she first scolded the temple caretaker for not offering her "cooling tea" (her favorite beverage), then scolded the anthropologist for taking an unwelcome photograph. As an enactment of her high status, she also insisted on the purity of her surroundings. Consequently, she criticized the caretaker for not being sufficiently pure, and when asking for tea, she demanded a clean cup. When not in trance, the Holy Mother's medium claimed that the Holy Mother was the Jade Emperor's elder sister, a possessing deity of very high rank.[24]

In contrast, consider the Vagabond Buddha, who is commonly called the "dirty Buddha" (though it is hinted that he is truly Maitreya Buddha). His robes are tattered, his hat is greasy, and he is said to bathe only once a year. He "likes to joke" and to "eat black dog," which means that he drinks Guinness stout, known as "black dog" in Pinang Hokkien slang. He also is a gambler and thus amenable to being approached for tips on lottery numbers. Clients enjoy his wit: he takes their problems seriously but also teases them, and his visits are filled with laughter.[25]

The Inconstant Uncle is one of the four assistants to the King of Hell. In the paper carnival image displayed during the hungry ghosts festival, he

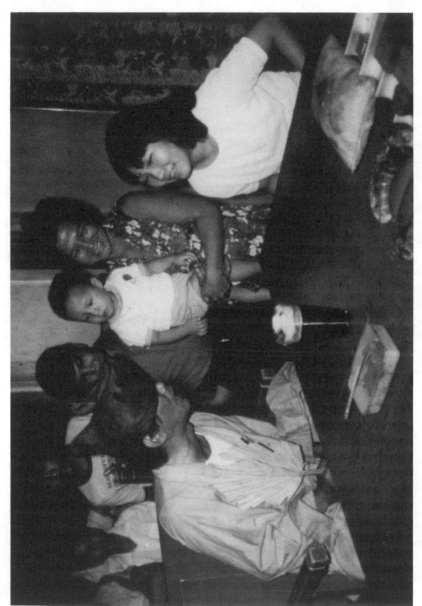

The Vagabond Buddha, with glass of Guinness stout at hand, entertaining his clients. Photograph by Jean DeBernardi.

wears mourning dress and a tall hat inscribed with the Chinese characters meaning "to see me is great luck." His tongue hangs out of his mouth, which Chinese suggest means that he died by strangulation. In the opening ceremonies of the festival, which "open the eyes" of the images, a street committee member smears his tongue with opium, the god's favorite intoxicant. When asked, members of the street committee usually said that the Inconstant Uncle was a filial son, and that prostitutes and gamblers worshiped him.

The stories told of his history confirm that he himself was a morally ambiguous character. A woman spirit medium (whose possessing spirit was Malay) gave his history. According to her account, the Inconstant Uncle was an unfilial son who hit his mother when she brought him food in the fields. However, he had a change of heart, and the next time his mother brought him rice in the fields, he ran to kneel before her. Frightened of him, she jumped into a well and died, and an ancestral tablet floated to the surface of the water. That is how the Chinese came to worship the ancestral tablet. Ultimately the Inconstant Uncle died of grief and was rewarded for his filiality by the Lord of Heaven with a bureaucratic appointment in hell. The spirit medium concluded by saying that prostitutes worshiped the god, and that his heart was very good.[26]

Thus the Inconstant Uncle (a ghost, really) represents both death and luck, and is the patron of socially marginal persons. This is symbolically apt, since prostitutes are "impure" (though ultimately perhaps filial) in their sexual behavior, and thus appropriately offer worship to an impure ghost. Unlike the Lord of Heaven, the Inconstant Uncle once was human. Like the human beings who worship him, he is fallible, but a "good heart."

In Chinese popular religious culture, heaven and earth, *yang* and *yin*, the spiritual and the material, represent complementary components of human society. The multileveled hierarchy of gods and ghosts is modeled on the human hierarchy, and heaven and hell at one level interpret the contrasting worlds of elites and the homeless poor.[27] The spiritual world linked to heaven is a world in which desire is overcome, passions are controlled, and purity achieved. Immortals and high deities such as the Buddha and the Goddess of Mercy have transcended cycles of life, death, and rebirth. Having no needs and no desires, they are in a state of peaceful bliss.

In contrast, spirits ranked lower in the spiritual hierarchy are susceptible to the desire to enjoy human pleasures and thus may be tempted to possess spirit mediums and to help humans. Low-ranking spirits frequently are approached by human beings who are drawn to a Pinang underworld that itself celebrates earthly pleasures—drinking, smoking, gambling, dancing, undomesticated sexuality, and song. The symbolic resources of Chinese popular religion thus link spiritual and human identities.

Mary Douglas has suggested that the human body is always an image of society, and that the relation among parts of the body expresses "the rele-

The Inconstant Uncle advises a client. Photograph by Jean DeBernardi.

vant patterns of hierarchy."[28] It would seem, however, that no single human body is adequate as an image of human society, which comprises male and female, old and young, aristocratic and plebeian. The body combines the spiritual and the material in a balance fashioned by society. Women differ from men both in their sexuality and their relative "purity." Elites whose self-cultivation, purity, and elegance earn them high social status contrast with nonelite members of society who labor with their bodies rather than their minds. Indeed, Douglas linked bodily control, ritualism, and formality with aristocracy and the performance of public roles; by contrast, she linked spontaneity, familiarity, and informality with lower social control and lower social status.

The Chinese religious pantheon provides a complex image of human society in which social difference is expressed through bodily dispositions, in particular through desires and appetites (or their transcendence). The trance performance provides a theatrical medium through which the gods can be engaged fully as embodied spirits with human interests and appetites. Attachment may be suffering, but nevertheless these gods turn back to the world to enjoy human pleasures once again.

NOTES

1. The field research that forms the basis for this essay was conducted in Pinang, Malaysia, from 1979 to 1981 and was sponsored by Fulbright-Hays and the National Institute of Mental Health. I would like to thank Stephen A. Kent and Jane Marie Law for comments on earlier drafts of this paper.

2. The Hokkien Chinese are an ethnic subgroup defined primarily by the Chinese topolect they speak. I follow Malaysians and other anthropologists in referring to the group as Hokkien Chinese but follow Chinese linguists in identifying the language spoken in this community as Southern Min.

3. See Jean DeBernardi, "Historical Allusion and the Defense of Identity," in *Asian Visions of Authority: Religion and the Modern States of East and Southeast Asia,* ed. Helen Hardacre, Laurel Kendall, and Charles Keyes (Honolulu: University of Hawaii Press, forthcoming).

4. Victor Turner, *The Forest of Symbols* (Ithaca: Cornell University Press, 1967), pp. 50–51.

5. Victor Turner, personal communication cited by Jerome Bruner in the introduction to *The Anthropology of Experience,* ed. Turner and Bruner (Urbana: University of Illinois Press, 1986), p. 13.

6. Victor Turner, *From Ritual to Theatre: The Human Seriousness of Play* (New York: Performing Arts Journal Publications, 1982), p. 13.

7. See Jane Marie Law's essay in this volume.

8. Interview with Lim Eu Liang, temple committee member, Pinang, Malaysia, March 20, 1981.

9. Interview with Lim Peng Eok, spirit medium, Pinang, Malaysia, March 14, 1981.

10. Interview with Master Khor, spirit medium, Pinang, Malaysia, January 13, 1981. During the interview, this spirit medium told a poignant story about Li Dok Kwai, the "Crippled Immortal." According to him, Li Dok Kwai meditated on a

mountain and left his body for forty-nine days. He had asked his disciples to come for him on the forty-ninth day, but they miscalculated, came early, and thinking that he had died, cremated his body. On his soul's return, he discovered that he had no body to take with him when he became immortal. Seeing a tattered beggar who was on death's door, he possessed his crippled body and took it to heaven.

11. Interview with Master Khor, spirit medium, Pinang, Malaysia (January 13, 1981).

12. Cf. Nietzsche's observation on the relation between the concepts "good" and "bad" and social class identity: "what was the real etymological significance of the designations for 'good' coined in the various languages? I found that they all led back to the *same conceptual transformation*—that everywhere 'noble,' 'aristocratic' in the social sense, is the basic concept from which 'good' in the sense of 'with aristocratic soul,' 'noble,' 'with a soul of a high order,' 'with a privileged soul' necessarily developed, a development which always runs parallel with that other in which 'common,' 'plebeian,' 'low' are finally transformed into the concept 'bad.' *On the Genealogy of Morals* (1887), reprinted in *Basic Writings of Nietszche*, trans. Walter Kaufman (New York: Vintage Books, 1966), pp. 463–64.

13. Despite this, even very highly ranked gods are sometimes drawn by desire to return to earth. See, for example, the story of Xian Tian Da Di in *The Journey to the North*, in which the god sees the beauty of the world and chooses to leave heaven and be reborn. Gary Seaman, *The Journey to the North* (Berkeley: University of California Press, 1987.)

14. Gary Seaman, "The Sexual Politics of Karmic Retribution," in *The Anthropology of Taiwanese Society*, ed. Emily Ahern and Hill Gates (Stanford: Stanford University Press, 1981), p. 389.

15. Ibid.

16. Gary Seaman, "Mu-lien Dramas in Puli, Taiwan," in *Ritual Opera, Operatic Rituals*, ed. David Johnson (Berkeley: Chinese Popular Culture Project, 1989), p. 178.

17. I discuss the symbolic structure of these two festivals, and argue that the festival cycle orders the syncretic diversity of Chinese popular religious culture through an ordering of space and time, in Jean DeBernardi, "Space and Time in Chinese Religious Culture," *History of Religions* 31, no. 3 (1992):247–68.

18. Ibid., p. 264.

19. Interview with Lim Eu Liang, Pinang, Malaysia, February 29, 1981.

20. Historically the Chinese state monopolized worship of Heaven, in a symbolism that represented the unity and harmony of the Chinese state. This historical myth suggests that the Hokkien Chinese appropriated this prerogative when they directly offered their allegiance to the Lord of Heaven. See DeBernardi, "Historical Allusion and the Defense of Identity."

21. Mikhail Bakhtin, *Rabelais and His World* (1965), trans. Hélène Iswolsky (Cambridge: MIT Press, 1967), p. 21.

22. Personal communication, Vivienne Wee (Sociology, National University of Singapore).

23. Interview with Tan Khee Huat, spirit medium, Pinang, Malaysia, November 4, 1979.

24. In this instance, the spirit medium was a woman; however, the Holy Mother frequently possesses male spirit mediums.

25. See also Jean DeBernardi, "The God of War and the Vagabond Buddha," *Modern China* 13, no. 3 (1987): 310–32.

26. Interview with Datok Yi, spirit medium, Pinang, Malaysia, August 20, 1980. For further discussion of the Inconstant Uncle, see Jean DeBernardi, "Tasting the Water," in *The Dialogic Emergence of Culture*, ed. Bruce Mannheim and Dennis Tedlock (Urbana: University of Illinois Press, forthcoming).

27. See Stephan Feuchtwang, "Domestic and Communal Worship in Taiwan," in *Religion and Ritual in Chinese Society*, ed. Arthur P. Wolf (Stanford: Stanford University Press, 1974), for a discussion of the homologies between religious and social landscapes in late traditional Chinese society. William LaFleur, "Hungry Ghosts and Hungry People: Somaticity and Rationality in Medieval Japan," in *Fragments for a History of the Human Body, Volume 1*, ed. Michel Feher (New York: Zone Books, 1989), pp. 271–303, discusses the medieval Japanese "ladder of being," in which the upper classes assimilated themselves to heavenly beings and the starving poor provided models for representations of hungry ghosts, in the context of a Buddhist theodicy which ratified social difference by reference to karma.

28. Mary Douglas, *Natural Symbols: Explorations in Cosmology* (London: Penguin, 1970). See esp. chap. 5, "The Two Bodies," pp. 93–112.

GLOSSARY

bai muikha (Southern Min) 拜門脚

Guan Yin 觀音

kuan (Southern Min) 款

lasam (Southern Min) 邋雜

lasam e mihkia (Southern Min) 邋雜的物件

Tai Shang Lao Jun 太上老君

tao 道

taoli 道理

yang 陽

yin 陰

REALITY AS EMBODIMENT
AN ANALYSIS OF KŪKAI'S
SOKUSHINJŌBUTSU AND *HOSSHIN SEPPŌ*

Thomas P. Kasulis

As an approach in the study of religion, philosophy focuses primarily on doctrines or ideas. We may wonder, therefore, what philosophy has to say about the human body. The body is, after all, a physical thing, not an idea. Admittedly it is material, and we can study it by empirical observation in an anatomy class. In fact, we often cite anatomical characteristics to define our species. Yet what also defines our species is how we think and feel about this body. We adorn it with clothing, jewelry, paint, tattoos. We shape it with hairstyles, exercising, and diet. We display it in sculpture, paintings, and photographs for yearbooks. This suggests that the body is more than a physical thing to us human beings; it is also an idea, a cultural and personal construct. Like other human constructs, the body is part of a view of reality, a world view. What are the interactions among concepts and values and how have religious traditions influenced them? That is the philosophical question concerning us here.

In this case, we will analyze the teachings of a particular religion in relation to its view of the body and how this tradition gives the body special significance and value. The religion we will examine is Japanese Shingon Buddhism, especially as articulated by its founder, Kūkai (774–835). Philosophers are trained to evaluate arguments, and one of our goals will be to see whether Kūkai's position is intelligible and consistent.

Philosophers of religion do not study only the philosophical arguments found in religious traditions, however. We may also make arguments of our own. By examining the doctrines of religious traditions, we may try to answer questions like the following: what is religion? what purposes does it serve (for society at large and for the individuals who participate in it)? in what senses can a religion (or an aspect of a religion) be said to be "true" or "false," "right" or "wrong"? what does the study of a particular religion tell us about human nature, either universally or as culturally defined in a particular society? In asking such questions, the philosopher may go beyond the study of doctrinal systems in a narrow sense to understand the larger contexts of those doctrines as embedded in religious ritual, community, and personal behavior. This is an important point to bear in mind. Philosophy differs from other disciplines in religious studies not so much for what is studied as for how it is studied. Let us consider a concrete example from a Western religious tradition.

Suppose several religion scholars decide to study the ritual of the Roman Catholic Mass. A scholar with an anthropological or phenomenological approach might carefully observe the ritual forms of the Mass, noting their internal structure and relevance to the life of the religious community. A historian, on the other hand, might trace the precedents for the present ritual, showing its roots in earlier forms of religion, both Christian and non-Christian. A philologist might study the text of the Mass itself, noting how its significance changed as parts of it underwent translation from Greek to Latin to English and other languages. A sociologist might examine the relation of the Mass to social class, gender, and power relations within the religious community. What might the philosopher analyze? She or he might try to look into the ideas expressed in the ritual: the notions of sacrifice, the "transubstantiation" theory that says the bread and wine become the body and blood of Christ, and so forth. In terms of the former, the philosopher might try to determine the assumptions about human nature and God that underlie such an idea of sacrifice. As for transubstantiation, the philosopher might try to understand its doctrinal formulation and defense. What other ideas does it assume? What distinctions are needed for making the idea intelligible and consistent? In the end, the philosopher might even argue whether the doctrine makes sense or not.

Another way of emphasizing this notable aspect of the philosophical approach to the study of religion is that philosophers seldom stop with the descriptive. Once it is clear what the people of a particular religion maintain or how they justify the ways they behave, the philosopher will generally take that description as a starting point for an evaluation. Are the justifications adequate? Are the reasons behind the religious beliefs sound? Is there something in this particular religion that has a universal relevance to our understanding of the human condition? Since world views usually imply ways human beings should live, what relevance does this religion's world view have on understanding the ideals of human community and personal experience?

Therefore, in our philosophical study of Kūkai's religious theory of the body, we will attempt two tasks. First, we will try to uncover the philosophical assumptions in his theory and test whether we can find consistency in his position. This will be our major concern. Our second goal is more evaluative. Does Kūkai's doctrinal position teach us something general either about ways of viewing the body or about ways of understanding doctrinal systemization in religious traditions? As we shall see, Kūkai's understanding of the body is a particularly intriguing one for our purposes. His theory of the body was not only central to his general theory, but also was a way of relating religious theory and religious practice. Let us begin our analysis, therefore, with a particularly trenchant, although dense, passage from his writings.

Kūkai wrote in his treatise *Sokushinjōbutsugi* (On the significance of "attaining Buddha in, with, and through this very body"):[1]

> The word "body" *(shin)* refers to one's own body, the [cosmic] Buddha's body, and sentient beings' bodies; these are called "body." There are four kinds of bodies: the self-nature body, the enjoyment body, the transformed body, and the emanating[2] body. Also, there are three kinds (of bodies): letter, mudra, and pattern.[3] These bodies are in manifold relationships and are like a lamp and its images in [offsetting] mirrors, each penetrating the other. That body is this body; this body is that body. The Buddha's body is sentient beings' bodies; sentient beings' bodies are the Buddha's body. They are the same and not the same, different and not different.[4] (p. 28; Ch: p. 12)

This passage, cryptic as it may at first seem, is typical of Kūkai's theory of embodiment. As an entrance into his thought, it gives us, if nothing else, one vital piece of information—for Kūkai, the term *body* is polysemous. It refers to our bodies and also to the body of Dainichi, the Buddha's embodiment as the cosmos. Body also includes the products of thought, word, and deed—that is, pattern, letter, and gesture. These in turn correspond to the ritual forms centering on the geometric mandalas, the incantational mantras, and the sacred postures or hand gestures called mudras. Yet, as the passage suggests, Kūkai thinks of those meanings not as separate significations in different contexts but as meanings which "penetrate each other" in one specific context. Like a lamp placed in the middle of an octagon of mirrors, each signification is reflected infinitely into every other signification. That mirrored context is esoteric Buddhism, in particular, Kūkai's version of Japanese Shingon Buddhism developed in the early decades of the ninth century. Hence, despite the polysemous character of the word, for Kūkai embodiment is essentially one thing, one simple thing reflected as a complex of interdependent profiles. In this essay we will explore what that one thing is and try to understand its main profiles.

First, who was Kūkai? Also known by his posthumous title, Kōbō Daishi (Great teacher who promulgated the true teachings), Kūkai was one of the most prominent cultural figures of ancient Japan. Artifacts throughout the country attest to his legendary miraculous powers: wooden buddhas that he carved and that survived unscathed the most devastating temple fires, solid rock into which he inscribed sacred characters with his fingernails, and so on. Most striking of all, however, is the mythos associated with his body. If we are to discuss Kūkai's theory of the body, we must first consider his praxis of the body. By that we mean not simply his bodily praxis of more than eleven centuries ago but also, strange to say, his praxis today. According to the faithful, Kūkai is not really dead. He still resides on Mount Kōya in the famous complex he established there, Kongōbūji (Temple of the Diamond Peak).

In Kūkai's era, it probably took two or three days to get from the capital of Kyōto to Mount Kōya. Today it is only a couple of hours by train and cable car. Yet it seems a journey back to a radically different time and place. Despite the hordes of visitors, there are no inns or hotels, so overnight guests must arrange to stay in one of the subtemples, where they can observe daily religious practices. Shingon religious training is well known to Japanese, if not personally at least via television documentaries.

The sensuality of Shingon ritual continues to attract Japanese pilgrims: the shimmering of gold-plated utensils on altars in darkened rooms; the sounding of bells, drums, and gongs; the rumbling rhythm of incantations; the precision of mudras; the pungent wafts of incense; the fascinating, terrible power of demonic sculptures; the geometrical intricacy of mandalas hanging from the ceiling or on a wall. Shingon ritual strikes us today as something ancient, mysterious, and magical. This overall impression is enhanced by a walk to Okunoin, Kūkai's mausoleum.

The path takes us through an extensive cemetery of moss-covered stone tablets among towering Japanese cedars over a hundred feet tall. Sprinkled here and there are imposing yet graceful Buddhist statues. On entering the temple building, we find a dark interior permeated with the fragrance of incense and vibrating with the priests' continuous chanting. As our eyes begin to adjust to the darkness, the golden ritual objects become visible. Yet our eyes are repeatedly drawn to the backlit, translucent white veil covering a large opening at the back of the hall. Later, when we go around behind the temple building, we see that the veiled window opens to a separate, simple hut with a thatched roof overgrown with moss. In that humble structure is Kūkai. Believers say Kūkai has not died but sits in a permanent state of meditation, merged with the Buddha's *hosshin* (Sanskrit: *dharmakāya*), the embodiment of the entire cosmos as identical to the Buddha.[5] Kūkai's body is the Buddha's body. The body of the cosmos is the body of the Buddha. Kūkai interpenetrates the cosmos, acting within it and as it. The faithful believe Kūkai's fingernails and hair are still growing.

Our first reaction might be to consider this belief a quaint example of the archaic and superstitious. It is hagiography gone berserk. We have the hallmarks of a mystic nature cult: the grove of cedars, the shadowy interiors, the earth's mossy reclamation of the gravestones and buildings. Amidst all this is a cosmic resonance between the religion's founder and the universe. Mount Kōya might be seen as the final fortress of folk religion in a society of technologists and business tycoons; it is where Japanese pilgrims can temporarily divest themselves of modernity's cloak and once again live among the naked magic of rocks, trees, and streams. From this perspective,

Kūkai is a Japanese Merlin and Mount Kōya a museum for the Druidic relics of Japan's ancient past.

But there is another side to the story. Merlin left us no books, and if he had, they probably would have been no more than recipes of spells and charms. Kūkai's writings, however, are both encyclopedic and critical. They more resemble the systematic philosophical scope of, say, the *Summae* of Thomas Aquinas. Kūkai organized and critically evaluated all the forms of religious thought known in Japan up to his time. He wrote treatises on Chinese poetry and was a noted poet himself. Not surprisingly, therefore, Kūkai's intellect was as much a factor in his charisma as his thaumaturgy. Even proverbs have recognized this quality: to console someone who has just made an error, one can say, "Kōbō ni mo fude no ayamari" (the writing brush may slip even for Kōbō Daishi). If even Kūkai could make a mistake, we should not expect perfection in ourselves.

So Kūkai was both a Merlin and a Thomas Aquinas, to us moderns an unlikely combination. Allowing that Kūkai is a religious figure, we might shrug off the thaumaturgy as the embroidery of devotees. Even Thomas's hagiographers have attributed to that saint various miracles, but we tend to disregard those accretions when considering his philosophical and theological contribution. Yet if we ignore Kūkai's thaumaturgy, we dissociate him from the social and cultural ground in which his thought took root. To appreciate Kūkai's brilliance, as we did with the golden Shingon implements, we must enter the shadowy hall to see the glimmer. We must allow our twentieth-century Western eyes to adjust to the dark and mysterious context of Japan's early history. If we can make this adjustment, our goal will no longer be to debunk the mythos of the mausoleum but to see the enduring philosophical theory behind it. Whether we listen to him with the paranormal hearing achieved in Shingon practice or through the words he has written in his treatises, Kūkai has, I believe, something to tell us. It is a message not about *his* body but about *our* bodies. After all, as he said in our opening quote: "This body is that body."

To explain Kūkai's idea of embodiment, it is useful to analyze two of his foundational ideas: *hosshin seppō* and *sokushinjōbutsu*. The former is a theory about reality—a metaphysics. The latter is a theory about praxis, how it functions and why it works—what we will call a "metapraxis."[6] The relation between the two generates the multiplicity of profiles in Kūkai's theory of embodiment. In other words, for Kūkai embodiment is simultaneously a theory about what is and about what we must do to comprehend or participate in what is.

Let us begin, then, with the profile of embodiment reflected in our metaphysical mirror. The phrase *hosshin seppō* might be translated: "the Buddha's reality embodiment (*hosshin* or *dharmakāya*) expounds *(setsu)* the true teachings (*hō* or *dharma*)." In his classic essay *Treatise on Distinguishing the Two Teachings: Exoteric and Esoteric (Benkenmitsu nikyōron)* probably written in 814 or 815 when he was in his early forties, Kūkai explained in detail the essence of esotericism as he understood it. The opening sentences establish the key point:

> Whereas the Buddha has three bodies, there are two kinds of teachings. Those delivered by the celestial (*ō*) and historical *(ke)* embodiments are called exoteric teachings *(kengyō)*. Being publicly expressed and abridged, those words are suited to the [audience's] circumstances. The speeches of reality embodiment *(hosshin)*, on the other hand, are called esoteric teachings *(mikkyō)*. Recondite and profound, those words are the authentic exposition. (*KZ* I:474; *KKZ* II:149)

Mahāyāna Buddhist thought generally recognizes three embodiments of the Buddha. First, the Buddha can be incarnated as a historical, flesh-and-blood figure such as Siddhartha Gautama, the founder of the Buddhist tradition in India 2,500 years ago. Second, the Buddha can be embodied in celestial forms, apprehended not empirically but through the spiritual or meditative powers of human beings beseeching their assistance. Many of the buddhas and bodhisattvas of Mahāyāna Buddhist art—such as Amida, Kannon, and Jizō—represent celestial embodiments. Finally, there is the embodiment of the Buddha as all reality. The reality embodiment *(hosshin)* is the cosmos itself understood as enlightened. On this level, the Buddha is generally considered formless, intangible, impersonal, and nameless. For most Buddhist schools, the reality embodiment is an abstract principle, a theoretical ground for the omnipresence of spirituality, what links together the enlightenment of all the personal buddhas. For the sake of suffering beings, the abstract reality embodiment manifests itself as the celestial and historical buddhas. This lends the Buddha a virtually infinite number of forms through which to respond to the needs of a particular audience.

Like the exoteric Kegon (Chinese: Hua-yen) school, however, Shingon maintains that the reality embodiment does have a name and is, in some sense, personal. Both Shingon and Kegon refer to the *hosshin* as the particular buddha Dainichi Nyorai (Sanskrit: Mahāvairocana), the Great Sun Buddha. In making this move, both Kegon and Shingon assert that the reality embodiment is more than a theoretically necessary linchpin for their metaphysics: the reality embodiment is the source and goal of Buddhist practice. To attain enlightenment is to have an interpersonal encounter with reality as the Buddha.

An exoteric school, Kegon does not assert the second part of the *hosshin seppō* formula, however. For Kegon, Dainichi Nyorai may be the personal name of the reality embodiment, but it is still so abstract as to be incapable of directly interacting with us: it cannot expound the Dharma. According to Shingon, however, Dainichi Nyorai himself teaches; Dainichi is the main speaker in the *Dainichi* and *Diamond Peak Sūtras*, for example. Even more important, however, Dainichi expounds the Dharma through all dharmas; that is, the Buddha's reality embodiment expounds the true teachings through all the phenomena constituting the cosmos.

> [Dainichi] Buddha's expounding *(seppō)* necessarily uses expressive charac-
> ters *(monji)*. These characters are located right in the world of our senses,
> the six realms [of sight, sound, smell, taste, touch, and introspection]. Their
> ground is the reality embodiment's three intimacies. These three intimacies
> even pervade at all times the entire world of dharmas. All five kinds of
> wisdom and all four manifestations of the reality embodiment are inherent,
> without exception, in each and every realm of the universe. (From *Shōjijis-
> sōgi, KZ* I:521; *KKZ* II:265)

In short, each item in the universe's inventory is only a sacred letter in
Dainichi's self-expression. The world is literally telling us something.

But how can we hear this message? How can we be intimate to Dainichi's
intimations? To answer such questions, we must consider Kūkai's understanding of the "three intimacies."

> The reality embodiment enjoys the dharma in and for himself. Accom-
> panied by his whole retinue of buddhas and bodhisattvas, he preaches the
> entrance to the "three intimacies" *(sanmitsu)*. This is the esoteric teaching.
> This entrance to the three intimacies is the so-called realm of the Buddha's
> innermost wisdom. (From *Benkenmitsu nikyōron, KZ* I:474; *KKZ* II:150)

The three *(san)* intimacies *(mitsu)* are the corporeal, the verbal, and the
mental. This threefold division derives from a general theory of karma or
action in traditional Indian thought according to which human behavior is
morally analyzed under three categories: action, speech, and thought or,
as the Western tradition has formulated the same distinction, thought,
word, and deed. The logic of the Shingon position is that since the reality
embodiment *(hosshin)* is in fact personal, namely Dainichi Nyorai, it too
must function in these three behavioral domains. What makes Dainichi a
person is his behavior, something an abstract principle (such as the exoteric
view of the reality embodiment) does not have.

We must take care not to construe Dainichi's personhood in the Western
sense of soul or ego identity. Given the general Buddhist perspective of no
ego, we can say that Dainichi is not an agent who acts but the act itself.
Dainichi, like any other person, is not what has a body; he is the corporeal
process. Dainichi is not what has speech; he is the verbal process. He is
not what has a mind but the mental process itself. In short, Dainichi is not
a thing but an event. But since Dainichi is a person and that person is the
cosmos, the universe is a personal event. We can say the universe is Dainichi's style: through Dainichi's behavioral expression the universe intimates the truth of Buddhist teachings, intimates what is innermost in
Dainichi's own being.

This may still be too abstract. To better grasp *hosshin seppō* and its relation
to the three intimacies, we can consider briefly how the metaphysical position is embodied in Shingon practice. Let us reflect initially on the general
principle linking its practice and theory.

If the entire cosmos is simply the words of Dainichi's own expressive style, we human beings are no more than letters or syllables in Dainichi's exposition of the truth. In this regard we are no different from anything else: everything is intimately related to Dainichi. Metaphysically speaking, in fact, there is only one reality: Dainichi's activity. Still, as human beings, our intimacy with Dainichi is special: it must be *achieved*. Both Dainichi and we are *persons;* we are defined by the same three forms of behavior: the corporeal, the verbal, the mental. Hence, as human beings, we can fathom the universe as an intimation of Dainichi's personal style; we can deliberately harmonize our own styles of being with Dainichi's. This interpersonal harmonization is the unifying theme in Shingon practice. As the *sanmitsu* theory implies, there are three parts to this harmony.

For the sake of brevity, let us consider just the verbal intimacy. In many ways it is the easiest for us to grasp and the most central to Kūkai's metaphysics. What is Dainichi's language of intimation? First, we must keep in mind that unlike the historical and celestial buddhas, the reality embodiment does not adapt its message to its audience; Dainichi expounds the Dharma not for our benefit but for his own enjoyment (*jijuyū*). Dainichi's intimations to us are not some revelatory voice calling out in the dark night of the soul; nor are they embedded in scripture or prophecy. Such techniques are expedients (*hōben*) to bring others to enlightenment—the verbal style of the Buddha's celestial and historical embodiments. The reality embodiment, on the other hand, just *is*. A sunset, a snowflake, a birdcall, a telephone pole, a worm, a chunk of cow manure—these are Dainichi's intimations. But what kind of speech or verbal expression is that? Kūkai took up this question in his essay "On the Significance of 'Sound-Word-Reality'" (*Shōjijissōgi*).

To follow Kūkai's analysis, it is helpful to think of Dainichi's verbal activity on three levels: the cosmic, the macrocosmic, and the microcosmic. Let us start with the cosmic. The entire universe is the Buddha's activity, whose reality embodiment—its purest and most universal meaning—is Dainichi Nyorai, a person. This cosmic person, we might say, practices Shingon Buddhism. To the uninitiated Westerner, this claim may seem ludicrous—like saying God is a Methodist or a Lutheran. But let us not too hastily project a Western category on an alien experience. Dainichi is, in effect, a Shingon practitioner because Shingon practice was designed to harmonize with Dainichi's activity. If Shingon is correct—and Kūkai naturally assumes it is—the Shingon Buddhist's practice is the same as Dainichi's activity. So Dainichi's activity, conversely, must be the same as the Shingon Buddhist's practice. The Shingon practice of verbal intimacy is to intone a sacred syllable (*mantra*) or phrase (*darani*). Hence Dainichi's verbal intimation is a sound. What sound? We can hear the sound of a birdcall, but what is the sound of a sunset or a telephone pole? The answer lies in the function of mantras, or as they are called in Japanese, *shingon*.

Of all the mantras and darani, Shingon ritual singles out six "seed mantras": A, Va, Ra, Ha, Kha, and Hūm.[7] When reciting these mantras in the correct posture and mental framework, one becomes attuned to the basic vibrations or resonances (kyō) constituting the cosmos. These seed mantras are not themselves the basic constituents of reality, but by intoning them within the proper ritualistic context, one becomes sensitive to the "truth words" (shingon) inaudible to ordinary hearing. This is the cornerstone of Kūkai's metaphysics: reality as vibration or resonance.

With these points in mind, we can better follow one of Kūkai's fuller comments on the metaphysics of hosshin seppō. This statement is from "Introduction to All the Sūtras" (Issai kyō kaidai).

> The material body is not the Buddha (nyorai). The material body has form, but the Buddha is without aspect. The material body is born, but the Buddha is not. The material body lives [and dies], but the Buddha is inexhaustible. Precisely because [Dainichi] does not have a material body, he is the Buddha. This material body is just the expedient manifestation of the historical embodiment and celestial embodiment. We call them the fulfilled material body, that is, the "wondrous material body" (myōshikishin).[8] This wondrous material body is the Buddha, that is, the reality embodiment. The reality embodiment embraces all things (dharmas) and is neither born nor extinguished, neither comes nor goes. Thus, we call it the "fulfilled material body."
>
> The Nirvana Sūtra (Nehankyō) says: "The Buddha is the dharmas; the dharmas are the Buddha." The interpretation is that the Buddha's body is the reality embodiment [literally, the "dharma-body"]. [The Kongō hannya kyō says that] "As the dharmas, the Buddha cannot expound, so we call this 'expounding dharmas' (seppō)." The interpretation is that in terms of the five constituents of the physical body, there are things taught. In terms of the reality embodiment itself, however, the reality embodiment orders all dharmas. This is called "expounding dharmas" (seppō). Another interpretation is that if we speak from the secular standpoint, this is the "reality embodiment expounds the Dharma" (hosshin seppō). But this expounding is just between the Buddha and the Buddha: Dainichi deigns to let it be known to us. The Abhidharma and Mahāyāna Buddhists have no knowledge of this. In people's minds, there is the distinction between high and low, but the way of the Buddha has neither. For the reality embodiment, consciousness is and always has been unproduced. Why then are there all these views? The way of the Buddha is not remote. It is just a matter of changing one's outlook. (KZ I:853–54; KKZ III:536–38)

Let us consider the above passage point by point. The first paragraph discusses what we could call the incarnation theory of Shingon buddhology. As the absolute, Dainichi himself cannot be simply material but must be what is behind the material, making the material what it is. Still, Dainichi materializes as celestial and historical buddhas, fulfilling (gusoku) them and making them wondrous (myō). In so doing, the reality embodiment identifies with the celestial and historical embodiments: "the wondrous material body is . . . the reality embodiment." The entire universe is embraced by this physicalized spirit.

If we follow this position through to its logical conclusion, the general embodiment theory of Mahāyāna must be radically reformulated: there can be only one body (the reality embodiment) and all other forms are simply the physical manifestations of this one body. For this reason, as in the quote from *Sokushinjōbutsugi* that opened this essay, Kūkai often referred to the "fourfold reality embodiment" *(shishu hosshin)* rather than the triple embodiment theory. According to this formulation, there is only one Buddha embodiment, but it has four forms. First, there is the reality embodiment standing alone as itself, the so-called "self-nature reality embodiment" *(jishō hosshin)*. Second, there are the celestial embodiments, the "enjoying reality embodiment" *(juyū hosshin)*. Third, there are the historical embodiments, the "transformed reality embodiment" *(henge hosshin)*. These three forms of the reality embodiment closely parallel the three kinds of bodies in the triple body theory. The fourth form suggests the distinctively esoteric twist: there is the universal form of Dainichi as everything not recognizable as a buddha. This is the so-called "emanating reality embodiment" *(tōru hosshin)*.[9]

What is the significance of this esoteric fourfold reality embodiment theory as distinguished from the standard exoteric triple body theory? This brings us to the main point in the second paragraph of the quotation. "The Buddha is the dharmas; the dharmas are the Buddha." In interpreting this passage, the primary sense of *dharmas* is "phenomena." All phenomena are equated with the Buddha and vice versa, in effect, a restatement of the meaning of the fourth form of the reality embodiment. In such a characterization all residue of transcendence is removed. The cosmos, at this moment, is the Buddha. Furthermore, as the Buddha, all phenomena themselves are the true expressions ("dharma" in another sense) of Buddhism. The Buddha is present here and now in every item of the cosmos, in everything available to us. We do not need to know something higher or deeper. This is the gist of the Shingon position, what the exoteric Buddhists do not grasp: "In people's minds, there is the distinction between high and low; but the way of the Buddha has neither."

Why is the Shingon vision of reality so hard to accept? Why do exoteric Buddhists not see that the world is the Buddha's teaching the Dharma (true doctrines) as the dharmas (phenomena)? Because when Dainichi teaches as the reality embodiment itself, Dainichi is expounding the dharmas not for us but for himself. Dainichi is making no explicit effort to communicate with us directly. (To the extent Dainichi does so, Dainichi is embodied as one of the celestial or historical buddhas, not as the reality buddha.)

Still, we are not left completely in the dark: "Dainichi deigns to let it be known to us." Although Dainichi does not communicate explicitly with us, he does let us read his intimations. Once initiated into the style of the universe, we can intimately know Dainichi's preaching. Through Shingon practice, through participation in the three Shingon intimacies, one can learn to read Dainichi's embodiment language, to see the entire universe as an intimate expression of enlightenment's act. This intimate vision of the cosmos is depicted in the two main mandalas associated with Shingon Buddhism.

The Sanskrit term *maṇḍala* (Japanese, *mandara*) means "circle," an appropriate one given the basic shape of mandalas: sets of circles, either concentric or juxtaposed within squared-off areas. In ancient Indian religious life whence the tradition evolved, mandalas were drawn as central places for the deities to locate themselves during rituals. In the Shingon tradition, the circles generally contain either images of buddhas or sacred letters. Shingon scholars often interpret the etymology of the word *mandala* to mean "possessing *(la)* the essence *(maṇḍa)*." The essence of what? Of the universe as the manifestation of Dainichi Buddha.

Shingon is known as a dual mandala *(ryōbu mandara)* form of esotericism.[10] For our purposes we can understand the first mandala, the *taizō*, to be a metaphysical depiction, in effect an expression of *hosshin seppō*. The term *taizō* (Sanskrit, *garbha*) means "womb," "embryo," or "matrix." The mandala, therefore, takes us into the innermost, most intimate structure of the universe, the source of everything. In effect, the mandala pictorially expresses the procreative, or more precisely emanative, function of the reality embodiment.

The Womb Mandala has the general configuration shown in figure 1. In each of the boxes are various pantheons of celestial buddhas emanating outward from the central square in which Dainichi is surrounded by his retinue of celestial buddhas. Each of the buddhas depicted (and the paintings may show hundreds) has his or her own specific symbolic connotations: posture, sacred hand gesture, and color. Visualization of the mandala is part of the Shingon meditative practice.

The structure of the Womb Mandala is a matter of almost infinite detail. Paintings are mere suggestions of the real mandala envisioned in years of esoteric practice under the tutelage of a master. For our purposes, a detailed exposition is not necessary. The significance for our interest in Kūkai is to know that this scheme intimates the resonance of Dainichi's enlightened activity as embodied specifically by the celestial buddhas, but ultimately by the entire cosmos. While chanting mantras, gesturing in mudras—each associated with various buddhas—one visualizes the entire scheme of reality emanating from Dainichi's activity at the center of the Womb Mandala. Hence the mandala is said to express the metaphysical principle *(ri)* of reality. The configuration of reality emanates concentrically outward from the center of the mandala where Dainichi resides.

But since Shingon Buddhism is a dual mandala tradition, any account of its mandalic view of reality should include some discussion of the other central mandala, the Diamond Mandala *(kongō mandara)*. Whereas the Womb Mandala represents the metaphysical principle, the Diamond Mandala depicts the attainment of wisdom *(chi)*, the dynamics of Shingon prac-

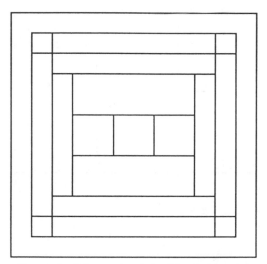

Figure 1. Schematic of the Womb Mandala.

tice. In other words, whereas the Womb Mandala is metaphysical as a schematic of reality, the Diamond Mandala is metapractical as a schematic of Shingon practice.

Like the Womb Mandala, the Diamond Mandala has multitudinous clusters of celestial buddhas and bodhisattvas, but unlike the Womb Mandala's concentric organization, the Diamond Mandala is interpreted as a spiral symbolizing the function of empowerment *(kaji)* in practice (see figure 2). Each aspect of Shingon practice has its place in the map of reality depicted by the mandala. Dainichi Nyorai is again at the center and the Buddha's empowerment moves clockwise around the mandala, starting at the middle (frame 1), proceeding downward (frame 2), and spiraling until reaching the lower right corner (frame 9). Conversely, from the practitioner's standpoint, the approach to Dainichi is counterclockwise, moving from frame 9 to frame 1 at the center. The configuration of the Diamond Mandala is based in the *Diamond Peak Sūtra* instead of the *Dainichi Sūtra*.

In short, the Diamond Mandala portrays the dynamics of Shingon practice. On one hand, the practitioner undergoes the practices of the three mysteries in order to reach the center of reality—Dainichi. On the other hand, the empowerment of the practice can also be seen as emanating from Dainichi and engulfing the practitioner's activity. After all, enlightened activity is ultimately Dainichi's enactment.

The principle behind the Diamond Mandala is obviously an interdependence of the embodied activity of Dainichi and the Shingon Buddhist practitioner. Whereas the Diamond Mandala depicts the metapraxis of embodiment in schematic form, the philosophical expression of the same point is in Kūkai's theory of *sokushinjōbutsu*. Let us turn our attention now to that theory.

5	6	7
4	1	8
3	2	9

Figure 2. Schematic of the Diamond Mandala.

Kūkai learned the principle of *sokushinjōbutsu*, as he learned *hosshin seppō*, in China, but he gave it his own emphasis, especially in his later years. As *hosshin seppō* explains the metaphysical profile of embodiment, *sokushinjō-butsu* articulates the metapractical profile. *Hosshin seppō* characterizes the structure of embodiment behind *(meta)* events *(physis)*, whereas *sokushinjō-butsu* characterizes the structure of embodiment behind *(meta)* practice *(praxis)*.

Shingon commentaries on Kūkai have found it convenient to explain his interpretation of *sokushinjōbutsu* in terms of three different ways to read the phrase. First, it means *sunawachi mi nareru butsu*, "this body in itself is the fulfilled Buddha." This is sometimes called the interpretation in terms of essence *(tai)* or "inherence of principle" *(rigu)*. The point is that self and Buddha are ontologically inseparable. The second reading of *sokushinjō-butsu* is *mi ni sokushite butsu to naru*, "I become the Buddha through my own body." This is the interpretation in terms of aspect *(sō)* or empowerment *(kaji)*. Although essentially one with Dainichi, I must participate in his empowerment to unify the outward aspects of self and Buddha. In other words, although I am always part of Dainichi's activity metaphysically, I can only experientially recognize this unity through embodied practice. Finally, *sokushinjōbutsu* is also read *sumiyaka ni mi butsu to naru*, "the body immediately becomes the Buddha." This is considered the interpretation from the standpoint of function *(yū)* or manifestation *(kendoku)*. My own actions, insofar as they have been identified through practice with Dai-nichi's actions, are manifestly enlightened. Through my own style, I mani-fest Dainichi's style.

Although the three readings of *sokushinjōbutsu* are not Kūkai's own exegesis, they do capture well the gist of his teaching. In particular, Kūkai emphasized this phrase as a way of affirming three major points. First, contrary to the teachings of some exoteric Buddhist schools that maintain enlightenment is available to us only after eons of lifetimes spent in assiduous practice, Kūkai wished to affirm that enlightenment can be attained by any of us in this very body, that is, in this present lifetime. In this regard, Shingon belongs to the Buddhist traditions emphasizing enlightenment as a sudden and complete, rather than gradual and cumulative, reversal of the ordinary understanding of experience. Enlightenment is available to everyone at any time.

Second, enlightenment is attainable to us in this embodiment because Dainichi is embodied right now as this world, including our very own bodies. As the quote opening this essay stated, "The word 'body' *(shin)* refers to one's own body, the [cosmic] Buddha's body, and sentient beings' bodies. . . ." In fact, Kūkai even claimed that our bodies, like Dainichi, are the six great elements: "Wherever the six great elements reach, that is my body" (*KZ* 6:758). Hence there is an identification between a person's enlightened body and the universe as the enlightened body of Dainichi.

Third, Shingon praxis is the path to identification with the Buddha. In "On the Significance of *Sokushin jōbutsu*," Kūkai quoted from the *Dainichi Sūtra:*

> Without abandoning this body,
> One attains supernatural power over the objective world,
> Wanders freely in the state of the great void.
> And, moreover, accomplishes the Bodily mystery *(shin himitsu)*. . . .
> If you want to enter Perfection (Siddhi) in this life,
> Comply with (you Buddha's) empowerment and contemplate on it.
> After receiving the Mantra (of your Buddha) personally from your
>   reverend teacher,
> Meditate on it until you become united with it. Then you will attain
>   Perfection. (P. 17 Ch: p. 4)

From such passages we can surmise that in Kūkai's theory, "body" *(shin)* is not equivalent to our Western sense of body as separate or distinguished from the mind. Consciousness *(shiki)*, for example, is one of the six great elements *(rokudai)* with which Kūkai identifies the body in *Sokushinjōbutsugi*. In earlier works, Kūkai referred to the five, not six, great elements, omitting the element of consciousness. Yet in the work in which he identified the idea that "this very body" is the Buddha, it is striking that he felt the need to expand the list of elements to include consciousness. This expansion of the list of elements also led him to extend the list of seed mantras, since each mantra is correlated with a single element. He added the seed mantra *Hūm*, itself the subject of another of his traditionally most respected treatises, *Unjigi* (Significance of the word *Hūm*).

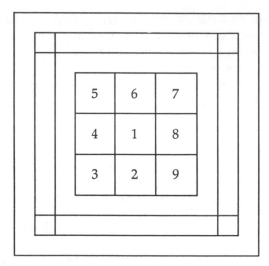

Figure 3. Schematic of the Dual Mandala.

Admittedly, in Kūkai's theory of the three intimacies the corporeal *(shin)* is distinguishable from the mental *(i* or *shin)* and the verbal *(go* or *ko)*. Yet Kūkai also claims that the three intimacies are continuous, not discrete. In fact, the later Shingon tradition sometimes refers to the theory of *sanmitsu soku ichimitsu* (the three intimacies as single intimacy) and *ichimitsu soku sanmitsu* (the single intimacy as three intimacies).

Furthermore, as we saw in our discussion of the passage on *hosshin seppō* from the treatise "Introduction to All the Sūtras," Kūkai explicitly said that "the material body is not the Buddha." Dainichi's embodiment of enlightenment as the three intimacies is what lies behind all physical, mental, and verbal phenomena. It cannot be reduced to any one of the three.

In discussing the nature of the body, we have found it useful to discuss *hosshin seppō* and *sokushinjōbutsu* together. We have indeed treated them as two profiles of the same theory of enlightenment. If we are justified in having the two theories interact in this way, it would follow that the two mandalas can be similarly superimposed on each other, just as the images of the lamp interpenetrate in the mirrors. Indeed, this is the case. Shingon is not simply a twin mandala theory; it also uses the Dual Mandala as one of its key schematic representations. If we look at the geometric structure of the Dual Mandala, we can see that it represents the insertion of the Diamond Mandala into the heart of the Womb Mandala. The common point between them is, of course, the central image of Dainichi (see figure 3, box 1).

Kūkai's philosophical insight behind this development is that in any religious system, the theory of reality (the metaphysics) must correlate with the theory of practice (the metapraxis). Both are, in the end, reflections of the praxis itself. Resorting again to the image of the lamp and the mirrors, we can say that at the heart of Shingon (and probably any religious tradition) is praxis. The praxis inherently raises questions in the minds of practitioners. This leads to philosophical reflection. Some of the reflections are metaphysical: what is the object of my religious concern? in performing this praxis, what realities am I affirming as real? how do those realities relate to the realities I affirm in my nonreligious life? Other philosophical reflections are more metapractical in nature: why is this praxis preferred over others such as those praxes found in some other religious traditions? why is this praxis done this way rather than that way? what in the praxis is arbitrary and what essential? Kūkai's entire system seems to affirm that these series of reflections cannot be completely separated. What makes a praxis work involves what it means to be human. Yet being human is also part of reality.

The praxis is the common element in the two directions of philosophical reflection. This observation may be generalized as a philosophical principle that could apply to the doctrinal systems of all traditions: The praxis must fit the metaphysics. I could not, for example, be a metaphysical monist and establish a praxis of empirical verification. The senses cannot ground a belief in a monism. Monism requires something like a meditative state that can reveal the illusion of the senses and establish an experience of oneness. On the other hand, the praxis must also fit the metapraxis. For example, I cannot establish a metapraxis that justifies the epistemic priority of trance states and then perform a praxis that emphasizes empirical verification. The theory justifying a praxis must obviously fit the praxis as it is enacted. Finally, since the metaphysical and metapractical theories both reflect the same praxis, the metaphysics and metapraxis must be coherent with each other. They will be different—as no two mirrors can reflect the same object in exactly the same way—but they must be different profiles of the same thing. As such, they should logically be mappable unto each other, just as Kūkai mapped the Diamond Mandala into the Womb Mandala to make the Dual Mandala.

What, then, does this tell us about embodiment in Kūkai's system? Embodiment is the foundation of Shingon praxis. Practitioners voluntarily impose a style on themselves—a style of verbal, mental, and physical action. The metapractical justification for this style is that it mimics the style of Dainichi's action; it harmonizes with the style of the universe. This is the principle of *sokushinjōbutsu*, the achievement of Buddha in, through, and with this very body. It explains the power of thaumaturgy, the ability to harmonize with the universe so well that the disharmonies of disease, drought, and political unrest disappear. In this we see the justification for practicing the three intimacies.

The metapraxis raises metaphysical issues as well, however. What exactly is Dainichi and how does Dainichi constitute the universe? That leads to the metaphysics of *hosshin seppō*. This metaphysics establishes a system of resonances, configurations, and modes of movement—the metaphysical equivalents of mantras, mandalas, and mudras. So the very same praxis that is reflected metapractically in *sokushinjōbutsu* is reflected metaphysically in *hosshin seppō*. As the image in one mirror ultimately reflects not only the lamp but also the images of the lamp in the other mirrors, the two theories also interpenetrate. Together the praxis, metapraxis, and metaphysics of embodiment form a coherent whole. The same terminology—mantra, mudra, mandala, resonance, pattern, and most of all, body—can apply simultaneously to the nature of the universe, myself, and the Shingon practices I undertake. In an important sense, therefore, for Kūkai embodiment is fundamentally a praxis. It can only be fathomed by being lived. The sacred relation between master and disciple assures the character of that lived experience. From this standpoint no reflection can ever capture its richness. Yet philosophical reflections—whether metaphysical or metapractical—are not necessarily false. They can capture accurately a profile of the praxis. Embodiment can be reflected in a multitude of ways. Here we have considered only the two main ones in Kūkai's system, the theories of *hosshin seppō* and *sokushinjōbutsu*. Still, the analysis, however limited, has been able to show us the function of the polysemous term *body* and has reminded us that embodiment is not simply what I do but what I am. In fact, ultimately the entire universe is embodiment.

As a philosopher of religion who works in a comparative context, I will close with a comment about an intriguing cross-cultural similarity. It is easy to think of Kūkai's system as alien, recondite, and—well, esoteric. I do not want to leave that impression, however. Although I will not develop the comparison here, we might think of the polysemous character of *body* in early Christian thought. Jesus sat with his disciples and said of the bread, "This is my body." The Eucharist represents the incorporation of Christ's body into the Christian's own. And Saint Paul thought of the community of the faithful as the "body of Christ," later often called the "mystical body of Christ." Paul also said the body was the temple of the spirit. So, for this strand of Christianity, what is the body of Christ? Is it the physical body into which he was incarnated? Or the spirit that unifies the church into a single personal act? Or is it the bread of the Eucharist? And what of the tradition of the stigmata? Is that not a mirroring of the body of the crucified Christ, the fullest expression of intimacy with the ultimate sacred reality? In this Christian tradition "body" has many meanings and each meaning reflects the others.

If a more detailed analysis would uphold such a parallel, the question now becomes why two such totally separate traditions would have such a comparable analysis of embodiment. Perhaps it is because the body is the twilight area between self and world, mind and corporeality, spirit and matter. My body expresses my style and, in so doing, becomes an intimation of what is most intimate to me. My body is given to me, yet I shape it, move it, and adorn it in my own personal manner. One kind of personality looks at the world and sees a mechanism with laws of motion; another sees an expression of style. For the second type, the impulse would be to coordinate the style of one's own expression with the style of the universe. The goal would not be to understand the cosmos but to participate in it. In one religious terminology, we call this a sacramental view. I suspect that wherever we find this kind of sacramental thinking, we will also find a theory of embodiment not unlike Kūkai's. Here we see one of the benefits of the philosophical study of religions. By analyzing the doctrines of a particular religion—understanding them in their own historical and cultural contexts—we often discover a rational structure that may illuminate the doctrines of other religions as well.

NOTES

1. When simple page numbers are given after a quotation, I have followed—with slight modifications detailed in the notes—the English translation of *Sokushinjō-butsugi* in *Kukai's Principle of Attaining Buddhahood with the Present Body*, trans. with an introduction and annotation by Hisao Inagaki (Kyoto: Ryukoku Translation Center, Ryukoku University, 1975). This translation is recommended for its completeness, accuracy, and excellent annotation. In addition, it includes the full original Chinese text (the page numbers cited in my text with the prefix "Ch"). A good but incomplete and not fully annotated English translation also occurs in Yoshito S. Hakeda's *Kukai: Major Works* (New York: Columbia University Press, 1972). For the Chinese text of Kūkai's complete works, see *Kōbō daishi zenshū* (Complete works of Kōbō daishi), 3d ed. (Kōyasan: Mikkyō bunka kenkyūjo, 1965). Citations of my translation from this text are designated *KZ*. Its limitations are sparseness of annotations and availability (it is out of print). For Japanese translations of the text, one may refer to *Kōbō daishi Kūkai zenshū* (Tokyo: Chikuma Shobō, 1983–85). In the text of this essay, citations to this work are abbreviated *KKZ*. The only edition of Kūkai's complete works in print, *KKZ* also has the advantage of including the *kambun* reading of the original (but not the original Chinese itself) on the top of the page and a modern Japanese translation at the bottom. The annotations and indices are also helpful. In vol. 2, pp. 219–62, Matsumoto Shōkei's Japanese translation of the *Sokushinjōbutsugi* fascicle is included. Another modern Japanese translation with extensive commentaries and notes is *Kūkai's Sokushinjōbutsugi*, trans. and annotated by Kanaoka Shūyū (Tokyo: Taiyō Shuppan, 1985). Still another modern Japanese translation of most of Kūkai's works with helpful notes is *Kōbō daishi chosaku zenshū*, ed. Katsumata Shunkyō (Tokyo: Sankibō Busshorin, 1979). *Sokushinjōbutsugi* appears in vol. 1, pp. 41–58.

2. Substituting "emanating" for Inagaki's "homogenous" to translate *tōru*.

3. Substituting "pattern" for Inagaki's "figure" to translate *gyō*.

4. Substituting "the same and not the same, different and not different" for Inagaki's "not-identical and identical, not distinct and distinct."

5. The technical term for Kūkai's present status is *nyūjō* (entrance into meditation). In his *Kōbō Daishi no nyūjōron* (A perspective on Kōbō Daishi's *nyūjō*), Morita Ryūsen brought the techniques of modern scholarship to bear on the history and doctrinal significance of this phenomenon. On the development of the Kūkai mythos, see also Joseph M. Kitagawa, *On Understanding Japanese Religion* (Princeton: Princeton University Press, 1987), pp. 182–202. Mummification of noted religious figures is not limited in East Asia to Shingon Buddhism. See the excellent discussion in Bernard Faure's "Substitute Bodies in Chan/Zen Buddhism" in this volume. Since our concern here is philosophical rather than phenomenological, however, our goal

in this essay is to see this phenomenon within the context of Kūkai's philosophical system. In what ways is such practice understandable in terms of Kūkai's doctrines about the body?

6. For a fuller discussion of my use of the term *metapraxis,* see my "Philosophy as Metapraxis," in Frank Reynolds and David Tracy, eds., *Discourse and Practice* (Albany: State University of New York Press, 1992), pp. 169–95.

7. In Kūkai's earlier works, only five such seed mantras are listed. The significance of adding the sixth mantra is discussed later in this essay.

8. In this concept of the "wondrous material body," we find a sharp contrast between Kūkai's (Mahāyāna-influenced) Buddhist view and that of the Southern Buddhist traditions. In Theravāda Buddhism, the "body" was usually understood simply as the material body *(rūpa).* As such, that tradition has typically emphasized its impermanence and its inappropriateness as an object for desire. See, for example, the two essays in this volume dealing insightfully with that tradition, by Sue Hamilton and Elizabeth Wilson. Once we introduce the Mahāyāna Buddhist theories of the triple or fourfold body of the Buddha, however, the material body can be transfigured into an emanation of the cosmic, spiritual ground—the *hosshin.* Hence it becomes a *wondrous* material body.

9. For a brief discussion of the threefold and fourfold theories of the Buddha's embodiment, see Kanaoka Shūyū, *Kūkai jiten* (Kūkai dictionary) (Tokyo: Tōkyōdō Shuppan, 1979), p. 191.

10. For further discussion of the philosophical theory behind the Shingon use of mandalas, see either chap. 6 of Taikō Yamazaki's *Shingon: Japanese Esoteric Buddhism,* trans. and adapted by Richard and Cynthia Peterson, ed. Yasuyoshi Morimoto and David Kidd (Boston: Shambhala, 1988), or chap. 4 of Minoru Kiyota, *Shingon Buddhism: Theory and Practice* (Los Angeles: Buddhist Books International, 1978). Both books give useful detail about Shingon doctrines and practices.

GLOSSARY

Benkenmitsu nikyōron 辯顯密二教論
Dainichi Nyorai 大日如來
gusoku 具足
henge hosshin 變化法身
hosshin seppō 法身説法
ichimitsu soku sanmitsu 一密即三密
Issai kyō kaidai 一切經解題
jishō hosshin 自性法身
kaji 加持
Kegon 華嚴
kendoku 顯得

kongō mandara 金剛曼荼羅

Kongō hannya kyō 金剛般若經

Kūkai 空海

kyō 響

mi ni sokushite butsu to naru 身に即して佛と成る。

monji 文字

myō 妙

myōshikishin 妙色身

nyorai 如來

nyūjō 入定

ri 理

rokudai 六大

ryōbu mandara 兩部曼荼羅

sanmitsu 三密

sanmitsu soku ichimitsu 三密即一密

shiki 識

Shingon 真言

shishu hosshin 四種法身

Shōjijissōgi 聲字實相義

sō 相

sokushin jōbutsu 即身成佛

Sokushinjōbutsugi 即身成佛義

taizō 胎藏

tōru hosshin 等流法身

Unjigi 吽字義

yū 用

THE TRANSFORMATION OF THE BODY IN TAOIST RITUAL

Poul Andersen

This essay in the hermeneutics of Taoist ritual focuses on the *jiao* liturgy in Taiwan to reveal a fascinating case of body symbolism and transformation. Its method is both comparative and historical, in the sense that several variants of the same rite—derived from different liturgical traditions and in some cases from disparate geographical areas—are considered in order to elicit what appears to be the essential and historically more original meaning of the rite, a meaning that may be absent from the interpretations of the priests practicing the rite today, though traces of this meaning are found in the texts they use. At the same time I emphasize the role of the interpretations of the priests in ritual performance and ritual change. The essay's sources derive mainly from ritual texts and oral explanations pertaining to the *jiao* liturgy, and the point of departure is the surviving forms of this liturgy in present-day Taiwan. References are also made to related elements found within forms of ritual theater in the same area.

The *jiao* Liturgy

The Chinese word *jiao* means "offering," but it is used specifically as the technical term for the large-scale ceremonies, lasting several days, performed by Taoist priests in Chinese communities on behalf of the people of these communities. Forms of this liturgy have been preserved in Taiwan, Hong Kong, and parts of Southeast Asia; in recent years they have also begun to reappear in Fujian and other parts of the People's Republic of China. In Taiwan a classical *jiao* is presided over by a priest of the Zhengyi tradition who is hired for the occasion. He is accompanied by a group of assistant priests and musicians to carry out a comprehensive program of rituals in the temple of the local tutelary god. The inside of the temple is rearranged for the occasion; the place of honor normally occupied by the tutelary god is ceded to the supreme Taoist deities, who are made present by the priests. Only a handful of selected representatives of the community may participate in these rites within the temple, the space within the temple having been designated as a closed, sacred area during the event. Outside the temple, however, there are simultaneous performances by other religious practitioners, notably local exorcists and spirit mediums who are possessed by the spirit of the tutelary god. There is a large variety of theatrical performances in front of the temple throughout the period, as well as enormous quantities of offerings, including food and spirit money. Processional plays follow the palanquin which carries the figure of the tutelary god through the streets of the "territory." In short, a *jiao* represents a moment of exceptionally high intensity in the religious life of a community, and a time when the presence of the divine forces within the community reaches its maximum.

The whole event may be characterized as a "definitional ceremony."[1] It is the means by which a Chinese community defines itself on the religious level and renews its contract with the gods. A *jiao* may function as a kind of "redressive action" (following major calamities, such as epidemics, drought, fires, and the like), but it also serves as a periodic restatement of the identity of a community. As such, it is repeated at fixed intervals of three, five, or more years. In either case, one of the core elements of the liturgy is a large document written on red paper and referred to as a *shu*, "memorial." It is a prayer for blessing addressed to the superior deities and is read by Taoist priests as a part of all the major rituals of the *jiao*. This document states, among other things, the specific circumstances of the ceremony in question: the name of the officiating high priest, the time, place, and duration of the ceremony, the names of the persons who participate in the ritual as representatives of the community, and the complete liturgical program. In its most complete form the document includes a number of appendices which together constitute an updated list of the totality of members of the community (or at least the names of all heads of household).[2] It thus is a precise delimitation of the community in terms of its population and corresponds on the level of territory to the array of lamps on high poles outside each of the participant households, which visibly indicate the boundaries of the community celebrating the *jiao*.

When asked about the purpose of it all, the ordinary members of the community—who organize and finance the whole thing—will often answer that they do it in order to obtain the "blessing" or "protection" (*baohu*) of the gods. They are aware of the fact that the ritual performances of the Taoist priests—which mostly take place behind closed doors but which are occasionally (especially toward the end of the program) transferred to temporary stages outside the temple—are essential to achieving this purpose. But in general they have little or no knowledge of the details and inner workings of these rituals. Prior to the event a contract has been negotiated between the leaders of the community and the high priest, stipulating the scope and duration of the ritual program and the consequent charge for his services, and reflecting the affluence of the community as well as the importance attached to the *jiao* in question. The rituals constituting a *jiao* may all be performed in more or less complete versions; the forms we shall consider here represent the parts of major rituals that are done most rarely, that is, only at especially "important" occasions. Whether or not the people of the community actually get their money's worth in terms of ritual content is largely a matter of trust between them and the high priest. However, as made clear to me by several priests, cheating in such matters would first of all constitute a serious offense against the gods (to whom the advent of the full program is constantly announced as part of the rituals themselves, that is, in the *shu*), and for this reason alone is utterly out of the question.

Knowledge of the details and specific meanings of Taoist ritual is the preserve of Taoist priests, who need this knowledge in order to be able to give a proper performance. It is embedded in the expertise transmitted from master to disciple (basically through practice and participation), and to some extent in the ritual manuals and other written material possessed by the high priest. The classical Zhengyi tradition of southern China has been transmitted to the present day in Taiwan through the hereditary priesthood of so-called *huoju*, or "hearth-dwelling" priests, that is, priests who have families and live like others, passing on the tradition to their oldest or most gifted son. The same tradition has survived—almost miraculously it seems—in many variations in several parts of the People's Republic, for instance in Fujian, where the authorities today are doing their utmost to deal with the "problem" of this highly undesirable type of Taoist religious professionals.[3]

Over and above the hereditary transmission of ritual expertise, the Taoists of southern China traditionally have been more or less directly associated with the Celestial Master Zhang (*Zhang tianshi*), the nominal head of the Zhengyi tradition who resides at the foot of Mount Longhu in Jiangxi. During the Yuan dynasty the Celestial Masters were imperially granted the monopoly to issue certificates of priesthood, and up to the present Mount Longhu has served as an ordination center for a large region of southern China. In Taiwan the Japanese occupation of 1895 effectively severed communications with the mainland and appears to have led to a strengthening of the position of important Taoist families, such as the Zeng and Chen families of Tainan and the Lin family of Hsinchu.[4] Access to the lore of classical Taoist liturgy was controlled by the leading members of these families, though in actual practice they were open to accepting disciples from other families who would serve first as assistant priests and might eventually establish themselves as independent priests. The basic principle seems to have been, however, that a high priest would transmit the totality of his tradition only to his sons.[5]

The total corpus of written materials connected with the performance of Taoist rituals may be classified according to a scale of accessibility. At one end of the scale we find the basic Taoist scriptures, such as the Scripture of the Northern Dipper *(Beidou jing)* and the Scripture of the Jade Pivot *(Yushu jing)* which are recited as parts of the *jiao* liturgy, and which are available to the public in printed versions that are for sale in any well-stocked bookstore in Taiwan. At the other extreme we find the supreme symbol of textual secrecy, the so-called *mijue,* "secret instructions," a small manual copied by the high priest himself and intended solely for his own use. It is usually bound in pocketbook format, ostensibly so that the high priest may carry it along hidden in his sleeve when he goes to perform a ritual. In my experience, however, the common practice is to leave this text behind and, if necessary, to prepare for any given event by rehearsing those parts of the contents to be used. In any case, it is inconceivable that the high priest would show the manual to anybody, including his assistant priests and disciples, during the ritual performance.

The *mijue* contains the formulas used in ritual by the high priest alone, including the inner parts of ritual, that is, the visualizations and inaudible, "faint" incantations *(weizhou)* executed inwardly by the high priest and complementing the series of visible, external acts performed by all the priests together as a group. Between the two extremes on the scale of accessibility, we find the bulk of ritual manuscripts which guide the performance of the priests as a group. Each contains the text, that is, the hymns, recitations, etc., of one particular ritual, and it is placed on the altar where it is leafed through by the priests as the performance of the ritual in question progresses. Like the *mijue,* the ritual manuscripts are usually copied by the high priest himself at his ordination, but they are guarded with far less secrecy, and it is likely that even a disciple from outside the family will be allowed to make copies for himself during the course of his training.

Traditionally, the high priest transmits the *mijue* only to the son who will be his successor. It represents the monopoly of the trade of a high priest: the final piece of the puzzle, without which it would be impossible to lay claim to the possession of a complete tradition and thus to attempt to establish oneself as a high priest. At the same time the *mijue* represents a separate dimension in the performance and conceptualization of Taoist ritual, and the manual therefore provides an essential key to the meaning of this ritual. It may be said that only in the mind and body of the high priest can a complete view of Taoist ritual occur, and it is thus natural that scholars wishing to study this ritual have most often approached their subject through the person of the high priest. For several reasons, it has in some cases been possible for foreign scholars to circumvent the social barriers outlined above and be permitted not only to observe the otherwise strictly closed ritual events, but also to copy the totality of textual materials of a high priest. Most important in this arrangement has probably been the fact that a foreign scholar, while lending local prestige to the high priest, is in no position to use the knowledge thus gained to compete with the priest in the ritual market. It should be noted, however, that the systematic publications during the 1970s and early 1980s of present-day Taoist ritual manuals, derived from those used by the dominant Taoist family lineages of Tainan and Hsinchu, have finally come to the attention of other local priests and are now being copied and reintroduced into the milieu from which they originated, thus contributing to the rapid change of this milieu.[6]

My own materials for the study of Taoist ritual were gathered during two years of fieldwork in Tainan (1978–79 and 1986–87). They are the manuals transmitted within two of the dominant families of priests in Tainan, the Chen and Zeng families, as well as the manuals used by the Lai family of Xishu (immediately south of Tainan), who are associated with the Zeng. Especially important in this connection are the *mijue* transmitted within these families and referred to here as *Chenjue, Zengjue,* and *Laijue,* respectively.[7] The totality of texts possessed by Chen Rongsheng, one of the two main exponents of the Chen family tradition, have been copied by the Japanese scholar Ofuchi Ninji and published in his *Chūgokujin no shūkyō girei* accompanied by his descriptions of the ritual acts as part of which the texts are used.[8]

In addition to the material from Tainan, I shall refer also to the texts compiled by Michael Saso in Hsinchu (and representing a closely related tradition), and to the detailed documentation of the Taipei area made available to me by John Lagerwey. However, my primary sources for describing and interpreting Taoist ritual are, first, my sustained observation of (and occasional participation in) ritual events in the Tainan area, during which I saw the same rituals performed again and again by the same priests in different ritual contexts; and second, my talks with different priests of this area concerning the precise details and meanings of what they do. This twofold approach is based on the conviction that the objective description of ritual cannot be separated from its interpretation. In particular, I believe it is essential that we take careful account of how a priest himself interprets what he is doing, if we are to understand how and why ritual changes over time.

It follows that I disagree with theories of ritual such as the one proposed by Frits Staal that attempt to establish a radical separation of the form and content of ritual. As Staal suggests in a discussion of classical Asian liturgies, "rituals are not only remarkably persistent *within* the alleged religious traditions, where they are provided with constantly changing interpretations; they also remain identical even across the alleged religious boundaries."[9] The implication here is that the meanings ascribed to ritual by those who perform it are secondary and totally arbitrary in relation to the fixed and essentially meaningless structures of the ritual.[10] Staal's view is problematic for several reasons. For one thing, there is no basis for inferring "no meaning" from "changing meaning." But even more important, the alleged permanence of ritual structures is contradicted by the facts of the histories of ritual traditions. Here we shall consider an example of how the sequence of some parts of classical Taoist ritual has changed in recent times, evidently on the initiative of the performing high priest himself, and clearly on the basis of an interpretation of the meaning of the elements of the rituals. In other words, we shall see how Taoist ritual may be restructured on the basis of the meanings of its elements. The study of the historical layers of Taoist liturgy, preserved in the *Daozang* and elsewhere, makes it quite clear that the creativity of individual masters has always played an important role in the development of Taoist ritual.

Few would deny that great liturgists such as Lu Xiujing (406–77) and Du Guangting (850–933) made important and conscious choices concerning the actual form of the liturgy. But is seems to be generally overlooked (especially among scholars who see systems dominating and determining human subjectivity) that a similar state of affairs exists even today, when the most influential living representatives of the Taoist priesthood reveal themselves to be consistently engaged in efforts to understand the basic purposes and ideas of the elements of ritual practice, so that they might be able to adjust the form of the performance in accordance with the insights reached. A clear example of this kind of activity is the case of Zeng Chunshou (b. 1913) of Tainan. After studying in Japan as a youth, he returned to Taiwan too late in life to consider establishing himself as a high priest, serving instead as an assistant priest. However, as the last scion of the Zeng family he has undertaken to revise and edit the ritual manuscripts of the Zeng tradition, and he further serves as a highly respected teacher and mentor of a number of priests from other families.

Revisions introduced by Zeng Chunshou include the addition of a piece of music (taken from another ritual) at one point in a ritual, where the usual drumming seemed inadequate as an expression of the sentiment of that moment. Such changes are apparently motivated by a strong desire to achieve perfection in ritual, though they are suggested only with great hesitation on the part of Zeng himself. His basic attitude (undoubtedly shared with Taoist priests in general) is clearly that the correct way of performing ritual is embedded in the tradition itself, wherein it may be discovered or deduced through attentive study and search for information. Taoist ritual is probably best understood as the product of an interplay between a given (more or less fully transmitted) tradition and the priests who perform according to this tradition. The meaning of ritual is suspended and arises between these two poles. It is not merely a function of the individuality of the priest but an element of the received tradition, partly embedded in the ritual structure and partly transmitted orally and in written texts.[11] At the same time the semiosis of Taoist ritual is sufficiently open to leave room for both "creative misunderstandings" and inventive combinations on the part of the performing priests.

The Transformation of the Body

The program of a *jiao* may be divided into three main parts, which in the case of a five-day ceremony last two, one, and two days each.[12] During the initial part the sacred area is established and purified. It comprises two major rituals, the first of which is the Proclamation (*fabiao*), done in the morning of the first day (or sometimes late at night the day before). Through this ritual the advent of the *jiao* is proclaimed in all parts of the universe by means of a large number of documents that are sent off by being burned. The second major ritual is the Vesperal Announcement (*suqi*), which is done in the evening of the second day, and through which the sacred area is established. It opens with the comprehensive purification and sealing of the sacred area (*jintan*), and continues with the implanting in the five directions of the ritual area of the five Lingbao talismans, that is, the five "perfect writs" (*zhenwen*) by which the world was created, according to the cosmology of the Lingbao tradition.[13]

The final part of the program likewise includes two major rituals, namely the Presentation of the Memorial (*jinbiao*), and the Formal Offering (*zhengjiao*). During the *jinbiao,* the priests move outside the closed ritual area and ascend a stage, on which they have an audience with the Jade Emperor and hand over a large document called a "memorial" (*biao*). The ritual is sometimes referred to as the Statement of Merit (*yangong*), and it seems basically to serve the function of reporting to the celestial bureaucracy, presided over by the Jade Emperor, on the merit acquired for the community through the performance of the ceremony as a whole. The final major ritual, *zhengjiao,* includes the sending off of the superior deities invited for the occasion and the distribution of offerings to all the assistant spirits in reward of their services, as well as the dismantling of the sacred area through "collecting the perfect writs" (*shou zhenwen*).

The initial and final parts of the program are referred to by Du Guangting as the basic framework (*gangling*) of the liturgy.[14] They represent the opening up and the closing down, respectively, of a sacred space, that is, a space for communication with the superior deities. Between these two parts, then, the actual communication takes place on the central day of the program. In a five-day *jiao* (and usually also on the second day of a three-day service) this communication is achieved through the performance of the three large Audiences, viz., the Morning, Noon, and Evening Audience (*zaochao, wuchao, wanchao*), each of them lasting as long as three to four hours. It is interesting to notice that in many ways the structure of an audience ritual parallels that of the *jiao* liturgy as a whole. For instance, the practices for the "transformation of the body" (*bianshen*), which are performed in the beginning of the Audiences, are found also in the opening sequence of the *fabiao,* the first ritual of the whole liturgy. In fact they occur much more consistently and with more elaboration here, and thus the written descriptions of these practices are included in the parts of the secret manuals of the high priest which relate to the *fabiao.*

The practices of *bianshen* form part of the sequence of "secret" rites that accompany the Declaration over the Water (*shuibai*).[15] The text of the Declaration is different in each of the Audiences and in the *fabiao;* it will be quoted here from the *fabiao*. The text of the Declaration is "intoned" (*kanbai*)—i.e., recited with a melody, but without a fixed beat—by the priests as a group. It is included at the beginning of the rituals, right after the opening hymn of *buxu*, "pacing the void," and before the purification of the altar (*jingtan*). The text describes the divine qualities of the water to be used in this purification, and it is accompanied by "secret" rites of the high priest directed toward the small bowl containing the water. The water is transformed into a divinely efficacious substance through the addition of the ashes of talismans burned in the air above it, and through the summoning of the forces of the sun, the moon, and the Big Dipper into the water.

Having thus prepared the water, the high priest hands the bowl and sword to the assistant priest who serves as "troupe leader" (*yinban*), and the latter leads the whole group into the performance of the purification (*jingtan*). Singing in unison they circle the altar, while the *yinban* sprays water over it from the bowl, and move in figure-eights in front of it. I have analyzed the cosmological symbolism of these movements elsewhere.[16] Suffice it here to say that they illustrate the harmonizing of the forces of *yin* and *yang*, and their union into the Supreme Pole (*taiji*). The overall idea clearly is that of an ascent, corresponding to the notion (in ancient times the reality) of the altar as a three-layered structure and expressed in the term *dengtan*, "ascending the altar," which still is used for the entrance to the sacred area.

The "secret" rites of the high priest performed in the beginning of the Declaration over the Water, prior to those directed toward the transformation of the water, serve the purpose of transforming the body of the high priest (*bianshen*). The idea clearly is that before entering the inner sanctum of the ritual area in order to communicate with the superior deities, the high priest must set aside his usual, limited identity, associated with the ordinary body (*fanshen*), and assume an immortal, cosmic identity. The opening phrase of the Declaration (*gongyi*), "We respectfully submit that . . . ," is accompanied by three commands of the high priest, each in the name of one of the Three Pure Ones (*Sanqing*), and directed toward the incense burner on the altar table in front of him.[17] They are followed by a sequence of practices of *bianshen* performed by the high priest while the assistant priests very slowly intone the first ten-character verse of the Declaration, "The calm of the universe necessarily relies on the auspicious light of the Nine Phoenixes." The practices of *bianshen* consist in a "faint incantation" (*weizhou*—also referred to as "secret recitation," *minian*), accompanied by a series of meditations. The high priest closes his eyes and holds his hands joined together, covered by the long sleeves, in front of his mouth. Slightly moving his lips, but barely emitting any sound, he inwardly pronounces the incantation, and for each line moves his thumb to an appropriate point in the plan of the cosmos in the palm of his left hand. The points are indicated by the names of the terrestrial branches distributed in the circumference of the earth, and in a few cases by the positions of the trigrams in the *Luoshu* arrangement. They are noted in the manual after each line of the incantation, sometimes along with meditation instructions, as shown in the following translation.

> The Emperor on High has a command!
> I wash my body with the moon (*you* [west]. I visualize the light of the moon at a distance of nine inches from my face. In it there is true water, which cleanses my body).
> With the sun I refine my perfection (*mao* [east]. I visualize the light of the sun at a distance of nine inches from my face. In it there is true fire, which refines and transforms my body).
> Immortals guard my shape (*chou* [north-northeast]. With the left eye I envisage an immortal to the left. It is the breath of true *yang*).
> Jade Girls protect my form (*zi* [north]. With the right eye I envisage a Jade Girl to the right. It is the breath of true *yin*).
> The three *hun*-souls are calm and orderly (*mao*).
> The seven *po*-souls are peaceful (*you*).
> The twenty-eight constellations stand beside me (from *chen* [east-southeast] counterclockwise all the way round to *si* [south-southeast]).
> The myriad perverse and filthy influences (*gen* [the trigram in the northeast, representing the Gate of Devils])
> are cleansed away by the water (*kan* [the trigram in the north]).
> My heart communicates with the Perfect Way (*zi*).
> I ascend and enter the formless *wu* [south], and "release" (*fangchu*, i.e. snapping away the thumb from the point).
> Hastily, hastily as commanded with the force of law!

The practices are concluded by the high priest's performing a turn around himself toward the left, that is, drawing the so-called Circle of the Supreme Pole (*taiji quan*), said in the manuals to represent his taking possession of the center. The next verse of the Declaration reads: "The cleansing of the sacred area necessarily draws on the divine water of the Five Dragons." It is accompanied by the stepping of the high priest through the Guideline of the Three Terraces (*santai gang*, i.e., the three pairs of stars also referred to as the Staircase of Heaven, *tianjie*, and situated below the Big Dipper). The walk proceeds from the Upper Terrace, nearest the Gate of Heaven, downward through the Middle to the Lower Terrace, and it has the function of bringing down the protective forces of the Three Terraces. It is preceded by the Incantation for Concealing the Body (*cang-shen zhou*), through which the Big Dipper is brought down so as to hide the body of the high priest.

The next verse of the Declaration reads: "It is that wherewith one wipes away perversity and expels filth, gets rid of the evil and hails the virtuous." It is accompanied by the Great Incantation for the Transformation of the Body (*da bianshen zhou*).[18] Again the high priest stands still, his eyes closed and with hands held together in front of his mouth, as he inwardly pronounces the words of the next incantation:

> My body is not an ordinary body.
> My head is like black clouds.
> My hair is like wild stars.
> My left eye is like the sun.
> My right eye is like the moon.
> My nose is like a fire-bell.
> My ears are like golden gongs.
> My upper lip is the Rain Master *(Yushi)*.
> My lower lip is the Earl of Winds *(Fengbo)*.
> My teeth are like a forest of swords.
> My ten fingers are like Inspectors of Merit *(gongcao)*.
> My left side is the Lord of Mount Min *(Minshan jun)*.
> My right side is the Lord of Mount Lu *(Lushan jun)*.
> My left foot is the General of the Thunders to the Left *(Zuolei jiangjun)*.
> My right foot is the General of the Lightning to the Right *(Youdian jiangjun)*.
> My spine is the Lord of Mount Tai *(Taishan jun)*.
> The thirty-six animals and the twenty-eight constellations all correspond to my body.
> Hastily, hastily (let it be so), as commanded with the force of law![19]

The idea clearly is that by reciting this incantation the high priest may transcend his limited ego and attain a cosmic identity. It is significant that the medium and locus for this transformation is the body, which is described as coextensive with the entire universe. The Taoist view of the body has been discussed by several writers, especially Kristofer Schipper, who rightly emphasizes the connection between the concept of the cosmic body, as expressed in a large number of Taoist physiological, meditational, and ritual techniques, and the ancient Taoist myth of the creation of the world. According to this myth, the universe arose from the body of Laozi, that is, the Old Master who wrote the *Daodejing*, but who in this connection is conceived of as a primordial cosmic deity and named *Taishang laojun*, Lord Lao, the Most High.[20] It should be noted, however, that very often the goal of the transformation of the body described in Taoist ritual texts is to assume the identity of less universal deities associated with specific types of practice. The term *bianshen* is written alternatively with the character meaning "spirit" (i.e., the transformation of the spirit), especially in texts of the Song dynasty (960–1279).[21] We find there that the priest begins a rite for expelling mountain goblins *(shanxiao)* by impersonating the True Warrior *(Zhenwu)*, the god of the northern cosmic pole (566 *Shangqing tianxin zhengfa* 5.1a), and that the elaborate rite of writing the three basic talismans of the Tianxin tradition opens with his impersonation of the first Celestial Master, Zhang Daoling, the founding father of the tradition (3.1a and elsewhere). The above two examples are representative of most variants of the transformation of the spirit/body found in the texts of this period. In the majority of cases the divine figure impersonated is the prototypical performer of the rite in question (the "exemplary model," to use the terminology of Mircea Eliade), that is, the first patriarch of the specific method or the deity from whom it is thought to have been transmitted to the world (and who in many cases is seen to be the active force operating in and giving effect to the method in question).

Similar forms are found both in the present-day *jiao* liturgy and in the Taoist funeral liturgy. Thus, for instance, in the great purification (*jintan*), which forms part of the *suqi* ritual in the initial part of the *jiao* liturgy, the high priest enters brandishing a sword, which he declares to be that of Zhang Daoling.[22] There is an obvious connection between exorcistic rites such as these, performed by Taoist priests as parts of larger liturgical contexts, and forms of ritual theater such as the Zhong Kui dances (*tiao Zhong Kui*). The latter may be performed by professional actors on the invitation of individuals or local communities, usually for specific exorcistic purposes. The similarities go beyond the mere borrowing of styles and elements of performance (such as types of movement, of singing and musical accompaniment). Even specific elements of the transformation of the body, used by Taoist priests as parts of the rites of entrance, are identical to elements in the Zhong Kui dances.

The initial rites for the transformation of the body, performed by the high priest during the intonation of the Declaration, continue with practices related to the issuing of the first of the three talismans and the walk along the Guideline of the Nine Phoenixes (*jiufeng gang*). Both elements serve the purpose of purifying the sacred area by means of the forces of the Nine Phoenixes, mentioned also in the beginning of the Declaration. The talisman represents the "true form" of the Great General of the Destroying of Filth by the Nine Phoenixes (*Jiufeng pohui da jiangjun*), and it is burned by the high priest while he holds it in the air between his fingers, finally blowing out the ashes over the altar.[23]

Right after the burning of the talisman and before the walk along the Guideline of the Nine Phoenixes, some final practices for the transformation of the body are included. First is a series of breathing exercises by means of which the high priest inhales the "life-giving breaths" (*shengqi*) of the five directions and brings them into the "five internal organs" of his own body. Finally there is a curious practice referred to as *jiaoer*, "stirring the ears." It is performed in several alternating, circular movements with the hands in front of the chest and past the ears, three rounds to the left and seven to the right, while pronouncing the names of the three *hun*- and the seven *po*-souls residing in the human body. Interpretations of this practice vary. It was explained to me by Chen Rongsheng as serving the purpose of ensuring that the souls may thereafter leave the body through the ears (in order to communicate messages to heaven) instead of through the eyes—the latter occurring when a person dies. Others have referred

An actor performs the Zhong Kui ritual on a theatrical stage facing the entrance of a temple being inaugurated in a small town south of Tainan, Taiwan, March 1987.

to a more general effect of achieving a certain stability of the souls in the body, but none of the priests of the Tainan area whom I spoke with offered—nor wished to confirm—the explanation which is indicated by one of the ancient secret manuals obtained by Michael Saso in Hsinchu and published by him as part of the *Zhuang-Lin xu daozang*. It is a manuscript in the hand of Wu Jingchun, who according to Saso arrived in Hsinchu from southern Fujian in 1823; part of it is dated 1839.[24] The description in this manual of the practices for the transformation of the body to be used in the beginning of rituals includes both a *jiufeng gang* and a *bianshen zhou* (the latter different from those discussed above, yet also found in manuals of the Tainan area), as well as the following incantation:

> The ancestral master [or: my personal master] arrives to let through the *hun*-souls.
> The seven ancestral and immortal masters arrive to let through the *hun*-souls.
> They lead the three *hun*-souls, the seven *po*-souls, and the twelve chronograms [25] in the body of this disciple, N.N., and let them enter and go for a walk in the palace of the Ancestral Master of Orthodox Unity *(Zhengyi zushi)*.[26]
> They go for a walk in the palace of the Imperial Lord of Purple Tenuity *(Ziwei dijun)*.
> They go for a walk in the palace of the Imperial Lord Who Governs the Altar *(Zhutan dijun*; or: the Saintly Lord, Sir Zhang, *Zhanggong shengjun)*.
> They go for a walk in the palace of the Inspectors of Merit throughout the Ages *(lidai gongcao)*.
> They have immortals as personal attendants serving tea.
> Jade Girls bring them their monthly rations.
> They suffer neither hunger nor thirst.
> Spirits and devils know nothing of them.
> Their transformation is complete.
>
> The ancestral master [or: my personal master] and the seven ancestral and immortal masters arrive to let through the *hun*-souls.
> They lead the three *hun*-souls, the seven *po*-souls, and the twelve stellar chronograms in the bodies of the complete families, male as well as female relatives and dependents, of the heads of the ceremony,[27] and let them enter and be concealed in the palace of the Great Emperor Governing the Stars *(Xingzhu dadi)*.
> They are concealed in the palace of the Celestial Master of Orthodox Unity.
> They have immortals as personal attendants serving tea.
> Jade Girls bring them their monthly rations.
> They suffer neither hunger nor thirst.
> Spirits and devils know nothing of them.
> Their transformation is complete.

This incantation clearly has to do with the theme of avoiding danger by depositing one's souls in a department of heaven,[28] and it seems warranted to infer that the rite of stirring the ears, occupying the same position in the rituals of the related tradition of the Tainan area, and likewise referring to the three *hun-* and the seven *po-*souls, expresses the same idea. In fact, this conclusion becomes inevitable when one compares it with the rite of entrance used by the Zhengyi priests of the Taipei area. Though the Zhengyi tradition of the Taipei area differs in many ways from that of Tainan and Hsinchu, the basic pattern of ritual is the same, and a large number of elements are identical.[29] The rite of entrance *(ruhu)*, used in the beginning of major rituals in the Taipei area, has the form of an approach in three stages. The high priest moves first to the altar table representing the seat of the officials and generals *(guanjiang*, i.e., the protective deities), then to that of the Jade Emperor *(Yuhuang)*, and finally to that of Lord Lao in the northwest, corresponding to the trigram *qian* and the Gate of Heaven. In front of each he burns a talisman, recites a silent incantation, and performs steps through the constellations (the Southern Dipper in front of the officials and generals, the Big Dipper in front of the Jade Emperor). From the position of the Jade Emperor he proceeds all the way across the ritual area, in nine steps, inwardly reciting a line for each step, until he reaches the Gate of the Capital *(dumen)*, that is, the Gate of Heaven and the seat of Lord Lao. There he steps through the five elements *(wuxing)* representing the five directions, and at the same time inhales the breaths of the directions. For each step he recites one character of the incantation: *Heming tiandi ri,* "My light is united with the sun of the celestial emperor."[30] Finally, with a sweeping movement of one hand from the breast and toward the incense burner on the altar table (pointing with the thumb inside the hand toward the position corresponding to the terrestrial branch of his year of birth, his "point of fundamental destiny," *benming wen*), he externalizes his souls and turns them over to Lord Lao for safekeeping.

Having thus deposited his souls, the high priest offers incense to the supreme gods of the five directions, the Five Ancient Celestial Worthies, *Wulao tianzun*, and formally enters the inner sanctum of the central altar *(dongan)*, the "cave table," while reciting the Incantation for Concealing the Body *(cangshen zhou,* a version of which is translated below). The interpretation of these acts as a rite of depositing the souls emerges perhaps less from the incantations involved than from the explanations offered by the priests themselves. It is confirmed, however, by the complementary rite of exit *(chuhu)* at the end of the ritual, when the high priest once again addresses himself to Lord Lao, now in order to collect his souls. He performs the same walk through the five elements as before, agitates the "point of fundamental destiny," and recites an incantation, which in the case of the Noon and the Evening Audiences reads as follows:

I go out of *yin* and enter *yang*.
The myriad ways are spread out.
The affairs of communicating are ended.
I ask to conclude [the rites of] the Yellow Chamber *(huangfang)*.
When the matters are ended, [the assistant spirits] resume their
    positions.
Please return my primordial chronogram *(yuanchen)*.[31]

The practices of depositing the souls used by performers of the Zhong
Kui dances have been studied by Qiu Kunliang.[32] Characteristic of the
forms described by him is the fact that the "hiding of the soul" *(canghun)*,
always takes place at the conclusion of walks through the seven stars of the
Big Dipper. In one case it is stated that the actor dressed up as Zhong Kui
"emerges and does the 'seven stars paces.' Then with the toe of his right
foot he draws the character for 'well' *(jing)* on the floor of the stage. By
placing his foot in the center of the character, the actor is symbolically
building a well and secreting his soul in it for safekeeping." More typically,
however, the soul is entrusted to the patron saint of the theater, *Xi-Qin
wangye*. As in the Taoist rite of entrance described above, the place it is
deposited is the incense burner of the master, and again the depositing is
accompanied by the pressing with the thumb in the hand toward the point
of the terrestrial branch of one's year of birth. In one case the incantation
used is a version of the *cangshen zhou*, mentioned above. It is translated as
follows by Qiu:

> . . . let the sun and moon hide my soul. Let the Southern Constellation
> protect my body and the Dipper cover my form. May the Exalted Holiness
> hide my shadow and the Myriad Divinities guard my heart. In motion I am
> like roadside grass; at rest I am like roadside vines. Let my three souls and
> seven spirits be hidden in the golden censer of the Master, where neither
> spirit nor ghost can find them.[33]

The version of this incantation found in the secret manuals of the
Zhengyi priests of the Taipei area differs most importantly in the reference
to the master found in the concluding sentence: "I obey the command of
the Most High, Lord Lao" *(Taishang laojun)*. Evidently Lord Lao, i.e., Laozi,
the original father of Taoism, plays the role of the founding master in the
ritual tradition of this area. It is interesting to compare the incantation
translated above from the ancient manual of Hsinchu, where it is the first
Celestial Master, Zhang Daoling, the founder of liturgical Taoism, who receives the souls in his palace in heaven. In the context of the Zhong Kui
dances, the purpose of depositing the souls clearly is to save them from
being harmed by the fierce persona of the demon slayer, who will occupy
the body, and who himself acts like an enraged madman. The informants
of Qiu, who are professional actors (along with some local Taoist priests,
who also provide performances of the Zhong Kui dances) of northern Tai-

wan, further emphasize the danger of having one's souls abducted by the demons being expelled. The Taoist incantations from the Taipei area refer to the passage of the priest into the other world, the world of *yin*, and seem to imply that the souls of human beings are unable to endure a stay in this region.[34] In both cases the depositing of the souls inaugurates a radical change of identity and character, which in some respects parallels the trance states and possessions of shamans and spirit mediums.

The Flight to Heaven

The practices for the transformation of the body as performed within the classical Zhengyi tradition of the Tainan area were described above from the parts of the secret manuals of the high priest referring to the *fabiao*, the first major ritual of a *jiao*. As mentioned, the same sequence of rites occurs in the beginning of other major rituals in this tradition, notably the Audiences, which include separate versions of the Declaration over the Water (*shuibai*). Thus in the ritual text of Chen Rongsheng for the Noon Audience, the text of the Declaration is preceded by a notice in small characters, indicating the accompanying "secret" acts of the high priest: *gaogong bianshen bugang*, "the one of high merit [i.e., the high priest] transforms his body and walks along the guideline." The implication clearly is that the Audiences should open with the same kind of entrance as used in the *fabiao*, and it therefore came as a surprise to me, during my first period of fieldwork in Tainan, when I noticed that in fact Chen never performed the *shuibai* or any of the accompanying "secret" rites in this place. His answer to my question about the reason for this was quite simple: "It is not done any more."

Having had the opportunity later to observe the performance of other high priests of the area, I noticed, however, that some in fact do the *shuibai* in this place, and include also a somewhat shortened version of the "secret" rites of the *fabiao*. Lai Longfei of Xishu, for instance, who continues the tradition of the Zeng family and receives instructions from Zeng Chunshou, does it this way. However, he does not always include these parts of ritual in his performance of the Audiences, and the reason for this was explained to me by Zeng. The transformation of the body in the *shuibai* is correlated with the "submission of the petition" (*fuzhang*), that is, the meditative flight to heaven in order to deliver the special written prayer of the ritual in question to the superior deities, performed by the high priest later in the Audiences. Thus, when the Audiences do not include a *fuzhang* (and indeed this is the case at all but the most important occasions), the practices for the transformation of the body are also omitted. In fact, as Zeng further explained to me, the performance by the high priest of the entrance rites of the *shuibai* in the beginning of an Audience serves also as a signal to the assistant priests that at the appropriate moment (later in the ritual) the high priest will extend the standard form of the transmission of the prayer (i.e., the burning of the concrete document) with the performance of a *fuzhang*.

The notion of a correlation between the "secret" practices of the *shuibai* and the *fuzhang* is supported by the evidence of the practice of Chen Rong-sheng. During the two years that I followed his performances, he did the *fuzhang* only twice, once as part of the Noon Audience and once in an Evening Audience.[35] In both cases the performance of the *fuzhang* entailed the inclusion of practices for the transformation of the body. They were not performed, however, as parts of the *shuibai* (which even then was omitted from the performance of Chen), but later in the ritual, right before the *fuzhang*. Being performed in this place, the practices for the transformation of the body very explicitly appeared as preparatory to the meditational flight to heaven. Having completed them while facing outward (i.e., away from the central altar and toward the ritual south), Chen turned around and performed the walk along the Guideline of Return to the Altar *(huitan gang)*, ending up before the central altar, where he crouched down as a turtle and executed the inner practices of the *fuzhang*.

The above facts are significant, in my view, as demonstrations of one of the ways that ritual may change. In the first place, it is clear that Chen's practice is contradicted by the actual ritual texts used by him, and for this reason the change may be assumed to be fairly recent (if not introduced by Chen himself, then possibly by his father). In the second place, the moving of the practices for the transformation of the body from the opening part of the ritual to right before the meditational flight to heaven clearly seems to be conditioned by the conceptual correlation of the two sets of practices. The joining of these two sets of practices radically alters the structure of the ritual and thus would seem to represent an example of a structural change occurring on the basis of an interpretation by the performers of ritual themselves of the meanings embedded in the ritual structure. If my interpretation of this instance of ritual change is correct, it goes against the assertion by Frits Staal of a permanence of ritual structure, independent of the varying meanings attributed to this structure.

It may be noticed that the conceptual connection between the transformation of the body and the *fuzhang* is particularly apparent in the Chen family tradition. In all traditions the *fuzhang* is performed as a form of inner practice executed by the high priest, as he lies down in the center of the ritual area and remains still for some ten minutes. And in all cases the chief cantor *(dujiang)* sings the Song of the Demon King *(mowang ge)* while the other assistant priests move the sword and the incense burner over the body of the high priest in order to protect it from being possessed by evil spirits during his absence. However, there is variation in the overall concept, as well as in the exact details of the journey. According to the ancient texts of the Tianxin tradition, the priest visualizes a journey through the different layers of the cosmos, reaching in the end the palace of the Most

High *(Taishang)*, with whom he has an audience. The Most High will read the petition, approve it (if all goes well), and order the Supreme Emperor *(Shangdi)* to add the character *yi*, "accordingly," to the document.[36] A very similar series of visualizations is prescribed for the *fuzhang* in the *Chenjue*, but with the difference that all the celestial departments are identified there with precise parts of the body of the priest. The journey starts from the heart, in which the priest himself emerges as the Great Lord of Long Life *(Changshen dadi)*, and ends at the top of the head, identified as the palace of the Three Pure Ones *(Sanqing)*. The linking of the meditational flight to heaven with the practices for obtaining a body that is coextensive with the cosmos thus seems particularly appropriate in the case of the *fuzhang* of the Chen family tradition.

The *fuzhang* taught by Zeng Chunshou and practiced by Lai Longfei differs from that of the Chen family in being a much more energetic and completely wordless form.[37] It consists of a long series of strenuous and extremely expressive movements, compared by Lai with the martial arts *(gongfu)* and said to serve the purpose of creating a state of total void or oneness, a state in which the whole outer world has actually disappeared.[38] However, the movements end in a stable position on the floor, in which the priest impersonates a mythical animal; depending on the audience, it is either the "unicorn" *(qilin)*, the Tortoise of Midday *(wugui)*, or the Vermilion Bird *(zhuque)*, that is, an animal thought to be capable of flying to heaven. The practice of *fuzhang* represents without question the most solemn moment in Taoist ritual, and probably for the same reason it is also a moment of exceptional symbolic and technical complexity. A more detailed account of the practice must be postponed for future work on this subject. Suffice it to say that in both of the traditions considered here the rite comprises a number of different (and to some extent, it would seem, mutually contradictory) symbolic statements. On the other hand, it is sustained by elements of physiological practices, such as the violent exertion in the Zeng tradition, which appear to serve the purpose of provoking an ecstatic or mystical experience in the high priest.

NOTES

1. See Barbara Myerhoff, *Number Our Days* (New York: Simon and Schuster, 1979), p. 32. Cf. Victor Turner, *The Anthropology of Performance* (New York: PAJ Publications, 1987), pp. 42–43 and 46–47, and "Are There Universals of Performance in Myth, Ritual, and Drama?" in *By Means of Performance*, ed. Richard Schechner and Willi Appel (Cambridge, 1990), pp. 8–18.

2. Cf. Kristofer M. Schipper, "The Written Memorial in Taoist Ceremonies," in *Religion and Ritual in Chinese Society*, ed. Arthur P. Wolf (Stanford: Stanford University Press, 1974), pp. 309–24.

3. Zhengyi priests of this kind are referred to in the People's Republic as *sanju*, "living dispersed among the people" (instead of being properly stacked away in a

monastery). Cf. Chen Yaoting, "Des systèmes religieux," *Cahiers d'Extrême-Asie* 4 (1988), pp. 189–98, and Kenneth Dean, "Revival of Religious Practices in Fujian: A Case Study," in *The Turning of the Tide*, ed. Julian F. Pas (Hong Kong: Hong Kong Branch Royal Asiatic Society, 1989), pp. 51–78.

4. The situation in Hsinchu has been described by Michael Saso in *The Teachings of Taoist Master Chuang* (New Haven: Yale University Press, 1978).

5. The logical policy for a scholar wishing to study Taoist ritual thus was to seek to be adopted into the family of a high priest, and this in fact was achieved by Kristofer M. Schipper, who opened research into the Zhengyi liturgy of southern Taiwan in the mid-sixties and was adopted by Chen Weng, the father of the now-famous Chen Rongsheng. See Kristofer M. Schipper, *Le Fen-teng: Rituel taoiste* (Paris: Ecole Française d'Extrême-Orient, 1975).

6. Cf. *Zhuang-Lin xu daozang*, ed. Michael Saso (Taipei, 1973), and Ofuchi Ninji, *Chūgokujin no shūkyō girei* (Tokyo, 1983).

7. A more detailed account of the histories of the families, and of the mentioned *mijue*, may be found in my "Guideline of the Eight Trigrams," *East Asian Institute Occasional Papers* 6 (1990), pp. 13–30.

8. Ofuchi, *Chūgokujin no shūkyō girei*. It should be noted, however, that these descriptions often seem to be based on conversations with Chen Rongsheng rather than on sustained observations of his actual practice. The result is that many misunderstandings have crept in, and several important elements of the ritual have been overlooked. In fact, the very important and probably the most solemn moment of the *jiao* liturgy, namely the meditational flight to heaven occurring as part of the Audiences, is not mentioned in Ofuchi's book.

9. "Substitutions de paradigmes et religions d'Asie," *Cahiers d'Extrême-Asie* 1 (1985), p. 28.

10. See also Frits Staal, *Rules without Meaning* (New York: P. Lang, 1989), in which he links his ideas with the concepts of transformational linguistics established by Noam Chomsky.

11. See the type of manual referred to as *mizhi*, "secret purports," usually possessed by high priests.

12. For an example of such a program, see Ofuchi, *Chūgokujin no shūkyō girei*, pp. 183–84.

13. On the *jintan*, see Kristofer M. Schipper: "Comment on crée un lieu saint," *Etudes Chinoises* 4, no. 2 (1985), pp. 41–61, and John Lagerwey, *Taoist Ritual in Chinese History and Society* (New York: Macmillan, 1987), pp. 90–105. The latter work contains a comprehensive account of the ritual practice of Chen Rongsheng, based both on the book by Ofuchi Ninji and on personal observations. See also my article "The Practice of *Bugang*," *Cahiers d'Extrême-Asie* 5 (1989–90), pp. 15–53.

14. *1224 Daomen dingzhi* 6.6a-b. The italicized numbers before the titles of books in the *Daozang* correspond to the numerical index compiled by Kristofer M. Schipper, *Concordance du Tao-tsang, titres des ouvrages* (Paris: École Française d'Extrême-Orient, 1975).

15. The term *secret* is used here to designate all the practices described in the *mijue* and performed by the high priest alone, whether truly hidden from others by being performed inwardly, or observable (at least to the assistant priests), yet secret in the sense that their precise content and meaning are unknown to all other participants.

16. *Cahiers d'Extrême-Asie* 5 (1989–90):20.

17. The rite is referred to as *boxiang*, "poking [the fire of] the incense."

18. This according to the *Zengjue*, p. 19. The *Chenjue* reserves the Great Incantation for a later part of the *fabiao*, the part where the high priest prepares for an exit from the sacred area to ascend a table or small bench in order to read and send off the General Summons (*zongzhao*), that is, the document through which the

totality of subordinate spirits assisting the high priest in his performance of ritual are commanded to be present for the *jiao*. In the present context the *Chenjue* prescribes the use of the Small Incantation for the Transformation of the Body *(xiao bianshen zhou)*, included also in the *Zengjue* as an alternative possibility. See Ofuchi, p. 243.

19. I follow the version given in *1227 Taishang zhuguo jiumin zongzhen biyao* 2.2b, the earliest preserved compilation of the methods of the Tianxin tradition, dated 1116. It is identical to the incantation used in the present-day *jiao* liturgy and differs only in minor details from the versions found in the secret manuals referred to in the present study.

20. Kristofer M. Schipper, *Le corps taoiste* (Paris: Fayard, 1982). See also the review article by Lawrence E. Sullivan, "Body Works: Knowledge of the Body in the Study of Religion," *History of Religions* 30, no. 1 (1990), pp. 86–99.

21. E.g., texts of the Tianxin tradition, compiled in the first half of the twelfth century.

22. In fact, in connection with the initial "transformation of the water" he also states: "This sword of mine is not an ordinary sword. It is the very sword of the Celestial Master, used for decapitating evil spirits" (see Ofuchi, p. 284). Note the legend (reported to me by Zeng Chunshou) concerning the origin of the most spectacular part of the *jintan*, the part in which the high priest and one of the assistant priests dressed as a demon stage a violent battle within the ritual area. The legend attributes this to an occasion when the Celestial Master himself was performing ritual. The spirit of a willow tree intruded, wishing to acquire the magical techniques of the master. It was driven out by him, and ever after the act was kept as part of the ritual.

23. The ashes of the other two talismans are added to the incense burner on the altar table and the bowl of water for purification.

24. *Shejiao daochang dengtai baibiao yujue keyi, Zhuang-Lin xu daozang*, pp. 5901–46. On Wu Jingchun, see Saso, *The Teachings of Taoist Master Chuang*, pp. 63–68.

25. Probably the "primordial chronogram" *(yuanchen)*, associated with the terrestrial branch *(dizhi)* of one's year of birth and conceived as a kind of personal soul in the body of each human being. See Hou Ching-Lang, *Monnaies d'offrande et la notion de trésorerie dans la religion chinoise* (Paris: A. Maisonneuve, 1975), pp. 109–23.

26. The first Celestial Master, Zhang Daoling.

27. The community leaders who participate in the rituals as representatives.

28. Rituals for depositing the souls of a family in crisis for a whole year in the Big Dipper, represented by a talisman which is buried in a jar, are described in the Song dynasty compilations of the methods of the Tianxin tradition. See, for instance, *1227 Taishang zhuguo jiumin zongzhen biyao* 9.12b–14b. Similar forms occur today as a normal element of the popular religion and have been observed by John Lagerwey as organized by Taoist priests in the Taipei area.

29. The tradition of northern Taiwan has been explored by John Lagerwey, from whom I have received copies of the manuals I refer to. See his "Les lignées taoistes du Nord de Taiwan," *Cahiers d'Extrême-Asie* 4 (1988), pp. 127–43. I have also had the opportunity to observe the performances of Zhu Mingli, one of the main informants of Lagerwey, and to discuss the meanings expressed in the rites with him. While the tradition of Hsinchu is based on largely the same corpus of ritual texts as are used in the Tainan area (apparently originally deriving from Quanzhou), a few texts are shared with the tradition of the Taipei area, notably the great purification *(jingtan)*. Also the style of performance, that is, the forms of movement and music, is in many ways similar to that of the Taipei area.

30. Some manuals give another sequence of the characters of this incantation, the meaning of which is not totally clear to me.

31. See n. 25.

32. See Qiu Kunliang, *Xiandai shehui de minsu quyi* (Taipei, 1983), pp. 265–87. An article by Qiu on the same subject was translated into English and published in a special issue on Zhong Kui of the *ECHO Magazine*, vol. 6, no. 7 (Taipei 1977), pp. 17–24. My quotations are from the latter source.

33. From Qiu's article, p. 24. The first line of the incantation, omitted by Qiu, is *Qian yuanheng lizhen*, the very first sentence of the *Yijing*, which is used very commonly as the opening phrase of Taoist incantations. It is translated as follows by Richard Wilhelm and Cary Baynes: "QIAN works sublime success, furthering through perseverance." See *The I Ching or Book of Changes*, 3d ed. (Princeton: Princeton University Press, 1967), p. 4

34. A notion of this kind is expressed in many historical texts, for instance in scriptures of the Shangqing tradition from the fourth century. See *1316 Dongzhen shangqing taiwei dijūn bu tiangang fei diji jinjian yuzi shangjing* 8a, which describes how one may ensure that the souls will follow the body to heaven, in spite of their initial "fear of the majesty of the seven stars" of the Big Dipper.

35. November 28, 1978, in a three-day *jiao* in the Zhen'an Temple in Maming shan, and February 17, 1987, in a five-day *jiao* in the Jintang Temple in Jiali.

36. *566 Shangqing tianxin zhengfa* 6.7b–8b; *1227 Taishang zhuguo jiumin zongzhen biyao* 5.9a–10b.

37. The traditions of the two families otherwise share most of their "secret" material and techniques of performance, and the basic ritual texts used are identical.

38. For a description of the state aimed at, Zeng referred me to a passage in the Scripture of the Jade Pivot *(Yushu jing)*, which describes the method of "entering the Way" *(rudao)* as a process of forgetting first one's form, then one's self, and finally that one has forgotten. The passage ends: "When the light of wisdom is born, then you are one with the Way. This is called true forgetting. Only the forgetting is not forgotten. The forgetting has nothing that can be forgotten. That which has nothing that can be forgotten is the perfect Way. The Way is in heaven and earth, but heaven and earth know not whether it has any feelings. It is only oneness, undivided" *(Ziwei yushu baojing*, Taichung, n.d., pp. 28–29).

GLOSSARY

baohu 保護

benming wen 本命文

bianshen 變身（神）

biao 表

cangshen zhou 藏身咒

Changsheng dadi 長生大帝

Chenjue 陳訣

chou 丑

dengtan 登壇

dongan 洞案
fabiao 發表
fangchu 放出
fanshen 凡身
Fengbo 風伯
fuzhang 伏章
gangling 綱領
gaogang bianshen bugang 高功變身步罡
gongcao 功曹
gongyi 恭以
heming tiandi ri 合明天帝日
huangfang 黃房
hun 魂
jiao 醮
jiaoer 攪耳
jinbiao 進表
jing 井
jintan 禁壇
Laijue 賴訣
laojun 老君
lidai gongcao 歷代功曹
Lushan jun 廬山君
mao 卯
mijue 秘訣
minian 密念
Minshan jun 岷山君
po 魄
qilin 麒麟
Sanqing 三清
santai gang 三台罡
Shangdi 上帝
Shangqing tianxin zhengfa 上清天心正法
shanxiao 山魈
shengqi 生氣

shu 疏
shuibai 水白
suqi 宿啟
taiji 太極
taiji quan 太極圈
Taishan jun 太山君
Taishang 太上
wanchao 晚朝
weizhou 微咒
wuchao 午朝
wugui 午龜
Wulao tianzun 五老天尊
Xi-Qin wangye 西秦王爺
Xingzhu dadi 星主大帝
yangong 言功
yi 依
yin/yang 陰／陽
yinban 引班
you 酉
Youdian jiangjun 右電將軍
yuanchen 元辰
Yushi 雨師
Yushu jing 玉樞經
zaochao 早朝
Zengjue 曾訣
Zhang tianshi 張天師
zhanggong shengjun 張公聖君
zhengjiao 正醮
Zhengyi 正一
zhenwen 真文
Zhuang-Lin xu daozang 莊林續道藏
zhuque 朱雀
Zhutan dijun 主壇帝君
Ziwei dijun 紫微帝君
Zuolei jiangjun 左雷將軍

IV.

Body Relics, Transpositions, and Substitutes

SUBSTITUTE BODIES IN
CHAN/ZEN BUDDHISM

Bernard Faure

Students of the branch of Mahāyāna Buddhism called Chan (better known under its Japanese reading, Zen) are often told that this teaching, which arose in China sometime during the sixth century, aims at a direct perception of the ultimate nature of things, namely, emptiness. The fundamental assumption of Chan practice is that the physical universe is an illusion, a mental construction. According to the idealist school of Buddhist philosophy, "The three worlds are mind-only." The Chan school, which subscribed largely to this ontological primacy of mind, was also known as the "school of the mind" *(xinzong)*. One will therefore not be surprised to find in its teaching a negative image of the body. However, Chan masters did not simply deny corporeality, as did early Buddhists; they claimed to be able to transcend the body with this very body. In other words, not unlike their Daoist colleagues, they attempted to transmute the physical, transient body into an incorruptible one. I would like therefore to question the Chan ideology of mind, transcendence, and emptiness and show that behind it lurks another ideology—of the body, of immanence, or presence. In the end, however, both ideologies turned out to be variants of the same dream of immortality, a dream constantly belied by the gruesome reality of death and decay.

I use the term *ideology* here both in the sense of an implicit or explicit system of ideas and in the usual Marxist sense of a discourse that presents an inverted image of its practice. Chan, as many know it through the work of the Japanese Zen scholar D. T. Suzuki, is usually characterized by a radical antinomianism and a denial of all the cultic mediations of traditional Buddhism.[1] There is, however, in this tradition a trend that has been largely neglected by orthodox scholarship, intent on arguing the originality and purity of "iconoclastic" Chan. This trend, which we may call sacramental, was repressed in the official discourse of "classical" Chan that developed at the end of the Tang. It later reemerged in Japanese Zen—and more particularly in the Sōtō sect founded by Dōgen (1200–1253). It appears, for instance, that the cult of relics and icons was at least as important in the allegedly "iconoclastic" Chan/Zen as in traditional Buddhism. Relics imply a mediation with the invisible realm that seems at first glance to contradict the Chan emphasis on immediacy, i.e., the sudden and unmediated character of awakening. In common practice, the virtue of the relics seems predominantly magical—they serve to bring worldly benefits to the worshiper. The mediation that they provide tends to become an end in itself, displacing the ideology of immediate transcendence (sudden awakening) by an ideology of thaumaturgic immanence—what I called the "ideology of presence." Although both ideologies (of immediacy and immanence/presence) apparently contradict each other, they reinforced the ideological grip of Chan/Zen on Chinese and Japanese Buddhism by allowing its adherents to "cash in on both sides."

The Chan Body

Before turning to the Chan cult of relics to illustrate the ideology of presence, some words about the Chan conception(s) of the body are in order. The common image of the body in Chan is indeed negative; it inherits the Indian Buddhist tradition vividly described by Elizabeth Wilson in her essay in this volume. Chan masters such as Linji Yixuan (d. ca. 867) often refer to the body of the practitioner as a "bag of excrement." The practice of early Chan, informed by the Mahāyāna notion of emptiness, aims at the realization of the emptiness of the body.[2] At the same time, the body is perceived as an indispensable instrument to achieve that realization, since no spiritual practice would be possible without it.

Despite transcendental claims, awakening is always localized: it needs a locus to "take place," and this locus is the body. The eponym practice of Chan is after all a bodily technique, and one could argue that the Chan school is primarily a gestural community. However, the body it acknowledges is no longer simply profane; it is already a means toward achieving the glorified body of a Buddha. The hieratic posture of the practitioner is modeled after the "majestic attitude" of the Buddha. Thus the perfect immobility of sitting meditation reaffirms clerical closure; it purifies the body from all defilement; it represses or suppresses all that could threaten corporeal borders.

As the Chan monk turns his aspirations toward the "Body of Law" of the Buddha, born from countless good deeds, his own body is supposed to become "without outflows." The term, referring metaphorically to the passions, was sometimes interpreted literally, as in the case of Master Wulou (No Outflows), who was believed never to urinate. Physical outflows, bodily fluids or excretions, were a reminder of the openness of the body, of its dependence on the outside world, and therefore of its mortality. By contrast with the open, porous, messed-up body of commoners, which is perceived as continuous with its environment, part and parcel of the great chain of being (the gods above, the animals below), the ascetic body tends toward perfection and autocracy.

This utopian goal of the closed, self-contained body of the ascetic is also expressed in the fictional body created by the ritual. The logic at work there is, however, slightly different: it is a synthesis of the two images of the body (as closed and open) that implies the notion of a dual or even plural body transgressing its own borders and disseminating itself into other bodies or objects (such as relics). Funerary rituals, in particular, define a double body—simultaneously mortal and immortal, individual and social. The purpose of these rituals is precisely to transmute the first (individual, mortal) body into the second (collective, immortal) body of the Chan patriarch. They aim at ritually creating an immortal body, one that, unlike the apparently self-enclosed body of the practitioner, is disseminated, fragmented, opened. In both cases, however, the goal is the same, to produce (i.e., create or reveal) a pure, adamantine body. Due to their practice of meditation and the resulting awakening, Chan masters are in a sense "twice-borns," mixed persons, whose dual nature is expressed symbolically by a double body, or rather, whose body manifests the twofold truth of impermanence/permanence. However, we will see that the ideological conception that commands Chan funerary rituals—where everything is done to shift from the single to the double, from the physical body of the practitioner to the "double body" of the Chan master—is undermined by the consciousness that death ineluctably reduces the double to the single, i.e., to the "single body" of a mortal human.

For now, suffice it to say that the body appears to be essential to the two forms of ritual immortality found in Chan and other Buddhist schools—meditation and funerary rites. In both cases, the goal is to operate a metamorphosis of the body, to obtain a kind of physical transmutation. This explains the symbolic value of the body fragments (relics) or of the entire body (in the case of mummies) that attest this metamorphosis. Despite its theoretical denial of the body, Chan, like Daoism, has dreamed of a corporeal immortality—or at least of an immortality based on the preservation of the body.

The Cult of Relics

One of the traces left by this dream is the central role of relic worship in Chan. In the strict sense, the term *relics* refers to those crystalline fragments (Sanskrit *śarīra*, Japanese *shari*) produced by the cremation of the body (*śarīra*).[3] They are, as the plural of the Sanskrit term implies, the fragmented "bodies"—by contrast to the "whole body," i.e., the corpse or, in some cases, the mummy or "flesh body." In this sense, the term *relics* is perhaps misleading, since it usually means something "left behind" (from the Latin *relinquere*), whereas the power that was embodied in the Buddha or in the Buddhist saint is believed to be still present in his *śarīra*.[4] However, because the term has been used in the Western context to designate a similar type of phenomenon, I will continue to use it here. We need also to differentiate between the relics of the Buddha and those of Buddhist saints, although for the sake of the argument we will consider them together. Thus, in the broadest sense, *relics* indicates anything that was associated with a saint: ashes, bones, "flesh-body," but also bowl, robe, text—even places. As Gregory Schopen and others have shown, *śarīra* were believed to be alive: being impregnated with morality, concentration and wisdom, they were fully endowed with all the powers of the Buddha or the saint.[5]

In China, the cult of the relics of the Buddha became prominent during the Six Dynasties, with the discovery of reliquaries allegedly erected by King Aśoka. One such reliquary was that of the Ayuwang Monastery (Monastery of King Aśoka), in Zhejiang. The cult reached its climax during the Tang and was actively promoted by eminent monks such as the Vinaya master Daoxuan (d. 667). Another famous relic was the finger bone of the Buddha, enshrined in the Famen Monastery near Changan. It was as a result of his protest against the imperial worship of this relic that the Confucianist Han Yu faced exile in 819. Despite various criticisms, the cult of relics played an important role in the legitimization of Chinese dynasties. *Śarīra* were produced not only by cremation but also by "materialization" through ritual, prayer or meditation—and their quantity and quality increased constantly. By the Song dynasty, an eminent monk usually left after his death (or sometimes produced while alive) several thousand grains of *śarīra*, some of them multicolored and the size of beans.

In Japan, the first relics are mentioned by the *Nihonshoki* (720). They played a significant role in Nara and Heian Buddhism and became even more important in the Kamakura period with the development of the ideology of the "Final Dharma" *(mappō)*. It is recorded in a fourteenth-century document how a tooth of the Buddha, which had been brought back to China during the Tang by the famous pilgrim Xuanzang (602–664), was brought to Japan and transmitted on Hieizan. The Sennyūji, a monastery founded in Kyoto by the Vinaya master Shunjō (d. 1227), also claimed to have the tooth of the Buddha transmitted by the Chinese Vinaya master Daoxuan.

Relics were also conspicuous in the Zen tradition, although scholars have tended to overlook them. We know, for instance, that Yōsai (var. Eisai, 1141–1215), the monk credited with the transmission of Rinzai Zen to Japan, gave three grains of *śarīra* of the Buddha to the shōgun and that these *śarīra* became the basis of ceremonies held at various Kamakura monasteries. It is also significant that the first text written by Dōgen upon his return to Japan dealt with the relics of his late master and friend Myōzen (d. 1225), which he brought back from China. Dōgen claims that after

Myōzen's cremation, three grains of white-colored *śarīra* were found and that during the six centuries since the introduction of Buddhism in Japan, this was the first time this had happened in the case of a Japanese monk.[6]

However, it is apparently among Yōsai's and Dōgen's rivals in the so-called Bodhidharma School (Darumashū) founded by Dainichi Nōnin (d. ca. 1195) that the cult of *śarīra* played the most prominent role. This role is now documented by the recent discovery of a scroll relating the transmission of the relics of the Six Chan Patriarchs (from Bodhidharma to Hui-neng) and of the Bodhisattva Samantabhadra (Fugen) at Sanbōji, the headquarters of this school (near present-day Osaka). The transmission was carried on continuously at least till the fifteenth century.[7]

The transmission of the Chan patriarchs' relics had not taken place in Sanbōji alone. We know that Gikai (d. 1309), a former Darumashū adept who became Dōgen's disciple and second successor, transmitted some of these *śarīra* to his disciple Keizan Jōkin (d. 1325). Keizan eventually placed them, together with relics of five Sōtō masters (including his own, *ante-mortem*, relics), in a reliquary that, in his mind, was to be not only the focal point of his newly founded monastery, Yōkōji (in Noto peninsula), but also of the later Sōtō school. After Keizan's death, both his and Dōgen's ashes were eventually dispersed among seven Sōtō monasteries.[8] The records concerning these relics clearly reflect attempts made by various monasteries to gain legitimacy and precedence.

Eventually, relics became a cheap commodity. A case in point is that of Shōgen (d. 1311), a disciple of the Kamakura Zen master Enni Ben'en. After Shōgen's cremation, his disciples were surprised to find several grains of *shari*. One of the disciples argued that relics were no longer respected and convinced his fellows not to mention them to anyone. The relics were therefore divided between the disciples and hidden. However, when wonders began to happen, the skeptical disciple had to admit that he had underestimated the efficacy of his master's relics. At any rate, his skepticism may be symptomatic of a growing tendency to treat relics as objects, not as "subjects" implying a real presence.[9]

The Rise of the "Flesh-Bodies"

Despite attempts to establish a hierarchy of various kinds of relics, the relic par excellence remained the mummy, or "flesh-body."[10] Buddhist mummies have attracted the attention of Japanese scholars since the discovery of a group of mummified monks in northern Japan (Yamagata Prefecture). Most of these monks were Shugendō practitioners whose practice was patterned after the legend of Kūkai (Kōbō Daishi), the founder of Shingon sect. According to this legend, Kūkai entered *samādhi* on Kōyasan in 835, thereby becoming a "Buddha in this very body" (*sokushin bu*). Self-mummification was usually achieved by entering the final *samādhi*

it is perhaps significant that in the Indian context, *samādhi* designates metonymically both the spiritual state of the ascetic and the grave in which he
is sometimes buried alive.[11]

The oldest of these Japanese Buddhist mummies in existence today is
that of Kōchi Hōin (d. 1363), preserved in Niigata Prefecture, the most
recent that of Bukkai shōnin (d. 1903), also in Niigata.[12] In his ethnographi-
cal essays on northern Japan, *Hokuetsu Seppu*, Suzuki Bokushi describes the
mummy of Kōchi Hōin—one of the twenty-four wonders of Echigo—as he
saw it in 1838 (477 years after Kōchi's death). In his commentary, Suzuki
notes: "There are, in China, mummies similar to that of Kōchi. When the
Tang-dynasty monk Yicun died, his corpse was placed in a casket, from
which it was lifted each month to have the nails and hair trimmed. The
body had not decomposed even after one hundred years. Later, during the
rebellions and uprisings at the end of the dynasty, it was cremated." Suzuki
concludes that "the whole idea is an insult to Sākyamuni's teachings of the
impermanence of all compound things, and cannot be praised."[13]

The Chinese monk to whom Suzuki referred, Xuefeng Yicun (d. 908),
is a well-known figure in the Chan tradition. His case is not exceptional:
beginning with the Fourth Patriarch Daoxin (d. 651) and the Sixth Patriarch Huineng (d. 713), many Chan masters turned (or were turned) into
mummies, or flesh-bodies, after their death. Although this phenomenon
is in no way restricted to Chan, it seems, rather paradoxically, to be in this
school that the majority of known examples are found.

I should first point out an important difference in the Japanese cases.
In Japan, the cult of the so-called *sokushin butsu* had a distinct eschatological
connotation. It was explicitly linked to the legend of Mahākāśyapa entering
into *samādhi* to wait for the coming of the future Buddha, Maitreya.[14] The
legend of Kūkai's "becoming a Buddha in this very body" on Kōyasan is
based on that of Mahākāśyapa.[15] With a few exceptions, however, this Mai-
treyan background is absent in the Chinese examples mentioned. Furthermore, the conspicuous lack of mummies in Japanese Zen forms a significant
contrast with Chinese Chan.

To shed some light on this contrast and its significance, it is necessary to
retrace briefly the Chinese evolution of the mummy cult. Kosugi Kazuo,
in a seminal article, has described what could be called the "iconization" of
the Buddhist mummies through the application of dry lacquer.[16] Perhaps
the first mention of a lacquered mummy is that of a contemporary of
Huineng, a Central Asian monk named Sengqie (d. 710), who not only was
adopted posthumously by the Chan tradition but came to be worshiped in
Chinese religion as a god of navigation. The preservation of his mummy
contributed greatly to his divinization. In the eleventh century, a Japanese
monk named Jōjin came to pay homage to Sengqie's mummy, and when
he himself died in China, his mummified body was in turn lacquered and
covered with gold dust.

The mummification of Sengqie marks a turning point: from that time

onward, mummies were usually lacquered. In most known cases, the lacquering took place relatively late, after the process of mummification had
followed its natural course. With the lacquering of the body, the attitude
toward the dead changed drastically. The corpse became more of a representation, and somewhat lost its gruesome character as a corpse. Thus it
gradually "surfaced," being brought from the grave or stūpa to a special
building called "image hall." In these halls, the portrait of the dead was
supplemented by the dead himself, who thus became his own effigy, an
autoreferential sign. However, the mummy did not supersede the portrait;
on the contrary, the presence of the dead was actually reinforced by his
dissemination into various "substitute bodies."

This "iconization" reached its climax in the subsequent development of
what has been called "ash icons," i.e., representations of the dead made by
mixing his ashes with clay to model realistic statues of him. This method
was probably adopted to meet the religious needs of the people and the
sectarian interests of the monks and to palliate the scarcity of "natural"
mummies. These ash icons appeared toward the mid–eighth century, when
lacquered mummies already had become popular. They mark the last stage
of the iconization of mummies in China, a process that was facilitated by
relic worship and by technical developments such as the technique of dry
lacquer. By the ninth century, mummies had become a special kind of icon:
as the mortuary associations receded to the background, they left the stūpas
for the memorial halls—or rather the *mausoleums*, since the function of
these halls was not merely commemorative.[17]

Once it had become an icon, the mummy could be challenged, and eventually replaced, by other icons. Whereas several types of "representation"
have vied with each other in the Chinese image halls, portraits seem to
have won out in Japanese monasteries.[18] Eventually the custom of inserting
ashes or relics (among other things) in a cavity made in wooden statues
prevailed. However, just as the mummy, once lacquered, acquired some of
the characteristics of the icon, the icon or statue acquired some of the
characteristics of the mummy. The iconization of the mummy was also a
"mummification" of the icon. This iconization process may explain why
there are practically no mummies in Japanese Zen.

Bones of Contention

We now turn to the "pragmatic" aspect—the use of mummies and relics
as commodities in the sectarian context, what we might call the "politics of
mummification." What factors contributed to such an evolution? Was relic
worship a concession to popular superstition, as scholars, following in the
wake of Confucianists, have tended to believe? Although there might be
some element of truth in this view, it is far from sufficient to explain the
change described above. The Chinese interest in relics and flesh-bodies was

primarily a concern of monks and expressed a highly structured awareness of death.

Behind these monastic concerns, we can discern intense sectarian stakes. Relics were from the outset "bones of contention." It is not by a mere coincidence that most of the mummies recorded in the Chan tradition happen to be the "founders" of new schools. In all likelihood, the mummies of these "patriarchs" were used by their successors (and owners) to attract the devotion of believers. One may even wonder whether these attempts at self-mummification were free decisions of individuals, or rather reflected the pressure and expectations of the community. Chan masters may have been strongly independent and undisputed in their lifetime, but they became after their death a collective property, and a much disputed commodity.

The case of Huineng (d. 713), the Sixth Patriarch of Chan/Zen, is particularly significant in this context. The Caoxi community in northern Guangdong, where he had taught and died, could boast of possessing a number of his relics, not only "contact relics," such as his robe, bowl, and staff, but also the supreme relic, Huineng himself—"in the flesh." The title of the work attributed to Huineng, the *Platform Sūtra*, one of the few sūtras not attributed to the Buddha himself, seems to reflect the confidence of his disciples that Huineng, because he had produced an incorruptible flesh-body, was a Buddha in his own right. Thereafter, Chan patriarchs were referred to as "old Buddhas," and abbots of Chan/Zen monasteries were often considered to be living Buddhas.

Huineng's mummy was allegedly threatened several times. In 722, a Korean reportedly attempted to steal its head. According to the Chinese tradition, this attempt failed. According to the Korean tradition, however, it was successful and Huineng's head was taken to Korea, where it has been until today enshrined in a mausoleum at Ssanggye-sa (on Chiri san). Whatever we make of this Korean claim, the desire to steal Huineng's head was clearly not intended to destroy the mummy but merely aimed at stealing its power. On this account, it did succeed: various wonders are said to have taken place at the sight of Huineng's Korean mausoleum, and so impressive were they that no one ever dared to open it. The relic of Ssanggye-sa was even compared to the frontal bone of the Buddha enshrined on Wutai shan, and in 1980 a delegation of Taiwanese Buddhists made a pilgrimage to Korea to worship it.

Among other coveted relics of Huineng were his bowl and his patriarchal robe *(kaśāya)*. Their importance as sectarian or dynastic regalia can be seen from the various attempts, by emperors and by followers of rival Chan schools, to acquire them. As in the medieval West, "translations" (transfers) of relics paved the way for "sacred thefts" *(furta sacra)*. The importance of these relics in dynastic legitimization is reflected in various reports that Tang emperors requested that these relics be brought to the imperial palace. The patriarchal robe also played a conspicuous role in the transmission of Chan.[19] According to Huineng's self-proclaimed successor, Shenhui (684–758), "The robe and the Dharma are transmitted by one another and there is no other transmission."[20] Thus it is clear that the robe is not just a symbol: like Huineng's other relics, including the *Platform Sūtra,* it is the *embodiment* of the Chan Dharma. However, Shenhui's emphasis on the transmission of the robe as the *only* valid one reveals the concurrence of these various relics and embodiments. Often these various "embodiments" (relics, robe, text, portrait, verse) reinforced each other in an "orgy" of presence and legitimacy.

Perhaps the most recent case of sacred theft is that of the alleged mummy of Shitou Xiqian (Sekitō Kisen, d. 790), in whom the tradition sees a second-generation successor to Huineng and the ancestor of the Sōtō lineage. It was brought to Meiji Japan at the time of the Chinese revolution (1911) by a Zen and Shugendō adept named Yamazaki Takeshi. Yamazaki had found the mummy in a monastery in Hunan and rescued it from a fire that devastated the monastery. He was eventually able to smuggle it to Japan in a Mitsui ship. After his death, the mummy was forgotten in a trunk, until rediscovered in 1960. After examination by a group of experts, it was handed over in 1975 to Sōjiji (in Yokohama), one of the two headquarters of the Sōtō sect, where it still is today. Although the Sōjiji authorities are somewhat reluctant to acknowledge its presence, I was able to see it in 1988. The body was lacquered, and the cloth on which the lacquer was applied remains visible. The preservation was not very good. The face has been blackened by fire and shows various wounds. The limbs, at one time detached from the body, had to be tied up to the torso. The mending, however, has been successful, and the mummy, in its brocade robe, looks quite impressive.

From all these examples, we may conclude that the cult of relics and flesh-bodies served a variety of purposes. It was a proof of the holiness of a master but also a source of power for his disciples and of worldly benefits for all. Relics permitted new religious foundations, made spiritual practice less abstract by giving it a focus, provided spiritual and political protection as well as communal prestige. Finally, the cult of relics, while it served well the popularization of Chan and Zen, also implied a "humanization" or "demythologization" that often went against certain local beliefs in cosmic or divine mediators, such as dragon-kings, stellar deities, and mountain gods. Sacred mediators became idealized men, Chinese patriarchs whose power or efficacy (*ling*) was manifested in the relics.

Icons and Portraits

The Zen tradition is known for the stern "realism" of its portraits (*chinzō* or *chinsō*). The term *chinzō* originally referred to the protuberance on the top of the head, one of the thirty-two marks of a Buddha. It is not clear how or when it came to designate the portraits of Chan/Zen masters. Art historians have often marveled at the "true-to-life" character of Zen portrait-sculpture. Even to the casual observer, these "representations" of the dead master, with their inlaid eyes glittering in the dark, produce an eerie feeling because, like a mummy, they look "as if alive." These sculptures are not portraits in the Western sense; like their aniconic counterpart, the *śarīra*, they constitute "substitute bodies." In other words, they are not merely "realistic," they are *real*, pointing to no reality beyond themselves. At first glance, the metaphoric logic of Western representation, in which one thing stands for another, seems apt to describe the two-tiered structure of Buddhist cosmology. As the fourth-century monk Huiyuan, speaking of the Buddha, put it: "There [in nirvāṇa] is his body, here on earth is his shadow."[21] However, this metaphorical logic gives way in ritual practice to the logic of metonymy and synecdoche, in which the shadow or trace becomes as real as the body, *is* this very body. Thus icons came to be perceived no longer as a "metamorphosis body" *(nirmāṇakāya)* "standing (or sitting) for" the true "Dharma-body" *(Dharmakāya)* but as the Dharma-body itself. Chan discourse, however, fluctuated between metaphor and metonymy, transcendence and immanence, endlessly replaying the game of absence and presence reminiscent of the Freudian notion of *fort/da*.

Buddhist icons are imbued with the powers of the dead, animated or empowered by them. This empowering results from a ceremonial "opening of the eyes" *(kaiyuan, kaigen)* of the statue. The rite was already known in early Buddhism and even in Brahmanism. It appears in Buddhist esoteric texts translated into Chinese during the Tang, and its performance is recorded in Japan for the *kaigen* ceremony of the Great Buddha of Tōdaiji in 753. However, no mention of it is found in earlier Chinese documents. This rite was parallel to that of "closing the eyes" of a statue to make it temporarily powerless. According to an esoteric document of the Sōtō tradition, the parallelism is such that one cannot "dispatch" the spirit of a statue if one does not know by which method it was empowered at the time of the *kaigen* ceremony. Briefly, the esoteric tradition defines two types of "eyes opening": the empirical and the noumenal. In the empirical opening, the priest, while pointing to the eyes of the icon, projects into it his own power *(jiriki)*, i.e., the Buddha within himself. In the noumenal opening, he summons into the icon the "power of another" *(tariki)*, that of the cosmic Buddha. Consequently, when "closing the eyes" of the icon, the priest dispatches the spirit within the icon back to its original abode, that is, the metaphysical realm in the noumenal ritual, or his own body in the empirical ritual. The latter is the most common in Sōtō Zen, while the former is used primarily in Shingon. Similar rituals are performed for mortuary tablets.[22]

The ritual animation of the icon is often supplemented by the actual presence of relics inside it. Sometimes these are not postmortem relics but relics left by the master while alive. A case in point is that of the statue of

Ikkyū Sōjun (1394–1481), on the head of which real hair—probably belonging to Ikkyū himself—was implanted. As the art historian Mōri Hisashi puts it, "The thought process involved in such a practice corresponds exactly to that involved when inserting the possessions or actual remains of the subject into hollow portrait statues."[23]

Mummies were only one modality—if the most impressive—of the lingering presence of the dead patriarchs. Even the so-called "*nirvāṇa* without remainder" turned out to leave a remainder after all. Ancestral tablets and icons were functionally equivalent to the flesh-body and eventually provided convenient substitutes. The portraits (*chinzō* or *shin*) of Chan/Zen were functionally similar to the Chinese mortuary portraits and other "seats of the spirit" (*shenzuo*) described by ethnographers.

Portraits thus became the locus and proof of immortality, if only because, like Christian icons, they were animate—and sometimes literally animated—like the Japanese puppets described by Jane Marie Law in her essay in this volume. They functioned according to the metonymic/synecdochal logic of the *pars pro toto*, a logic that was manifested in the case of statues by the presence of "live" relics within them. In Japan as in China, statues and portraits were believed to be alive, once the rite of the "opening of the eyes" was performed. Many cases have been recorded of statues that sweat, cried, moved, or walked. A similar rite of "pointing" empowered the ancestral tablets (*ihai*) or the steles of deceased masters, which also occupy a prominent place in Zen temples.

All these hierophanic artifacts (portraits, mortuary tablets, stūpa), like the Greek funerary slabs (*colossoi*) analyzed by J.-P. Vernant, can be seen as "substitute bodies" or "doubles."[24] The consecration of an icon is a birth, but simultaneously, by its "suspended animation" in *samādhi*, it amounts to the creation of a living dead—in other words a kind of mummy.[25] In this way, death is controlled and serves to regenerate life. Like mummies, icons provided a channel between immanence and transcendence, between the visible and the invisible, and at the same time renegotiated the demarcation between the two realms. Not only could they be looked at; they themselves were endowed with the power of vision—a power so great that at the time of the "eyes opening" ceremony, the priest must in some cases be shielded from the icon's gaze and looks at its reflection in a mirror.[26] However, most of all, their vision is transformative.[27]

On the other hand, as in the case of relics, the power of the icon depends on the faith and karma of the worshiper and/or on proper ritual reactivating. The latent power of the icon becomes manifest only under certain objective and subjective circumstances. As the Kamakura monk Myōe (1173–1232) put it, "When you think of an object carved of wood or drawn in a picture as a living being, then it *is* a living being."[28] A Chinese poem entitled "The Gate of Worshiping Relics, Images and Stūpas" suggests that the icon serves as a support for the Buddha as well as a focusing mechanism for the believer: "[An image] will express our feelings, concentrate our thoughts, [make them] compassionate and loving; / It brings down [the Buddha's] spirit and portrays his likeness, wiping clean all dust and doubt."[29] In India, the body of an ascetic who has "entered *samādhi*" (in both senses of the grave and the spiritual state in it) while alive is believed to be still the occasional habitation of his soul, which wanders freely through the three worlds.[30] Even in the case of Zen texts such as the "Recorded Sayings," it is as relics or aniconic icons that such artifacts are able to "bring the Buddha down to earth"—in a sense quite different from that intended by Judith Berling in her article on the "Recorded Sayings" genre entitled "Bringing the Buddha down to Earth."[31]

Transmission or Diffusion?

As the individual master had been an embodiment of the Dharma during his life—or, to borrow the title of Thomas Kasulis's essay in this volume, "Reality as Embodiment"—so was his *chinzō* after his death. The *chinzō* thus came to play, like the relics, an important role in the transmission, or rather the diffusion, of the Dharma. It is well known, for instance, that, through the mediation of two disciples, Dainichi Nōnin received in 1189 a portrait of Bodhidharma, on which the Chan master Fozhao Deguang had written a eulogy, together with the robe of Dahui Zonggao. Furthermore, before returning to Japan, Nōnin's disciples had also a portrait of Deguang made, on which they asked the master to inscribe a verse. As we saw earlier, Nōnin had also, probably on the same occasion, received the *śarīra* of the six patriarchs and the bodhisattva Samantabhadra. The writing of a verse by a Chan master on a portrait (his own or that of an earlier patriarch) may be seen as an alternative form of "pointing" an icon. Likewise, Dōgen returned to China in 1227 with a portrait of his master Rujing. Although he later complained about the commodification of *chinzō*, to which he attributed the decline of Rinzai Zen, he clearly shared with his contemporaries the "ideology of thaumaturgic immanence" that caused the vogue of icons. He was in all likelihood merely reluctant to share its symbolic gains with other schools—in particular with the Darumashū. Similar in this sense to the patriarchal robe, these portraits were not simply proofs of transmission—as is generally believed—but, in some cases at least, its medium and palladium.

As Griffith Foulk and Robert Sharf have pointed out, the possession of a *chinzō* was in itself insufficient to claim spiritual transmission or awakening.[32] However, it was the device that allowed the ritual transmission of the master's charisma to take place and provided access to it, thereby linking magically the possessor of the *chinzō* to the mainstream of the tradition perpetuated by his master. The *chinzō* thus lays the ritual ground on which the rarefaction of legitimate authority through succession documents (*shisho*) could take place as a specific case. The *chinzō* must be placed in the funerary context, but so must the patriarchal transmission: by receiving the seal *(inka)* of the master, the disciple becomes his double, symbolically killing him. Likewise, the transmission of the patriarchal robe was never merely the "proof" of the "mind-to-mind" transmission; it functioned rather as a relic, a ritual device transforming the disciple into his master (i.e., into the Buddha). This logic of metonymy and dissemination is not negated by the multiplication of *chinzō* or robes and "seals of transmission." Instead of transmitting his Law to a single successor, the master is disseminating it—and himself, too, since the *chinzō*, being his "Body of Law," is both his Law and his body. However, with their multiplication and diffusion to monks and laymen alike, *chinzō*, like relics, lost their privilege of conferring legitimacy upon a specific lineage and came to serve merely as instruments of ritual affiliation with the Chan "blood lineage," or even as talismans and amulets, forms of "objectified charisma" somewhat similar to the effigies of Thai monks studied by Stanley Tambiah.[33]

Functionally interchangeable with the *chinzō*, the *shin* (literally, "truth" [in painting]), or portrait of the dead master, is said to be "the substantial image of the Dharma." That this mortuary portrait or effigy was perceived as a double is clear from the fact that it was the center of the funerary ritual, even while the dead body was in the coffin nearby. As in the case of Roman emperors or French kings, the body of the Chan/Zen master seems divided into *ossa* and *imago*, into a physical, mortal body and a social, immortal, metonymic body. Studying royal funerals in sixteenth- and seventeenth-century France, Ralph Giesey describes the process that led to dissociation of the "two bodies," i.e., the coffin and the effigy of the dead king.[34] In Zen funerals, too, it is for the second, immortal body of the master that the ritual is performed: as in the funerals of the king, the focus of the ceremony shifts away from the encoffined body and centers upon the lifelike representation of the deceased. Thus the portrait serves as support for the social body of the deceased master until the latter is properly reincorporated—through cremation or mummification—into his purified body (the relics or the flesh-body), thereby becoming a "collective" ancestor and a source of regeneration for the collectivity. The portrait anticipates this state of affairs and continues to operate in parallel with the relics afterward. In a sense, the growing "realism" of Zen portraiture marks a decline of the ritual symbolism. The utterly "realistic" portraiture of the Ōbaku sect in Japan can be seen as the end of the iconization process of the double that leads from relics and symbolic relics through flesh-bodies to *chinzō*.

As Foulk and Sharf have shown, the primary function of portraits is a funerary one, and the traditional claim that they served as transmission devices must be questioned; it can be seen to represent a minority view.[35] Nevertheless, these two functions are not exclusive; they seem rather to imply each other, and to imply a similar belief in the "ideology of presence." That the use of portraits as instruments of transmission was criticized by

Zen masters such as Dōgen suggests that this ideology came to be perceived for what it was, namely, a fiction that was no longer very useful.

Similar in many respects to the *chinzō* of the Chan/Zen master, the icons of the gods worshiped in Chan/Zen monasteries nevertheless differ by their ritual function; they protect the monastery or some part of it. The presence of these gods in their icons is achieved by ritual empowerment through invocation. As a result, these icons are believed to possess "spiritual power" or "efficacy" *(ling)* and they belong to what we could call the "category of the double." This heuristic category provides a common link among relics, mummies, gods, and icons. All these "doubles" are functionally or psychologically related. The icons are, in the strict sense, the visible bodies of the gods, their "traces"—although *trace* here implies an invisible presence, not a mere absence. Just as, according to William Blake, the body is the visible part of the soul, the icon or relic is the visible part of the Buddha's or Zen master's Mind or "Body of Law."[36] On the basis of the Platonic conception of mimesis, art historians have tended either to devaluate or to idealize these images as "artistic representations," in both cases missing the point (i.e., the pupils in the icon's eyes).

Despite the radical difference of soteriological context, the Chinese "question of icons," like its Christian counterpart, appears to have been a controversy over the position of the sacred in society. Chan's much-vaunted "iconoclasm" was aimed essentially at "superstitions" which seemed to result in "hemorrhage" of the sacred—and, by the same token, in a routinization of charisma and a devaluation of sectarian legitimacy.[37] Accordingly, a purely rationalist reading of Zen iconoclasm or a purely aesthetic interpretation of Zen iconism would be misleading. Chan/Zen monks were apparently trying to limit the proliferation of sacred symbols and to reserve to themselves the privilege of the possession of selected symbols or icons such as relics and mummies. Their iconoclasm was generally well-tempered, even if the most radical among them, carried away by their rhetoric of immediacy, attempted to deny any symbolic mediation. Even then, they still relied on the notion of a lineage of Zen patriarchs having realized one by one the formless truth. Such a notion made sense only in the context of a funerary ideology centered on ancestor worship, an ideology for which every patriarchal generation is essentially the *lex incarnata*, the embodiment of a perennial Dharma. Each patriarch is thus himself already an icon, a particular form of the formless, a metamorphosis of the primordial double—the Buddha. Sitting cross-legged on his chair, the Chan master appears as a double of the Tathāgata, and he is in turn reflected in his cross-legged disciples; conversely, the Buddha manifested in his icons may be seen either as a mental projection of the individual monks or as a ritual projection of their Buddha-nature. In this way, the logic of dissemination has come to supplement—and to displace—the early Chan metaphysics of presence. Between these mirror images, power circulates endlessly—not only from mind to mind but also from body to body. Through such an ideology of disseminated presence, Chan/Zen, the "School of the Mind," gives voice to the body and leaves the ethereal realm of spiritual contemplation for the corporeal realm of ritual.

However, it is precisely in this corporeal realm that the ideology finds its limitations: despite ritual precautions and dissemination, bodies do eventually decay. Thus the body of the Chan master, even when mummified, is, like the body of the French kings, clearly single, not double. Alain Boureau has questioned the theses advanced by Ernst Kantorowicz and Ralph Giesey regarding the ideology of the "king's two bodies," or rather the actual impact of this ideology in French history. Boureau, in analyzing the profanation by the French revolutionaries of the royal graves at Saint Denis, refers, on the contrary, to the "impossible sacrality" of the French kings. He describes in particular the "great indifference" of the Roman Catholic Church vis-à-vis political sacralization.[38] Although borrowed from an entirely different context, this example brings to light the similar, if not quite as gruesome and massive, failures of the Chan attempt to sacralize the bodies of the patriarchs. In both cases, we observe a failure to reach the "immutability within time," i.e., to achieve the transcendence of death within worldly immanence or to reconcile in one single (yet dual) body the ideologies of transcendence and of immanence. However, the Chan theory was perhaps more successful than the French juridical fiction in its attempt to sacralize the body: the production of mummies, and their religious function, suggest that we have in the Chan case more than a purely discursive fiction; it implies an actual belief on the part of some (if not all) of the protagonists. The naïve belief in the symbols of permanence cannot be simply dismissed in light of the evidence of impermanence (even mummies decay), and of the conflicting historical reality—the fact that these bodies were "bones of contention," stakes in an ongoing struggle for power.

In actual practice, people do not necessarily believe that there is power in the relics. Their worship, when contextualized, shows petty sectarian, political, or other psychological motives. In this sense, Boureau is right to argue that Kantorowicz and Giesey, in their analysis of the French royal ideology, put too much emphasis on a theological theory which does not really explain the behavior of the agents. However, the theology is nevertheless operative at a certain level. Otherwise, one cannot explain why kings, at the time of death, are so concerned with having their body dispersed into several relics, in order to have more intercessions and gain immortality. Clearly, there is a time to be skeptical and a time to believe, and sometimes the two attitudes coexist within a single (or dual?) individual. Therefore it is necessary to take into account both levels, the ideological and the political, and to remember that each type of interpretation presents its own insights and blindness.

Ultimately, the utopian attempt to create a double seems bound to fail. The Chan master's attempt to stage his own death and thereby to elude it reminds us of the impossible dream of Herman Herman, the tragicomic character in Vladimir Nabokov's *Despair*. Herman's plan to start a new life ultimately fails, because, contrary to what he believes, the double which he had found to replace him in the grave bears no resemblance whatsoever to him. Even if, in the Chan ritual context, resemblance is less important, a similar discrepancy is likely to be perceived by the participants. Reality is stubborn, and it can undo the best-woven ideological constructs. Mummies, however well lacquered, seem to retain the stink of death and serve as a vivid *memento mori*. Other attempts to preempt death through ritual means, such as the production of portraits and other "substitute bodies," paradoxically ended up establishing more firmly the grip of death on a tradition that eventually became a dominant trend of "funerary Buddhism."

NOTES

1. For more details, see Bernard Faure, *The Rhetoric of Immediacy: A Cultural Critique of Chan/Zen Buddhism* (Princeton: Princeton University Press, 1991).
2. For the Mahāyāna description of the body as empty, see, for instance, Etienne Lamotte, trans., *L'enseignement de Vimalakīrti* (Louvain: Institut Orientaliste, 1962), pp. 132–33.
3. A Sanskrit term used as synonym for śarīra is *dhātu*. Concerning these terms, see Bernard Faure, "Dato," in *Hōbōgirin: Dictionnaire encyclopédique du bouddhisme d'après les sources chinoises et japonaises*, vol. 7 (Paris: Adrien Maisonneuve, forthcoming), and Gregory Schopen, "On the Buddha and his Bones: The Conception of a Relic in the Inscriptions of Nāgārjunikoṇḍa," *Journal of the American Oriental Society* 108 (1988): 527–37.
4. The point was made forcefully by Gregory Schopen in his discussion of the papers read at a panel on the theme "Theravāda Buddhism and the Idea of 'Tradition': Books, Relics, Images," at the 1993 American Academy of Religion Meeting in Chicago. Incidentally, the use of the masculine pronoun here is intentional: women usually do not leave relics, as in orthodox Buddhist doctrine a woman must be reborn as a man before reaching Buddhahood.
5. Gregory Schopen, "Burial 'Ad Sanctos' and the Physical Presence of the Buddha in Early Indian Buddhism: A Study in the Archeology of Religions," *Religion* 17 (1987): 193–225.
6. See *Shari sōdenki*, in Ōkubo Dōshū, ed., *Dōgen zenji zenshū*, vol. 2 (Tokyo: Chikuma shobō, 1969–70), p. 395.
7. See Bernard Faure, "The Daruma-shū, Dōgen and Sōtō Zen," *Monumenta Nipponica* 42, no. 1 (1987): 25–55.
8. These monasteries are Eiheiji, Yōkōji, Daijōji, Shōboji, Sōjiji, Kōshōji (during the Edo period), and Hōkōji (during the Meiji era).
9. See *Genkō shakusho*, in Suzuki gakujutsu zaidan, ed., *Dai Nihon bukkyō zensho*, vol. 62, no. 470 (Tokyo: Kōdansha, 1970–73), p. 110.
10. The "body" of literature on Buddhist mummies in China and Japan has grown since the seminal study by Kosugi Kazuo, "Nikushinzō oyobi yuikaizō no kenkyū" (Studies in "flesh-body icons" and "ash icons"), *Tōyō gakuhō* 24, no. 3 (1937): 93–124. See in particular Paul Demiéville, "Momies d'Extrême-Orient," *Choix d'études sinologiques (1929–1970)* (Leiden: E. J. Brill, 1973), pp. 407–32; Doris Croissant, "Das Unsterbliche Leib: Ahneffigies und Reliquienporträt in der Porträtplastik Ostasiens," in Martin Kraatz, Jürg Meyer zur Capellen, and Dietrich Seckel,

eds., *Das Bildnis in der Kunst des Orients* (Stuttgart: Franz Steiner, 1990), pp. 235–68; Faure, *Rhetoric of Immediacy*; and Robert H. Sharf, "The Idolization of Enlightenment: On the Mummification of Ch'an Masters in Medieval China," *History of Religions* 32, no. 1 (1992): 1–31.

11. See Jonathan Parry, "Sacrificial Death and the Necrophagous Ascetic," in Maurice Bloch and Jonathan Parry, eds., *Death and the Regeneration of Life* (Cambridge: Cambridge University Press, 1982), pp. 74–110.

12. Also in existence are the four twelfth-century mummies of the Fujiwara family in northeastern Japan. The fact that all these mummies were found in northern Japan has to do with cultural conditions (the development of Shugendō in Hokuriku and Tōhoku), but perhaps also with climatic conditions necessary for their preservation. The southernmost *sokushin butsu* actually preserved seem to be those of Myōshin at Yokokuradera (near Gifu) and of Dansei in Ōhara (on the northern outskirts of Kyoto).

13. Suzuki Bokushi, *Snow Country Tales: Life in the Other Japan*, trans. Jeffrey Hunter (New York: Weatherhill, 1986), pp. 281–83.

14. On the Maitreya cult in East Asia, see Alan Sponberg and Helen Hardacre, eds., *Maitreya, the Future Buddha* (Cambridge: Cambridge University Press, 1988).

15. The legend appears in textual form at the turn of the eleventh century. One case of mummification that had nothing to do with Maitreya was that of Yutei Hōin (1591–1683), a Shingon monk who identified himself with the Buddha Yakushi and became the object of a healing cult at Kanshuji (Fukushima Prefecture). Matsumoto Akira points out a number of other Japanese cases (among which he includes that of Zōga and of his disciples) apparently related to the Pure Land doctrine. See Matsumoto Akira, *Nihon no miirabutsu* (Tokyo: Rokkō Shuppan, 1985).

16. See Kosugi, "Nikushinzō oyobi yuikaizō no kenkyū"; Demiéville, "Momies d'Extrême-Orient"; and Sharf, "The Idolization of Enlightenment."

17. See Kosugi, "Nikushinzō oyobi yuikaizō no kenkyū."

18. A few ash icons are recorded in Japan, for instance, those of Daidō Juen of Jijōji (Yamaguchi Prefecture) and Zuigan of Ankokuji (Gifu Prefecture). In China, the most famous example is that of the Chan master Wuxiang (alias Kim *heshang*).

19. See Bernard Faure, "Alternative Images of Pilgrimage: Sung-shan and Ts'aohsi," in Susan Naquin and Yü Chün-fang, eds., *Pilgrims and Sacred Sites in China* (Berkeley: University of California Press, 1992).

20. See Jacques Gernet, trans., *Les entretiens du maître de dhyāna Chen-houei du Hotsö* (Paris: Adrien Maisonneuve, 1949), p. 110.

21. See Walter Liebenthal, "Shih Hui-yüan's Buddhism as Set Forth in His Writings," *Journal of the American Oriental Society* 70 (1950): 258.

22. See Sugimoto Shunryū, *Zōtei Tōjō shitsunai kirigami narabini sanwa no kenkyū* (Researches on the esoteric *kirigami* and *sanwa* of the Sōtō tradition) (Tokyo: Sōtōshū shūmuchō, 1982 [1938]), p. 92.

23. Mōri Hisashi, *Japanese Portrait Sculpture* (Tokyo and New York: Kōdansha International, 1977), p. 44.

24. See Jean-Pierre Vernant, *Mortals and Immortals: Collected Essays*, ed. Froma I. Zeitlin (Princeton: Princeton University Press, 1991), pp. 186–92.

25. This is discussed by Michel Strickmann in "The Animate Icon," unpublished paper.

26. See Richard Gombrich, "The Consecration of a Buddhist Image," *Journal of Asian Studies* 26, no. 1 (1966): 23–36.

27. See Jan Gonda, *Eye and Gaze in the Veda* (Amsterdam: Verhandelingen der Koninklijke Nederlandse Akademie van Wetenschappen, 1970).

28. Robert E. Morrell, trans., *Early Kamakura Buddhism: A Minority Report* (Berkeley: Asian Humanities Press, 1987), p. 60.

29. Richard Mather, "Hymns on the Devotee's Entrance into the Pure Life," *Journal of the American Oriental Society* 106, no. 1 (1986): 93.

30. See Jonathan Parry, "Sacrificial Death and the Necrophagous Ascetic," in Maurice Bloch and Jonathan Parry, eds., *Death and the Regeneration of Life* (Cambridge: Cambridge University Press, 1982), p. 96.

31. See Judith A. Berling, "Bringing the Buddha down to Earth: Notes on the Emergence of *Yü-lu* as a Buddhist Genre," *History of Religions* 21, no. 1 (1987): 56–88.

32. See T. Griffith Foulk and Robert H. Sharf, "On the Ritual Use of Ch'an and Portraiture in Medieval China," *Cahiers d'Extrême-Asie* 7 (1993–1994): 149–219.

33. See Stanley Tambiah, *The Buddhist Saints of the Forest and the Cult of Amulets: A Study in Charisma, Hagiography, Sectarianism, and Millennial Buddhism* (Cambridge: Cambridge University Press, 1985).

34. See Ralph Giesey, *The Royal Funeral Ceremony in Renaissance France* (Geneva, 1960). On the ideology of the "king's two bodies," cf. Ernst H. Kantorowicz, *The King's Two Bodies: A Study in Medieval Political Theology* (Princeton: Princeton University Press, 1957).

35. See Foulk and Sharf, "On the Ritual Use," pp. 194–202.

36. "Man has no Body distinct from his Soul; for that call'd Body is a portion of Soul discern'd by the five Senses, the chief inlets of Soul in this age." William Blake, *Complete Writings*, ed. Geoffrey Keynes (Oxford: Oxford University Press, 1972), p. 149.

37. See Peter Brown, *Society and the Holy in Late Antiquity* (Berkeley: University of California Press, 1982), p. 263.

38. Alain Boureau, *Le simple corps du roi: L'impossible sacralité des souverains français, XVe–XVIIIe siècle* (Paris: Editions de Paris, 1988).

GLOSSARY

Ayuwang Monastery 阿育王寺

Caoxi 曹溪

Chan/Zen 禪/禅

Changan 長安

chinzō 頂相

Daoxuan 道宣

Darumashū 達摩宗

Dōgen 道元

Hokuetsu Seppu 北越雪譜

Huineng 慧能

ihai 位牌

Ikkyū Sōjun 一休宗純

inka 印可

kaigen 開眼

kaiyuan 開眼

Kōbō Daishi 弘法大師

Kōchi Hōin 弘智法印

ling 靈

Linji Yixuan 臨濟義玄

mappō 末法

Myōzen 明全

Nihonshoki 日本書紀

Rinzai Zen 臨濟禪

shari 舍利

Shenhui 神會

shenzuo 神座

sokushin butsu 即身佛

Sōtō 曹洞

Suzuki Bokushi 鈴木牧之

Wutai shan 五臺山

Xuefeng Yicun 雪峰義存

Yōkōji 永光寺

Yōsai 榮西

Zhejiang 浙江

GURU'S BODY, GURU'S ABODE

Daniel Gold

In the history of religions of the last several decades, few concepts have found wider applicability than that of Mircea Eliade's sacred space: someplace set apart as sanctified, often conceived as the center of the universe, in any event a place where the human world meets the divine.[1] Another important concept, featured particularly in historical studies of early Christianity and anthropological studies of Near Eastern Islam, is that of the holy person.[2] In these studies, we often find ideas of sacred space intersecting with those of holy person after the holy person's death: in saints' tombs and places sanctified by their physical relics. When we move beyond the Near East and Christian Europe to Hindu tradition, however, we find the intersection of place and person frequently occurring while holy persons are still alive, in their living presence and the space in which they interact with devotees. Linking the immanent spiritual presence to the concrete physical place is the holy person's body.

Hindus call a living person who is revered by devotees a guru. This word literally means "heavy." Most devotees, while not necessarily aware of the literal sense of the word, see the guru as heavy in many ways: a guru's authority is weighty; a guru's presence is imposing. In some Hindu traditions, moreover, this personal weightiness of the guru is understood to derive from a subtle physical density. The guru's body itself is taken to have been transformed through devotion and ascetic techniques into a conduit of divine power. Devotees interact with the divine by interacting with the guru. One of the central places for this interaction is the guru's abode, the ashram.

In the experiences they offer devotees, both the guru and the ashram differ from the other repositories of the sacred discussed in this section of the volume: the Awaji puppets by Jane Marie Law and the relics of Zen patriarchs by Bernard Faure. Although gurus may on occasion be treated as images of a deity, they have important dimensions lacking in inanimate objects seen as infused with life—even if, like Awaji puppets, these images seem to speak and move. Gurus are neither controlled by any puppeteer nor bound to any script. Capable of unexpected personal interaction with devotees, a living guru can startle them into new personal realizations. Ashrams, extending the field of the guru's physical presence, provide diverse ways in which these realizations can take place. As extensions of the master, the ashrams thus differ from the relics of Zen tradition, which appear to displace spiritual awakening with magical power. Instead of radically altering the power of the living guru after his death, a temporal change, the ashram broadens its range in space, if necessarily in an attenuated form.

Ideally sylvan retreats, ashrams have been increasingly set in urban environments as modern Indian city life has led to new developments in Hindu tradition. Busy, middle-class Hindus often find it difficult to practice complex traditional rituals; educated in Western science, they may find it hard to take seriously elaborate Hindu myth. Many have turned to new forms of devotional and yogic practice that are grounded less in ritual and myth than in direct personal experience. The gurus teaching these practices are often strong individuals whose personal appeal can stand independent of a traditional authority that may no longer be taken at face value. What they generally offer are streamlined forms of old Indian internal practices that can be carried out by large numbers of people under modern urban conditions. Because neither the practices of these gurus nor their spiritual authority depend on acceptance of the whole complex of Hindu tradition, their religious influence has also been able to spread among Westerners in search of religious alternatives.

Of contemporary holy persons who underscore the necessity of a living guru, one of the most vital lineages was made known to the West by Swami Muktananda. He founded an ashram in South Fallsburg, New York, that has since grown very large. He was succeeded after his passing by his female disciple, Swami Chidvilasananda, known as Gurumayi, who continues to spend time there as well as at the main Indian ashram in Ganeshpuri, Maharashtra. Deriving from Indian traditions that highlight the power of holy persons, continuing to maintain a succession of charismatic gurus, and supporting substantial ashrams in both India and the West, this lineage provides particularly apt examples of the ways in which the guru's powerful body makes the ashram a field of sacred space.[3]

The Power of the Guru in the Lineage

Ganeshpuri, the principal Indian center of the lineage, is about an hour or two by road from Bombay in the state of Maharashtra, a large region in western India that boasts a long tradition of popular holy persons. The Maharashtrian devotional tradition is one of many that swept through India from the seventh century on. All of these devotional traditions produced great poet-singers in vernacular languages whose verses and life stories form the bases of commentary by later figures with lesser poetic gifts. Within these traditions, different gurus made their own religious syntheses, drawing on their own experiences and sometimes on new textual sources as well.[4]

Characteristic of the Maharashtrian devotional tradition is a very early assimilation of aspects of the Indian yogic heritage. Indeed, the first great poet in the tradition, Jnanadeva (born ca. 1275), claims a spiritual lineage from legendary yogis called Naths. Like most other traditions of popular devotion in India, the Maharashtrian did not, in theory, discriminate according to Hindu caste, but at the same time it was more open than some to traditional Hindu ritual forms.

Swami Muktananda and his successor have long revered the great Maharashtrian poet-singers and commented on their verses. In their synthesis of yoga and devotion, their admittance of all Hindu castes (and even of traditionally impure foreigners), and their acceptance of what they deem worthwhile in Hindu ritual, the gurus in the lineage stand squarely within the socioreligious tradition of Maharashtrian devotion.

Distinctive to the lineage, however, is a particular type of yoga that seems to derive in part from sources outside the Maharashtrian mainstream. The gurus refer to it as siddha yoga—a name with precedent in broader Hindu tradition but which outside India has become particularly identified with these gurus' teachings and practices.[5] To link this yoga to the larger Indian heritage, the gurus in the lineage have turned, in part, to selected texts of Kashmir Shaivism. A complex tradition with many rich philosophical and ritual texts, Kashmir Shaivism presents much on which devotees may reflect if they are so inclined.[6] Most devotees, however, are content with the central experience of siddha yoga, which can be described in general terms as an experience of the divine power perceived to flow through the guru, who thus becomes a living object of devotion. *Siddha* here means "a perfected one," and the name *siddha yoga* emphasizes the importance for the yoga of a perfected guru who is understood to be able to channel divine power.

The Bodies of Perfected Persons

Deriving from a Sanskrit root (*sidh*) that means to attain, complete, or be fulfilled, siddha and related terms cover a wide semantic range in Hindu religious traditions. At the most elevated reaches of this range is the siddha referred to in siddha yoga: a living person who has attained life's final goal. That goal itself can then be referred to as siddhi, meaning "ultimate spiritual perfection." Having achieved union with the divine while embodied on earth, siddhas do not immediately leave the body behind. Instead, they continue to fulfill their destined roles in the human world—roles that frequently, but not always, entail nurturing disciples along a spiritual path.[7]

Spiritual accomplishment, however, also has explicit psychic and physical dimensions. While moving toward the highest goal, the adept may acquire a number of lesser attainments, psychic powers of different kinds that are frequently referred to in the plural as siddhis. Lists of psychic powers are many,[8] but those most commonly perceived by disciples are those entailing holy persons' ability to extend their subtle persons. Gurus occasionally appear to disciples in ways that are not only concrete but collective—appearing more substantially real than most images seen in individual meditation. In Swami Muktananda's lineage, these appearances often accompany initiation sessions. At an intensive group session held in the absence of Gurumayi, for example, a number of disciples reported concrete visions of her. The hall monitor at the door saw her go through the wall. "I'm going inside to give Shaktipat," the monitor heard Gurumayi say, referring to the "descent of power" disciples experience at initiation, "and you will be the first one."[9] Even deceased yogis can appear in this way. When Gurumayi asked a visitor to the Ganeshpuri ashram to meditate in the room next to Swami Muktananda's shrine, the devotee accompanying the visitor had a vision of the Swami: "He came striding directly through the wall . . . stood in front of the man, and gave him full Shaktipat." Just at that point the two were called away by Gurumayi, the visitor obviously having had a powerful experience.[10] At crucial times, the guru's subtle presence is understood to pervade substantially a particular physical space.

A distinctly bodily attainment is found in the stories of several legendary yogis who are thought to be eternally active on earth. Like most other siddhas, they can reveal themselves to the devout through subtle senses like gods. But they are also understood to be present on earth in a more densely physical way—eternally embodied—roaming the Himalayas, perhaps, or hidden in the jungle. Some say that Gorakh Nath, an illustrious yogi who may have lived about the ninth or tenth century, might still be living hidden in the forest ashram of the sage Dattatreya, who is also said to be eternally embodied. Many yogic texts refer not only to bodily postures but also to alchemy, both of which offer techniques understood to alter the substance of the body, enabling it to hold spiritual power as well as prolonging its duration.[11]

While the goal of a physically conceived immortality is not widely held by Hindus and is not advocated in Swami Muktananda's lineage, admitting its very possibility reflects other, more widely held yogic understandings. For although Hindu ascetics commonly speak of the renunciation of material life, many yogis also see the material body itself as a source of spiritual power. Yogic philosophies frequently take physical matter ultimately as concentrated spiritual energy, and yogis who have learned how can in their persons manifest a conscious continuity between the two.[12] Through spiritual practices, moreover, the yogi's body undergoes subtle changes and can thus be understood to be very special, imbued with consciousness in a way that the bodies of ordinary people are not. Thus one of Gurumayi's disciples, entrusted with serving at large public audiences of devotees, has remarked that Gurumayi's "every pore, her every cell is so refined that I can see in the way she holds her hand whether or not she wants to hold" a particular offering.[13]

Even if a yogi has not achieved physical immortality, his or her body is usually understood to have undergone a transformation—sometimes conceived in alchemical terms—that makes it particularly valuable. At death—unlike most Hindus, who are regularly cremated—yogis in some lineages are buried: their bones are powerful; the places where the bones rest are special. And more important, during life, yogic power is transmitted to disciples through embodied gurus. In order to progress quickly on yogic paths, disciples with bodies are understood to need spiritual power that is manifest at their own level of physical density. Almost universally, yogic traditions are explicit about the need for a living guru.[14]

Contemplating the Guru

While the necessity of a physically embodied guru is widely acknowledged in yogic traditions, many disciples have little chance to be in the guru's physical presence for any length of time. And even when they do, they realize that the "principle of guruhood" is something much more than the body, a "mystery" "very hard to comprehend."[15] More familiar to many than the guru's physical person is what is understood to be the guru's subtle presence. At initiation the guru is understood to implant something of himself or herself into the disciple, a consciousness that spans the most sublime heights and the most physical depths. Through techniques of meditation, disciples identify with this consciousness. By identifying with the guru, whom they see as having become divine, disciples may achieve a divine identity themselves. "In the course of time," says Swami Muktananda, "the disciple comes to absorb the guru's perfection into his being, and then he radiates it."[16]

The Swami goes on to elaborate the dynamics of the disciple's transformation. "The transition takes place through constant absorption of the Guru's light and by constantly following the practices"[17] he or she recommends. A practice particularly conducive to absorption of the guru's light is a meditation on the guru's image. "The root of meditation is the Guru's image" begins an oft-quoted verse from the Guru Gita, a popular text from the Skanda Purana that the Swami enjoined disciples to chant daily. The verse continues to reveal the singular role that disciples can see their gurus playing in their spiritual practice: "The root of worship is the Guru's feet. The root of mantra is the Guru's speech. The root of liberation is the Guru's grace."[18]

While such sentiments are found in many yogic traditions, they are subject to some dilution in traditions with strong mythological components and complex meditation practices. In those contexts, the guru can be regarded as an incarnation of a mythic deity—usually Shiva for Hindus, or a Buddha in Tibet. While the guru's image may be seen as a particularly vital meditation object, other images, from mythic tradition, may be contemplated more frequently.[19] Alternatively, the guru's physical image may remain a frequent object of contemplation, but is visualized alongside the iconic forms of mythic deities, with various gods identified at different parts of the body.[20] Swami Muktananda's lineage, however, falls outside any one sectarian fold; and since it remains socioreligiously rooted in popular devotion, most devotees are not expected to perform complicated visualization practices. As an object of contemplation, the guru's image has no rival. The form and significance of that image itself, however, is subject to considerable variation.

Images in Succession

Vivid inner images of the guru often appear in response to crises of succession, which are endemic to lineages of gurus and disciples. Successions are regularly disputed, and even when a successor has been generally recognized, individual devotees may not find their psychic allegiance transferring quickly to the new guru. Thus disciples' visions of old and new gurus in close relationship can mark the resolution of doubts and the affirmation of their lineage's continuing power.

Two such visions were reported at a large group session of Indian devotees in Nasik, Maharashtra, in November 1986. "When we sat for meditation," reports one devotee, "I saw Baba Muktananda standing by a cradle, gently rocking it. I looked inside and the baby Gurumayi was in the cradle. Then, suddenly, the scene was changed and Gurumayi, grown up, was standing, rocking the cradle. Again, I looked to see what was inside, and the world was in the cradle. As the divine mother, she was rocking the whole world—taking care of the whole world."[21] Here the image of Gurumayi appears finally as the divine mother. But images of gurus in a lineage can also give them a different kind of religious significance, presenting successive gurus as repeated embodiments of a lineage's divine transformative force. Thus another person at the same meditation session, looking a generation further back, takes the succession as an identification among divine beings that become transformed one into the other. He saw Nityananda, Muktananda's guru, giving the blessing of fearlessness, conventionally represented in Hindu iconography by a raised arm and open palm. The figure changed into Muktananda and then into Gurumayi, all the while giving the same blessing.[22]

The place and time of these visionary experiences make them particularly pertinent. They occurred among local Maharashtrian devotees about a year after the major succession crisis in the lineage had come to a head. For three years after Muktananda's passing in 1982, Gurumayi and a brother-disciple of hers were treated as his co-successors. Although yogic gurus may have a number of successors who move away and make disciples of their own, joint authority within a single ashram establishment is unusual in Hindu tradition. And even though siddhas and their disciples tolerate

Gurumayi Chidvilasananda. SYDA Foundation.

unorthodox ways, this particular arrangement, with obvious potential for
conflicts, was not destined to last. In early November 1985, the other successor declared himself unqualified, leaving the ashram. After Gurumayi
was installed as sole successor, however, he sought to regain his position.
Although he failed, he made public claims that kept the succession question
alive through much of the next year. By the time of the visions reported
at Nasik, many devotees were no doubt ready to have any lingering
doubts resolved.[23]

The Guru's Photo

Appearing unique and exalted to mark the end of a succession crisis,
the guru's image can in other situations also seem personal, intimate, and
enchanting. Indeed, in a devotional tradition without a clear mythic focus,
it is the guru that becomes the primary object of religious emotion.[24] Attracted to their gurus, devotees enjoy seeing their gurus' pictures. Hindu
iconographical enthusiasm thus develops in the contemporary setting into
an efflorescence of photography of the guru. Different photos present
different expressions, which have their own evocative effects: laughing,
serene, authoritative, ecstatic. Most contemporary Indian ashrams prominently display pictures of the present guru and their predecessors in their
lineage. This is especially evident at Gurumayi's ashrams, where photography and photographic archives are well developed.

The photos themselves come into devotees' religious experience, and are understood by them, in different ways. Certainly their most common role is inspirational, helping to put devotees in touch with their feelings for the guru, reminding them of the guru's presence. Sometimes the photos can appear as conduits of spiritual power—like some Hindu images and the portraits of Zen masters discussed by Bernard Faure in his essay in this volume. This heightened perception of the photo can figure as part of a meditation experience: "Finally, I opened my eyes," says one disciple. "I saw light coming out of Gurumayi's picture. It just kept sparkling, this light, and flowing from her picture into me. Then I saw light coming from me and going into her picture. It was an exchange of energy. . . ."[25]

Even outside meditation experience, a guru's photo can appear to some as an object with extraordinary powers. Indeed, Swami Muktananda himself spoke of the potencies of a holy person's photo in concrete terms, presenting the photo as a form in which the holy person's consciousness can be embodied. "A picture has great power," says Muktananda. "The kind of power the picture has depends upon whose picture it is. . . . The state of the one whose photograph was taken remains inherent in the photograph."[26] The power in the photograph is understood to be so concrete that it can also be perceived by nondevotees. Thus a relative visiting a devotee sees the photo moving. "There's some kind of electrical device attached to it, right?" he asks. No, he is told, just "the Guru's grace."[27] A photo, moreover, may even arouse potent emotions in people who threaten devotees, thus serving as objective protection. We hear of thieves accosting one of Gurumayi's disciples as he returned to his village. The disciple, declaring that his guru was protecting him, displayed her picture. The thieves "took one look at the picture and they became scared and left."[28]

Experiencing the Guru in the Body

If even the photo of the guru can manifest so much power in the material world, how much more so can the guru's material body. Because disciples understand divine power to be emanating from the guru's body, they often want simply to be around it, ready to receive any blessings that may naturally come their way. At the same time, because they desire to approach spiritual perfection in their own bodies, they often participate enthusiastically in the guru's concrete work, transforming their corporeal selves into instruments of the divine. The assimilation of the guru's divinity through simply being around him or her is covered by the Hindu concept of darshan, the "blessed vision" of a divine being. Participation in the guru's work comes under the heading of seva, religiously motivated "service."

In addition to their practical, external forms, darshan and seva can both also refer to internal experiences: visions of the guru within, like those of a god, are regularly called darshan; similarly, the performance of meditation practices enjoined by the guru can be thought of as seva, work that contributes to the guru's spiritual mission. For devotees living outside an ashram, these inward experiences are more easily accessible than the corresponding outward ones. But opportunities for outward darshan and seva, when available, are valued very highly, and are very frequently what draw devotees to ashrams.

The Guru's Physical Presence: The Power of Darshan

Darshan is a phenomenon widespread through Hindu tradition. Referring to almost any kind of transmission of grace through sight or vision, the term is commonly used by ordinary worshipers to refer to their encounters with the Hindu deities they see manifest in traditional images.[29] The sense here is that grace flows to worshipers from a visual contact with a divinely empowered image. A similar dynamic is understood to occur through contact with a spiritually powerful person, who can also move spontaneously in the world and interact with devotees. In reference to a holy person, then, darshan can have two senses. It can refer to specific, organized occasions in which a devotee may have personal contact with a guru—sometimes routinized in ways that present parallels to ritual adoration of a deity. But it can also refer to any occasion of individual contact with the guru—perhaps unexpected—in which disciples feel they have been blessed.

Unexpected blessings through personal interactions with the guru usually occur amid everyday experience. On tour with Gurumayi, for example, a disciple is suddenly asked by the guru to accompany her in the car to a nearby meditation center. The disciple is "stunned. It was just me, Gurumayi, and the driver. I was instantly in another state."[30] Just being alone in close contact with the guru seems to transport the disciple beyond normal consciousness.

When disciples in an exalted state observe the guru living in the world, moreover, they are likely to have new realizations about the guru's nature—about what it means for a living person to be an embodiment of the divine. "Even after achieving perfection," says Swami Muktananda, a good devotee "keeps learning from his Guru by making the Guru reveal himself to him by the force of his devotion."[31] In this case, as in many, the disciple's realization is triggered by the guru's interaction with others—here with two young boys from families of local devotees. When the two boys wave vigorously at the car in which Gurumayi and the disciple are riding, Gurumayi opens the door, then sits them down next to her. After one makes a fuss about waving out the window, she takes his hand and looks at his palm. "If he has good guidance," Gurumayi notes, "he could become a good renunciate."[32] The disciple riding with Gurumayi is awestruck. How can the young boy not receive good guidance when he is "practically sitting in [Gurumayi's] lap?" In pondering this question, the disciple comes to look at Gurumayi in a new light, as someone who is herself less an agent in the divine play than a participant in it, who acknowledges lines of destiny like those written in the boy's hand. Gurumayi "doesn't look at the world with a view toward changing it," the disciple comes to understand; "she just witnesses the world as it unfolds."[33] Embodied divinity here appears not so much to generate divine grace and guidance as to serve as a vehicle through which they pass.

As a living vehicle of divine grace, the guru can move around to distribute blessings to devotees in their own homes and villages. In doing so, he or she can turn these ordinary places—at least temporarily—into sacred places. Thus, returning from the meditation center with the disciple, Gurumayi stopped at the boy's family's house to give them some prasad, ritually sanctified food offerings. Immediately invited inside, she followed her hosts as they pushed away the clotheslines in front of their very modest dwelling. Although the house itself was "tiny and very dark and cool,"[34] everyone crowded in, the entire extended family and all of Gurumayi's accompanying devotees. Seated in the place of honor—on a swing in the center of a room, above devotees sitting on mats on the floor—Gurumayi was offered ceremonial worship as if a divinity. The small dark living room is transformed into a shrine.

If a house can thus appear to be a temple while the guru is there, a village can take on the aura of an ashram. The visits during which these new perceptions of the familiar take place are usually inspired by devotees' common desires to have the guru grace their abode. One devotee tells how Gurumayi's visit to her village was preceded by a dream.[35] Gurumayi was singing and playing the harmonium in front of a big crowd in the devotee's village; she called the devotee close and hugged her. The devotee "was so full of love" that a few days later she composed a prayer-song: "At least once, at least once, Gurumayi, please come to our village." Eventually Gurumayi did accept the devotee's invitation to come to the village, which was famous for its mangoes. Walking around the mango orchard, she remarked: "In this orchard I feel just like I'm in the Ganeshpuri ashram."[36]

In temporarily transforming familiar surroundings, the darshan given by the guru on tour is often a collective experience for family groups and local communities; but for those living under spiritual discipline at ashrams, darshan of the guru is likely to spark intense individual experiences. These experiences can be personally intimate even in the routinized forms they take at large establishments, where rare occasions of spontaneous encounter with the guru are supplemented by regular opportunities for brief one-on-one contact. Often the outward encounter is no more than a bow from the disciple and eye contact from the guru; sometimes a few words pass between them. There may also be some regular physical contact: Swami Muktananda would touch devotees with a wand of peacock feathers, a practice continued by Gurumayi. At Ganeshpuri and South Fallsburg, as at other large ashrams, the "darshan line" can move on slowly for hours.

One devotee tells of how his experience in darshan line led to both spiritual and personal realizations. The night before, the disciple had been reading about spiritual lineage, pondering with difficulty the relationships between generations of gurus and disciples. He then dreamed that he "was looking out the back window of [his] house and Gurumayi was in the back yard. She came to the back door and tried to open it. It was locked. . . . [He] said, well, Gurumayi, that's the way I was raised; my mother always wanted the doors locked. She said, I was here before your mother; I was here even before Baba [Muktananda] and Bhagwan Nityananda. How come your door has always been locked?"[37] In darshan line at Ganeshpuri, the devotee told Gurumayi the dream. Understanding that the dream linked his lack of spiritual understanding to his personal closedness (he kept the doors locked), he also asked Gurumayi for the ability to be devoted.

The disciple's experience in the darshan line came both from his own narration and the guru's response. Just relating the dream to the living guru resolved the disciple's intellectual questions about spiritual lineage: "When I told Gurumayi this dream, I had the experience of her expanding in front of me, and I understood that . . . the whole lineage of all the sages . . . is within Gurumayi."[38] The guru's response to his request for devotion led to new puzzlement. "Just do your seva," she said, repeating her answer to his second imprecation that "devotion . . . is all I want."[39] At one level this response could mean simply that there was nothing special Gurumayi was about to do; the disciple must "keep doing [his] seva," his daily work at the ashram. Still, to the devotee in his heightened state at darshan, the response probably carried more complex meanings: what relationships might he draw between seva and devotion?

The Disciple's Physical Work: The Virtues of Seva

Certainly the semantic range of the term *seva* has grown very wide. It can refer to any work done for the sake of some higher religious authority: a respected elder, a teacher, or divinities conceived in mythic as well as abstract terms. Everyday service to religious teachers is mentioned in the early Upanishads,[40] which date from about 600 B.C.E. By the beginning of the Common Era, with the emergence of the forms of devotional religion still prevalent in India, seva developed an important specialized meaning. Seeing divinity embodied in a mythic image of the Lord, many Hindus would treat material icons of gods respectfully as persons, dressing them, offering them food, and washing their feet. These ritual actions of service to the embodied image have since been known technically as seva, which is in this sense a liturgical term, referring to the ceremonial worship of the deity. The concept of seva thus links ideas of everyday service to a teacher with those of regular devotional worship.

Seva, then, represents a counterpart to darshan, another way of inter-acting with one's object of devotion. While darshan refers largely to a sense of assimilation of power, a passive experience, seva entails devotees' activity, often activity of a very physical nature. Service for the guru becomes a way of identifying with him or her: devotees are doing the guru's work, participating in the guru's earthly mission. And since the end of devotion in Hindu tradition entails merging one's identity into a devotional object, physical service to the guru can be a highly effective devotional practice. Through performing service to the guru, devotees can see themselves extending the spread of the guru's spiritual power in the material world, their own bodies becoming extensions of the guru's material nature.

The assimilation of the guru's power in the body entailed by this perception can be experienced with particular intensity through physical work, which may help devotees overcome resistance to menial service they might otherwise see as distracting them from their goals. One devotee on kitchen duty at South Fallsburg, unhappy about a new assignment that would necessitate missing darshan, ended up getting a welcome surprise: "my supervisor gave me a cart to be cleaned. . . . As soon as I began to clean the cart, a strange energy went through my hands and into my body and I felt an incredible and indescribable ecstasy. Gurumayi was inside that cart. As soon as I surrendered myself to seva, Gurumayi entered me. Now I very much like to clean carts."[41] Indeed, service itself is said to evoke religious emotions that can lead people to discipleship. One person, who "didn't know anything about Siddha Yoga," was a friend of the devotee at whose house Gurumayi was going to stay during her visit to Nagpur. There "was so much going on there to prepare for her visit," the person writes, that "I began to do guruseva. I didn't know why, but I started to feel an intense love for Gurumayi even though I had not yet met her."[42] This person went on to become a devotee.

In addition to the ecstasy and love that comes from guruseva, "service to the guru," devotees also speak of trials and transformation. The situations in which disciples find themselves in seva may be taken to derive ultimately from the guru's will, which is understood to be rooted in a higher reality. Difficulties encountered are thus likely to lead disciples to question their own shortcomings instead of the situations themselves. Limitations to creativity, we hear, can then be overcome: doing iconography under the guru's guidance, a trained artist faces creative block but eventually enhances her talents;[43] a professional singer learns to stop worrying about her voice when she's performing hymns at the ashram.[44] Frequently, everyday tasks become spiritual lessons for a disciple and are sometimes held up as examples for others. A disciple doing ashram business in Bombay, for instance, gets into an argument, which Gurumayi hears about and mentions in a talk. "He's got such a big ego," she says, "he doesn't know how to communicate."[45] The overcoming of an inflated ego through service is no doubt its most frequently reported benefit.

When direct interaction with the guru occurs during service, the experience can be particularly intense. One devotee, from the context obviously a Western woman, tells of an unexpected encounter with Gurumayi during a group construction project at South Fallsburg. Her account brings together experiences of seva and darshan with a somatic experience of the guru's power. "I'm not really used to shovelling," writes the devotee. "About an hour into it my arms were ready to fall off my body. . . . Then . . . [Gurumayi] walked all the way up a little hill right next to where I was and picked up a pick and shovel. I thought, Oh my God, she is going to dig! Wow this is nice. . . . I knew that if I didn't pull it together, my body would fall apart, because I couldn't do it anymore. Something else was taking over. . . ."[46] Working so close to the guru thus leads to a sense of being physically taken over by her force.

After about half-an-hour of working beside Gurumayi, who joked with her a bit, the disciple feels she should move, to let other disciples have a similar experience. She decides to finish up, but even though she "was taking dirt out of the last hole . . . it wasn't getting any deeper." A Swami[47] came to measure the hole and told her, "It's not deep enough, go deeper." Her account continues: "Suddenly my mind said, Go deeper. What a metaphor! . . . in one minute the hole was finished." This spiritual realization is followed by an intense physical sensation: "As I walked down the hill, my body felt as if I had put it into a microwave oven; heat was coming out of it and my whole body was vibrating. My breath was coming fast, panting in and out."[48] An experience of the guru in the body like this—with an intensity coming from simultaneous seva and darshan—is, as here, most commonly accessible at an ashram.

The Ashram as Guru's Abode

The term *ashram* derives from a Sanskrit root meaning "to exert one's self" *(shram)*. Etymologically, the term implies a place where people make special efforts, where they lead a disciplined life. Set apart from the everyday world, an ashram typically provides a place where individuals can devote themselves to spiritual practice under the guidance of a guru. As the physical seat of the guru's body and psychic presence, moreover, the ashram can be experienced as a concentrated center of the guru's transformative power. "Wherever a great saint dwells," writes Swami Muktananda, "he endows that place with the character of his profound inner state. . . . There is no distinction between a holy place and its presiding saint."[49]

Once established, an ashram can have an attraction of its own: "The atmosphere of a siddha's abode is charged with enormous force. It makes its impact on a person as soon as he enters it and begins to recast him in its own mold."[50] In contemporary movements, established ashrams are able to play an important role in extending the practical range of the guru's physical presence and psychic influence. Just by living at the ashram, devotees who have little personal contact with the guru can experience the guru's power, which continues to be focused there even when the guru is temporarily away.

Traditional Types

As a secluded abode of religious practitioners and their disciples, the institution of the ashram has long precedent in Indian tradition.[51] This ideal is regularly portrayed in classical literary texts, where the ashram is depicted as the home of a wise teacher who lives with his disciples in sylvan surroundings.[52] The students imbibe the teacher's knowledge and do service to him, which in the rural environment often included common labor. Under the teacher's direction, they lead a disciplined life devoted to sacred learning and spiritual practice. Despite the historical diversity of ashrams in India, the image of the ashram as the peaceful abode of a wise teacher living in harmonious order with his disciples remains the cultural and religious ideal. Indeed, this was one of the reasons, they say, why Swami Muktananda was attracted to the forested Catskill region as a place for his U.S. retreat.

While the different historical variants of Hindu tradition that have emerged over the last two millennia have not all built ashrams in forests, they have often located their establishments in places physically distinct from everyday reality. Many ashrams have been located in remote villages, supported by lands donated by wealthy patrons or tax revenues assigned by a sympathetic ruler.[53] Others have been located on the outskirts of large towns, where they receive support from local householders impressed by the sanctity of a particular guru.[54] Still others have been located in particular pilgrimage centers such as Banaras and Rishikesh, where they are supported in part by pious travelers. In all these cases, the ashram through its location represents a refuge from the ordinary world, even while often remaining accessible to interested urban householders. The guru's abode is a place apart, distinct from one's own.

Swami Muktananda pointedly contrasts the ashram with the home: "While at home, you spend your time filling your stomach, gratifying your senses, occupying your mind in all kinds of wild hopes, anger and irritation, cunning, intrigue, and carnal indulgence. You continually conduct yourself in the same manner when you leave your home—in your office or factory, or in the company of friends. . . . Do not carry this mentality to an ashram. . . ."[55] Certainly the new mentality imbued by devotees at the ashram may ideally be carried back into the everyday world, but the sharp contrast drawn here by the Swami nevertheless suggests two corollaries. First, at the ashram devotees form a special community that transcends the mundane world of family and work. Second, undergirding this new community is a relationship that transcends mundane ties: that between disciple and guru.

Specific senses of community and perceptions of gurus differ, however, in ashrams from yogic and devotional traditions. Yogis typically treasure their disciplined individual solitude and look to the guru as a source of psychic wisdom and spiritual power. Devotional traditions are likely to complement individual discipline with shared celebration and spontaneity coming from the interjection of the guru's personal presence into devotees' lives. Like other medieval and modern holy persons, Swami Muktananda was adept at synthesis, and the ashrams he founded bring together ideals of yoga and devotion in ways that have parallels in other large international establishments.

A Powerful Place for Individual Practice

The isolation from the world provided by yogic ashrams is often a preliminary to meditation practices that flourish with individual solitude. A cave, providing an atmosphere of complete silence, is frequently considered an exemplary meditation place for a yogi. Although natural caves are not usually available at ashram sites, artificial caves are sometimes made—either newly dug underground or, as at South Fallsburg, created from specially designated basement rooms. At crowded ashrams, moreover, a sense of inner solitude can be fostered through the observance of a common daily discipline, which usually entails early rising, meditation, daily work, and evening activities. Swami Muktananda comments about life at Ganeshpuri: "I try to ensure that everyone in the ashram sleeps, gets up, and eats punctually, remains silent and alone even while in the midst of a crowd . . . talks softly and a little . . . and lives a pure and austere life."[56]

Silence and solitude are particularly appropriate to meditation practices that draw attention inward toward the subtle physical body. As in many yogic traditions, Swami Muktananda's Siddha Yoga leads to new perceptions of the energies contained in the body, which is conceived in terms of traditional yogic physiology. A passage from the Swami's autobiography relates some of his early experiences of the chakras, places where energy is concentrated in the body:

> Sometimes I would see a beautiful, slender, silver-colored tube, standing like a pillar from the muladhara [chakra at the base of the spine] to the throat. It was fascinating, and I wondered how such a slender tube could be permeated with the silvery light. Sometimes I would see a god in each chakra, and feel a slight pain there. Sometimes I would look right into my body at the nervous, circulatory, excretory, and digestive systems.[57]

This passage seems to show a twentieth-century reconciliation of subtle yogic physiology with other, grosser physiological systems, but the former is definitely more alluring. Described in different versions in a number of Hindu treatises,[58] it is also subject to visual display. Yogic meditation can thus be enhanced by the frequent availability of textual and iconographic materials at ashrams: images of deities, maps of inner worlds, and line diagrams (called yantras) that can help focus the mind.

More important to many practitioners than these obvious outward supports to their meditation is the less obvious inward one they find at ashrams: the spiritually charged atmosphere generated from the presence of the guru and the continuing practice of fellow disciples. For while the subtle energies of the guru can extend infinitely in space, they are densest at the place where the guru is physically located and may even continue to be concentrated there after his physical passing. Referring to his own guru, who once lived at Ganeshpuri, Swami Muktananda extols the benefits of the place: "This is the impact of the Ganeshpuri atmosphere—the magic of the power of spiritually charged particles . . . emanating from Sri Gurudev."[59]

A Place of Interaction with the Embodied Divine

Although temporary visitors to Siddha Yoga ashrams often attempt a strict yogic regimen, those who live there for longer periods are likely to adopt an attitude that draws in part from devotional movements that began to burgeon in India in the seventh century. Crucial to the sense of ashram life fostered in these movements are two central concepts in Hindu devotional traditions: lila, "divine play," and satsang, "good company." The latter term refers to the community of disciples who keep "good company" with the guru and with one another. To the devotee, the universe appears as the continuing divine play of the Lord, with the guru as the Lord's veritable embodiment. Devotees with high spiritual qualifications are attracted to the "good company" of the guru and his circle, and life within the ashram is experienced as purified and highly pleasurable divine play.

Not just a seat of the guru's power apart from the world, the ashram as a place of divine play should also reflect heavenly enjoyments. Tasty food, celebrations, and beautiful surroundings all have a place there. Swami Muktananda waxes eloquent about the natural wonders of the Ganeshpuri ashram: "the orchards and trees, the fertility of the branches bending to the ground with their rich fruits, the loveliness and fragrance of abundant flowers, the holiness of the cows. . . ."[60] People living at the ashram, he affirms, should be open to the beauty that is there.[61]

The divine play at an ashram is given significance according to specific devotional traditions. In some, divine play is understood in graphically mythic terms, with the guru taken to be an incarnation of a fabled figure like Krishna, and his close disciples as the incarnations of Krishna's intimates. In this case the ashram may be seen as the present earthly replication of a mythic realm: an "earthly Vrindavan," for example, corresponding both to Krishna's earlier legendary playing field on earth and his eternal heavenly realm.[62] In other traditions, including those of many of the medieval poet-saints cited by Swami Muktananda, the link with mythic lore is less direct. The guru is seen as a divine being of his or her own distinct nature and the disciples as fellow sojourners on a spiritual path. The interaction of individual disciples with the guru and with one another can lead to great heights of wisdom and experience.

A good deal of this interaction among gurus and disciples comes through the dynamics of seva—which, though oriented toward the guru, in large ashrams more frequently involves the interplay of devotees with one another. The supervisor who gives the order to clean the cart, the Swami who urges the digger to "go deeper"—these fellow disciples also play roles in the ashram drama, one that is frequently joyful, sometimes unsettling, but always revealing hidden truths beyond surface realities.

Modern Transformations

The ashrams at Ganeshpuri and South Fallsburg are examples of the many large establishments that have grown out of Hindu tradition in the twentieth century. As modern means of transport and communication have radically transformed a guru's possible sphere of influence, particularly compelling spiritual personalities often attract large numbers of people from India and abroad. Although the role of the popular holy person has immediate precedent in Hindu tradition, the scale of popular followings is now often of a much greater order. Like popular holy persons of the past, many contemporary gurus frequently have a relatively limited group of devotees with whom they interact regularly and a much larger circle of devotees with whom they do not have close outward relation.[63] These latter devotees, recognizing an inward relationship with the guru, contemplate the guru's image from afar and treasure any interaction they can have with the guru in the physical world.

To renew contact with far-flung groups of devotees, many gurus make periodic tours. In addition to providing opportunities for brief encounters with many disciples, the tour also makes for intense experiences for those accompanying the guru. Indeed, touring with the guru can be a highly prized form of service. Most devotees who want to spend time near the guru, however, must go to an ashram.

Many of the transformations in the modern ashram thus entail extending the range of opportunities through which large numbers of devotees can understand themselves to be interacting with the guru in a concrete way. When the guru is present, "darshan lines" and their equivalents are held. In addition, large collective gatherings are organized with the guru in attendance. Devotees of Siddha Yoga talk of "evening programs," an adaptation of Indian English that refers to a particular elaboration of the common Indian devotional gathering called satsang, a Hindi term that in other contexts refers to the community of devotees itself. Like traditional satsangs, evening programs can feature lectures, the chanting of hymns, and meditation. When the guru is away, a focal center for devotion can be provided by certain physical articles seen as embodying the guru's presence and power. These may be objects connected with the lineage, a grave or consecrated image of the past guru, or objects with which the present guru has been in close physical touch, frequently sandals or a particular chair. Whether or not the guru is present, arrangements can be made to let devotees feel that they are interacting with the guru through concrete service.

As a place of physical interaction between a single mobile guru and a multitude of disciples, the contemporary ashram has undergone changes in both its socioreligious and its symbolic significance. Since at a large ashram the guru is a physically distant figure for most inhabitants, the religious significance of the community of disciples is likely to increase. At the same time, the sense of community provided by the ashram collectivity is often more crucial for contemporary urban devotees than for traditional Hindu ones. Among urban Hindus, ties to region and to extended kin and caste networks have frequently loosened. Isolated urban Westerners may never have had much sense of community belonging at all.

Serving urban devotees, ashrams are now often found in the middle of major metropolitan areas in India and abroad. These city ashrams are frequently limited in size and serve a specific community. In residence at these ashrams are often longtime dedicated disciples—whom other devotees may take as the guru's representatives or as elder spiritual siblings whose guidance is valued. Like some yogic ashrams in earlier days, these are often supported by urban devotees who see the ashram as a place to which they can retreat for spiritual practice and experience of community. Even in the city, then, the ashram can still appear as a place of refuge from worldly distraction. Concurrently, outside large cities, ashrams serving as major centers of a guru with an international following have grown quite large. In India, the Ganeshpuri Ashram has parallels among other movements in Beas, Punjab; and Pondicherry.[64] Extensive establishments become necessary because these ashrams not only house a core of regular residents and those who come for temporary stays during ordinary times but must also be able to accept much larger numbers for extraordinary events. At some of these ashrams—like the one at South Fallsburg—the most important of these extraordinary events is the extended stay of the guru.

The major transformation of the ashram's identity in modern times is indeed in its significance as the guru's abode. With contemporary gurus frequently on tour all over the world, no one place may serve as a regular residence. Ashrams may be set up in many places, and all may be seen at least figuratively as the guru's abode—graced by the guru's physical presence at least occasionally and continuing to serve as a seat of the guru's power. Moreover, major national and international headquarters, where the guru spends extended periods in residence, are clearly the guru's abode in more than a figurative sense.

Even as the literal significance of the ashram as the guru's abode decreases in an age of touring gurus, its practical religious significance grows. In movements rooted in popular Indian traditions that highlight the holy person, interaction with the guru is a very precious resource. But the guru's finite body has limited capacities. Large ashrams then serve to maximize the interaction that disciples are able to have, distributing it broadly and giving it added intensity when it occurs. Moreover, for the many devotees in residence with little concrete contact with the guru, the ashram itself can serve as a more diffuse field of interaction, a means for experiencing the guru's presence in a way more physically intense than could be had anywhere else. "Reflect on the significance of an ashram," writes Swami Muktananda. "It is the extended body of a Siddha, yogi, saint, seer, or sage."[65] Containing the guru bodily, the ashram is enveloped by the guru psychically, and continually makes the guru's presence immediate to devotees.

NOTES

1. An accessible presentation of the concept is found in Mircea Eliade, *The Sacred and the Profane: The Nature of Religion*, trans. Willard Trask (New York: Harper and Row, 1961), pp. 20–65.

2. On early Christianity, the work of Peter Brown stands out, esp. his *Cult of the Saints: Its Rise and Function in Latin Christianity* (Chicago: University of Chicago Press, 1981). See also Patricia L. Cox, *Biography in Late Antiquity: A Quest for the Holy Man* (Berkeley: University of California Press, 1983). On Near Eastern sufis, see Clifford Geertz, *Islam Observed: Religious Development in Morocco and Indonesia* (Chicago: University of Chicago Press, 1971), and Dale F. Eickelman, *Moroccan Islam: Tradition and Society in a Pilgrimage Center* (Austin: University of Texas Press, 1976).

3. A brief, analytic history of the lineage as the basis of a new religious movement is given by Gene R. Thursby, "Siddha Yoga: Swami Muktananda and the Seat of Power," in *When Prophets Die: The Postcharismatic Fate of New Religious Movements*, ed. Timothy Miller (Albany: State University of New York Press, 1991), pp. 165–81.

4. On Maharashtrian devotion, see R. D. Ranade, *Mysticism in India: The Poet Saints of Maharashtra* (Albany: State University of New York Press, 1983); Anne Feldhaus, *The Deeds of God in Riddhipur* (New York: Oxford University Press, 1984); and Eleanor Zelliot, "A Historical Introduction to the Warkari Movement," in *Palkhi: An Indian Pilgrimage by D. B. Mokashi*, trans. Philip C. Engblom (Albany: State University of New York Press, 1987). On the related Hindi tradition and on poet-singers in general, see Daniel Gold, *The Lord as Guru: Hindi Saints in North Indian Tradition* (New York: Oxford University Press, 1987).

5. In the literature of the lineage in English, the term is usually capitalized ("Siddha Yoga"), a convention I follow when referring more narrowly to lineage matters.

6. The complexities of Kashmir Shaivism are well presented by Paul Eduardo Muller-Ortega, *The Triadic Heart of Shiva: Kaula Tantricism of Abhinavagupta in the Non-dual Shaivism of Kashmir* (Albany: State University of New York Press, 1989), and Mark S. G. Dyczkowski, *The Doctrine of Vibration: An Analysis of the Doctrines and Practices of Kashmir Shaivism* (Albany: State University of New York Press, 1987), and *The Canon of the Shaivagama and the Kubjika Tantras of the Western Kaula Tradition* (Albany: State University of New York Press, 1988).

7. Traditions with more philosophical orientations frequently describe a person in a comparable state as jivanmukta, "alive while free."

8. Perhaps the best known list of siddhis is in the *Yoga Sutras* of Patanjali, book 3. Tempting to disciples, siddhis are regularly de-emphasized by yogic masters, including those of Swami Muktananda's lineage.

Guru's Body, Guru's Abode

249

9. *Transformation: On Tour with Gurumayi Chidvilasananda* (South Fallsburg, N.Y.: SYDA Foundation), vol. 3 (1987), p. 107.

10. Ibid., p. 105.

11. These particularly physical aspects of yoga are emphasized in Nath tradition, which is seen to come down from Gorakh Nath and is an important strand in popular Maharashtrian tradition. George Weston Briggs, *Gorakhnath and the Kanphata Yogis,* 2d ed. (Delhi: Motilal Banarsidass, 1973; Calcutta, 1938), provides an overview of the tradition and a translation of the Gorkashashataka, a basic treatise on the physical practices known as hatha yoga. Other hatha yoga texts attributed to Gorakh Nath include *Amaraugha Shasana,* ed. Pandit Mukund Ram Shastri (Srinagar: Research Department, Jammu and Kashmir State, 1918), and *Yogabija,* ed. Keshava Ram Chandra Joshi (Puna: Keshava Ram Chandra Joshi, 1974). The best-known work of hatha yoga is Svatmarama, *Hathayogapradipika of Svatmarama* (Adyar, Madras: Adyar Library and Research Center, 1972). *Goraksha Samhita,* ed. Janardana Shastri Pandey (Varanasi: Sampurnanada Sanskrit University, 1978), is a text in that tradition dealing with alchemy.

12. For introductions to Tantric traditions, see Agehananda Bharati, *The Tantric Tradition* (New York: Samuel Weiser, 1975), and Douglas Renfrew Brooks, *The Secret of the Three Cities: An Introduction to Hindu Shakta Tantrism* (Chicago: University of Chicago Press, 1990).

13. *Transformation* 3:13

14. Gold, *Lord as Guru,* pp. 104–10, presents scholarly opinions on this subject.

15. Swami Muktananda, *Satsang with Baba: Questions and Answers with Swami Muktananda,* vol. 4 (Ganeshpuri: Gurudev Siddha Peeth and Oakland: SYDA Foundation, 1978), p. 9.

16. Swami Muktananda, *In the Company of a Siddha* (South Fallsburg, N.Y.: SYDA Foundation, 1985), p. 102.

17. Ibid.

18. *Guru Gita,* v. 76, taken as the basis of a discourse by Swami Muktananda in his *Perfect Relationship* (South Fallsburg, N.Y.: SYDA Foundation, 1980), p. 2, and by Gurumayi in *Transformation* 3:173.

19. See, for example, H. H. the Dalai Lama, Tsong-ka-pa, and Jeffrey Hopkins, *Deity Yoga: In Action and Performance Tantra* (Ithaca, N.Y.: Snow Lion, 1987).

20. Sir John Woodroffe, *The Serpent Power,* 7th ed. (Madras: Ganesh, 1964), translates two important visualization texts from Hindu tantra with extensive commentary: *Shat-chakra-nirupana* and *Paduka-panchaka.*

21. *Transformation* 3:79.

22. Ibid., pp. 79–80.

23. See the account by Thursby, "Siddha Yoga," pp. 175–78 (n. 3). The institutional succession, completed within a few years, should be considered a smooth one in comparative perspective. For much more prolonged and bitter succession disputes in modern and medieval Indian lineages, see Gold, *Lord as Guru,* pp. 98–104, 149–69.

24. This theme is developed at length in Gold, *Lord as Guru.*

25. *Transformation* 3:76.

26. *Satsang with Baba,* vol. 5, p. 2.

27. *Transformation* 3:78.

28. Ibid., p. 25.

29. For the importance of darshan of images in Hindu traditions, see Diana L. Eck, *Darshan: Seeing the Divine Image in India* (Chambersburg, Pa.: Anima Books, 1981).

30. *Transformation* 3:18.

31. *Satsang with Baba,* vol. 5, p. 126.

32. *Transformation* 3:19.

33. Ibid.
34. Ibid 3:20.
35. Since it is not always obvious whether the narrators are male or female, I have sometimes been arbitrary in assigning genders to them.
36. *Transformation* 3:21.
37. Ibid., p. 205.
38. Ibid., p. 206.
39. Ibid.
40. See, for example, the story of Satyakama Jabala in the Chhandogya Upanishad, 4:4.
41. *Transformation* 2:88.
42. Ibid. 3:259.
43. Ibid., pp. 206–9.
44. Ibid., pp. 152–53.
45. Ibid., p. 153.
46. Ibid. 2:85.
47. During Swami Muktananda's lifetime, about six dozen Indian and Western devotees were initiated as "Swamis," celibate renunciates in the traditional Hindu Saraswati order. Those who remain with the movement serve as respected elders, often working in educational projects and giving personal guidance to devotees.
48. *Transformation* 2:86.
49. Swami Muktananda, *Ashram Dharma* (Ganeshpuri: Gurudev Siddha Peeth, 1968), pp. 3–4.
50. Ibid., p. 16.
51. The early Upanishads, among the oldest and most venerated Hindu scriptures, refer to students living with teachers for up to twelve years to learn sacred lore; see Chhandogya Upanishad, book 6. During his period of exile, the hero of the epic Ramayana (ca. 500 B.C.E.) stayed for a time at the forest ashram of the sage Agastya (Aranya Kanda 11–13).
52. See, for example, Kalidasa's *Shakuntala*, ca. 300 C.E.
53. In *The Mughals and the Jogis of Jakhbar* (Simla: Indian Institute of Advanced Study, 1967), B. N. Goswamy and J. S. Grewal present an interpretive account of Mughal records documenting state patronage of a rural yogi establishment. See also their *Mughal and Sikh Rulers and the Vaishnavas of Pindori*.
54. Khaliq Ahmed Nizami, *Some Aspects of Religion and Politics during the Thirteenth Century*, 2d ed. (Delhi: Idarah-i Adabiyat-i Dilli, 1974), p. 261.
55. Swami Muktananda, *Ashram Dharma*, p. 33.
56. Ibid., p. 29.
57. Swami Muktananda, *Play of Consciousness* (South Fallsburg, N.Y.: SYDA Foundation, 1978), p. 114.
58. See, for example, *Shat-chakra-nirupana*, in Woodroffe, *Serpent Power* (n. 19).
59. Swami Muktananda, *Ashram Dharma*, p. 7.
60. Ibid., p. 11.
61. Ibid., pp. 11–12.
62. See David Haberman, *Acting as a Way of Salvation* (New York: Oxford, 1988).
63. On the inner and outer circles around popular holy persons in medieval Indian Islam, see Nizami, *Religion and Politics*, pp. 205–14, and Richard Maxwell Eaton, *The Sufis of Bijapur* (Princeton: Princeton University Press, 1978), pp. 165–67. The relevance of this evidence to Hindi traditions is discussed in Gold, *Lord as Guru*, p. 208.
64. In Beas, the Radhasoami Satsang; in Pondicherry, the Sri Aurobindo Ashram.
65. Swami Muktananda, *Ashram Dharma*, p. 32.

THE PUPPET AS BODY SUBSTITUTE
NINGYŌ IN THE JAPANESE *SHIKI SANBASŌ* PERFORMANCE

Jane Marie Law

According to a legend from the Inland Sea of Japan, a fisherman named Hyakudayū was out at sea one day when suddenly the sky grew dark and lightning flashed all around his tiny boat. Overcome by fear, he saw another boat floating nearby in the waves. He looked closely and realized that the only being on it was a child about twelve years old, with a remarkable countenance. As the storm raged about them, the child turned to face Hyakudayū. Identifying himself as the abandoned child of the world-creating pair Izanagi and Izanami, he spoke: "I am the Leech Child of Long Ago. Until now, I have been floating on the waves with no worship hall where I can be worshipped. Build me a worship hall on the shore near Nishinomiya."[1] With that, the storm died down. Hyakudayū realized that this was no ordinary child, and that he had heard the words of a deity, and so he hastened to do as instructed. He built a worship hall at Nishinomiya in honor of the Leech Child. (It later came to be known as Nishinomiya Daimyōjin Ebisu Saburō Den.) There, a priest by the name of Dōkumbō served the Leech Child faithfully, until one day, the priest died. With no one to serve Him, the Leech Child grew restless and angry and caused numerous disasters at sea and on land. Hyakudayū learned of these disasters and, following an imperial edict, made a puppet with the same face and posture as the deceased priest Dōkumbō.[2] He manipulated this puppet in front of the worship hall of the Leech Child in Nishinomiya, and the child deity, satisfied that his faithful servant had returned, ceased making trouble. Hyakudayū then traveled the country performing his appeasement rites using puppets and eventually settled on the island of Awaji in the village of Sanjo, where, it is said, he married, had a son, and eventually died.

That, so the legend goes, is the origin of deity propitiation rites using puppets in Japan.[3] This essay further examines the use of a body substitute in ritual practice by focusing on this ritual puppetry tradition of the Inland Sea area. Performances by puppeteers hailing from the ceremonial center in the divination district known as Sanjo on the island of Awaji were common occurrences throughout Japan from early medieval times up until the early post-World War II period. The puppeteers were itinerant performers who specialized in sacred rites of deity propitiation, purification, and revitalization and the delivery of oracles and presentation of dramatic skits.

This ritual puppetry tradition presents a series of what I call body concerns: (1) the destruction of a physical bond between people when one of them dies, expressed in this origin myth by the appeasement of an angry (and, I maintain, grieving) deity through the creation of a body-substitute puppet which makes possible a return of the deceased; (2) the possession of the human form by a spiritual force and the implications of this possession for our understanding of the Japanese folk conception of the body and soul relationship; and (3) the periodic revitalization of the community through the parallel process of vitalizing the human body substitute, the puppet. This represented human form reverses the action of death, and in this ritual realization, the life-giving power of the spiritual world is made available to the human community. The puppet as a representative of the human being becomes the nexus where these powerful body-related and body-dependent religious concerns are enacted. The ritual context creates a forceful presentation of the existential problem of death and revitalization. The ritual tradition of Awaji puppetry both poses the problem, as we have seen in the origin myth, and dramatically presents an experience of renewal, which is then generalized into repeatable performances. The puppet, in the hands of a sacred specialist, serves as a vessel for invited sacred forces temporarily "embodied" in the phenomenal realm. The vitalization of the human form represented in the puppet body becomes a powerful ritual substitute enabling those present at the ritual to gain access to sources of vitality in the spirit realm.

The method of analysis used in this discussion is based on insights and formulations achieved in two related and overlapping enterprises, the history of religions and ritual studies. As a historian of religions, I am most interested in how a given religious phenomenon, in this case Japanese ritual puppetry, expresses an understanding of the fundamental and agonizing existential fact of death, and the human yearning to escape its final pronouncement.

Methodological Considerations

In Daniel Gold's essay, "Guru's Body, Guru's Abode," in this volume, he demonstrates how the concept of sacred space as described by Eliade can be elaborated by understanding the role of the guru's physical body in contemporary Hinduism. His case is an interesting example of the transposition of the body onto a physical as well as an imaginary landscape. In this essay, we look at another form of body transposition. We examine how a body substitute becomes the locus of a creative act of cosmogonic proportions—inert matter is brought to life as the sacred possesses the puppet. This revelation of the sacred in the body of a puppet becomes an event around which the meanings of daily life can be organized. Of this orientation, Eliade writes, "The world (that is, our world) is a universe within which the sacred has already manifested itself, in which, consequently, the break through from plane to plane has become possible and repeatable. It is not difficult to see why the religious moment implies the cosmogonic moment. The sacred reveals absolute reality and at the same time makes orientation possible; hence it founds the world in the sense that it fixes the limits and establishes the order of the world."[4] As we shall see, this ritual makes direct references on a number of levels to the cosmogonic acts of Izanagi and Izanami.

Scholarly discussion of ritual is anything but a new field of inquiry. The field of ritual studies, however, an interdisciplinary inquiry formally still in its infancy, can best be typified by the new primacy it gives to ritual within the study of religions.[5] Earlier studies of ritual and religion tended to subordinate ritual action to belief, myth, or text, separate ritual from thought as "mindless action," or contrast ritual with rational behavior. Rituals were deemed worthy of study because they could be seen as reflections of given dogmas, beliefs, or myths within a religious tradition. Psychologists studying ritual tended to view it as the opposite of rational behavior. In other words, rituals were seen as secondary expressions of a more primary experience, whether that experience was one of belief in a given system of meaning or the experience of neurosis.

Ritual studies, on the other hand, explores ways in which ritual action, behavior and performance not only encode and synthesize meanings but also create experience and bring about transformations in people's lives and entire communities. Ritual, then, is not merely an expression of a prior understanding but a way for a new understanding of an existential reality to come about. Rituals display meanings and symbols, but they also transform meanings and understandings. Participants in rituals are both recipients of culturally constructed and staged meanings and, reflexively, agents in the creation of those very meanings. Rather than being mere expressions of myths, beliefs, and texts, rituals interact with these components of religious traditions. Ritual is its own mode of experience, not simply reducible to texts or belief systems.

While the myth of the puppeteer and deity appeaser Hyakudayū claims to recount the origins of the tradition of ritual puppetry in Japan, the actual puppet ritual examined here plays with the motifs and nuances from this myth and develops them beyond the meanings the myth prescribes to them. Because the case of puppetry is presented in a ritual context, a number of specific concerns of ritual studies come to our attention. The first feature of the ritual context which must be considered is the fixed nature of the ritual content. Certain features of the rite—the utterances in the rite, the puppets, the order in which performers do things, the costumes—remain the same every time the ritual is performed. Not only does this allow for continuity in the ritual, it also enables the ritual itself to assume meanings beyond each occasion it is used. Richard Schechner refers to this quality of ritual as "restored behavior."

> Restored behavior is used in all kinds of performances from shamanism to exorcism to trance, from ritual to aesthetic dance and theater, from initiation rites to social dramas, from psychoanalysis to psychodrama and transactional analysis. In fact, restored behavior is the main characteristic of performance. The practitioners of all these arts, rites and healings assume that some behaviors—organized sequences of events, scripted actions, known texts, scored movements—exist separate from the performers who "do" these behaviors. Because the behavior is separate from those who are behaving, the behavior can be stored, transmitted, manipulated, transformed.[6]

The ritual becomes a repository of symbols and meanings which, when enacted, interact with the larger contexts of individual rituals. So whether the ritual we look at is presented at a wedding, a boat launching, during the new year, or at a rainmaking rite influences the nuanced meanings attributed to it.

Another issue we must address is how a ritual operates as a unified system of meaning with its own inherent logic. In this regard, we look at the dynamics between different components of the ritual within the ritual itself. We examine the interaction between the myth describing the origins of the rite, the bounding of performance space, timing of the rite, perception in the community of the performers and the relationship between performers and audience, medium of the performance, various symbols used in the rite, the ritual chant in the performance, and ritual paraphernalia. As we shall see, the ritual is designed to envelop the participant and control his or her conscious and unconscious processing of the ritual's message. Although the puppet dominates one's conscious and central experience of the rite by its uncanny movements and flashy costume, the other elements of the rite—movement, sound, language, symbols, music, timing, even weather—appeal to and even overload many channels of sensory input simultaneously. All seem to be redundantly reinforcing the same overlapping themes: fecundity, vitality, longevity. Herein lies an important feature of ritual: the synesthetic nature of ritual communication.[7]

Though all elements of this rite, and perhaps any rite, need to be understood holistically as they relate to one another, one specific element has a special status as the cohesive point of the rite. In this case, the puppet body has this status among the other aspects of the rite, for it is the puppet which renders the diverse motifs and meanings of the ritual coherent. I refer to this element of the rite which has this ability to cohere diverse motifs and symbols and absorb different meanings in various contexts as the *nexus* of the ritual.

Furthermore, we must ask how a rite is used within the larger society in which it occurs. In the case of Japanese puppetry rituals, the event is at once ritual and performance. We are interested in how the ritual context provides a concentration, integration, and dissemination of the deep existential meanings being addressed in the rite. The ritual is understood to be efficacious on a spiritual level. Are we to call this ritual magic? Why does the ritual work? To understand the answer to this very important question, we must look at what is supposed to result from the rite and what physically and concretely does happen in the rite. The dynamic relationship between these two levels, intentionality and actuality, reveals how the ritual works. The intentionality of this rite is revitalization of the cosmos and the bestowing of fecundity on the human community and agricultural (and sometimes fishing) realms. What actually happens in the rite is that a puppet is transformed from inert matter to a moving being. The relationship between this intentionality and this actuality, then, is at once enactment and analogy. I call this feature *analogical realization* of a desired end. It is because the analogical realization is symbolically and spiritually satisfying for those involved that the ritual can be seen as efficacious. In this case, the puppetry rite is concerned with the existential and religious problem of death and revitalization of life. The ritual context gives this deep issue a force, referred to in ritual studies as "performative force," enabling members of the human community to understand an otherwise inaccessible or unarticulated part of themselves and their own inner experience. The performance, and the participants' responses to it, become a new experience, around which other meanings in life can be organized. One has not merely been told that the spiritual realm is the realm capable of vitalizing the human world. One has experienced it with one's very senses in a powerful aesthetic context.[8] Each element in the rite—puppet, symbol, utterance, movement—assumes the status of paradigmatic event.

We also look at how the ritual interacts with myths describing it. The dominant event in the Hyakudayū myth is the death of a priest and his recreation in a body substitute. This mythic event both informs and reverberates throughout the ritual.

This threefold focus—on the dynamics within the rite, the rite within the culture, and the rite in relationship to myth—can be seen as the domain of ritual studies.

Ritual Puppetry in Japan: An Overview

Throughout Japanese history, effigies and body substitutes of different types, from simple sticks, clay figurines, straw effigies, and stone sculptures to the elaborate and lovely puppets of the classical puppet theater stage have been used to guard tombs, purify the emperor, imitate sexual union to instill fecundity in rice seedlings and fields, ensure safe pregnancies and childbirth, protect tiny infants and growing children by becoming surrogates for their illnesses, remove pollutions from both bodies and homes, ward off plagues, and act as spirit vessels for deities summoned from beyond the human realm. The sacred specialists capable of luring and harnessing powerful forces and concentrating them into the form of the body substitute or effigy were regarded with a mixture of fascination, awe and dread. Their magical abilities to make contact with and even control sacred forces marginalized them from mainstream Japanese society, and by the Tokugawa period (1603–1868), when formal social status codes were drawn up and written into law, ritual puppeteers were classified as outcasts (*hinin*, literally "nonhuman").[9] Concerning the magical power of these specialists, the eleventh-century writer Oe no Masafusa noted, "They can change sand and stones into gold coins, and grasses and twigs into birds and beasts."[10]

The topic of ritual puppetry can seem deceptively limited as an angle from which to understand Japanese views of the body, owing to a commonly held assumption in the United States that puppetry is a degenerate art intended for children or a form of religious expression long outdated with the introduction of less magical forms of ritual. As Michael Malkin wrote in his 1977 book, *Traditional and Folk Puppets of the World*, "For many of us, puppets belong to a world of alphabet blocks, little red wagons, and rainy Saturday recollections of squeaky voices and tangled strings."[11] But this Japanese case is interesting precisely because it challenges a number of such assumptions about drama, religion, and the understandings of the human form and its relationship to the world of spirits and divine beings.

The Japanese word *ningyō* can be translated literally "in the shape of the human" and the term, unlike our word *puppet*, loosely refers to any effigy of the human form[12] and is not restricted to those which are moved by a human agent.

The scale and variety of ritual puppets used throughout Japanese history is staggering. One of the most common types of puppets is the *ayatsuri ningyō*, or manipulated puppet, made to move by up to three puppeteers in ritual performances and dramas from a ballad tradition known as *jōruri*. The noted scholar of Japanese ritual performance and puppetry Nagata Kōkichi, in his *Ikite Iru Ningyō Shibai*, (Living Puppetry), limiting himself only to *ayatsuri ningyō* troupes still performing in 1983, lists 141 puppetry groups in all regions of Japan, with a combined total of 5,900 *kashira*, or elaborately carved puppet heads.[13] These 141 troupes are merely those which have survived the demise of folk performances in the postwar period. Although no such comprehensive figures exist for the Tokugawa period, it is likely that at that time, the number of small troupes throughout the country was considerable, perhaps even ten times larger. These figures, leaving out the classical *Bunraku* puppets with which so many non-Japanese are familiar, indicate that dramatic and ritual puppetry in Japan was a widespread phenomenon.

The period from the late sixteenth century until the early twentieth century constitutes what can be called the heyday of ritual puppetry in Japan. Puppetry rites were a common occurrence before the worship halls of Hachiman and Ebisu shrines[14] and on beaches, docks, rice paddy dikes, and homes throughout the country. Although puppetry performances as entertainment became more widespread, bands of ritual puppeteers continued to practice spirit pacification and purification rites until the early postwar years.

Owing to the hardships of the war, by the late 1940s the practice of ritual puppetry had all but died out. Ritual puppetry on Awaji declined from the nearly forty active troupes in the late nineteenth century to scattered performances scraped together for local festivals. During the 1980s, the tradition was reestablished on the island, though the contextual meanings have been dramatically altered.[15]

This discussion of ritual puppetry is based on fieldwork conducted by the author in Japan on Awaji, which spanned the period from 1984 through 1991.[16] During this period, I watched the transformation of this tradition as it moved from being a loosely organized group of enthusiasts intent on keeping their tradition from disappearing altogether, performing in a small theater above a souvenir shop, to the well-established theater with a modern performance hall and government subsidy. The present theater, known as the Awaji Ningyō Jōruri Kan, under the directorship of Umazume Masaru, recruits young persons from around the island of Awaji and provides them with a salaried position in the theater. My discussion is informed in part by extended observation of puppetry ritual and performance over this seven-year period, presented for the most part by the same core of artists. In my analysis, I have woven together the observations from my field studies with both the understandings of the rituals by the performers, participants, and local people and the larger textual and contextual evidence from Japanese folk ritual performance.[17] Because I am here describing an aspect of this rich tradition which has largely died out, however, I have relied heavily on analyses of old texts and descriptions, on recordings and on films of the prewar performances. I have compared these examples of the ritual with the current-day versions of it and have tried to minimize the discussion of minute points of theatrical variation. When possible, in addition to secondary sources in Japanese, my interpretations have been heavily informed by elderly persons on Awaji who remember the prewar rituals.

The Shiki-Sanbasō Rite: An Itinerant Performance

The focus in this essay is on the sacred rituals of the itinerant puppeteers who hailed from the ceremonial center of ritual puppetry, Sanjo, on the

island of Awaji. These performers are, the tradition maintains, the professional descendants of the fisherman-turned-deity-appeaser Hyakudayū
mentioned at the start of this essay. They performed appeasement, purification, and fecundity rites from door to door at homes at set seasons of the
year, before audiences from all levels of society, from the poorest peasants to
the imperial family. Historically, while many of them also presented scenes
from dramatic ballads (jōruri) to augment their incomes, they drew sharp
distinctions between these performances and their ritual duties, referred
to as shinji or kamigoto (literally, "sacred matters"). Their ritual performances were of two types: humorous deity plays depicting and honoring the
deity Ebisu, and magical purification and revitalization rites depicting three
deities who visit the human realm. The former rite has a rich narrative
describing the life of the Leech Child into adulthood as the deity Ebisu,
and presents his drunken nature in a most comical fashion. The latter rite,
solemn and graceful, called Shiki-Sanbasō (literally "'ritual' or 'ceremonial'
Sanbasō"), is the subject of this discussion. While it is impossible to prove
because the history of the development of these rites remains unclear, I
suggest that the two rituals form a pair connected with Leech Child/Ebisu
worship: Shiki Sanbasō appeases the child deity (as recounted in the myth)
and the Ebisu dance entertains the deity and spreads the story of the deity's
life to worshippers.[18]

Versions of the Shiki Sanbasō rite can be found in the ritual repertoire
of other Japanese performing arts, such as Kagura and Noh, and later,
Kabuki and Bunraku. These ritual performances have the overriding
theme of the creation of the cosmos and the establishment of the cosmic
order. All the characters in the performance—Okina (the old man), Senzai
(the youth of one thousand years), and Sanbasō (the third old man)—are
understood to be visiting deities from across the sea (marebito) who bring
special blessings and curses with them in their seasonal visits.[19]

In these other performing arts, there is a strict distinction between the
dance of Okina (Okina mai) and the dance of Sanbasō (Sanbasō mai). In the
case of ritual puppetry, however, the Sanbasō performance has absorbed
the dance of Okina[20] and the terms are used interchangeably at times,
leading to no small amount of confusion among scholars not familiar with
puppetry rituals but aware of the ritual repertoire in other performing art
forms in Japan. In this tradition, the same performance is at times called
Okina watari ("Okina crossing over"), or Shiki Sanbasō, and rarely Kuro-
Okina ("Black Okina," as Sanbasō wears a black mask). In the tradition of
Sanbasō performance, Sanbasō is often closely identified with the Leech
Child. Some variations of the oral tradition even equate the two, and thus,
the actions of this character in the performance, which are graceful and
ritually potent, show the power of a failed creation (abandoned on the sea
by his parents), an example of "negative capability" par excellence.

Though common throughout the Japanese performing arts, the origin
of the Sanbasō rite is in the Sarugaku tradition and it was originally pre-

Itinerant Awaji puppeteers present the Shiki Sanbasō rite before a roadside shrine, circa 1935. One performer presents offerings before the shrine while another prepares the puppets packed in the carrying box.

sented by Shushi performers. Most scholars agree that the earliest versions of the rite probably used puppets. This ritual performance was presented throughout Japan by itinerant performers from as early as the late eleventh century up through the postwar period, with, needless to say, considerable variation and development in ritual context and performance style. The fundamental structure of the ritual, from the puppets and ritual chant used to the various symbols displayed during the rite, shows remarkable continuity throughout Japanese history.

While Awaji puppetry as dramatic entertainment has made a comeback in the last several years, the practice of itinerant puppeteering by ritual specialists died out abruptly after World War II, when economic pressures made such forms of livelihood impossible. Most itinerant puppeteers, who before the war would spend the first several weeks of the new year and periods surrounding the planting of rice wandering from location to location performing, settled down permanently and put their puppets away in boxes or sold them to collectors. The puppet manipulation and narration of the ritual chant *(tonaegoto)* was maintained among puppeteers and presented as stage performances, but these performances were no longer presented in their traditional settings. In the middle 1980s, however, an interest in reviving these rites began to develop, and younger professional puppeteers from the Awaji Puppet Theatre, as well as amateur puppeteers

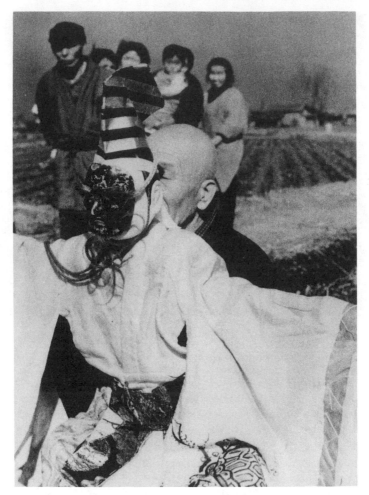

An Awaji puppeteer presents the Shiki Sanbasō rite, with
Sanbasō masked, while farmers and passersby look on.

from the village of Sanjo on Awaji, began once again to present Sanbasō
and Ebisu rites door to door and before worship halls in shrines. In many
cases, the performances had not been presented in these traditional out-
door locations in nearly forty-five years. The two older photos here are
from the period when ritual puppeteers still traveled about early in the
new year.

The Awaji ritual puppets are nearly life-size representations of the human form, and each puppet is manipulated by a sacred specialist called
either *Ebisu-kaki*, *Ebisu-mawashi*, *ningyō mawashi*, *hako mawashi*, or *Sanbasō
mawashi*. Unlike later *jōruri* puppets of the type used in dramatic performances, which are handled by three people, one puppeteer handles one

puppet and does not wear a *kuroko*, or black hood. The puppeteers carry the puppets and ritual implements with them in boxes on their backs. The puppet is understood to be the *shintai*, literally "deity body" or "sacred body," capable of being possessed by any number of deities invoked in the rite. While the deity is not mentioned by name, the deities most commonly summoned are the *ta no kami*, the deity of the fields who is called back in the spring to instill the rice seedlings with new life, and Ebisu, connected with fortune and fishing, and as already noted above, understood to be the adult Leech Child. The puppeteers performed in villages—at entryways to homes, in shrines, on roads—received prayers offered to the deity in the form of the puppet, and performed purification rites of homes, places of work, and boats.

Locus and Meaning: The Significance of Itinerant Performance

Itinerant performers have been a common feature throughout the history of Japanese performing arts. Performances of these wanderers are given the name *kadozuke*,[21] which means literally "attached to the gate" and refers to rites performed door to door, in the precincts of shrines, and "on the road." The term isolates the itinerant nature of these performers, indicating that they did not perform in theaters but presented their pieces on the road, the metaphorical gateway between the known and settled world of everyday life and the wild, unknown world "out there." Neither inside the home nor part of the street itself, the gate is the no-man's land to which all meanings can be attached and onto which all projections of potentiality and danger can be projected.[22]

While not all *kadozuke* performances are of an overtly ritual or religious nature (some are merely humorous skits), it is possible to demarcate some common features of the *kadozuke* context.[23] First, *kadozuke* performances were presented by itinerant artists. Second, because they were not members of the communities in which they were performing, they were regarded as outsiders.[24] Because they were not situated in a familiar social setting, their nature was a mystery, and thus a number of societal meanings were projected upon them. Third, as outsiders, these performers were regarded with a certain degree of ambivalence at best and even fear and loathing. The itinerant performer represented an unassimilatable dimension of life—the realm beyond ordered space and meaning—and was hence potentially dangerous. Fourth, the ambivalence with which the itinerant performer was regarded also led to his or her being perceived as having special magical powers—the ability to cure illness, bring or ward off plagues, cause or prevent calamities, and so on. Fifth, the performers were frequently given some form of payment for their services. Usually the host in the village where the artist performed would pay the performer with food, money, or temporary lodgings. Far from being merely payment for services rendered, this exchange of money or goods must be understood as a ritual exchange between two realms of existence—the settled realm of everyday, profane life and the realm of sacrality, represented by the itinerant ritual artist. Those living in the settled and established world of meaning (the villages and towns) had need of the services of the ritual performers, but were also afraid of them. The payment of goods was in part a gift to send the performers away. Last, the arrival of these performers was usually seasonal. In the case we are discussing here, ritual puppeteers presented the Shiki-Sanbasō rite at weddings and boat launchings, and during the period of time when rice seedlings are being germinated in nurseries and transplanted to the paddies in the spring. Most common, however, was the performance during the first fifteen days of the new year. This time period is interesting for a number of reasons. It is the time when the new year is still not fully formed, and hence the first days are marginal time. As the order of the cosmos is being recreated, these days are regarded as powerful and sacred. The rites presented by these puppeteers served to harness the dense sacrality of these days and channel it for the benefit of the community or home—to revitalize the life forces of the communities and instill good health, prosperity and longevity on people living in the area. So common was the appearance of *Sanbasō mawashi* during this time that one informant noted, "It just isn't New Year's anymore without Sanbasō."

The puppeteers who presented Sanbasō rites would travel from door to door within prescribed territories agreed upon by the puppeteers them-selves, carrying their puppets and ritual implements in boxes on their backs. The road became an important geography which underwent a trans-formation from profane space to ambiguously powerful space. The "world out there" became the space from which powerful outsiders with sacred powers would arrive. Concerning the power of these visitors, Hori Ichirō writes:

> Through careful comparison and analysis, . . . scholars have drawn the con-clusion that much of the present-day lore about mysterious visitors derives from the original belief that strangers who appeared at harvest time or at the turn of the year were life-givers from the other world in heaven or from the eternal land overseas. The ancient Japanese believed that these visitors came to instill new life power in rice seeds and in human beings in order to ensure vigorous germination in the approaching spring.[25]

Sanjo Districts, Death, and the Abreaction of Grief

The next component of this ritual practice we turn to is the interrelation-ship of the ritual itself and the myth/legend describing its origins.[26] As noted at the outset of this essay, it diminishes our understanding of any ritual to see it merely as an "acting out" of a text, belief or myth. However, by looking at the mythical account of the tradition itself, we can glean interesting hints about the meanings to be elaborated and played upon in the rite. The founding myth and ritual penetrate one another and are ultimately inseparable in any meaningful analysis.

The mythical origins of ritual puppetry, cited in legendary form at the beginning of this essay, are recounted in a document dated 1638, based upon an oral tradition which clearly dates from a much earlier time. The text, entitled *Dōkumbō Denki*, is a 1,067-character Japanese text written solely in Chinese characters. As the founding narrative of the tradition, it was recopied and carried by the puppeteers who journeyed from Awaji presenting their performances. Like the puppets used in rituals invoking a divine presence, the scroll was understood to be sacred. Before the puppeteer would present the rite of Shiki Sanbasō, there was frequently a presentation of the scroll on which this legend was written. Therefore we must consider the presentation of the myth scroll prior to the puppetry performance of Shiki Sanbasō as part of the ritual itself. The myth serves as a legitimation of the puppeteer,[27] for he can trace his profession back to Hyakudayū, and a warm up for the performance. The motifs in the myth sensitize the human audience to those in the ritual about to be performed with puppets. What motifs stand out in this myth?

The myth raises a number of important topics for discussion: the name of the place where Hyakudayū settles on the island of Awaji, the meaning of the deity's "misbehavior" after the death of the priest, and the use of a body substitute puppet to appease the upset deity. Let's look first at the meanings associated with the name Sanjo.

Sanjo, rather than being merely a proper place name, refers to a *category* of special districts existing in Japan from the late Heian up through the pre–World War II periods.[28] Morita Yoshinori suggests that the history of marginalized peoples in Japan can be studied by dividing this group into two categories, based upon their domicile. These two groups, he writes, are the "riverbed people" *(kawara no mono)* and the "Sanjo people" *(Sanjo no mono)*.[29] Sites with the name Sanjo can still be found throughout western Japan, almost invariably attached to shrine or temple precincts or nearby tombs. The characters used to write the place name could be pronounced either Sanjo or Sansho (though the former is standard), and can be written with the characters meaning "birthing place," "place of divination," "scattered place," "third district," or "tax (free) district." The earliest text using the term Sanjo is from Eishō 3 (1048) and indicates the Sanjo districts of Yodo and Yamazaki, using the characters "scattered place."[30] The ambiguity concerning the characters reflects the various ways these places participated in a liminal world, for all these possible character compounds imply a quality of experience radically outside ordinary life. Most places with the name Sanjo have undergone changes in the character compounds used to write the name and have settled upon the neutral "third district," as their inhabitants sought to escape the highly negative associations and subsequent discrimination living in these districts call forth.[31] In many of the cases, the present-day inhabitants of these areas called Sanjo have no connection with the historical conditions of the sites.

Hayashiya Tatsusaburō suggests that these districts originated as special compounds for ritual performers (musicians, diviners, deity pacifiers, etc.) attached to major ceremonial centers, and that during the medieval period, such people were the dominant residents of Sanjo districts. He notes that ritual performers attached to Tennōji in present-day Osaka lived in a Sanjo district attached to the shrine and suggests that these performers had a large impact on ritual performance in other areas of Japan. As the demand for ritual performers specializing in shamanistic activities (healing of sickness, calling back the dead, etc.) began to decline and residents of these districts suffered the inevitable fall from status, they dispersed throughout Japan, and specialists originating in the Tennōji Sanjo district could be found as far away as northeast Japan. Hayashiya cites a selection from *Chūyūki* (dated 1114) which discusses the presentation of dances at Byōdōin in Uji (near present-day Kyoto). The passage clearly shows that even from this early date, Sanjo residents were discriminated against and were denied equal treatment.[32]

This "fall from status" is a complicated chapter in Japanese history. Briefly, as the system of legitimating government shifted from a ritual "theater state" to a more militaristic model of government (a process well in place by the start of the Tokugawa period in the early seventeenth century), ritual performers no longer were so essential to the art of statecraft. The ritual activities of the Sanjo residents became more varied over time, and the people and their arts became increasingly marginalized. By the early Tokugawa period, a demographic analysis of Sanjo would look quite different, with the inhabitants of these districts differing over time and even from season to season. Taoist diviners *(onmyōshi)*, wandering sacred specialists *(hijiri)*, midwives, parturient women,[33] prostitutes, handlers of corpses, executioners, slaughterers, falconers, puppeteers and healers all found themselves at times affiliated with these districts. A Tokugawa-period source entitled "Sensha Ko" ("Reference to the Outcasts") explains that places called Sanjo were associated with great taboos and pollution *(imi)*, and people from these districts were not allowed to marry people from other districts of Japan. The text explains that birthing women, performers, *nembutsu* dancers, and shamanesses lived in Sanjo districts.[34] Because these types of occupations were tied to removal of dirt, handling of death and killing, childbirth, and contact with powers from beyond the human realm, these districts and the people who lived in them were regarded as polluted *(kegare)*, dangerously powerful, even sacred, and to be feared.[35] One did not venture into Sanjo except on the most pressing of spiritual or physiological business: the need to make contact with or dispose of one's dead, have a baby, or have one's fortune read or illness treated. Sanjo, then, was a quality of space, an island of pollution, spiritual power, and ambiguity in an otherwise settled world of meaning. The meanings of Sanjo were those defying assimilation into the routine of daily life.

That the ceremonial center of Awaji puppetry is located in a zone called Sanjo is of special importance. The centering of puppetry in a zone with this name indicates yet another level of meaning for our understanding of the relationship between puppetry and death.[36] Quite near the ceremonial center of Awaji puppetry are two large shrines, one dedicated to Hachiman and the other to Ebisu. It is my theory that this district was the divination district where ritual performers attached to one or both of these shrines lived. Most likely this aspect of the myth reflects the relationship between puppetry and the process of divination, appeasement and delivering of the oracles of the dead. The practice seen in the myth, namely, using a body substitute of a deceased person to return the person to those who missed him (or her), may have been a more widespread role of these ritual puppeteers.

In the ceremonial center on Awaji, the effigies of the main figures of the legend are enshrined as the patron deities of puppetry: Dōkumbō, Hyakudayū, and the Leech Child as an adult—the deity Ebisu.[37] The Dō-kumbō myth is synonymous with this district on the island of Awaji. The narrative itself is enshrined in the precincts of the Sanjo ceremonial center.

In my fieldwork, I was curious about how people living on Awaji now, in this district, understood the events of the legend of Dōkumbō. I conducted a series of interviews over several months in the precincts of the ceremonial center—where, every morning from about eight to ten o'clock, the elderly people of the area would gather to play gateball. While none of the people I talked with knew of the written version of the text referred to here, they all were very familiar with the outlines of the legend. One of my leading questions concerned why the Leech Child caused disasters after the death of the priest. This seems to be a question suggested in the legend. A common interpretation among people living on Awaji in and near the special zone called Sanjo is that the deity was moved to rage because of his intense grief. One of the universal problems with death is that no matter how well one can remember a deceased person, the person's physical absence can be excruciating. One informant, eighty-seven years old, put it very well: "The Leech Child was abandoned by his parents as a small child. His closest companion died on him. The grief he suffered because of the priest's death made him remember what his parents had done to him when he was a helpless child who could not walk." The text suggests this as well, for the term used for appease, *nagusameru*, carries the strong connotation of consolation of grief or calamity.

Another interpretation of the raging deity's behavior has to do with who the deity lost. The deity lost more than a friend. He lost the human officiant capable of mediating between the world of the sacred and the human realm. This myth strongly suggests that the sacred realm, though necessary for the well-being of the human community, is inherently dangerous and even overpowering and chaotic. When key sacred specialists are not there to mediate its entry into the human realm, all hell literally breaks loose. The puppeteer Hyakudayū, using a ritual body substitute, assumes the role of deity pacifier.

This, it seems, is the most remarkable feature of the myth. What does this say about perceptions of the body? The text specifically tells us that the effigy was fashioned with the face and posture of the deceased Dō-kumbō—two intimate and identifying aspects of a person's body. The text does not drag it out, but we are meant to understand that this body substi-tute—this represented form of the priest's body—was acceptable to the Leech Child, and his malevolence was adequately appeased. Furthermore, we are meant to understand that the recreation of the physical body makes possible the return—or ritual recreation—of the priest as companion and mediator, enough to calm the angry deity down. This originating event in the myth becomes the model for further appeasements, and the foundation of the art the mythical Hyakudayū teaches to the people of Awaji.

From this information, we are able to understand the use of puppetry in this tradition—with its insistence on the recreation of the body of the deceased—within the context of a well-developed type of Japanese rite, generically known as *chinkonsai*, literally meaning "rite for calming the spirit" and loosely translatable as "appeasement ceremony."[38] This type of rite is usually understood by scholars of Japanese religion and folklore to arise out of near death and mourning practices, and the desire to do one of a number of things: retain the soul in a dying person, call the soul back into a recently dead person, or soothe the soul of an unhappy and malevo-lent deceased (or living) person. Fudō Takashi, in *Nihon Geinō no Shigen teki Kenkyū* (A study of the origins of Japanese performing arts) notes that there are basically four types of *chinkonsai* which follow these agendas: (1) *tamafuri* (literally "shaking the spirit"), performed to revive a sick or weakening (near death) person; (2) "spirit shaking," performed immediately after the death of an individual for the purpose of trying to call back the deceased, also called *tama yobai* ("calling back the spirit"); (3) *tamashizume*, performed to neutralize the curses *(tatari)* of a malevolent ancestor, with *uramitama*, or a vengeful spirit; and (4) the rites performed to appease an angry deity.[39] The Dōkumbō story points to a *chinkonsai* of the last type but includes shades of meaning from the other types of *chinkonsai*. It has been widely observed that these rites of spirit shaking and spirit pacification are among the earliest forms of ritual performance in Japan.

The Hyakudayū myth is of particular interest because in addition to being a story about the appeasement of an angry deity, it tells us that a deity responds to a human death. It suggests that a ritual performance powerful enough for a deity must certainly be effective for human beings. At this level, the reenactment of the myth in the form of a puppetry per-formance is a ritual insistence on this understanding of the human-divine relationship.

Furthermore, if we think about the implications of the story—and people on Awaji certainly do—it tells us something about the primacy of a person's corporeal form. It suggests that emotional ties are woven between body and body—even if one body is human and one body is divine. As such, the grieving deity, or even the raging deity in need of a mediator, becomes a model for human grief, its abreaction and appeasement, and the need for physical proximity.

Myths recounting the origins of puppetry in other parts of the world often present a similar dilemma of bereaved loved ones who cannot be consoled. In fact, the prevalence of such a motif in the legends of puppetry suggest that there is something about puppetry as a ritual medium which lends itself to bringing back the dead from beyond the grave, to deliver oracles, offer consolation, and provide companionship and a transition period in grieving for bereaved people.[40]

Whether one wants to accept the mythical origins of Japanese ritual puppetry as historical fact is not the point. Historical origins and existential originating experiences can be discussed as two separate concerns. Inherent in the use of puppets as a medium in this Japanese ritual performance, however, is a central concern with the inextricable problems of death and grief. The puppet is a means of rendering continuity in an ongoing present with an inescapable fact of the death of some individual. In the case of the Ebisu-kaki, the puppet allows for a continuity with the Leech Child's caretaker and mediator, Dōkumbō, after his death. It is the artist, Hyakudayū, who makes possible the bridge between the time when the priest was physically present and the ongoing present. So, embedded in this puppetry tradition is a concern with what death takes away and a means of bringing that back, even if only in the constructed world of meaning of the puppetry ritual.

Possession and the Vitalization of Matter

This rite raises another issue: the vitalization of matter and possession of an inanimate object by a spiritual force. What makes things come alive? And conversely, what has happened when things die? A discussion of this issue involves looking at the details of the performance itself: the significance of the use of puppets (as opposed to human actors) as the medium for the performance, the timing of the rite, the movement of the puppet during the rite itself, the symbols displayed during the rite, and the magical use of language in the ritual chant recited during the performance. These components interact with one another to create a unified experience for performer and audience.

A question which occurs to me again and again in studying these puppetry rituals is of the most basic nature. Why puppets, and not human performers? While puppets have their advantages, they also come with their own set of problems: they are heavy (weighing up to twenty-five kilograms when in full regalia), they have to be carried around, and they are expensive (and were, even in the Tokugawa period). There are, on the other hand, many advantages of puppets as representational forms—they can portray everyone, for they are in essence no one person, and they can fly, be dismembered, change into animals and demons, enact dramatic special effects, and still pull themselves together for the next presentation. But these aspects do not account for the deep fascination—or deep discomfort—people feel for puppets. This has been one of the interesting discoveries of several years of fieldwork in Japan on puppetry. Unlike people in the United States, who, as Malkin suggested, consider puppets as beings of the toyroom, many Japanese I talked with had strong feelings about puppets. They either loved them or hated them. Among those who hated them, the most common reason I heard was that they give people the creeps. They are associated with eeriness, ghosts, and half-lit places. Something *other* happens with puppets. This positive side of this otherness of puppetry was well expressed by the director of the Budapest Puppet Theatre, Dezso Szilagyi, who wrote that

> the audience at a puppet show witnesses action which satisfies an urge present since time immemorial. On the puppet stage, before the spectators' eyes, the supreme act of creation is taking place—lifeless dead matter is turned into life. In his own activity, man, as a rule, achieves the opposite. In order to create anything, he has to watch part of his living environment suffer death. To clothe himself, to make a chair, to put his ideas down on paper, to represent the world with brush and paint—to do any of these things, he must turn living organisms into lifeless minerals. At the same time, his yearning and wish to create life are in fact far stronger than the compulsion of his destructive instinct. This creative urge is translated into other spheres and satisfied by the puppet brought to life.[41]

The puppets of the ritual performances presented by Awaji puppeteers can be understood as expressions of a deeply held and elaborate belief in the life-giving power of the spiritual realm in the world of matter, represented in this case by the substitute human body.

In general, possession of a human agent by a spiritual force is dramatic, but prior to and after possession, a shaman or shamaness can speak and move, albeit with his or her own voice and gesture. A puppet, however, is quite visibly merely the sum of its parts when it is inanimate. In fact, Awaji puppets do not have formal bodies, but consist instead of incomplete torsos, a *kashira* or head, hands, and in some cases, feet. The puppet head, *kashira*, considered the most important part of the puppet (not to mention the costliest), can be addressed separately, since the process of its creation is understood to be a birth. Puppet head carvers, like the late Tengu Hisa, or Oe Minosuke, speak of *kashira* as being either well-born or not well-born.[42] A well-born *kashira* is one which has spirit in it.[43]

A puppeteer performs the Shiki Sanbasō rite at the Omidō Hachiman Shrine on Awaji, July 1991.

The illusion of a body is constructed by draping an outer garment over the assembled body parts, which then must be held gracefully in unison by a skilled puppeteer. A puppeteer is considered a failure if, when he or she manipulates this collection of body parts (sometimes in conjunction with other puppeteers), the parts still appear disparate. Through the special abilities of the puppeteer, this sum of bodily parts is transformed into a living, moving, and even ecstatic being. Body parts come alive through manipulation. This "coming alive" becomes the key analogical event giving this ritual its force.

This transformation of assorted body parts into a body with a being inside it belies the close relationship between puppetry and fecundity and death. This seems to be the greatest fear in fecundity rites, namely, that life won't happen when it should, and the world—whether seeds or human wombs or fish from the sea—will remain nonproductive and dead. With every gesture, the puppet indicates the other side of life, for in a moment, as soon as the puppeteer puts it down in its proper sleeping position, the puppet is again no more than the sum of its parts: like a dead body. Display of the inert puppet body before and after the manipulation is a part of the performance presented before the eyes of the audience. Perhaps the invocation of death in a rite of fecundity is intentionally ironic.

Details of the Rite

Although human beings were witnesses to the rite, the intended audience was understood to be the deities summoned to the space and honored and entertained by the performance. Human beings were what Origuchi Shinobu referred to as "the uninvited guests" at the rite.

In the hands of a puppeteer, the puppet—an inanimate form settled in a carrying box—comes to life and becomes a vessel to be possessed by another force. One, two, or three performers can present this rite. When one performer works alone, events described below have to happen sequentially. Three puppets are used in the rite: Okina, Senzai, and Sanbasō. At the beginning of the puppetry rite, before the puppets are picked up, a flute and drum are played, inviting the spirit, in most cases understood to be the deity of the rice fields, to draw near to the spot, so it can be invited to enter the puppet. The puppets, preparing to be possessed, each in turn cover their faces with the sleeves of their elaborate costumes, indicating their submission to the greater spirit which has been summoned.

The initial movements of the first puppet are intended to purify space prior to the possession which will take place when the deity enters the puppet's body. First, the arms of the puppet move in the four directions, creating a dramatic effect as the long sleeves of the costume snap with each gesture. The puppet shakes a rattle to further purify the space and bless the audience. This gesture is also understood as a *tamafuri,* a spirit shaking, which invigorates the performance (although many farmers with whom I spoke said it was an imitation of sowing seed.) One puppet, Sanbasō, slowly begins to dance and eventually goes into a frenzied and ecstatic trance.[44] His ecstasy and trance are made apparent by a change in the shape of his eyes: they go from normal human eyes to round eyes which look into the other world—eyes of fear, pain, wonderment, intense rage, frenzy. As the preparation for the possession goes on, the movements of the puppet become erratic: he stamps his feet, rolls his eyes, and waves his arms about. This foot stamping (*ashibyōshi*) is also understood as an act of driving out evil and summoning up powers from the earth. All this is to show the powerful transformation about to take place. This is but a preparatory stage to the actual possession. In this way, the puppet becomes a body substitute on yet another level: he takes the place of the shaman or shamaness, who also may undergo such ecstatic transformation in preparation for possession. It is understood in this rite that the deities summoned are too powerful to be contained within the body of a human mediator, and so the puppet stands between the human and divine communities as a bridge.

The actual possession in full form is made apparent by putting masks on the puppets (or sometimes just on the puppet Sanbasō) in the middle of the rite. If we consider that puppets are once removed from the realm of human performers, we have another layer of removal from the ordinary, profane world of meaning when a puppet has a mask on its face. Even though puppets are substitutes for actual human beings in the rites, even they must be symbolically insulated from the sacred. This is accomplished by the donning of a mask. After the mask is put on the puppet,[45] their movements become more controlled, although more forceful. Another level of power has settled into the puppet and the deity is now in full control.

The purpose of this possession of a puppet, drawing from a tradition which situates the origins of puppetry at the revitalization of a deceased being, and continually hearkens back to these origins, is to bring fecundity and new life to the people in the audience, their homes, their rice seedlings, and the community in general. Just as the puppet, consisting of lifeless matter, is brought to life when he is made to move onstage and then "ontologically upgraded" to a being possessed by the divine, so too is the community's vital energy restored and strengthened.

Further evidence that the puppet embodies a hope for vitalization—or revitalization as the case may be—can be seen most clearly by examining the puppet's costume. The costumes consist of a series of superimposed images referring to longevity and eternity. The most identifying aspect of Sanbasō, so much so that it has become his trademark, is the hat. On it, we see thirteen stripes of dark and bright, indicating the waxing and waning moons, images of both the passage of time, and a cyclical renewal.[46] On one side of the hat is a full moon, and on the other, the crescent moon, further reinforcing the temporal, cyclical, lunar aspect of the hat.

The turtle, symbol of ten thousand years, appears on the costume, as does the crane, which signifies longevity to one thousand years. Sanbasō's two companions, Okina and Senzai both show the parameters of age, as Okina is old and Senzai (a mere thousand years of age) is youth. On Senzai's costume, we see the six-sided shape which indicates the felicity of longevity expressed in the turtle's ten thousand years. These images are often beautifully drawn on the costumes and sometimes are crudely embroidered. As the puppets perform and move their sleeves about, these visions of temporality flash in and out of view. One sees a turtle, then a crane, now and again a waxing or waning moon.

Perhaps the most problematic aspect of this rite is the ritual chant (*tonaegoto* or *jiuta*) used in it. It seems to defy any logical translation, and at times

272 Jane Marie Law

appears to be a medley of symbols and a salad of words. The problem with the text, however, lies perhaps in our expectation that it behave like a more conventional text—have a narrative structure, be translatable, etc. As Maurice Bloch correctly noted concerning the unique nature of language in ritual contexts, "Ritual is . . . a place where, because the ordinary forms of linguistic communication are changed, we cannot assume the semantic processes of more ordinary communication."[47]

On one level, the text can be seen as the "speaking parts" for the human officiant (the puppeteer as shaman) and the deities who enter the puppets during the rite. The use of poetic image and literary references, however, with ritual utterances of untranslatable meaning suggest that another level of language is at work here.

Ritual language, and ritual poetry in particular, is understood to have the magical capacity to create the realities it describes. This understanding is not an uncommon feature of ritual language in the history of Japanese religions. Two celebrated cases from the history of Japanese religions eloquently underscore this point:

An early reference to the power of language to create realities can be found in the *Kojiki*. In chapter sixteen of the text, the god Susanō, brother of the sun goddess Amaterasu, declares he has won a match for power with his sister, and he "rages with victory" by destroying the order his sister has created in the form of dikes between rice paddies, and defecates in "the hall where first fruits are tasted," then spreading his excrement about the hall. His sister's response is incomprehensible, unless we consider the power of language. She says, "That which appears to be faeces must be what my brother has vomited and strewn about while drunk.[48] Also, his breaking down the ridges of the paddies and covering up the ditches—my brother must have done this because he thought it was wasteful to use the land thus." The text continues: "*Even though she spoke thus with good intentions, his misdeeds did not cease*, but became even more flagrant."[49] As Philippi notes concerning this passage, her attempt to "speak good words correctively" (*nori-naoshi*) most probably reflects the belief that "one could turn evil into good by speaking well of it."[50] This example, it has been widely suggested, reflects this view of uttered words.

Second, the Japanese preface by Ki no Tsurayuki to the early tenth century text *Kokinshū* (or *Kokinwakashū*, "A collection of ancient and modern poems") directly refers to this capacity of the Japanese language properly used:

> The seeds of Japanese poetry lie in the human heart and grow into leaves of ten thousand words. Many things happen to people of this world, and all that they think and feel is given expression in descriptions of things they see and hear. When we hear the warbling of the mountain thrush in the blossoms or the voice of the frog in the water, we know every living thing has its song.
> It is poetry which, without effort, moves heaven and earth, stirs the feel-

ings of the invisible gods and spirits, smooths relations with men and women, and calms the hearts of the fierce warriors.

Such songs came into being when heaven and earth first appeared.[51]

A further reflection of an ancient Japanese conviction of the magical efficacy of ritual language, absorbed into many later Japanese ritual contexts, can be seen in what is referred to as *kotodama shinkō*, or the belief *(shinkō)* in the spirit *(dama)* of words *(koto)*. According to Konishi Jin'ichi this archaic and ancient view of the power of ritualized speech, when uttered in the proper context, and with the proper tone and pronunciation, survived in Japan well into the medieval period, at the time the rite under discussion here was being formed. Konishi specifically notes a feature we will see shortly in the Sanbasō chant, writing that

> priests composed [poems] in the belief that speaking a great many longevity-related phrases would propel the *kotodama* in their utterances toward their sovereign and grant him long life. . . . The priests were aware that their [poem], a virtual list of auspicious things, was recited in anticipation that the *kotodama* would function.[52]

Konishi sees the medieval Japanese perception of the spirit of words as influenced by another strain of magical language in Japanese religions, the concept of *dhāraṇī* from Esoteric Buddhism.[53] This ritual device used in esoteric Buddhist ritual practice maintains that elements of speech such as particular syllables (usually from Sanskrit), rather than entire words, can produce magical effects and reveal the ultimate nature of reality. Kūkai, the founder of Shingon Buddhism in Japan (discussed at greater length in the articles in this volume by Bernard Faure and Thomas P. Kasulis) wrote, "By reciting the voiced syllables with clear understanding,[54] one manifests the truth."[55] This emphasis on the power of meaningless sounds, or elements of speech rather than semantic units, became a dominant concern in Shingon Buddhism (the meaning of which, "True Word," reflects this point), and undoubtedly plays an important role in shaping views of ritual speech after the ninth century.

We cannot overlook the way in which these various views of the power of language came to express religious and political power relationships themselves. Gary Ebersole, in *Ritual Poetry and the Politics of Death in Early Japan*, writes, "Song was frequently used and experienced as a form of the exercise of power. It was a linguistic means of manipulating religio-political power in the human sphere as well as of manipulating the spiritual powers, including the *kami* and the spirits of the dead. Song was sung and poetry recited not only for aesthetic pleasure but as a means of ordering and controlling potentially dangerous aspects of the world. This sense of the efficacy of poetic language survived until much later in Japanese history and was prominent in the Heian and medieval periods. Indeed, it is still found in the present in attenuated form in certain rural areas and ritual practices."[56]

The Text

The text for the Sanbasō rite has often been neglected by translators and commentators precisely because it relies so heavily on notions of language extremely foreign to most people living in Japan and the West today.[57] Part of the difficulty in understanding this text, it seems, comes from the expectations modern readers have brought to it as text alone, divorced from its ritual context. When seen as an expression of ritual speech, the incomprehensible opening lines, lack of narrative, and layering of symbol upon symbol and literary reference upon literary reference make sense. The realities of vitality, longevity, and harmony are being invoked through the use of potent language in a ritual setting.

The text which I translate here is based upon the performance used by the Awaji puppet theater today. I have carefully compared it to a film made in the late 1940s of two elderly *Sanbasō mawashi* from Awaji, and the text is identical. Only slight variations in ritual action between the present-day Awaji puppeteers and the elderly men from the 1940s are apparent, and beyond the interests of this discussion.[58]

Sanbasō Jiuta

INVOCATION
Okina:
Tō tō tarari tarari ra
Tarari agari rarari tō
Chorus:
Chiriya tarari tarari ra.
Tarari agari rarari tō.[59]
Okina:
Live a long, long time[60]
Chorus:
We will also serve a thousand autumns—
Okina:
as long as the crane and the tortoise live[61]
Chorus:
Let us enjoy good fortune.
Okina:
Tō tō tarari tarari ra
Chorus:
Chiriya tarari tarari ra
Tarari agari rarari tō
Okina:
The sound of the waterfall,

the sound of the waterfall,
even if the sun is shining,
Chorus:
will not cease[62]
tō tari ari u tō tō tō

SENZAI'S DANCE AND POETRY INTERLUDE
Senzai:
It will not cease
tō tari ari
It will go on forever.
(Senzai performs a slow dance, waving his sleeves from side to side to purify the space.)
Senzai:
May you live a thousand years.
A heavenly maiden's robe of feathers[63]
Even if the sun is shining,
the sound of the waterfall will not cease;
Chorus:
It will not cease
Tōtari ari utō tō tō
(Senzai is put down, and Okina is picked up and made to dance slowly.)

OKINA'S DANCE AND POETIC INTERLUDE
Okina:
Ah, my lover with the braided hair!
ya ton do ya
Chorus:
Only a short distance from me![64]
ya ton do ya
(The drumming continues and the Okina puppet bows, spreads its arms, and then thrusts its hand holding a fan forward in an aggressive fashion and flips both sleeves behind its head.)
Okina:
Although we're seated,
Chorus:
let's begin!
Okina:
We have been celebrating together for a long time, since the age of the gods.[65]
Chorus:
Soyo yari chiya ton dō ya.
Okina:
The thousand-year crane sings the Manzairaku song of longevity[66]
And the turtle who has lived in the pond for ten thousand years

carries heaven, earth, and humankind on its shell.
The color of the morning sun glistens
in the rustling, spreading sands of the seashore.
The evening moon floats clearly
in the cool, pure water of the falls.
Peace under heaven! Tranquility throughout the land.
This is today's prayer.

ARRIVAL OF THE SACRED
(Okina pauses briefly, as if to listen to these following lines. These lines are
skipped in the stage version.)
Chorus:
Who are those old men?[67]
Who are they?
Where are they from?
Okina:
Since this dance is for a thousand autumns,
ten thousand years of bliss,[68]
Let's do one *Manzairaku* dance of longevity,
the Dance of Ten Thousand Years!
Chorus:
Manzairaku!
Okina:
Manzairaku!
Chorus:
Manzairaku!

TRANCE DANCE AND APOTHEOSIS OF SANBASŌ
(The puppeteer puts Okina down to his left and picks up Sanbasō. This
puppet has feet, as opposed to the other two, with only trousers. Sanbasō
is holding a rattle made of small bells with streamers attached. It is inserted
into a small hole in the puppet's right hand. Shaking the rattle serves to
purify the space, and the rattle itself serves as a *torimono,* an object into
which a sacred force will descend. When the puppet's arm moves, the rattle
sounds. He does a brief dance to drum accompaniment, which includes
feet stamping to drive out evil and rapid movements of his eyes to indicate
he is undergoing a transformation into sacred status.

(When Sanbasō's dance is finished, the puppeteer puts the doll down
and puts a black mask over his face. The "drummer" puts aside his drum,
puts a white mask on Okina, and both puppets are manipulated without
accompaniment. Note that in the following discussion, Okina serves as the
"straight man" for Sanbasō. In the Noh versions, this part is played by
Senzai or a minor actor [*omote*]. The conversation is carried out with both
puppets being held with their faces covered by their sleeves.)

Sanbasō:
Oh! Such joy, such joy, such joy!
I won't let it slip out of here!
Okina:
How felicitous![69]
Sanbasō:
I will summon that *ado* actor who takes care of things![70]
Okina:
I came at just the right time.
Sanbasō:
Aha!
Okina:
You are to dance the felicitous Thousand Autumns and Ten Thousand
Years for today's blessing. You, the black-faced old man.[71]
Sanbasō:
This black-faced old man will be happy to dance the felicitous Thousand
Autumns and Ten Thousand Years piece for today's blessing. There is noth-
ing I would like more to do! But first, sir, you must return to your seat
and settle down.
Okina:
After the old man's dance I will be happy to return to my seat. First,
perform the dance.
Sanbasō:
First, return to your seat.
Okina:
First, you dance!
Sanbasō:
No! Return to your seat!
Okina:
How felicitous. All right, I will give you the bell.
Sanbasō:
What a great deal of trouble this is!
(The conversation is thus concluded, and Okina is put down. The per-
former who manipulated Okina now picks up his drum for the masked
dance of Sanbasō, called in the Noh versions, the "bell scene." Both the
mask and the bell indicate that Sanbasō is now fully possessed by sacred
forces.)

THE WORDS OF BLESSING[72]
(Sanbasō dances frenetically to the following chant. His rattle cuts through
space and shakes wildly from side to side. He leaps about in the air. The
energy intensifies as the performers chant the text, beat the drum, the
voice cadence calls.)
Chorus:
Oh how grateful we are for this manifestation of the deity.
How blissful to give thanks to the deity with this sacred rite.[73]

Indeed, at Suminoe we will hear the clear lovely voices
of the many dancing girls
The blue waves of the ocean[74] are said
to there reflect the shadow of the Sumiyoshi pines
The road of the kami and the road of the sovereign should lead straight
to the capital in springtime.
This is the dance of "Returning to the Palace."[75]
In the Dance of Ten Thousand Years,
we use pure white robes.
Sweeping arms
purify you of all evil,
Outstretched hands
receive longevity and good fortune
The Dance of a Thousand Autumns caresses the people
The Dance of Ten Thousand Years lengthens our days.
We enjoy the voices of the wind in the pines.
We enjoy these gentle voices.
(As the chant concludes, the puppet ceases his dance, shakes his rattle from
side to side as if to bless the space and then is placed down in the sleeping
position in the carrying box. The performers clap their hands together
and bow and the rite is concluded.)

Motifs and Ritual Speech

The use of highly poetic and felicitous language presented in a ritual
context unleashes the power of the words themselves to create the realities
they so beautifully describe. Let us direct our attention to three types of
language use in this ritual text: the magical use of language as sound, the
use of language to invoke nostalgia and tradition, and the phenomenological use of language to create imaginary and visual experience.

The first stanza opens and closes with the nontranslatable syllables *tō tō
tarari tarari* and closes with similarly untranslatable syllables. While these
syllables have no readily available meaning, they serve a number of purposes in the text. First, they sensitize the listener to the onomatopoetic
qualities which come up in the rest of the text, and hence to the magical
use of language. Second, they set the stage for some later puns in the text,
when the same verb ending "rari" and the syllables "tō tō tō" come to have
meaning. This allows the listener to move between two levels of language—
the level of meaning and sense and the level of sound and sensation. We
see a subtle shift from this use of language, to the incorporation of these
syllables into meaningful phrases. And lastly, we see them used again ono-
matopoetically. So by prefacing the entire piece with ritual utterance of
this sort, the participant or audience is immediately forced to move through
various levels of comprehending ritual sound. This ritual use of language
I call the magical use of language as sound.

The next element in the text is what I have chosen to call the medley effect. A medley, a song or piece which borrows and places in seemingly random order famous and readily recognizable bits and pieces of songs of the day, is capable, in a few minutes, of conjuring up an entire mood and creating a powerful ambiance. It becomes unnecessary to reinvent the wheel for each new ritual event. One has only to think of the intentions behind and mood created by a brief medley of "The Star Spangled Banner" and other patriotic songs and the frequent use of such medleys in Memorial Day parades and Fourth of July celebrations. Indeed, when a medley is effectively used, it is often preferable to new pieces of music with the same theme, as new pieces lack the power of nostalgia and the authority of tradition. Another important aspect of the medley effect is its *economy*. The more brief and famous the reference to another work, the better. A good medley uses only enough of the piece to set the mood and then moves on to another piece.

This Sanbasō chant employs such an apparatus to condense a number of meanings into one ritual moment. A series of famous one-liners from classical Japanese poetry, names of famous *kagura* and *gagaku* performances, references to myths, legends and felicitous symbols, are all thrown into the text. For example, "the sound of the waterfall" is a line from the *Ryōjin Hishō,* and "Ah, my lover with the braided hair" (Agemaki) and "Only a short distance away from me" (Irobakari) are lines lifted directly from a Saibara poem with an overt sexual theme. The simple line "A heavenly maiden's robe of feathers" calls forth an entire myth and a profound notion of eternity, the Vedic idea of a *kalpa* as a measurement of time: a maiden descends to earth once every one hundred years and brushes a rock (forty *li* in breadth) with her robe of feathers. As long as it takes to wear down this rock is one *kalpa,* defined by Sir Monier Monier-Williams's Sanskrit-English dictionary as "a fabulous period of time (a day of Brahmā or one thousand Yugas, a period of four thousand, three hundred and twenty millions of years of mortals, measuring the duration of the world; a month of Brahmā is supposed to contain thirty such kalpas; according to the *Mahābharata,* twelve months of Brahmā constitute his year, and one hundred such years his lifetime; fifty years of Brahmā's are supposed to have elapsed, and we are now in the Svetavārāha-kalpa of the fifty first; at the end of a kalpa the world is annihilated. With Buddhists, the kalpas are not of equal duration."[76] Whether one accepts the orthodox Sanskrit definition of a *kalpa* or defines the term as the length of time needed to wear down a rock with a robe of feathers, the reference is to a long, long time. Since it is an incantation for longevity and fertility, it is optimistic indeed. The result of this "medley effect" is a high degree of ritual condensation and efficiency. The ritual is literally packed with the substance of each of these references.

A well-educated listener in medieval Japan might have been familiar with a number of these references. Today most people at this rite will be largely unaware of these references and must rely on the power of the images and poetic utterances themselves, without recourse to their original contextual origins. It is still possible, however, for a person witnessing this rite to have a profound experience of the rite at the level of language, because the initial chant includes a third use of language, an appeal to a phenomenology of the senses. References to waterfalls, the sun, turtles, and cranes, and lovely lines such as "The color of the morning sun glistens in the rustling, spread-ings sands of the seashore. The evening moon floats clearly in the cool, pure water of the falls" have an evocative power. One is able to visualize the realities described, and through visualization in the ritual, these peace-ful and vibrant images become reality at the level of the spirit. When rein-forced by the other simultaneous events in the rite—the movement and transformation of the puppet, the flute and drum music, the presentation of visual images on the costume, and the incessant ringing of tiny bells—the full meanings of these linguistic images can be felt. I have interviewed people who have come to watch the Sanbasō performance, and many often remark that the lovely visual images, understandable even today, create a soothing and pleasant mood.

So if we look to this text for a narrative, we will find a thin one: a few old men show up from the land of the gods and perform a dance after a bit of humorous negotiation. If, on the other hand, we direct our attention to these three ritual uses of language, we see that this text is not about narrative but about the creation of mood, image, and effect. Language is in the service of the larger analogical realization taking place in the rite: death is being turned into life. And for the mood to be fully felt, the text cannot be separated from the other ritual elements—myths, symbols, timing, perceptions of the performers.

I noted earlier that this case is appropriate for exploring a Japanese folk conception of the human body, as the puppet as ritual body substitute serves as the nexus of meaning in this rite. A final and appropriate question concerns the relationship between the body of the puppeteer and his (very rarely, her) puppets, and the soul of the puppeteer and the potential for soul in puppets. Around the world, stories abound of puppeteers falling in love with puppets, only to be destroyed, or at least greatly inconve-nienced by the puppets when they actually come to life. We have only to think of Pinocchio as a good example.

The actual practice on Awaji reveals a different sensibility to the puppet body. In my fieldwork, I asked two questions along these lines: Do puppets come to have souls of their own, or are they merely empty body vessels for the sacred? and "If they do come to have their own souls, are they eternal, or can puppets, too, die?" The first question was always the source of inter-esting discussions of the relationship between matter and spirit. A series of practices within the world of the performers reveals an attitude which an-swers this question in part. First, there is the case of puppets which are used repeatedly. As puppets are used time and again in rites, often for several generations, the lines of demarcation become a bit blurred. Sanbasō puppets come to be sacred in and of themselves, because they have come in contact with the spirit world.

Second, there is the attachment of puppeteers to particular puppets and puppet body parts. Most puppeteers develop intense attachments to particular *kashira* and have a sense of which body parts work best with which heads. It is more than a matter of technicality, but has to do, as one puppeteer put it, with "helping the puppet find its body."

Last, there is the interesting attitude toward the broken puppet. Until the late nineteenth century, when a puppet head could no longer be used, and was beyond repair, it could not simply be thrown away or recycled. Rather, the head, and frequently all the other assorted body parts as well, were buried, and a full funeral was performed. Near the Sanjo ceremonial center on Awaji, there is an area which was once the puppet cemetery, called the *dekozamma*. The practice of burying these images suggests an awareness that while matter and spirit may appear to be separate orders, once spirit has encountered a material form, the latter cannot return to being merely matter, but becomes matter set apart. A dilapidated puppet—a head, arms, perhaps a costume, rattles, flutes and masks—will never again be merely the sum of its parts. Today they are put in museums or glass cases, a practice which worries many older puppeteers.

The process of revitalizing the tradition of puppetry on Awaji is unlikely to fully reconstruct the meanings and understandings embodied in this rich ritual performance tradition. These beings "in the shape of the human" have in the past reflected deeply held understandings of the relationship between the human and the divine worlds. Although the rites are being revived, the understandings today are different from those of a hundred or even two hundred years ago. But as long as puppets are picked up and made to move in the hands of skilled puppeteers, the potential for transforming the world of matter into life is still there. It will, in the words of the Sanbasō chant, "live a long, long time."

NOTES

1. According to Japanese mythology presented in the *Kojiki* and *Nihongi*, the deities Izanagi and Izanami created the Japanese archipelago. Their first attempt at creation failed, however, since the woman spoke first. The result was a leech, which at three years of age could not even walk. They set the being adrift in a reed boat on the waves and, rectifying their ways, proceeded to create the rest of the cosmos. See Donald L. Philippi, trans., *Kojiki: A Record of Ancient Matters* (Tokyo: University of Tokyo Press, 1968; fifth printing, 1989), pp. 47–73.

2. I translate the Japanese term *ningyō* (literally, "in the shape of the human") as "puppet." While our English term *puppet* is not as inclusive as the Japanese term, it most accurately places the Japanese phenomenon in a meaningful comparative context. Further, this is in keeping with the practice of other scholars of Japanese theater.

3. Numerous oral versions of this myth exist throughout the Inland Sea of Japan. A text entitled *Dōkumbō Denki*, dated 1638 recounts the myth. I discuss and translate the text and its variants in "Religious Authority and Ritual Puppetry: The Case of *Dōkumbō Denki*," *Monumentica Nipponica*, 47, no. 1 (Spring 1992): 77–97.

4. Mircea Eliade, trans. Willard R. Trask, *The Sacred and the Profane: The Nature of Religion* (New York: Harcourt, Brace and World, 1959), p. 30.

5. See Catherine Bell, *Ritual Theory, Ritual Practice* (Oxford: Oxford University Press, 1992).

6. Richard Schechner, *Between Theater and Anthropology* (Philadelphia: University of Pennsylvania Press, 1985), pp. 35–36.

7. Lawrence Sullivan, "Sound and Senses: Towards a Hermeneutic of Performance," *History of Religions* 26, no. 1 (1986): 1–33.

8. I am indebted to Avron Boretz and his work on Taiwanese Taoist exorcism ritual for drawing my attention to new ways to think about this aesthetic dimension of ritual as experience.

9. For a discussion of the history of Japanese outcasts, see Ninomiya Shigeaki, "An Inquiry concerning the Origin, Development, and Present Situation of the Eta in Relation to the History of Social Classes in Japan," *Transactions of the Asiatic Society of Japan* 10 (1933): 47–154. Emiko Ohnuki Tierney discusses the increased marginalization of outcast groups in her *Monkey as Mirror: Symbolic Transformations in Japanese History and Ritual* (Princeton: Princeton University Press, 1987), pp. 75–100.

10. This line is extracted from Oe no Masafusa's famous text "Kugutsu Ki" (Chronicles of Puppeteers). The text is transcribed in its original Chinese with an exhaustive and excellent discussion in Tsunoda Ichirō, *Ningyōgeki no Seiritsu ni kan suru Kenkyū* (Osaka, 1963), pp. 332–48. For a complete annotated translation, see my article, "Of Plagues and Puppets: On the Significance of the Name Hyakudayū in Japanese Religions," in *Transactions of the Asiatic Society of Japan*, 4th ser., vol. 8 (1993): 114–20.

11. Michael Malkin, *Traditional and Folk Puppets of the World* (New Brunswick: A. S. Barnes, 1977), p. 11.

12. When used to refer to a puppet or doll which is a representation of an animal, the term *ningyō* is modified with the name of the animal. For example, a fox puppet is called a *kitsune ningyō*. The use of this term in this way, however, is relatively late.

13. Nagata Kōkichi, *Ikite iru Ningyō Shibai* (Tokyo: Kinseisha, 1983), 191–203.

14. Hachiman and Ebisu are two important deities incorporated into the standard Shinto list of deities. The most exhaustive work on Hachiman is Nakano Hatayoshi's *Hachiman Shinkō Shi no Kenkyū*, 2 vols. (Tokyo: Yoshikawa Kōbunkan, 1975). In English, see Ross Bender, "The Political Meaning of the Hachiman Cult in Ancient and Medieval Japan," Ph.D. dissertation, Columbia University, 1980, and Christine Guth Kanda, *Shinzō: Hachiman Imagery and Its Development*, (Cambridge: Harvard University Press, 1985).

15. I discuss the transformations in the meanings of this tradition in my forthcoming book.

16. The essays by Poul Andersen, Jean deBernardi, and Daniel Gold in this volume are similarly based on fieldwork by the authors.

17. For a discussion by Poul Andersen of his uses of fieldwork, see his essay in this volume.

18. In fact, the Hyakudayū legend is important for the history of Japanese ritual performance precisely because it renders this hypothesis credible and sheds light on the development of Hiruko (Leech Child)/Ebisu worship, the Sarugaku tradition, and the spread of deity appeasement rituals throughout Japan.

19. Note the parallel between this conception of the characters in the rite and the perception of the performers as itinerant others, discussed later in this essay.

20. Furthermore, it is possible that since puppeteers tended to specialize in one dance, the separation of the Okina and Sanbasō dances became rigid, and eventually only the Sanbasō performance remained.

21. The term *kadozuke* also includes a number of performances which do not use puppets. An exhaustive study of this interesting class of performances is Park Jon Yul, *Kadozuke no Kōzō* (Tokyo: Kōbundō, 1989).

22. Many readers will be familiar with the famous Japanese film directed by Kurosawa Akira entitled "Rashomon" (literally "Gate Rasho"). The eerie narrative of the film is framed by the large gate of Rasho, as two speakers meet under the shelter it provides and discuss the strange times they are experiencing. In using the gate as the stage for this film, the director is appealing to a common Japanese perception of gates as liminal places.

23. My discussion of these aspects of *kadozuke* is informed in part by Origuchi Shinobu's analysis, cited in Jacob Raz, *Actors and Audience: A Study of Their Interaction in the Japanese Theatre* (Leiden: E. J. Brill, 1984), pp. 36–41.

24. For a discussion in English of the meanings associated with "outsiders" in Japanese religion and folklore, see Yoshida Teigo, "The Stranger as God: The Place of the Outsider in Japanese Folk Religion," *Ethnology* 20, no. 2 (1964): 87–99.

25. Hori Ichirō, "Mysterious Visitors from the Harvest to the New Year," in Richard Dorson, ed., *Studies in Japanese Folklore* (Bloomington: Indiana University Press, 1963), 76–77.

26. I have intentionally avoided entering into a discussion of the question of "which came first, myth or rite." This "chicken or the egg" discussion seems futile. The dynamics between the two, however, are of great interest.

27. I discuss this issue of legitimation in my article "Religious Authority and Ritual Puppetry."

28. For a list of twenty major Sanjo districts, see Toyota Yorihisa, "Sanjo Hōshi Kō: Kodai Shakai Sōshiki no Kenkyū," *Minzoku to Rekishi* 3, no. 4 (1921): 1–10. Ohnuki-Tierney briefly mentions Sanjo (Sansho) districts in *The Monkey as Mirror*, pp. 85, 92, and 93.

29. Morita Yoshinori, *Chūsei Senmin to Zatsu Geinō no Kenkyū* (Tokyo: Yūzankaku, 1986), p. 65.

30. Toyota, "Sanjo Hōshi Kō," pp. 5–6.

31. The Sanjo district in present-day Kyoto was most likely always a "third district," since it exists in a series of numbered districts.

32. Hayashiya Tatsusaburō, *Chūsei Geinō Shi no Kenkyū* (Tokyo: Iwanami Shōten, 1975), pp. 269–80. The *Chūyūki* text fragment is presented on p. 271.

33. Menstruating women and women giving birth were commonly separated from the rest of the community in Japan until as recently as the postwar period. For a discussion of these practices, see Kiyoko Segawa, "Menstrual Taboos Imposed Upon Women," in Richard Dorson, ed., *Studies in Japanese Folklore* (Bloomington: Indiana University Press, 1965), 239–50.

34. Morita, *Chūsei Senmin to Zatsu Geinō no Kenkyū*, pp. 66–67.

35. A common, though highly derogatory term for Japanese outcasts is *eta*, written with the characters "much pollution" (much *kegare*).

36. For a discussion of some of the meanings of these zones, see in Japanese, Yokoi Kiyoshi, *Chūsei Minshū no Seikatsu Bunka* (Tokyo: Tokyo Daigaku Shuppankai, 1982), pp. 337–339.

37. According to Japanese mythology, when the Leech Child became an adult, he was known as Ebisu.

38. A fine discussion in English of this type of rite is Jacob Raz, "Chinkon—From Folk Beliefs to Stage Conventions," in *Maske und Kothurn: Internationale Beiträge zur*

Theaterwissenschaft 27 (1981): 5–18. Susan Klein mentions this type of rite in her essay in this volume.

39. Fudō Takashi, *Nihon Geinō no Shigen teki Kenkyū* (Tokyo: San'ichi Shōbo, 1981), pp. 30–31.

40. In the Chinese chronicles of Ssu ma Ch'ien, a story about the emperor Wu Ti has a similar motif. After the death of the emperor's wife, a sorcerer is brought in to console the emperor. The sorcerer casts a shadow in the likeness of the deceased woman on a screen and imitates her voice. See René Simmen, *The World of Puppets* (London: Elsevier, Phaidon, 1975), p. 79. During my fieldwork in 1989, I encountered a tragic example of a doll being used as a body substitute. A young child of five had been struck by a car and killed, and her disconsolate mother maintained that the little girl's doll was grieving. Each morning the doll's dress was said to be soaked in tears. A Pure Land priest was called in and explained that the spirit of the child had entered the doll, longing for a continuation of her mother's affection and nurturance. The woman was instructed to rock the doll at a set time each day for a prescribed period of time, after which the doll was brought to the temple and a service was conducted to appease the child. A body substitute, in this case the little girl's doll, can make possible the bridge of healing that enables life to go on. And indeed, in other places in Japan, such as the *ningyō no o-tera* in Ueno Park, funeral services are customarily conducted for dolls—though not necessarily under such dramatic circumstances as the case of the little girl from the kindergarten. Psychoanalytically, this event suggests the healing power of a projection identification. On one level, while it may seem very foreign—spirits entering dolls and doll funerals—it is not completely unlike the healing power of the transference in the psychoanalytic tradition. What the priest clearly understood was that for some people, unmitigated grief does not come under control in the usual mourning practices. The transition from physical presence to memory is a difficult one.

41. In Margareta Niculescu, ed., *The Puppet Theatre of the Modern World*, trans. Ewald Osers and Elisabeth Strick (Boston: Plays, Inc., 1967), p. 35.

42. I interviewed Oe Minosuke at his home in Naruto-shi, Tokushima-ken, in August 1988.

43. This is also true of masks in the Noh theater.

44. In versions of the Sanbasō rite in Kagura, Kabuki, and Noh, the dance of Sanbasō is largely seen as a humorous skit. This is probably a later interpretation of the earlier shamanic dance, perhaps to make fun of the frenzied gestures of shamans in trance. A number of other Sanbasō dances, however, are quite ribald. (For example, he is present at his own conception and crawls up between his parents as they are making love.)

45. Sometimes masks are put on two or even three of the puppets, and they all get possessed, although this seems to be a variation of the performance dependent largely on the number of performers available and the desire for real dramatic force.

46. This is my interpretation of the significance of the hat's design.

47. Maurice Bloch, "Symbols, Song, Dance and Features of Articulation: Is Religion an Extreme Form of Traditional Authority?" *European Journal of Sociology* 15 (1974): 55–87.

48. The implication here is that vomiting, unlike defecation, is beyond one's control, and hence he should not be seen as guilty of an offense.

49. Philippi, *Kojiki*, pp. 79–80 (emphasis mine).

50. Ibid., p. 80f.

51. Laurel Rasplica Rodd, trans., *Kokinshū: A Collection of Poems Ancient and Modern* (Princeton: Princeton University Press, 1984), p. 35.

52. Konishi Jin'ichi, *A History of Japanese Literature*, vol. 2, *The Early Middle Ages*, trans. Aileen Gatten and ed. Earl Miner (Princeton: Princeton University Press, 1986), p. 113.

53. Ibid., p. 117.

54. I.e., with a clear understanding of the power of ritual sound.

55. As cited in Yamasaki Taikō, *Shingon: Japanese Esoteric Buddhism* (Boston: Shambala, 1988), p. 77.

56. Gary L. Ebersole, *Ritual Poetry and the Politics of Death in Early Japan* (Princeton: Princeton University Press, 1989), p. 19. In chap. 1 of this book, "Ritual Poetry in the Court," Ebersole discusses the ritual potency of song and poetry. See esp. pp. 17–23.

57. Frank Hoff, in "The 'Evocation' and 'Blessing' of *Okina:* A Performance Version of Ritual Shamanism," *Alcheringa/Ethnopoetics* (New Series) 3, no. 1 (1977): 48–60, translated a number of ritual chants used in related Okina rites. He correctly situates these poetic texts within their performance context to render the cryptic lines meaningful.

58. I wish to thank Dr. Kyoko Selden of the Department of Modern Languages and Literature at Cornell University for her advice and careful corrections in translating this piece. Many of the subtle references were brought to my attention by her. Further thanks to Karen Brazell for pointing out the complexities and influences of the Noh version of this rite.

59. These utterances are untranslatable. The Russian linguist of Japanese and Ural-Altaic languages Sasha Vovin has suggested that the words come from ancient Korean and are references to the moon.

60. This piece was probably originally intended as a longevity rite for the sovereign and is written as though addressed to this august person. The blessing extends to all present.

61. These two animals are said to live one thousand and ten thousand years respectively.

62. These are lines from a popular song *(imayō)* recorded as song number 404 in the *Ryōjin Hishō*. In the song, the waterfall makes the sounds rendered onomotopoetically as *tōtae*. The implication is that even if there is a lot of sunshine, there will still be water in the rivers, and hence no drought.

63. The popular legend of a heavenly maiden in Japan (the subject of the Noh play *Hagoromo*) makes use of a classical Indian notion of time.

64. These lines are from a popular Saibara song ("Agemaki," no. 57). A man and a woman sleeping a short distance apart (only one "iro," *irobakari*) toss and turn during the night, eventually roll toward one another, and, presumably have sexual relations. The poem also includes the syllables *tō tō*.

65. This line is most likely tied to the reference in the *Ise Monogatari* in which an emperor, on a journey to Sumiyoshi, encounters there the Sumiyoshi deity who manifests itself and recites to him, "Do you not know of the tie that unites us? Since times as ancient as my sacred fence have I protected you." The implication of this line in the poem is that the sovereign (or more precisely, the imperial line) has been in direct interaction and celebration of unity with the sacred forces of Sumiyoshi. The Sumiyoshi deities are those being invoked in this rite. See *Ise Monogatari, #117*.

66. *Manzairaku* (10,000 year music) is the name of a *bugaku* piece imported from China and popularized into many forms in medieval Japan. It is frequently performed on felicitous occasions.

67. These "old men" refer to Okina, Senzai and Sanbasō who have been summoned by the music, chanting and felicitous imagery.

68. *Sensu* (also *Senshu*) *Manzai* (one thousand autumns, ten thousand years) refers to dances performed at the imperial court as a New Year's ritual from the Nara period on. The form was popularized by medieval itinerant performers called *sensu manzai hōshi*, and their art has influenced the itinerant puppet tradition.

69. In the Noh version, the still unmasked Sanbasō performs a dance called *momo no dan* at this point. The reference to "how felicitous" which here would seem incomprehensible, is to that part of the Noh piece.

70. *Ado* is a secondary kyōgen actor. In the Noh version, Sanbasō, played by the

primary (*omo* or *shite*) kyōgen actor has this discussion with the secondary (*ado*) kyōgen actor who serves as mask bearer. Here, the role of the secondary character is played by Okina.

71. The "black faced old man" refers to Sanbasō who is wearing a black mask. That his mask is black is often interpreted that since he represents the visiting deity of the rice fields, his face is covered with dirt.

72. This final section, not included in the Noh Okina piece, is borrowed from the final scene of the Noh play *Takasago*. While in the Noh piece the lines are divided between the Sumiyoshi deity and the chorus, in the puppet version these lines are presented as a single poem and blessing with no divisions. In addition to its lovely imagery of peace and tranquility, this section refers again to the relationship between the Sumiyoshi deities and the imperial line. The "wind in the pine trees" is understood to be a manifestation of the deity, meaning peace and harmony in the realm.

73. The term *kami asobi*, literally "playing with the sacred" refers to the aspect of a *matsuri* which is intended to entertain, and thus appease, the deity who has been invoked. It implies that the deity is a participant in the festivities. The term is also synonymous with *kagura* in early texts.

74. The term "blue waves of the ocean" (*seigaiha*) refers to a bugaku dance performed by two dancers to entertain a deity. It is thought to have originated in China as an imperial dance, and was popular in Japan during the Nara period. As Suminoe is famous for its beautiful blue waves and the pine trees on the shore, this reference is very apt.

75. *Genjōraku*, literally "returning to the capital music," refers also to a type of Gagaku dance, derived from the tale of King Pedu from the Vedas, in which the king subdues a snake. In the dance, a wooden snake is played with by a person with a red face and deep set eyes wearing a jaw mask. The snake subduer jumps about playfully on the stage during the performance. In the Sanbasō text, the name of the piece is merely invoked, perhaps to underscore the theme of purification and placation of evil being presented.

76. Monier Monier-Williams, *Sanskrit English Dictionary* (Oxford: Oxford University Press, 1979), p. 262, s.v., "kalpa."

GLOSSARY

Amaterasu 天照

Awajishima 淡路島

ayatsuri ningyō 操り人形

Bunraku 文楽

Byōdōin 平等院

chinkonsai 鎮魂祭

Chūyūki 中右記

dekozamma 木偶ザンマ (三昧場)

Dōkumbō 道薫坊

Dōkumbō Denki 道薫坊伝記

Ebisu 夷/恵比須

Ebisu-kaki 夷舁き

Ebisu-mawashi 夷廻し

Gagaku 雅楽

Genjōraku 還城楽

gohei 御幣

Hachiman 八幡

hako-mawashi 箱廻し

hijiri 聖

hinin 非人

Hiruko 蛭子

Hyakudayū 百太夫

imi 忌

jōruri 浄瑠璃

kadozuke 門付け

Kagura 神楽

kami asobi 神遊

kashira 頭

kawara no mono 河原の者

Kojiki 古事記

Kokinshū 古今集

kotodama 言霊

kotodama shinkō 言霊信仰

Kugutsu no Ki 傀儡記

Kuro-Okina 黒翁

Manzairaku 万歳楽

marebito 稀人（マレビト）

nembutsu 念仏

Nihonshoki 日本書紀
ningyō 人形
ningyō-mawashi 人形廻し
Nishinomiya 西宮
Nishinomiya Ebisu Saburō Den 西宮恵比須三郎殿
nori-naoshi 宜直し
Oe no Masafusa 大江匡房
Okina 翁
Okina-watari 翁渡り
onmyōshi 陰陽師
Ryōjin Hishō 梁塵秘抄
Sanbasō mai 三番叟舞
Sanbasō-mawashi 三番叟廻し
Sanjo 散所・産所・算所・三条
Sanjo no mono 散所の者
Sensha ko 賤者考
Senzai 千歳
Shiki Sanbasō 式三番叟
shinji/kamigoto 神事
shintai 神体
Susanō 須佐之男
ta no kami 田の神
tama-furi 魂(霊)振
tama-shizume 魂(霊)鎮
tama-yobai 魂(霊)呼ばい
tatari 祟り
Tennōji 天王寺
urami 怨み(恨み)

CONTRIBUTORS

Poul Andersen has done two years of fieldwork on Taoist ritual in Tainan, Taiwan (1978–79 and 1986–87). He obtained a Ph.D. from the University of Copenhagen in 1991 with a thesis entitled "Taoist Ritual Texts and Traditions." His works in English include *The Method of Holding the Three Ones: A Taoist Manual of Meditation of the Fourth Century A.D.* (Copenhagen, 1980), "The Practice of *Bugang*," *Cahiers d'Extrême-Asie* 5 (1989–90): 15–53, and a number of contributions to the forthcoming *Handbook of the Taoist Canon* (University of Chicago Press). He currently teaches Taoism and the history of science in China at the Technische Universität, Berlin.

Ioan P. Culianu's degrees included two doctorates from the University of Paris-Sorbonne, in 1980 and 1987, in 3eme Cycle en Science Religieuses and Lettres et Sciences Humaines, and a Dottore in Lettere in the History of Religions at the Catholic University in Milan in 1975. He published more than ten books in Italian, French, and English and wrote more than seventy-five major articles. His most recent publications in English are *Eros and Magic in the Renaissance,* translated by Margaret Cook (Chicago: University of Chicago Press, 1987), and *Out-of-the-World: A History of Otherworldly Journeys and Out-of-Body Experiences, from Gilgamesh to Albert Einstein* (Boston: Shambhala, 1990). At the time of his death in May 1991, he was Professor of Christianity and History of Religions at the Divinity School, the University of Chicago.

Jean DeBernardi is Assistant Professor of Anthropology at the University of Alberta. She received her Ph.D. in Anthropology from the University of Chicago. She teaches and publishes in the fields of cultural and linguistic anthropology and has done field research with Chinese communities in Malaysia and Taiwan. She is writing *Empire over Imagination: Chinese Popular Religion in Colonial and Post-colonial Malaysia.*

Howard Eilberg-Schwartz is Associate Professor and Director of Jewish Studies at San Francisco State University. Drawing on anthropological theory and gender and feminist criticism, his interdisciplinary work on ancient Judaism seeks to reimagine the meanings of ancient rituals, myths, and symbols. He is author of *The Savage in Judaism: An Anthropology of Israelite Religion and Ancient Judaism,* which won the American Academy of Religion's Award for Excellence, and *The Human Will in Judaism: The Mishnah's Philosophy of Intention.* He also edited *People of the Body: Jews and Judaism from the Embodied Perspective* and is co-editor of *Off with Her Head: The Female Head in Myth, Religion and Culture* (forthcoming). In addition, he edits a book series at SUNY Press entitled "The Body in Culture, History and Religion."

Bernard Faure received his Ph.D. from the University of Paris VII. He is Professor of Religious Studies at Stanford University. In addition to numerous scholarly articles in French, Japanese, and English, his publications include *Le bouddhisme Ch'an en mal d'histoire: Genèse d'une tradition religieuse dans la Chine des T'ang* (Paris Publications de l'Ecole Française d'Extrême-Orient, 1989), *The Rhetoric of Immediacy: A Cultural Critique of Chan/Zen Buddhism* (Princeton University Press, 1991), and *Chan Insights and Oversights* (Princeton, 1993).

Daniel Gold is Associate Professor of South Asian Studies and Director of the South Asia Program at Cornell University. He received his Ph.D. from the University of Chicago in the History of Religions and has done extensive fieldwork in India. His recent publications include *The Lord as Guru: Hindi Saints in North Indian Tradition* (Oxford University Press, 1987) and *Comprehending the Guru: Toward a Grammar of Religious Perception* (Scholars Press, 1988).

Sue Hamilton received her Ph.D. from Oxford University and is Lecturer in Indian Religions at King's College, London, where she teaches Hinduism and Buddhism. Her area of research is the constitution of the human being in early Buddhism, and she is preparing a book on this subject.

Thomas P. Kasulis received his Ph.D. from Yale in Philosophy and is Professor of Comparative Studies and Humanities and Chair of the Department of East Asian Languages and Literature at Ohio State University in Columbus. In addition to dozens of scholarly articles, his publications include *Zen Action/Zen Person* (Honolulu: University of Hawaii Press, 1981), and *Person as Body in Asian Theory and Practice,* co-edited with Roger T. Ames and Wimal Dissanayake (State University of New York Press, 1993). He edited and co-translated a work by Yuasa Yasuo, *The Body: Toward an Eastern Mind-Body Theory* (SUNY Press, 1987). A former president of the Society for Asian and Comparative Philosophy, he has been the Numata Visiting Professor in Buddhism at the University of Chicago and a Mellon Faculty Fellow in the Humanities at Harvard. His current research is on the historical development of Japanese religious thought.

Susan B. Klein received her Ph.D. in East Asian Literature from Cornell University. She is Assistant Professor of Japanese Literature at University of California, Irvine. Her primary research interests are premodern and modern Japanese theatre and dance, Japanese religions, and feminist critical theory. Her publications include *Ankoku Butoh: The Premodern and Postmodern Influences on the Dance of Utter Darkness* (1989) and a translation of the Noh play *Kakitsubata* in *Twelve Plays of the Noh and Kyogen Theater* (1989), both published by the Cornell East Asia Monograph Series. She is preparing a book on secret allegorical commentaries and their use in medieval Noh theater.

Jane Marie Law received her Ph.D. from the University of Chicago in the History of Religions. She is Assistant Professor of Japanese Religions at Cornell University, where she teaches and publishes in the fields of history of religions, Japanese religions and folklore, and ritual studies. Since 1984 she has done extensive field research in rural Japan, translated plays and performances from the Jōruri tradition, and published widely on Japanese ritual puppetry. She is writing *Ningyō: The Imagination of the Otherness in Japanese Ritual*.

Fedwa Malti-Douglas is Professor of Arabic, Semiotics and Women's Studies and Chairperson of the Department of Near Eastern Languages and Cultures at Indiana University. She has published extensively in Arabic, French, and English on classical and modern Arabic literature and Islamic civilization. Her latest books are *Blindness and Autobiography* (1988) and *Woman's Body, Woman's Word* (1991), both with Princeton University Press. With Allen Douglas, she co-authored *Arab Comic Strips: Politics of an Emerging Mass Culture* (Indiana University Press, 1994). Her book, *Men, Women, and God(s): Nawal El Saadawi and Arab Feminist Poetics,* will be appearing as A Centennial Book with the University of California Press in 1995.

Pheme Perkins received her M.A. and Ph.D. degrees in New Testament and Christian Origins from Harvard University. She is Professor of Theology (New Testament) at Boston College. In addition to more than sixty articles in scholarly and popular journals, she has written fifteen books, including *Reading the New Testament, The Resurrection, Hearing the Parables of Jesus, Love Commands in the New Testament, The Gnostic Dialogue,* and *Epiphany: Proclamation 5 Series A.* Her newest books are *Peter in the New Testament and Early Christianity* (University of South Carolina Press) and *Gnosticism and the New Testament* (Fortress Press).

Elizabeth Wilson received her Ph.D. from the University of Chicago in the History of Religions and is Assistant Professor of Religion at Miami University in Ohio. Her research focuses on cultural constructions of gender and the body in the religious traditions of South Asia, particularly Buddhism. Her dissertation is entitled "Charming Cadavers: Horrific Figurations of the Feminine in Post-Ashokan Buddhist Literature."

Michael Winter is Professor of Middle Eastern and African Studies at Tel Aviv University. He has published extensively on the Arab countries during the Ottoman period and on Sufism and other Islamic topics. He is author of *Society and Religion in Early Ottoman Egypt: Studies in the Writings of ʿAbd al-Wahhab al-Shaʾrani* (New Brunswick: Transaction Books, 1982) and *Egyptian Society under Ottoman Rule, 1517–1798* (London and New York: Routledge, 1993).

INDEX

A, 174
Abihu: elder of Israel, 140
Ablution, 40
Adam, 24, 25, 26, 27, 28, 31, 32, 33, 35f;
creation of, 22, 29, 30; sin of, 42
Adam, Light, 26-28
Ado: secondary kyogen actor, 277, 286f
Adornment, 67, 72, 73; of women, 67, 68; of
face and body, 67-68; as transgression, 71;
Islamic material on, 72
Adultery, 31
Agastya: sage, 250f
Agemaki: Saibara song, 279, 285f
Ahkam al-Nisa', 70
Ahmed, Leila, 74f
Ahorai, 144
'Ajb al-dhanab, 43
al-ākhira, 37
Akumil: flower, 86
Albert the Great, 6
Alchemy, 233, 249f
Allen, Prudence, R.S.M., 5, 15f
Allison, Dale C.: W. D. Davies and, 33f
Altars, 153, 155, 156; temporary, 157
Ama: diver, 107, 117, 118, 126, 132f, 135g;
Noh play, 116, 117; nun, 131f
Āmaka, 98f
Āmaka-susāna, 98f
Amaraugha Shasana, 249f
Amaterasu: sun goddess, 272, 286g
Amida, 171
Amos: prophet, 140
Amputation, 79
Analogical realization, 255
Ānanda: friend of the Buddha, 53, 85, 96f
Anāsava, 92
Anattā, 48
Anattatā, 51
Androgynous, 25
Angels, 22, 25, 28, 30, 31, 35f, 39; Gabriel, 71
Anguttara Nikāya, 47, 55, 96f, 98f
Aniccata, 51
Ankle, 14, 38
Anklets: Arabian, 17f
Anorexia nervosa, 4, 5
Antrum, 5
Anus, 91
Aoi no Ue: Noh play, 102, 125, 127f
Apperception: faculty of, 49, 51, 52
Apsaras, 81, 82c
Aranya Kanda, 250f

Aratī: Discontent, daughter of Mara, 97f
Archons, 22, 24, 25, 26, 33
Arhat, 81, 92
Ariake no tsuki: dawn moon, 121
Arié, Rachel, 16f
Aristotle, 6
Āsava, 92
Āsaya: habitat, 58
Asceticism/Ascetic(s), 11, 21, 22, 32, 42; ma-
nipulation of the body, 30; practice, 31;
Christian, 21, 33
Ashibyōshi: foot-stamping, 270
Ashoka, King, 80, 97f, 214
Ashoka: Mauryan emperor, 94f
Ashokāvadāna, 80, 98f
Ashram: abode of a guru, 230, 231, 235, 238-
48; contemporary Indian, 236; of Guru-
mayi, 236; of Muktananda, 236; city, 247
Ashubha-bhāvanā: Sanskrit, 77
Ashuci, 77
Ashvaghosha, 97f
Assaka, 99f
Assakajataka, 99f
Asubha, 58
Asubha bhāvanā, 60, 78c, 85, 86, 87, 94f, 98f;
Pali, 76
Asuci, 47, 58; impure, 54
Ata, Abd al-Qadir Ahmad, 74f
Ātmabhāva: Buddhist Sanskrit, 56
Attabhāva, 56
Attabhāvato, 56
Attar, Fariduddin: Persian mystic, 42
Aubha, 60
Augustine, 4, 6, 9, 46
Authoritative Teaching: gnostic tract, 23
Awaji, 230, 251, 252, 257, 258, 260, 263, 265,
267, 280, 281
—puppets/puppeteers, 230, 268 (*see also* Pup-
pets; Puppeteers); Puppet Theater, 259;
people of, 266; ceremonial center of, 265
Awaji Ningyō Jōruri Kan: Awaji puppet the-
ater, 257
Awajishima, 286g
Awareness: faculty of, 49
Awaresa, 135f
'awra, 70, 74f
Ayatsuri ningyō: manipulated puppet, 256,
286g
Ayuwang Monastery, 214, 228g
Aziz, Philip, 16f
A'isha: wife of Muhammad, 39